THE
END

THE
END

*80 YEARS OF LIFE ON
ARSENAL'S
NORTH BANK*

TOM WATT

Foreword by
DAVID O'LEARY

MAINSTREAM
PUBLISHING

EDINBURGH AND LONDON

The moral right of the author has been asserted

First published in Great Britain in 1993 by
MAINSTREAM PUBLISHING COMPANY (EDINBURGH) LTD
7 Albany Street
Edinburgh EH1 3UG

This edition 1995

ISBN 1 85158 793 4

A catalogue record for this book is available from the British Library

Typeset in Perpetua by Litho Link Ltd, Welshpool, Powys
Printed in Great Britain by Butler and Tanner Ltd, Frome

Contents

Acknowledgments

This book would not have been possible without the goodwill afforded by so many people in the course of the past 14 months during which I've written *The End*. At every stage, a willingness to offer time, effort and resources as soon as the North Bank was mentioned was the immediate response from everyone I asked for help.

Research benefited from the wholehearted support of Arsenal Football Club, through David Dein, Ken Friar and archivist Ian Cook. Another member of the Arsenal staff, community sport co-ordinator Alan Sefton, helped with early discussion about the shape of the book I was starting work on. Islington Central Reference Library gave me the run of the local history section and Mr Arthur Peakell lent me his collection of *GunFlash* (which the Supporters' Club has been happy for me to draw on). I am indebted to Robson Books for permission to quote from *Alex James* by John Harding, to Sidgwick & Jackson for permission to quote from Terry Neill's *Revelations of a Football Manager*, to Souvenir Press for quotes from *Arsenal From The Heart* by the late Bob Wall, and to Brian Glanville for an extract from his book *Arsenal*. I have been unable to discover the copyright holders of *Tom Whittaker's Arsenal Story* and *Allison Calling* by George Allison but will gratefully acknowledge their contributions if they contact me.

Contacting supporters, players and other contributors was made easy with the help of Kevin Connolly, editor of the Arsenal programme, John Cross at the *Islington Gazette*, Barry Baker at the Supporters' Club, Tony Willis, editor of the fanzine *One Nil Down*, Jeff Weston, Richard Stubbs, Charlie Robinson, John Birt and Ron Pilcher.

Apart from photographs credited elsewhere to commercial archives, the help and advice I received about pictures from the *Islington Gazette*, Doug Poole, Bill Smith, Tony Ward, Rob Ashman, Kelvin Meads, Damien Harris, and the Jales family were invaluable.

Putting *The End* together was a task shared in great part with Judy and Simon Spector – at all hours of the day and night! – who transcribed and word processed much of my 'raw material' with unfailing enthusiasm and accuracy. Their support matched that I received from other sources as diverse as my endlessly patient and constructive publishers, Mainstream, Hilton UK, Fred Perry Ltd, Roos UK, Paul

Windle and my literary agent, Bill Hamilton. I hope, too, that the cast and crew of *An Evening with Gary Lineker* (particularly Rob Palfrey) will now see why I was so preoccupied during our six months with the show, on tour and in the West End.

Since delivering my manuscript, I've had generous help and advice from my editor, Peter Frances, and from Simon Whittam, Anna Arthur and Jerome Anderson. Thanks are due, too, to Charlotte Erickson and Ann Jackson and – above all – to those who took the time and trouble to tell me the stories that make up *The End*. My book is the story of their experiences and, with gratitude, I dedicate what follows to them.

Tom Watt, 24 August 1993

Foreword

by DAVID O'LEARY

When I first arrived at Arsenal, half the first team were products of the youth side. The Club made a policy of bringing on their young talent. Also, there were two young Dublin lads here already, Liam Brady and Frank Stapleton, who seemed to be doing well. I thought that I wouldn't feel like I was away from home! I'd looked at other clubs but just liked the feel of Highbury and was impressed by what Bertie Mee had to say about the way Arsenal set standards and conducted themselves. Of course, my parents were Arsenal supporters – my dad was over here working when I was born – and growing up in Stoke Newington, Arsenal were the local team. Mind you, in spite of all that, my mum didn't want me to leave home – we were back in Dublin by then – but when I came over to sign, on my fifteenth birthday, 2 May 1973, I already knew that Arsenal was the only place I wanted to be.

I had 20 great years at Highbury – passing the 700-appearance mark was the big thing for me – and when people are surprised that I stuck it that long I can only explain how simple it was: I never wanted to be anywhere else. Whenever it came time to discuss new contracts my solicitor, Michael Kennedy, always joked that I made it too easy for the Club, that I'd walk into the manager's office with the pen ready in my hand! They always knew I wanted to sign and so did I. And, to be fair, I was always looked after. Arsenal never took advantage.

The Highbury fans, too, took to me straight away. I made my debut away to Burnley when I was 17 and then played at Highbury against Stoke City the following Saturday. People say the Arsenal crowd are a grumpy, moaning lot – and maybe they are – but they and I always had a great mutual feeling for each other that I think was to do with loyalty. They were 100 per cent Arsenal and so was I and, especially after Liam and Frank left with me the one that decided to stay behind, it was as if I could do no wrong in their eyes.

When Andy Linighan arrived at the Club and it looked as if, after 18 years, I was on my way out the door, I'll never forget the reception the crowd gave me when I came on as a sub against Chester a few weeks into the new season. The fans had heard I might be going. They knew I didn't want to go and that night was their way of letting me – and everybody else – know they didn't want me to leave. Again, at last year's

Coca-Cola Cup final, going behind the goal after we'd won and seeing thousands of Arsenal fans – so much goodwill coming my way – shouting for me to hold the Cup up to them was just unbelievable. And the farewell game against Manchester United when that huge crowd made the effort to be there – I'm still months behind with the mail! And I saw so many fans actually crying as I walked round the pitch saying goodbye that it started me off too. You just can't buy that kind of experience. Unbelievable.

I can remember standing to watch football from the terraces when I was a kid and, although I've always preferred to sit, I know how much people like to stand. A good mate of mine, the jockey Willy Ryan, often used to phone me up at the last minute after I'd arranged tickets for him to say that he was sorry but he wanted to go and stand on the North Bank, to enjoy the crack and be with the crowd. And him a jockey, only a midget, too!

Of course I'm worried that by moving to all-seater stadia we're maybe going to lose the supporter who comes down with his boy and holds him in his arms on the terrace until they can stand there together. With the rise in prices (and the cost of a Bond at Highbury) it's not easy for a dad to afford to come with his kids, and those kids are the Arsenal supporters of the future. Atmosphere, though, won't be a problem: I've played in places like Seville and Naples where a seated crowd's been so loud you couldn't hear what your team-mates were shouting to you. But I do wonder if we'll ever see regular capacity crowds again.

We had some great times in front of the old North Bank and I hope we'll see some great times in front of the new North Bank stand. All of football's changing – players are earning big money and the sport's become a big business – and I suppose we have to move with the times. No one knew the Hillsborough tragedy was going to happen or that Taylor's report would come through. Arsenal had no option but to build the new stand: the alternative would have been the North Bank and nobody allowed to stand on it! But in the same way, many supporters have said they can't imagine me in another team's colours, I won't ever be able to think of Highbury without seeing the old North Bank in my mind's eye, thousands of Arsenal supporters packed in and cheering us on.

Introduction

I once ate some funny-tasting mushrooms in the ruins of a Mayan temple in Mexico. I met the girl of my dreams in an Italian restaurant in Raynes Park. And last year I played Richard the Third at a castle overlooking the M6 in Staffordshire. These personally memorable episodes apart, the most intense experiences of my life have all taken place at football grounds: Highbury, White Hart Lane, Wembley Stadium and Anfield. Afternoons and evenings so significant I would forget to breathe for the best part of two hours, and so emotional I imagined my little heart was going to burst. Ray Kennedy or Charlie George or Michael Thomas have a finger on the button and what follows is like that climactic scene in the sci-fi movie when the control centre overloads: consoles explode, sirens wail, cables burst into flames and every dial in the place charges up to *RED FOR DANGER!* Or, in this case, *RED FOR GOA-A-A-L!*

These *are* dangerous moments: complete disorder of the senses, no fear, no control, no law of gravity. Hundreds, thousands of hours of boredom, frustration, anxiety and disappointment – watching Arsenal, living your life – then, at that one moment, the big hand covers the little hand, the counter says: *00:00*, and the whole bloody lot goes off. You and thousands of others are out there together, the same mind – no mind – just blind, screaming, effortless delirium. I'm a reasonable man, but enjoying football is the art of forgetting that from time to time. The point is that, of course, it doesn't matter. It's just the most important thing there is.

I started watching my local team – Highbury was a 20-minute walk from Hartham Road – in 1966. (I've a different address now, but it still takes 20 minutes.) Either side of Sir Alf and England's glorious World Cup summer, Arsenal won just 11 of 53 competitive games. Had the year been a season, running Christmas to Christmas, I would have spent 1967 watching Second Division football. Supporters of other clubs sneer at Arsenal fans' idea of hard times. Fair comment. At ten, though, I didn't have the mature perspective afforded since by regular contact with followers of Crystal

Palace, Stoke and Bishops Stortford. I didn't know either, for that matter, that this was the most ineffectual Arsenal side Highbury had ever seen. All I was sure of was that I'd spent weeks persuading Dad to take me and that now we were here, cold and wet on the Clock End as often as not, neither of us was going to budge. It was horrible but we liked it. Surrounded by old blokes who plumbed new depths of despair as defeat followed defeat – convinced they'd died and gone to Hell since the last Championship in 1953 – me and Dad looked for signs of life and stuck to our guns.

Raised on county cricket in Dover but now with Bob Wilson on his staff and young Charlie George a headache on his register at Holloway School, Dad looked on the South Terrace as an interesting and relevant place to spend his Saturday afternoons. For me, one Jon Sammels half-volley from the edge of the area was sufficient. I happily resigned myself to hours in the playground trying to explain that Ian Ure's effortless grace as our captain on TV's *Quizball* in midweek somehow made up for the complete mess he invariably made of keeping track of any half-decent centre-forward he was asked to mark come Saturday. These were the dark days when, in desperation, we all agreed that Furnell was better than Yashin. We may even have hoped that Roy Pack was a young man with a future as we watched him make his debut in a 3–0 capitulation to Leeds in front of 4,500 diehards, Highbury's smallest-ever crowd. Days later, Chairman Dennis Hill-Wood gave it the old *Next, Please* and Manager Billy Wright (and Roy Pack) disappeared ignominiously into the night.

By the spring of 1970, it had all been turned around. Although the old blokes were frantic (sullen-frantic) by now – it was 17 years since they'd watched Forbes, Lishman and Logie score and beat Burnley to win the League, while two Wembley defeats in the past two years had only made things worse – me and Dad were happy enough. We'd blamed the ref against Leeds in '68 and cried with Bobby Gould against Swindon in 69, Bob Wilson and Charlie George were in the first team and I could wear my Arsenal scarf to school every other week, it seemed, as Glentoran, Porto, Rouen, Bacau and even the legendary Ajax of Amsterdam were whacked out of sight under the lights at Highbury on the way to the European Fairs Cup final.

The week leading up to 28 April, though, was just about too much for everybody's nerves. Down 3–1 from the first leg against the excellent and experienced Belgian side Anderlecht, that one away goal was enough, we thought, to give us hope at home or enough, by way of rope, to hang ourselves. Certain, anyway, that we weren't sure, the Tuesday evening saw us out of the house by half past four: eating, conversation, homework all completely out of the question tonight. Four years on, we could now have walked this blindfolded: down to Caledonian Road, left into McKenzie Road, across Holloway Road and around Drayton Park, right up Aubert Park and to the top of Avenell Road.

The hill down towards the turnstiles is already teeming at five o'clock. Hundreds of people, soon to build to 50,000, are milling around with drawn faces, aimless, brittle, unconvincingly cheerful. Swarming under the shadow of the Main Stand, so many details of individual lives, lived elsewhere: families, homes, jobs, responsibilities; histories, futures, ways of making do; suits, overalls, anoraks, school blazers, butcher's coats and Doctor Martens; a confusion of races, dialects and accents – Stoke Newington and Nicosia, Thornton Heath and County Wicklow, Hertfordshire, Devon, Norfolk and, tonight, Brussels too; no one, save the twos and threes, the little bands of family and friends, anything to do with anybody else except for this – for what is going to happen here this evening. Thousands now, whoever they are, wherever they've come from, squeeze into a street in north London to wait for the turnstiles to open, wishing away the two-and-a-half hours of their lives to kick-off time in the company of familiar strangers, and starting to allow themselves to believe tonight might just turn out to be The Night.

On the terrace, pressed up against our end of the barrier, as people finish work and, arriving, stream out across the Clock End around us, Dad and me can't manage more than half a dozen consecutive words between us. Our spot packs in with its regular crowd but there's no chat, no cracks, just the odd breathless *Alright?*. I can't read the programme, or the paper. I feel sick, I'd like to lie down and go to sleep. All I can manage is to stare intently at the concrete between my feet or to look away past the left-hand goalpost towards the North Bank at the other end and count the minutes until half past seven.

Down there, the covered terrace is filling up fast as well. At first, you can pick out individuals: it's still light as fathers in macs lead little boys in red and white bobble hats down towards the rails behind the goals; clumps of lads in white sta-prest and short-sleeved Ben Shermans disappear into the gloom at the back under the roof, briefly silhouetted against the huge open doorway at the very top of the terrace. It's like watching a hive: constant movement, apparently at random, but each individual intent on finding the place in the whole that is their own. As the evening falls and lights come on under the roof, you lose sight of legs, then bodies, until the Bank is just a crop of heads, spread out in swathes of light and shadow, flickering as countless desperate hopeful cigarettes spark in the gloom. You can hear it fill up, too. During the years since 1966, Arsenal have found themselves a decent football team and the North Bank has found its voice: Highbury has an End. At first, tonight, it's all a little strained. Songs start, or a voice booms: *A-a-y-eh! A-r-r!*, only for another chant to cut across it. Accidents of timing, the network pegged out across the top steps not quite complete, the whole thing collapses into laughter and ironic cheers. All the while, more people pack up under the roof by the minute. Probably an hour before kick-off, the big voice starts to spell out *A-R-S-E-N-A-L* again and, this time, everybody's with him at the instant. From the moment a thousand voices hit the comedy bass-note for *E-e-e-ee!*, the North Bank comes loudly to life: the old pub songs, *When You're Smiling* and *Mother Brown*; the pop songs twisted into shape around the players' names – Radford, Sammels, Armstrong, Charlie George. The Belgian fans away in the West Stand may not catch every word, but they'll get the general drift: *We are the Arsenal and we are the best, we are the Arsenal so FUCK ALL THE REST!*

It's taking longer and longer for those arriving now to pick their way through to the places they want to stand. Little landslides of teenagers tumble down from the back after every knees-up, every song, sending ripples out and down the terrace towards the bright, hissing green of the pitch. As the seats fill up, this fever that's boiling up under the roof spills round the rest of the ground. Down at the Clock End, me and Dad and the old blokes are shouting our heads off, too. By quarter past seven, all doubts have been roared out into the North London air, replaced by swagger, bravado and belief: *And now you're going to believe us – We're going to win the Cup!* Highbury crackles and the roar that greets the players is scary and irresistible, so loud your ears ring and your teeth ache. We've never made a noise like this before!

Like all the best drama, the game's every move unfolds with all the gravity and significance of the inevitable. Kicking towards us in the first half, after a nervous 20 minutes Eddie Kelly snaps in a shot from just inside the penalty area for the first goal. One more will do it and from that moment, on the pitch and off it, belief becomes absolute conviction. The Arsenal players, though perhaps technically less accomplished, run faster, tackle harder and just want it more through the din. Every touch by a red shirt sparks roars of approval and encouragement. Each time an Anderlecht player has the ball at his feet, two or three Arsenal players and 50,000 spectators conspire to worry it away from him. As a game, the first 45 is tight, exciting to the point of suffocation, and seems to go on for ever. By twenty past eight the play and our voices are a little ragged. As the whistle blows for the break, the crowd seems to take a deep breath for the first time in an hour before applause crashes around the stands.

Where two hours before our little group had stood and stared, speechless with apprehension, now you can't get a word in edgeways. Nobody quite believes how well the team is playing, how much noise the crowd is making, how likely it appears this story is going to have a happy ending. While the roar that had greeted the teams at twenty past seven had been a gunshot, triggered by the hours of expectation, their appearance for the second half shakes out a wave of noise which begins in the West Stand, opposite the players' tunnel, and swirls round the ground as people, realising, turn away from the middle of thousands of excited, wide-eyed conversations to add their voices to the tide. Frank McLintock stands in front of the North Bank, shouting for effort and commitment from the supporters with the same ferocity, the same familiarity with which he shouts at his team-mates. The End responds with a roar that burns into everybody's memory of the second half, rolling around the terrace like thunder, dropping away in one corner only to take a fresh charge from somewhere else, relentless and thrilling. It's as if Arsenal have several more players on the pitch than Anderlecht. Certainly none of theirs are anywhere to be seen when John Radford arrives on the penalty spot in front of the North Bank, hanging in the air as if he'd just flung himself between the swings of a trapeze, and meets Bob MacNab's cross from the left with a perfect header past the Belgian goalkeeper. Charlie George, who'd been watching Radford play from the terraces just a couple of years before, runs in now to meet him and they both disappear into the heaving, jubilant mass behind the goal. Minutes later, taking a George through-ball in his stride, Jon Sammels carves into the right-hand side of Anderlecht's penalty area and slides a shot precisely into the opposite corner of the goal. Frank McLintock has sprinted from the halfway line to reach the goalscorer before anyone else. The pair of them stand on the running track, screaming at the North Bank while the North Bank screams back.

Even though the Belgians hit a post – and a goal now would send the final into extra time – the last stages of the match are fifteen minutes in football paradise: the world no longer exists beyond this brightly lit rectangle, the desire of 50,000 fans rolls down the terraces and breaks, deafening, across the pitch. These are perfect moments: you want the game won and to be over, but you don't want this to end.

Looking past Bob Wilson to the goalmouth at the other end, the North Bank boils: 17,000 faces turned up to the light, 17,000 bodies jiggling, bumping, swaying like some fierce, hysterical, happy chemistry; a great pot, struggling to contain the energy of 17,000 people's dreams; and the roar, no words, no tune, but endless and bottomless.

At the final whistle, the fragile formal barrier between the spectacle and the spectators is joyfully brushed aside. The kids, their dads, the lads pour from the terraces on to the pitch. Players give up their shirts, Wilson and McLintock bob up and down on the shoulders of the crowd. Somehow, precariously, a huge and ridiculous piece of silverware changes hands and is swallowed up in the throng. Goodwill, relief and disbelief unlock the Home of Football and the stadium, old and staid, gives way to cheerful mayhem. Having willed these moments for so long, stood behind the goals, we lay siege to the stretch of green on which all hopes and fears had focused. This is ours – me and Dad's, and the old blokes' and the North Bank's. The Arsenal done us proud. Running, jumping, hugging, laughing and cheering, Highbury belongs to us tonight, and this feeling will belong to us forever.

George Graham, who wore the number 11 shirt the night Arsenal beat Anderlecht, returned to the club as manager in the summer of 1986. The hope was that Graham, as demanding and disciplined as a boss as he had been relaxed and flamboyant as a player, might halt the slide into factionalised and irresponsible mediocrity that had followed the loss of Liam Brady – Arsenal's outstanding individual talent since the days of Alex James – to Italian football in 1980.

All expectations were quickly exceeded. Putting his faith, as had his boss in 1970, Bertie Mee, in the fire and promise of young players on the staff, Graham had his hands on the Littlewoods Cup a few months after taking charge. Within a couple of years, he had fashioned a side that had a realistic chance of bringing the League Championship to Highbury for the first time in 18 years. Indeed, Arsenal have subsequently enjoyed the club's most sustained period of success since the 1930s.

By the spring of 1989, the raw ability of a handful of home-reared teenagers had matured into the core of a reliable and often exciting side. Away from Highbury, particularly, Arsenal were playing as well as they had for a decade. Here was a team without stars, products of the youth system alongside careful purchases from second and third division clubs that supporters could feel 'belonged' to them: loyal, hard-working and unpretentious, like the Double side of which the manager had been a member. While Graham held himself aloof, a little unapproachable, the team he sent out on a Saturday was very much within the reach of the fans on the terraces: talented players but, apparently, men without a trace of ostentation – workers who applied themselves to the job each week with the same pride and sense of purpose that supporters felt as they took their places behind the goal. We could see, of course, that this was a team that could win things but it was also a team we could take to our hearts. Huge numbers of North Bank and other Highbury regulars were travelling away every week, feeling part of the effort and part of the club in a way they hadn't for a generation.

In April 1971 Arsenal had been the team coming up on the rails, tracking an increasingly nervous Leeds United for months before hitting the front at the very last. Come April 1989 Arsenal had been setting the pace since the turn of the year, watching over one shoulder as rivals Liverpool made up the ground on what had, at one point, been a 19-point advantage. Saturday the 15th brought an opportunity to ease the tension at the top of the table: Newcastle United came to Highbury on FA Cup semi-final day with our second and third-placed rivals both involved. Norwich were playing Everton at Villa Park, Liverpool met Nottingham Forest at Hillsborough. Arsenal, stuttering, were having their least inspired weeks of the season and United, struggling to avoid relegation, weren't potentially attractive opposition. Still, nearly 40,000 people were happy enough to head for Highbury in the hope, at least, that the team could grind out another important result.

The North Bank had been filling up since one o'clock and under the roof, at least, was packed in tight by the time I got to my seat in the Lower East Stand at ten to three. It was a bright, still afternoon, the ground a third short of its capacity and the crowd tense, a little restless, sensing that, with a victory of some description at this stage of the season counting for more than the means used to achieve it, they were in for an anxious, difficult afternoon. All round the ground, and on terraces all over the country, transistors and Walkmans were tuned in to keep track of events at the day's big games in Birmingham and Sheffield. What people began hearing and passing on to their neighbours over the course of the next hour would change football – and watching football – forever.

Before Arsenal had even kicked off, word was going around that something was amiss up at Hillsborough. The phrase people heard at first was 'crowd disorder', the official euphemism for it going off at football. The 1985 European Cup final, before which three dozen Juventus fans died after crowd disorder involving Liverpool fans, was a recent memory – especially at grounds like Highbury which were still denied competitive European football as a result. The incidents at the Heysel Stadium had often been referred to as a 'disaster' – inappropriately and irresponsibly because those deaths had been caused, after all, not simply by a coincidence of negligence and unforeseen circumstances but by the malicious intent of a small number of spectators in the middle of a large crowd. The Heysel Stadium outrage had been the most spectacular chapter in a history of fighting at football grounds which had plagued the English game since the mid-60s. This afternoon, with Liverpool supporters apparently involved, many at Highbury when they heard the first reports, while the Arsenal and Newcastle players warmed up, jumped quickly to the wrong conclusion.

It was not until the game was underway that it began to become clear that a real disaster was taking place 200 miles north at Hillsborough. What was happening in Sheffield, too, was to some extent a result of the violence at matches that had become, until recently, a regular part of our Saturday afternoons. Ill-judged forward planning, mismanagement on the day and the actions of an irresponsible minority may all have played a part, but the Hillsborough Disaster, surely above all, was a stark and horrifying testimony to a culture that placed the priority of crowd control over that of crowd safety. It has been spoken of as tragedy, but tragedy is inexorable, inevitable, predestined. Unlike Heysel, which happened because a few people, at least, wanted it to, Hillsborough need not – should not – ever have happened.

At Highbury, during a first half punctuated by whispers among the crowd and strained announcements over the public address system, a shocked silence was settling over the terraces. Every fan on the North Bank that afternoon had known a moment of fear, pressed into the heart of a capacity crowd on a square foot of concrete somewhere, when – even if only for a few seconds – the sense of benign chaos, excitement, of freedom, that was part of the thrill of standing on a packed end had given way, in a sudden crush, to blank, dry-mouthed panic. Those moments had always flashed by as the crowd swayed back, a deep breath, a nervous laugh and: *Now, where were we?* Every fan on the North Bank, and on terraces all over Britain, had an inkling there and then of how terrifying the crush on Leppings Lane became when, for once, the crowd wasn't able, wasn't going to, sway back or along because fences at the front and ignorance at the back meant the crush had nowhere to go but down.

By half time, as it became clear that people in Sheffield had died and were dying, the blood ran cold. The mass of people, young, old, men and women of all races, from all walks of life, spread out in red and white across the North Bank disintegrated into so many thousand individual lives. Their pasts and futures, brought to Highbury and forgotten for a couple of intense, occasionally joyful, hours on a Saturday afternoon, were thrown into sharp relief: threatened, frighteningly precious and fragile. Suddenly, this marvellous spectacle – a great adventure that every week led up to – was lost in shadow. The game began again (Arsenal scored, Newcastle didn't), happening in dull enervating slow motion, a meaningless sequence seen through the wrong end of a telescope, strange and a long way away. Life, indeed, may have been something we'd come to the stadium that afternoon to escape from or, at least, to put to one side. But that was done never thinking we might not return: we could let go of what we were from day to day, easy in the knowledge that the routines and tyrannies, the tangibility of our ordinary lives, would still be there waiting at twenty to five.

For those who died at Hillsborough, the afternoon was an adventure they couldn't come back from. Football was at the centre of their lives like it is at the centre of ours. The idea of something so beautiful and so important being the agent that took those lives away is a bleak, sobering, heart-breaking prospect. All of us – all football supporters – know that those deaths at Hillsborough might easily, might just as well have been, our own. That is said not to undermine, in any way, the very personal loss experienced by the families and friends of the Hillsborough victims, but to explain the fear and the vague sense of shame which, I'm sure, all other football supporters were to feel in the coming months when time came to mourn those who lost their lives on the Leppings Lane End on 15 April 1989.

Lord Justice Taylor, asked to report on the Hillsborough Disaster and to make recommendations for future policy on crowd safety at football grounds, came to the conclusion that standing up to watch matches was fundamentally dangerous. The legislation drafted by the Home Secretary in response to the Taylor Report means that all Premier League and First Division grounds, at least, must be all-seater by 1994.

Policy framed in regard to crowd safety at football in this country has, traditionally, been ill-advised on two counts. Firstly, any prescription for change has always been crisis-led. Ibrox, Bolton, Bradford and, now, Hillsborough were all profoundly disturbing incidents which followed – and arose from – the years of ignorance, neglect and mismanagement which preceded them. Our history of crowd safety legislation is simply that of a succession of responses to these famous disasters, drafted after hasty analysis in a highly charged atmosphere – grief, anger, and recrimination setting their own agenda. This is not to suggest that Popplewell, Taylor and their predecessors did not produce intelligent, imaginative and important contributions. But the spectacular incidents which provoked their reports were themselves symptoms of the long-term disinterest of government, the football authorities and fans themselves. Not once have the parties concerned sat down, without the storm cloud of a headline incident hanging over them, to determine a coherent workable policy for the future. Instead, legislation has invariably found its way on to the statute as a desperate attempt to avoid being haunted by the past. Of course, once the dust has settled, traditional disinterest has crept back once more. Hillsborough, it is true *may* prove a watershed in relation to this. Many of Taylor's recommendations on safety regulations and its enforcement are now already working practice. British football grounds will be less dangerous places for it. It remains to be seen, however, whether his analysis of the culture of mistrust which really makes disasters like Hillsborough possible will have a similar impact. There remains a lot of work to be done to improve the important relationships, identified in the report, between football clubs, the fans and the civil authorities. In many respects, indeed, this is work on which we haven't even made a start.

The second basic flaw in our development of crowd safety policy follows naturally from the high-profile nationally important stature of the committees that have laid the groundwork for change over the years. No matter how thorough the analysis, the study made always relates to the particular situation, the particular set of circumstances which have made the headlines. Always implicit in the remit given to these committees, however, is the requirement that, whatever their conclusions, one size must fit all. The lessons learned must be applicable across the board, without exception. This is tidy, politically glamorous. Something is seen to be being done. What the process ignores is the incontrovertible fact that every football ground – and every football crowd – is different. Each has its own architecture, its own culture, its own history, any or all of which may render 'catch-all' legislation unnecessary, inappropriate or insufficient. The truth of the matter has long since been recognised by some clubs, police forces and civil authorities – arrangements at Highbury are a model of this – but is still wilfully ignored by many others. The well-being of a large number of people enjoying a football match together, at a particular place and at a particular time, can only be ensured by the specific and local exercise of responsibility by those concerned in the particular circumstances. Needless to say, that responsibility lies with the individual member of the crowd as much as it does with everybody else.

Summary observation of the existing rules and regulations will prevent nothing. No one broke the law at Hillsborough, after all. Breaking down the traditions of fear and mistrust that have dominated relations between the clubs, police and fans for a generation, and finding ways to develop working local models of co-operative practice should be recognised as the essential principles of the programme for change set out by Lord Justice Taylor: the only lastingly relevant means to ensure football grounds a safe future. It is to be hoped that Taylor will not simply be remembered as the man who made football crowds sit down. Unfortunately, it remains possible that the blustering demands of political expediency will again have helped us miss the chance to really put things right.

Players play, managers manage, everybody else involved does what they do. But there's no point to football without fans. The game is the world's most important professional sport; more people are prepared to pay to watch it than any other. It's exciting because it's relatively unstructured, involving because it's relatively simple, and profitable – potentially at least – because it appeals to so many kinds of people on so many different levels. The bulk of football's audience has, traditionally, watched the game standing up. A place on the terrace, culturally and economically accessible to everybody, has offered the spectactor a regular and local opportunity for fast, colourful entertainment enriched by a unique sense of *participation* in the event. From this perspective, the move to the all-seater stadium may be seen as the most significant development to date in the history of football as a professional spectator sport. At the very least, it offers concrete evidence of a change, for good or ill, that has blown through the game and society as a whole over the past decade.

What is certain is that the experience of watching football from the terraces has been a profoundly important part of millions of lives for over a century. The game itself has been a ragged thread running through our cultural and social history since the late 1800s. Developed by the Victorians as a means to entertain and improve the labouring classes, football soon proved to have a life very much of its own and, well before the First World War, had grown up into something far more passionate and partisan than its forefathers had ever had in mind: a fiercely professional sport watched by huge and often very disorderly crowds.

> The one topic of conversation this week in football circles and in all circles at Woolwich and Plumstead, has been the assault committed upon Mr Brodie, the official referee in the match on the Manor Field, Plumstead, last Saturday, between the Woolwich Arsenal and the Burton Wanderers Clubs. About 7,000 spectators were present . . . Of course the great multitude of people felt profound regret for the outrage, not only for the sake of the principal sufferer and the true spirit of the game, but from well founded apprehensions of consequences.
>
> **The Kentish Independent**, January 1895

The popular terraces were not only places of entertainment but safe, sociable environments, offering the paying customer a sense of community and a safety value for the release of emotion and the relief of daily tedium. Their importance to the people who stood on them explains why many of the ends became as famous as the players, teams and clubs that they supported: Anfield's Kop, the Holte End at Villa Park, Old Trafford's Stretford End and, at Highbury, Arsenal's North Bank.

These great sweeps of concrete terracing, with their enormous, passionate and loyal populations, have now disappeared to be replaced by tip-up seats. 1994 marks the end of a very important story: how football – the national game – has been experienced by, and what it has signified to, the millions for whom a place on the End could make the rest of life worth-while. What follows is the history of one such terrace, the North Bank, told in the words of the five generations of Arsenal supporters to whom the story belongs.

A Note on Method

The End tells the story of Highbury's North Bank in the words of the fans who've watched football from its steps since Arsenal moved to north London in 1913.

In large part, it is a work of oral history: recollections, opinions and impressions recorded in personal interviews during late 1992 and early 1993. These interviews were arranged after Arsenal fans contacted me in reply to articles in the club programme, the local press and supporters' fanzines. In a few instances I have used letters instead of, or in addition to, the interviews arranged after my appeal for assistance. Respondents themselves, Arsenal staff, the Arsenal Supporters' Club and the Independent Arsenal Supporters' Association all furnished me with further personal introductions.

To reflect life on the North Bank from other perspectives, I was able to interview players, ex-players, Arsenal's MD and past and present members of the police force and St John's Ambulance Brigade. Where relevant, and whenever possible, I have set my oral evidence in the context of first-hand written accounts relating to the North Bank's history: press accounts, archive material, programme notes and minutes from Arsenal Board meetings. These latter exemplify the enlightened co-operation I received from the club at all stages of my research.

I believe that, for the most part, the story of The End is told most effectively by simply editing the first-hand oral and documentary material into a pattern of narrative and around specific themes. I have therefore restricted my own comments to introductory paragraphs to each chapter which, I hope, will establish a structure for what follows. I also take the opportunity, where necessary, to discuss any areas which obviously require further clarification or elaboration.

It is in the nature of *The End*, the book no less than the North Bank, to be full of contradictory descriptions, perceptions and explanations. I expect everything in these pages, save some of the more objective documentary evidence, to be called loudly and (I hope) passionately into question. It's a book about football, after all, and should therefore start as many arguments as it may help to settle.

CHAPTER ONE

'We Have Had Our Troubles'

THE LAUNDRY END, 1913–30

Woolwich Arsenal Football Club turned up on north London's doorstep over the summer of 1913, in search of a crowd. Until 1904 they had been London's best supported League team: they had been London's only League team. The club's early embrace of the professional game and the brave – perhaps foolhardy! – decision to compete against the Football League's northern-based heavyweights, rather than their peers in the Southern League, lent the Manor Ground in Plumstead a unique glamour. The surroundings, on the other hand, did not: it was possible to watch games in Arsenal's early days from a perch on sewage pipes that ran along the back of one side of the enclosure. But, although Second Division football was the standard fare, Woolwich's League membership helped ensure that the contemporary giants of English football, the likes of Aston Villa, Newcastle United and Blackburn Rovers, were regular visitors to the Manor Ground, if only for prestige friendlies.

In the early years of the twentieth century, especially if the team was playing well, supporters appear to have been willing to make the awkward journey down into one of south-east London's least accessible backwaters. Indeed, on Woolwich Arsenal's promotion to the First Division for the first time, season 1904–5 saw huge crowds drawn to the Manor Ground: only Newcastle United could better the club's average home gate of 19,980.

Unfortunately, both on the pitch and off, 1904–5 was to prove a short-lived high-water mark for the achievements of the Woolwich club. Mid-table mediocrity, it turned out, was the best the team could manage in the top flight. Worse, with the elections of Chelsea, Tottenham Hotspur and Fulham to the Football League over the next few years, the metropolitan spectator was offered the opportunity to watch football in surroundings considerably more comfortable and more accessible than Plumstead's Manor Ground. By 1910, Chelsea and Spurs were already attracting gates nearly three times as big as Woolwich Arsenal's. Even Fulham, still languishing in the Second Division, were proving a more popular attraction. The inevitable consequence was the development of a sell-to-survive policy which saw the club's better players sold off to pay the mortgage on the Manor Ground. This in turn, inevitably, hampered the team's capacity to perform and thus depressed the dwindling attendances still further. Woolwich Arsenal stumbled on, losing money as quickly as the team lost games. Season 1912–13 was an unmitigated disaster: only one victory at the Manor Ground all season – only three in all – as an average crowd of below 10,000 suffered the team's relegation back to the Second Division.

That would probably have been the end of the story but for the unlikely and, by all accounts, imposing presence of Henry Norris, who had stepped in and bought the club when, £3,000 in debt, it had been forced into liquidation in 1910. Quite why this man – a property developer of enormous, though not limitless, wealth, Mayor of Fulham and a director at Craven Cottage – should have taken the future of Woolwich Arsenal on to his shoulders (and his debit sheet) must remain a matter for conjecture. Perhaps the whole business was simply a manifestation of his huge and preposterously ambitious personality. Possibly the development of Highbury was an expensive second-best option, after Norris's grand scheme to merge the Woolwich and Fulham clubs at Craven Cottage was blocked, carried through on the strength of the pride and entrepreneurial ability of a man used to getting his own way. Whatever his motives, Henry Norris deserves the posthumous thanks of all who have enjoyed football from the North Terrace since those early days.

The move to north London cost a lot of money, upwards of £125,000 (a small fortune in contemporary terms), recoupment of which was halted before it could really begin with the outbreak of the 1914–18 war. Nor was it popular: Norris faced opposition from near-neighbours Spurs and Clapton Orient who disapproved of this prospect of local competition, from Islington Council who disapproved of the business of football, and from local residents who disapproved of the ruffians who they saw making up the traditional football crowd. In spite of all this, however, the move to Highbury was an immediate success: over 20,000 people turned up to watch Arsenal's first game at their new half-finished ground and kept coming, in spite of the spartan surroundings which prevailed, throughout the season. Some of these visitors were, of course, loyal Woolwich diehards finding their way across the river, as their descendants still do. By and large, however, Norris' argument that a new audience could be found for football in N5 was immediately and thoroughly vindicated.

Furthermore, while the outbreak of war dealt a severe blow to Norris' ambitions, its conclusion offered him no little consolation. He was able not only to wangle a place for his club, against all odds and against all common sense, in the First Division, but also to take advantage of the upsurge in enthusiasm for watching football which followed the return of peace-time in 1919 (much as it would again in 1946). Although attendances at Highbury of 30,000-plus helped keep the recently knighted Sir Henry's and Arsenal's heads above water, the team's performances were unimpressive. The situation became critical in season 1924–25 when, finishing in 20th place, the club only just avoided a return to the Second Division which might have proved the final straw for the owner's finances or his patience or both. Instead, Norris dumped his secretary-manager, the hapless and long-suffering Leslie Knighton, and secured the services of the already legendary Herbert Chapman.

Here was a man with the ambition, imagination and will to match Sir Henry's own. Success on the field was not long coming as Chapman assembled many of the team that would go on to dominate the next decade: Hapgood, Roberts, Hulme,

Jack and Bastin. By 1930, Arsenal had won their first major trophy, the FA Cup, beating Chapman's old club Huddersfield 2–0 in the final, and were the best-supported team in the country, with an average of 35,500 spectators packing into Highbury every other week to watch the first flower of the greatest football team the world had ever seen.

Sir Henry Norris, though, was not in a position to enjoy the fruits of his labour, having been barred, in February 1928, from any future involvement with football after the High Court found in favour of an FA inquiry into financial irregularities at Highbury in the early 1920s.

Arsenal's success as the decade closed gave the club the economic stability it required to turn Highbury into the stadium of which Norris and, now, Chapman dreamed. By 1930, plans were in place to build a new stand on the site of the Spion Kop, the west-side banking which had been the 'popular' terrace, holding the vast majority of the ground's standing customers, since 1913. At the same time the size of the north-side terrace, the Laundry End, was to be increased. Its banking would be fully concreted for the first time and its facilities improved to cater for the huge increase in attendances which Chapman and the club correctly foresaw for the coming decade. Arsenal – and the thousands who now swarmed out of the underground station next door and into Higbbury through the Gillespie Road turnstiles – stood on the threshold of a new era.

'AND WE GOT IN FOR NOTHING, SEE!'

This is an inside account of the alarums and excursions, in 1913, when the Arsenal football ground was being made. In those days we clinked golden sovereigns in our pockets, bought cigarettes 20 for 6d, and I believe Arsenal's big signing of the time was George Jobey. Times have changed.

In about 1908, Archibald Leitch, a consulting engineer and commercial architect, who had his office in Glasgow, had created a practice in Scotland for the building of football grounds. Rumours of likely similar happenings in Lancashire and Yorkshire caused him to move his practice to Manchester, the Glasgow office being maintained for other work in the shipyards. I joined the firm as second assistant and the 'battle' commenced. The main objective was to capture and consolidate the market for the Manchester United ground at Old Trafford, one of the few grounds constructed inside a symmetrical perimeter wall and originally laid out for 100,000 spectators, but shortage of money caused only part of the plan to be carried out for about 70,000 spectators.

The business sprouted and the chief assistant was called back to Glasgow and I was promoted to chief assistant and designer. Mr Leitch's time was taken up chasing likely financiers to support various works that might be influenced our way, and at this time you might say that probably about only half a dozen football clubs in the country were really solvent – Woolwich Arsenal being one of the 'others'. He spent a long time in London at Stamford Bridge, Tottenham, etc., and during 1911–12 began to bring back, from his London journeys, large-scale Ordnance plans of some of the sites in London, on which to plan and lay-out a new ground for 100,000 people. The purpose was to provide a ground for the Cup Final to replace Crystal Palace.

Most of these schemes were found to be too expensive and special considerations were necessary, not the least of which was the proximity of an Underground station, and so the last site to be considered, and planned, was the area south of the London College of Divinity bounded by Avenell Road, Highbury Hill and Gillespie Road.

I was made head cook and bottle-washer of the project and on a certain Friday early in 1913, Mr Leitch informed me that interested people had come to terms and that the job was to proceed forthwith, and I was ordered to London immediately. I asked about drawings and specifications and was told that I would have to do them on site as the ground was to be ready for opening in the coming September. It was at this stage that I found out that it was to be the new home of Woolwich Arsenal, then tottering at Plumstead, and that the people behind the scheme were Messrs Henry Norris and William Hall who, I discovered, had done a lot of dwelling-house building in the Fulham district, Mr Norris then being Mayor of Fulham.

Monday morning saw me getting into what was probably a two-cylinder Renault taxi at Euston with my rods, poles and perches, plus personal luggage, and later being deposited on the pavement in Avenell Road outside a forbidding brick wall which, at that time, ran the whole length of Avenell Road on the westerly side. I felt rather like, as the catch line in pantomime had it in those days, 'The only one saved from the wreck'. I found a large timber entrance gate on which I pounded as I had not been told who to contact, and I was very grateful when it was opened by two representatives of Messrs Humphreys Ltd, Civil Engineers of Knightsbridge, who were just installing the builders' hut. They looked after me and after a couple of days I found some very fine accommodation in Sotheby Road, and I discovered that the area around was a theatrical quarter, being an off-shoot from the Finsbury Park Empire. I was all set to start and as hardly anything had been planned, except a small perspective which I had put together for my own diversion, the job was just in my head and in my hands.

The first move I made was to get down to the LCC Engineer's Office (then in Spring Gardens) which was before County Hall was built, and to try to make arrangements to see if they would pass my plans piecemeal, preliminary to the building committee's monthly meets. They agreed and we were off. I had one foot at Highbury and the other in Spring Gardens, rushing each drawing I got passed, back to the site and fixing up the setting out with the foreman. The first plans were to get the pitch laid out, and remember there were no such things as bulldozers, scrapers, mechanical diggers, etc. It was all navvies, picks, spades and barrows. The College end was about six foot higher than Gillespie Road and the first job was to take a line across the centre of the pitch dug into the Aubert Park, and have the spoil wheeled to the other end to level out the pitch space. We then started to form the embankment at the other end. Then a bombshell dropped. The hang-over of the Victorian era still clung to Highbury, although the city VIP's had more or less left their villas and coaches and horses, etc. The suburbanites were still feeling superior however, and a bright boy in Highbury Hill started a petition to get the Islington Borough Council to put a stop to this 'vulgar project'. It appeared that we hadn't a chance, but Mr Norris pulled some strings behind the scenes and I was able to get on once again. Tons of material were required for forming the embankment and news of the 'tip' soon went round. Dozens of people brought us stuff from all over London and the yellow London clay, dropping from the carts, left the streets and roads all around Highbury dyed yellow for many weeks.

More trouble started when we wanted to build the high brick retaining wall at the College end, when the LCC Office 'passed the buck' and referred me to an out-of-date Parish Council office in Holloway Road, where two or three old gentleman of the 'father to son' type of ancient officials of officialdom were in charge. They did not know the difference between a retaining wall and a retaining fee – so now what? Once again Mr Norris came to the rescue and told me to forget them, and I did.

Then another bombshell: we commenced building a high boundary wall abutting Highbury Hill back gardens, when we received a solicitor's letter threatening an injunction because we were over the building line. It was a trick because we were not over the building line, but we could not afford to be held up so we pulled the wall down and rebuilt it six foot further in on our own side. So another threat was dealt with.

At the Gillespie Road end we needed an entrance opposite the Tube station, so two houses were bought and pulled down, giving us a good passage and leading to a large area where turnstiles and exit gates could be constructed to feed out up to the 'Spion Kop'. So we progressed: everyone but myself becoming more pessimistic and depressed, wondering whether the chaos could be got ready. Mr Norris, who was later to be knighted, was a tough nut; testy and a one-way man – his way. I did not let him worry me for I was too busy, but all the staff of Messrs Humphreys Ltd gave me wonderful co-operation and, although it wobbled on numerous occasions, the job went on. In those days anything incongruous was referred to as 'a proper Fred Karno's' after the music hall Crazy Gang of those days, and so this title was tacked on to our project at Highbury. Time was getting on and looking to the future we began to plan the position of the exit gates and turnstiles. The latter were delivered but we could not get the pay boxes ready for the opening. A week or so before September, I got the contractors to supply me with hundreds of feet of rough timber and many carpenters who, at danger points, made rails and passages guiding people into the turnstiles and out to the exits. Offices, dressing-rooms, bathrooms, etc., were roughly ready. Baths were in position but were not connected to supplies and drains. A couple of army field kitchens were brought in for heating water and the contractors' handymen were really first class. Even the players and officials of the club fell in with the spirit of the affair and treated it like a picnic, working hard here and there wherever their services were required, and getting a wonderful kick out of everything they did. They worked like Trojans.

As 'D' Day neared, Mr Leitch, possibly thinking that discretion was the better part of valour, made himself scarce and on the week previous to the opening he could not be found. The testy Mr Norris did everything to find him, without success, and was beside himself, for although the ground was still a hive of activity we were not really ready.

About 11 a.m. on the Saturday morning of the opening, things looked grim, for the exit gates were still open and carts were hanging around, going in and out on their various business, and Mr Norris almost threw in the sponge and insisted on taking myself and Humphreys' representative to lunch at a very large Italian restaurant next door to Finsbury Park gates. I gave instructions that all exit gates were to be closed, for a sprinkling of people were coming along to see what was happening, but on returning from lunch, I found the exit gates were still open and hundreds of people were lining up at the entrances four or five deep in Avenell Road. I rushed in and arranged for all the exit gates to be closed and then the spectators came in. I shall never know why they did not just walk in the exit gates and gate crash without paying, but it says much for the sportsmen of those days that they did not. Thank goodness the weather kept fine and the match was played – the crisis was over. I stayed on for four or five weeks helping with the completion until a proper clerk of works and foreman were appointed to take over for the finishing arrangements.

A.G. Kearney, *AFC Programme*, 21.12.63

Sirs, you are very welcome to our house. It must appear in other ways than words. Therefore I scant this breathing courtesy.

It is our pleasure today to welcome you for the first time to our new ground. That pleasure, great though it is, would have been greater had we been able to welcome you to a ground thoroughly equipped and laid out to its full holding capacity.

Whilst apologising to all and asking for their generous forbearance for such inconveniences as they must necessarily experience on this our opening day, we venture to think, when we state we have only actually been in possession for some 60 working days, that our patrons will admit we have got as near completion as has been humanly possible.

AFC Programme, 1913

As a kid, my pals and I used to walk from City Road to the ground frequently to watch progress, eagerly looking forward to the first match, for which if my memory serves me correctly the Arsenal team was captained by Percy Sands.

A.E. Smith, *AFC Programme*, 26.1.74

You can help to restore the Arsenal's pristine glory almost as much as the players can, for the loyal and whole-hearted support of a crowd means so much to a team. And I feel sure you will give it, wholly and unreservedly.

Percy Sands, *AFC Programme*, 6.9.13

The first game at Highbury? Well, that game – I would only have been about eight years old. In them days, the lad I used to knock about with – I used to be the leader. From Gillespie Road, there used to be an entrance there where you used to go up a slope. There was big doors up there to let the motors and that through to improve the ground, and we used to be able to crawl round the doors, sit under the planks of wood. We'd sit under there until the gates opened and we got in for nothing, see? Oh, I've done a lot for the Arsenal!

George Stinton

Thou though'st to help us; and such thanks we give,
As those near death to those that wish them live.'

Our first duty this week – and it is an exceedingly pleasant one – is to tender you one and all our sincere and hearty thanks, for it was more than gratifying to us to see some 20,000 friends, who had the welfare of the Club sufficiently at heart, brave the unknown discomforts of an incomplete ground, and so greatly assist in making the opening day last Saturday the success some few of those present have been kind enough to say it was.

AFC Programme, 13.9.13

The moment is opportune for me to tender you our very hearty thanks for the generous support you have given to the Club during the eight months now drawing to a close. Whatever may be our fate I am sure you will agree with me that the management have done everything they could to deserve your patronage and your good wishes. We have had our troubles; you have had to put up with your trifling discomforts. Such things were inevitable and you took them in good grace, which is just what a sporting crowd would do.

There have been carpers who wanted the earth and the fullness thereof all in the space of a few minutes, but, like Rome, our new ground could not be completed in a month, nor yet a few months. You have only got to pause for a few moments and realise what a stupendous undertaking the Arsenal management had to handle. It was a bold move to bid farewell to Plumstead and plant the old club in a new area, among a new people. But faith in the enthusiasm of the London football public was strong enough to overcome all obstacles. We came to Highbury, you saw, we conquered. I think it safe to assume that the end of the conquest is not yet.

If the good fates should favour us and take us back to the First Division great times will be in store. Even if we have to wait a little longer for the attainment of our ambition, we feel secure in the knowledge that you will continue to rally round the Arsenal banner. Much remains to be done before we can display our new home in its complete state. Rest assured that much will be forthcoming. Our directors have set themselves a big task, and they are determined to carry it through, no matter what the cost may be.

Throughout the long summer months – long, that is, to those who find pleasure only in the great winter game – a small army of workmen will be busy building up the ground and making it what it will soon be – the finest enclosure in London. It may be that we will have to wait some time before we can reach the limits of the ground's holding capacity, but when all the huge banking has been put in, we will have a home of which you will be proud. When August comes again and you call round to see our players disport themselves in strenuous practice, we hope to show you a picture of what has hitherto been left to the imagination.

AFC Programme, 18.4.14

'THE MOST GET-AT-ABLE GROUND IN LONDON'

The accessibility of our new home is indisputable. It can be reached from the city and places adjacent thereto in less time than any other ground, and should, therefore, prove a great boon to the cosmopolitan enthusiast who finds himself in the city during the kick-off at 2.30 p.m. season, when every moment saved in travelling is valuable.

AFC Programme, 6.9.13

In regard to our claim that we rejoice in the most *get-at-able* football ground in London, I think that there were 20,000 people within the confines of our new ground on Saturday, 6 September, who will heartily endorse that view. Even in our incomplete state there was not the slightest confusion when our patrons came, nor when they departed, and in the matter of catching trains they were in the happy position at Gillespie Road, Drayton Park, and Finsbury Park, of finding their trains actually waiting for them when they entered the station. The railway companies concerned recognise the wisdom of catering for the Arsenal's patrons, and I learn that the Metropolitan alone carried 5,000 extra passengers to Drayton Park.

AFC Programme, 13.9.13

It used to cost about a penny to go in those days. I was living in Holloway, Harvist Road, just across the railway. All the time I was at school – I left in 1922 – I used to go to Arsenal. My dad was a shareholder, you see, he had a seat. I used to stand on the North Bank, when it was called the Laundry End, all the time I was a boy I used to go with a bunch of school-friends. It was only 15 minutes walk, either round by Drayton Park or by Finsbury Park, either way.

Arthur Peakell

'JUST EDGES OF CONCRETE WITH THE DUST PACKED DOWN'

Till they got straightened out it was a mud bank, clay. And you can imagine with the wet weather, the winter, it was murder. I mean when you try and visualise what it was like then and see what it is now!

George Stinton

It was way back in 1913 that I attended my first game at Avenell Road. It was a reserve match and in those days these matches were played on Thursday afternoons. Being a schoolboy I paid half price for admission, which was two pence. My first sight of the ground was the old East Stand, with a few rows of terracing behind each goal, made up of wood and clinker. But along the west side there was just a long high mound of earth and rubble, being built up to form the foundation for the original terracing along that side of the field.

I can still recall the names of some of the first-team players of that time, such as Livesley (G); Benson and Shaw (Bs); Liddell (CH); Ducat, Grant, Gregory (HBs); Lewis (LW) and centre-forward Hardinge. When the latter was not available (because he also was a Kent cricketer), his place was filled by a Lieutenant North.

G.W. Gale, *AFC Programme,* 22.9.73

I was born in the pub. And when I was eight or nine, a fellow used to come down and take me out and about with him. Of course, as my mum and dad were busy in the pub they were quite pleased to get me out of the way. And the fellow said: *Can I take him over the Arsenal?* And so he took me over there. Up the North Bank, which was then called the Laundry End. Some matches you used to get clouds of smoke come up over the pitch from the laundry at the back there. We used to stand right on that corner where we used to come in off Gillespie Road, right up on the corner so we could look across everything. It was just terrace, all open terrace. Like it was on the side, too. All open. There was like edges made in the terrace and otherwise just black dust or something. Just edges of concrete with the dust packed down.

Tom Jales

We are sorry to say that the Assessment Committee of the Islington Borough Council are placing a most prohibitive value on our ground, and one which must materially restrict our efforts in the future, and we are afraid we shall have to limit our desires in the way of making our ground a delight to the eye, as well as a source of enjoyment. It is difficult to credit that even in its present incomplete state it is rated higher than the Spurs' magnificent enclosure, very much higher than the Millwall ground and the Fulham ground at Fulham, and nearly six times as high as the Clapton Orient ground. Indeed, we are rated higher than the magnificently appointed Kennington Oval.

AFC Programme, 1.10.13

A number of our patrons have asked us what we propose to do in the matter of providing refreshments on our new ground, at the outset we would say that it is our one and only desire to cater for the full comfort of our patrons. In the matter of refreshment booths we have been handicapped by the fact that the banking and building operations on the ground have not allowed us to allocate any special buildings for this purpose. But we hasten to assure our supporters that the matter will receive the fullest attention immediately circumstances make it possible. The buildings beneath the rear portion of the grand stand are nearing completion, and when the banking work is finished in other parts of the ground the provision of refreshments will be the first matter taken in hand.

AFC Programme, 8.10.13

We have been greatly troubled by unauthorised vendors of sweets and newspapers, who have managed to elude the vigilance of the police.

Newspaper sellers have no right to sell inside the ground, and our friends would confer a very great favour on the club if they would refrain from purchasing during the progress of the match. A club ground is private property, and we have the right to say who shall or shall not trade upon it.

AFC Programme, 28.8.26

Arrangements have been made with Messrs Gilbarts, the popular confectioners, to purvey their toothsome commodities in the Highbury ground. Their salesmen will wear distinctive attire, and I would remind our patrons that any other person trying to dispose of confectionery or other wares in the enclosure must be regarded as an unauthorised intruder.

AFC Programme, 18.9.26

The question of the erection of a refreshment stall on the unused ground at the Gillespie Road entrance was left to the manager for further report.

AFC Board Minutes, 9.5.28

One of the greatest sights was all the out-of-works – because you had no big diggers then – went down Liverpool Road to the Council who provided them with shovels. There was about 200 blokes out there digging. Coming into that end, into the middle there was a sort of a ramp and the lorries used to come in on that. That end of the ground used to be ten foot lower. They had it all built up with new drains and clinker and everything up to the height it is now. And all the lorries would go out and down Gillespie Road, dumping all the muck. So we had it all built up. All the turf come from Cumberland, beautiful Cumberland turf.

Ron Pottage

Since the close of last season many important ground improvements have been carried out at Highbury and the alterations that have been made under the supervision of our efficient clerk of works, Jack Campbell, who is to be heartily congratulated upon the success of the undertaking, will add enormously to the comfort of our patrons. Extra terraces have been built at the Gillespie Road end of the ground so that accommodation is provided for at least an additional five thousand people and a large portion of the old terraces have been concreted, an improvement that will be greatly appreciated in wet weather. Structural alterations have also been made on the stands but the biggest and, incidentally, the best scheme has been the erection of concrete steps leading from the Gillespie Road entrance to the top of the terraces. We have in the past received many complaints from supporters who use this entrance of the rough and ready state of the approach to the terraces. Now they can reach their favourite vantage points in perfect comfort and the provision of these steps will enable the crowd to distribute themselves over the terraces with much greater facility than formerly.

AFC Programme, 25.8.28

'WHEN HERBIE CHAPMAN CAME TO ARSENAL'

I first went in the 1920s. I remember there were crowds of 50 sometimes 60,000, so we always got there at least an hour before the kick-off. Times varied in those days, without floodlights. They kicked off anytime between two and three. We had a particular place my brother Ted used to stand, about halfway up the terraces behind the goal. We always went, whatever the conditions. I can remember going just in the hope that they'd play. We've been up there when it was so foggy that you could just about see the notice on the door that said *Match cancelled*. We'd still gone, though! We wouldn't risk them playing and us not being there.

George Williams

I remember when Herbie Chapman came to Arsenal from Huddersfield in the 1920s. Mr Chapman made the Arsenal, of course. Over the years there were some outstanding players: Doughy Baker – they used to call him the 'Rubber Man'; Eddie Hapgood, England full-back, he come there as an outside left; Doctor Paterson; Jack Rutherford. I always remember Dr Paterson. Him as a player, he was an individual – and if the referee wasn't certain if it was a corner or a goal-kick, well, he would know Dr Paterson for what he was and he would ask him. Where a lot of players might say it was a corner, he would say: *It's a goal-kick.*

Where we used to stand, we'd get up a bit high so we could look down. Because, otherwise, if you were a smaller bloke like me, it was a waste of time going. You did wonder for your safety sometimes, all swaying, pushing down when there was a goal. And of course, when you went out, you had to go out with the tide sort of thing. If anybody went down it was a bit naughty.

George Stinton

One of the most anxious times I had cropped up in season 1925–26. We were due to play an FA Cup replay with Aston Villa on a Wednesday at Highbury. I left home with, I thought, plenty of time to get to the match. Instead, about 20 minutes before the game was timed to start, I was stuck in Highbury Tube station approach, wedged in among the crowd. Luckily for me, a policeman came to the rescue, hoisted me over an iron railing partition and I got to the ground in time. Dr Paterson, Arsenal outside-left, soon made me forget that little trouble. He scored one of the most brilliant goals I've ever seen in the very first minute. (See plate 8.)

Charles Buchan, GunFlash 5

Shall we ever forget the memorable scene at Highbury on Wednesday. Had our ground been big enough I imagine we would have established a record in attendances at Cup-ties other than the finals. It is difficult to estimate the size of the crowds who were left outside the ground when the gates were closed, but such scenes have never before been witnessed at our enclosure. Happily everything went off without a hitch and I would congratulate the police upon their tactful and efficient handling of such a mammoth throng. I would also pay a tribute to the crowd for its exemplary behaviour. To attract 72,000 to Villa Park on Saturday and 55,400 on Wednesday, with receipts respectively of £5,457 and £4,020, is a wonderful tribute to the popularity of the two clubs.

AFC Programme, 27.2.26

Re: Mr Wright, landlord of house next to Tube, had fence damaged as supporters left Villa Cup-tie. Decided the manager should interview him and point out in a friendly manner we cannot be held responsible for damage at such a distance from our ground.

AFC Board Minutes, 21.2.28

When I started going it was a shilling to get in. Don't know how much the programme was, we could never afford one! 3d, maybe?

Rose Jales

For the man in the crowd who pays his bob every week, scraping the money together at some personal sacrifice, Mr Chapman has the greatest admiration. That man is a great sportsman. It is a great pity that that fine fellow cannot get a Cup final ticket but Mr Chapman is helpless.

Islington Gazette, 23.4.30

'NOTHING IF NOT PROGRESSIVE'

The cost of laying out the ground and all other incidental outlays has not been a small item, and further heavy expenditure will be necessary before it is complete. We want to cover in the end of the field backing on to St John's College in order to provide further protection against bad weather, and this we will do if you will help us.

AFC Programme, 6.9.13

Arsenal's policy is nothing if not progressive. We are ever on the lookout for improvements and are not afraid of trying experiments. It has been suggested to us by the firm responsible for the scheme that entrance to the ground can be expedited – and greater accuracy secured in checking the numbers admitted – by the installation of a ticket system such as in operation on the Underground railways. The experiment is being given a 'try-out' at the Gillespie Road entrance for the first-team matches and we ask for the co-operation of our supporters in order to make it a success. Briefly, the scheme is this: pay boxes are installed from which supporters will purchase their tickets of admission which will be given up as they pass through the turnstiles. Please note that one spectator can purchase all the tickets required in cases where a group of friends arrive together, just as is done on the Tube.

AFC Programme, 27.8.27

You will notice that since last season a new scoreboard has been built and we feel sure the change will be appreciated by our supporters. It is a most up-to-date structure and no one should experience the slightest difficulty in reading the half-time scores of the principal matches of the day.

AFC Programme, 27.8.27

To the Arsenal FC fell the distinction of being the first of the big professional League clubs to be chosen by the British Broadcasting Corporation as the medium of broadcasting an account of a 'soccer' football match. The epoch-making experience was made last Saturday and, from what I can learn about it, a distinct success was achieved, though it was particularly unfortunate that the conditions kept the crowd down to 18,000 and thus materially minimised the volume of sound which the community singing would ordinarily have provided. I would congratulate the BBC officials upon their enterprise and would assure one of my pessimistic friends that the dissemination of descriptive accounts of football matches in this way is not likely seriously to affect the revenue from the turnstiles nor to cause the football-reporting newspapers to go into liquidation. On the contrary, the BBC are doing a service to countless thousands of football enthusiasts who cannot attend the big matches through illness or other causes. This extension of the activities of the BBC will be heartily welcomed by the sporting community at large and, in my opinion, will be an important factor in adding still further to the popularity of our great national winter game.

AFC Programme, 29.1.27

Estimate for extending and roofing College end from Boulton Paul Ltd for £3,800 was accepted.

AFC Board Minutes, 12.5.30

Again given careful thought and resolved nothing be done further in the matter at the moment. Chapman's authority to sign contract cancelled.

AFC Board Minutes, 17.7.30

Decided not to allow the Omega Watch Co. to erect a football timing clock on the ground (as they) insisted on advertising on the structure to be erected. Chapman to contact Mr Fisher of Newcastle instead.

AFC Board Minutes, 7.8.30

It is our intention to erect near the scoreboard a 45-minute clock on the lines of those which have long been most useful on Continental grounds. The clock will be started at the kick-off, and only 45 minutes are marked on it, i.e. the length of a half a game. We had wished it to be ready by this afternoon, but it is probable that we may have to wait a bit longer. But in this respect I must bring one point specially to your notice. This clock is purely to help spectators to have a *rough* idea of how far the game has progressed. *It does not usurp the duties of the referee* who, by the wise provisions of the Laws of the Game, is the sole timekeeper. If the clock reaches its 45th minute and the referee does not signal 'time' do not abuse him or think he is a fool. There are certain to have been stoppages, etc., which the clock has not recorded.

AFC Programme, 6.9.30

The huge clock starts functioning immediately the whistle starts the ball rolling. The dial only marks 45 minutes, in the second half the dial goes back to zero. It has been decided not to use the hooter when the 45-minute periods are up. It can be seen all over the ground by players and spectators.

Islington Gazette, 19.9.30

Manager read a letter from the secretary of the Football Association calling the club's attention to the following resolution passed by the council at their meeting on 13 October 1930.

The council deprecates the use on football grounds of clocks purporting to indicate the duration of play and order their immediate removal.

The vice-chairman wrote a letter which was approved by the Board claiming that the above resolution was *ultra vires* and asking that the members of the council should personally visit the ground and inspect the clock, reconsider the whole matter and receive a deputation from the club. In the meanwhile instructions were given that the clock was to be covered and stopped pending the reply from the FA.

AFC Board Minutes, 23.10.30

Manager asked for estimate on changing 45-minute clock to ordinary clock.

AFC Board Minutes, 13.11.30

Chapman authorised to switch to ordinary clock. £180.

AFC Board Minutes, 29.1.31

Of course Chapman's idea was to move this ground up (to where the flats behind the Clock End are now) because you've got a natural grandstand there, haven't you? He wanted to take the West Stand back to the road in Highbury Hill, there'd be room for a running track, a great big bowl. All the stands were going to be closed in to make one big bowl.

Ron Pottage

'PEOPLE WERE JUST MORE SENSIBLE THEN'

What does it cost to watch football now? £8? What's that, for a season ticket? It used to cost us 7d and, of course, that 7d would last a few weeks because we used to bunk in. That was what you call a long-term policy! We'd go up to the turnstile and the bloke on the turnstile used to say: *Shove up!* Like, two for one. I used to say: *Right!*

And he'd let it go and we'd run and he got nothing. I mean, we used to get a kick out of getting in for nothing, the excitement of beating the 'two-for-one' business. I mean, he was dishonest and we were honest weren't we?

Get caught? No, of course not. You didn't expect to. The policeman didn't worry about you as long as you didn't do any harm. They knew you didn't have a lot of money, and they knew you was enthusiastic. What we were doing wasn't interfering with anybody! We might have been keeping a few bob from the Arsenal till but we thought they could afford it!

When we used to go to Highbury then we had to get there a couple of hours before they kicked off. We had a spot in that corner where they couldn't come in from the back and push you down. So we always stood there and got to know everybody around there.

George Stinton

When my brother Ted used to take me to reserve matches we used to move around at half time, because he used to like to stand with the Arsenal players coming towards you. That's a good thing about standing behind a goal, that feeling of the team coming towards you.

George Williams

There used to be more away supporters on the North Bank, because they'd come in from Gillespie Road Tube station, as it was then.

Tom Jales

Now a word to the people who come to our ground at Highbury and whom we want to see regularly. The ground was supposed to be full last Saturday. It was, in some places, but in others it wasn't. In this connection the spectators can help the club and assure themselves greater comfort in a simple way. The first great point is to keep the gangways clear, because it is the gangways which provide the means of distribution. There have been 60,000 people on our ground. That number can be taken again if the gangways are kept clear and you move round. This little lecture is for your benefit just as much as the benefit of the club.

AFC Programme, 3.9.25

During the close season special attention has been given to the playing pitch and whatever may be its fate as the season proceeds, we shall have a good green crop of grass to start with. In order to preserve it, it is essential that it should be kept free from unnecessary tramping over and we beg of our patrons to restrain the few unruly and perhaps unthinking boys who occasionally endeavour to run over the ground at the conclusion of the match.

AFC Programme, 27.8.21

Again we have to request boys and others to refrain from running over the field at the conclusion of the matches, particularly on reserve match days. If this request is not complied with, it will mean that we shall be compelled to withdraw the lower charges for admission now allowed to boys. There is neither sense nor reason in this scampering over the field whilst the damage done to the playing pitch should be obvious even to you boys.

AFC Programme, 15.10.21

The pitch has recovered nicely after the invasion by a large crowd last Saturday.

Islington Gazette, 17.1.30

I was delighted with the sporting attitude of the huge crowd, which filled the lofty terraces and the vast resounding stand. They were naturally anxious to see the home team win, and they had their heart's desire. But they gave the visitors a warm welcome, and loudly applauded every piece of fine play, whether it was to the credit of a 'Gunner' or a 'Toffee-maker'.

Morning Post, 14.11.25

'At Highbury it is extremely difficult to feel that one is not playing at home so generous are the spectators to the players of the visiting side.' Thus writes John Crosbie, the famous Scottish international and Birmingham player.

AFC Programme, 24.2.25

An 'Arsenal Supporter' writes that: 'It was good to read Pantling's statement in the *Daily Express* that he numbers the Arsenal's crowd among the best he has played before.'

'It is, I think,' adds 'Arsenal Supporter', 'a reputation Highbury's ground has earned, and one I hope will never be smirched, that whoever plays the game there will always be assured of a hearty reception, be he on the home or the visiting side. It may sound partisan, but anyone who witnessed the recent Bolton–Arsenal match would not dispute it that Vizard had as great an ovation when he beat us on the post as if Buchan had scored. This is as it should be. It is the honour of sport, and more of it is wanted on the football field. It is easy enough to applaud the winner on your side, but it is far nobler to applaud the winner on the other side. Let us make our grounds as welcome to visitors as we do our homes.'

Daily Express, 31.10.25

When a side builds up a reputation such as Everton have done this season there is always a danger that one or two members of the hitherto successful combination may lose their heads if the fortunes of the game run against them. Unfortunately it was so in this match and an incident arose of an unpleasant and regrettable kind. I am assured, however, by those who were in the best position to judge that the foul which Cresswell committed on Hoar midway through the opening half looked a good deal worse than it really was. What happened was this: Cresswell and Hoar went for the ball simultaneously and both missed it; Hoar was the quicker to recover whereupon Cresswell, in a moment of peevishness, lunged out blindly with his foot. It was a palpable case of a man losing his head in the heat of battle and I am sure no one regretted it more than Cresswell who has the reputation of being one of the most gentlemanly and most sportsmanlike players in the game. At the same time the act was inexcusable and I was not in the least surprised that the onlookers demonstrated long and loudly against the offender.

Many referees would have given Cresswell marching orders but Mr Harper exercised a wise discretion; he realised what we in the crowd did not at the time: that there was no viciousness in the foul. But once the anger of a crowd, sporting or otherwise, is aroused it insists on expressing its indignation in a way that cannot be mistaken and the next time Cresswell approached the ball after he had fouled Hoar he was booed and hooted. Probably they would have been content to let it go at that – we pride ourselves on the fact that Highbury houses one of the most sporting and fair-minded crowds in the country – but the referee took the unusual course of suspending play and addressing a section of the people in the stand. Personally I have always doubted the wisdom of such action. For one thing you may never be quite sure whether you are admonishing the real demonstrative spirits and in any case not more than a handful of folk hear a word of what is said. However, when the game went on, there was no more 'barracking' so that in this instance the referee's action had had the desired effect.

AFC Programme, 31.12.27

Re: An incident vs Everton 24/12 involving Forshaw Cresswell: A further letter from the FA was read, also the referee's report upon the demonstration by our crowd following the Cresswell incident. Resolved to reply that our crowd as a rule are far more sportsmanlike than the average football crowd (and that our management would always endeavour to give the referee the fullest possible support).

AFC Board Minutes, 10.1.28

I seem to remember we were more restrained. We used to shout loud when they scored and that but I don't recall the results being as vital as they are now.

George Williams

In them days, it *was* the only outlet for the working man. There was no betting, that sort of thing, so they went to football. Today they've got the television and the betting shops. In those days, for the average worker, football was his Saturday's enjoyment. Majority worked a half day on the Saturday, too.

People were just more sensible then. We never had all that jumping up and down and singing. When a player scored they'd shake hands and a pat on the back. Now they go barmy, don't they? Nearly kill the player for scoring the goal, don't they? I think: *what a lot of bloody fools*. And it was a more tolerant crowd. There was none of this chanting and that. I'd like to go up there now. Maybe George Graham would take pity and say: *You can have my seat, I'll go and stand.* When you think about it, we're the backbone of them, aren't we? When they come to Highbury it was us boys that kept them going, weren't it?

George Stinton

Islington was *en fête*. Great crowds thronged the pavements in Upper Street, Essex Road and Caledonian Road. Red and white favours were everywhere. Young enthusiasts leaned over the sides of buses twirling rattles and there were cheers from groups of jubilant supporters. At midnight there was still a big crowd outside the ground. And in the West End traffic had to be diverted. *Bravo Arsenal!* was the slogan of the evening.

The unprecedented scenes of enthusiasm happened again on Monday when the victors were given a civic welcome at the Town Hall, in Upper Street. The whole road from Cross Street to Compton Terrace was just a surging mass of people. A group of Arsenal supporters, decked from top to toe in the club colours, were waiting on the Town Hall steps. So were the Pearly Kings of Holloway and Covent Garden. There was a torrent of cheering when the Arsenal mascot – the famous White Duck – arrived. So there was for the arrival of a replica of the Cup designed in red and white flowers. But the greatest cheers of all were for the moment when the players arrived in two motor-coaches.

Islington Gazette, May 1930

CHAPTER TWO

'They Come to Marvel at the Arsenal'

THE LAUNDRY END, 1931–39

In the nine seasons before the Second World War, Arsenal dominated English football to a degree unheard of before (or since, until Liverpool's remarkable decade of achievement in the late 1970s and early 1980s). The League Championship was won five times and the FA Cup, again, in 1936. In 1934 an England team fielded seven Arsenal players for a match against Italy. In Alex James, the Scottish inside-forward, the club possessed arguably the most gifted player of the generation. In Herbert Chapman they possessed, without question, the finest manager. The latter was to die suddenly in 1934, his Arsenal team probably at their very peak and halfway through a three-season run of title victories. He was succeeded by the estimable George Allison, an Arsenal servant of such long standing he could remember touting desperately for custom outside the Manor Ground in Plumstead.

Crowds turned up at Highbury to marvel in huge numbers, on foot from the densely populated residential areas within walking distance of the ground or, from further afield, by underground railway to the renamed Arsenal station in Gillespie Road which opened almost directly on to the Laundry End's turnstiles. For eight of these nine seasons, Arsenal's attendances were higher than at any other ground in the country. Meanwhile, the stadium which welcomed spectators simultaneously underwent a transformation which would have staggered the 20,000 who had turned up to watch Arsenal's first game at their half-finished Archibald Leitch-designed enclosure in 1913.

In 1931 the terracing at the north end of the ground was built up, deepened and secured towards a capacity of nearly 20,000. This work was undertaken – without undue haste it seems – by the Cearns family building concern, which was later to acquire control of West Ham United. In the course of the rebuilding, the story goes, local residents were asked to bring in refuse by way of landfill on which the new higher banking could be based. One coal merchant, apparently, backed up too close to the edge and watched his horse and cart tumble down to become a part of the Laundry End's new foundations. Indeed, a horseshoe was found in the debris dug out of the old terrace during excavations over the summer of 1992. Although it spoils the story, it must be said that the shoe discovered was so small that it would be difficult to imagine its owner dragging coal around Islington, even in the underfed years of the early 1930s.

In 1932 the Prince of Wales opened a new West Stand on the site of the Spion Kop which had been Highbury's first 'popular' terrace. In 1935 the 'Bobites' on the Laundry End were rewarded for the team's success and their own loyalty with a roof over their heads which was itself not without a whiff of the grandeur that now trailed in Arsenal's wake. Simon Inglis describes the structure in his *Football Grounds of Great Britain:*

> '. . . covered by a simple pitched black roof, but far from seeming plain it has a white ripple fascia all round, with red and white corners and two Arsenal crests at the front.'

This gentrification of the Laundry End was soon followed by the opening of a magnificent East Stand to replace the old, gabled main stand which Archibald Leitch had rushed to get ready for the start of business over 30 years before.

If the idea for a new Highbury was Chapman's, the vision belonged to architect Claude Waterlow Ferrier whose design for the new West Stand was a contemporary landmark in stadium architecture. His careful art deco outlines have ensured that the stadium remains unique – and uniquely recognisable – in world football. Just as the secretary–manager's ambitions were to be put in the safe hands of his assistant after his untimely death, responsibility for the completion of Ferrier's work passed to his partner William Binnie on the architect's death before a schedule was in place for completion of the new East Stand which remains arguably the finest grandstand in Great Britain.

Change, too, affected the nature of the enormous crowds that made their way to Highbury. Better transport and the developing trend towards a full-day holiday on Saturday meant people could get to Arsenal in time for an afternoon kick-off in greater numbers and from further away as the decade progressed. The glamour associated with the team's success and the comforts afforded to wealthier patrons at the improved stadium meant football, at Arsenal at least, became no longer the chosen pastime exclusively of the working man. George Allison, sentimental perhaps but probably not wildly inaccurate, described the throng that crowded into Highbury to watch the world's most famous football team at the finest football ground in Britain:

> Football is the greatest show on earth, the social leveller which has the man in the cap and muffler and the noble in the silk hat urging on his favourite team. There is the man with the rattle, the man with the handbells, the man with the outsize rosettes, the man in a suit in the club's colours, the ladies with club scarves. There's the civil servant who wears a bowler all the week but sports a cap on Saturday so that Bill behind won't have to yell: 'Take that ruddy 'at orf!' The little knot that congregates in the same corner and runs a shilling sweepstake on the first goal, the winner being the one who draws the name of the player who scores it. There are the continual early-comers, the hail-rain-or-snow supporters. The continual late-comers who you can see threading their way to the top of the terraces. And the thousands of schoolboys, excited youngsters who dream one day of trotting out in their team's colours.

> **George Allison,** *Allison Calling*

'A BOB'S WORTH OF ALEX'

A great save by Frank Moss, a clearance off the line by Eddie Hapgood, the driving force of Wilf Copping, the magic of Alex, the body swerve of David Jack, the thrusting scoring wingers, Joe Hulme and Cliff Bastin, and Ted F. Drake blasting his way through the middle. Rarely, in those days, did Arsenal get beaten at Highbury. It was an event when it happened.

AFC Programme, 8.1.74

We used to go along in the 30s expecting Arsenal to win, because they nearly always did! We would come home very disappointed if they didn't win, because all through the 30s we always expected them to win the Championship or the Cup. Of course they won three Championships on the trot. They built up the ground on that success.

Arthur Peakell

I used to live in Hornsey Rise and all the mob would come down by me mum's and call out to me: *Coming down for a bob's worth of Alex?* Alex James.

Ron Pottage

One game that stands out: when they played Aston Villa in a Cup-tie. They were two down. And they came back – I think Bastin scored and David Jack got the equaliser and they drew 2–2. The atmosphere was terrific. It was one roar all the time. Especially after they scored the first goal and got back in the game.

Tom Jales

One goal which constantly crops up when people write and talk about Arsenal in the 1930s is the one scored by David Jack in the last few minutes of a home FA Cup-tie against Aston Villa. All sorts of dates are given but, from the records, it could have been only one particular occasion.

It was in 1931 when we drew 2–2 at Highbury and won the replay 3–1. The weather was bad; Villa were despondent because 'Pongo' Waring was not fit to play. But they were two goals up, through George Brown and Billy Walker, within 15 minutes. We soon pegged one back through Jack Lambert but we remained one down until the closing minutes of the game. When Bastin put a corner behind with four minutes to go, all seemed lost. But a fighting finish was at hand! James and Bastin took the ball forward and got it to David Jack who pounced upon it, weaved through the Villa defence and drove it into the Villa net with what was almost the last kick of the match.

The ex-Bolton star who is down in the record books as the first-ever goalscorer at Wembley had a body swerve that looked very simple but was almost ghost-like. He had the ability of effortlessly changing feet in front of goal and frequently seemed to hit the ball off the wrong foot. Strangely enough he was practically a chain-smoker and had a great liking for chocolates yet he kept as fit as the next man! It was nothing to see him with a cigarette in one hand and a chocolate in the other but, of course, not on the field!

AFC Programme

We had that pride. The players had that pride. I suppose the money was there but it was: *I'm playing for the Arsenal.*

Frank Martin

A booking would have been a big talking-point. I don't remember an Arsenal player ever being sent off at Highbury all through the Chapman era.

George Williams

We were different. We came from a different time. We loved the Club. You were proud of being an Arsenal supporter, we had the cleanest players. Nobody was bigger than the Club.

Geoff Gilbert

The Arsenal's away record this season — only one point left behind from six matches — is eloquent of their strength; but you have to see them away from home to realise what a team they are. People who have seen them several times in the North this season told me that the football they played at Liverpool on Saturday was their normal form. All I can remark is that we have never seen anything like it at Highbury. Never. And the players themselves could not tell me why it was.

I discovered other reasons for the popularity of the Arsenal abroad. Never once, despite some 'hair-line' decisions which robbed them of goals, did the Arsenal make any visible protest. They played to the whistle. They played a model of clean and clever football, never talked and never wasted a second over a throw-in or fetching a ball in the closing stages. Even Huddersfield, at their great heights, were apt to kick the ball over the stand when the game was tight.

Keen as provincial crowds naturally are to see such a side beaten, they come to marvel at the Arsenal and go away satisfied. You can't barrack a team like that. And that is why the Arsenal have achieved their priceless 'away-from-home' complex. Away, they are confident: at Highbury they are 'on view' and a trifle anxious.

Newspaper, 28.10.32

I dare say some people are wondering if the great crowds which put up new records for almost every ground we visit these days are a little bit upsetting. Not a bit of it. We should find small crowds much more trying. And, anyway, most of the old members of the side are 'crowd-tough', as an American would say.

The little tip from our manager, Mr Allison, that there is no need to shake the hand of the player who happens to score, has been much appreciated by all of us. What does it matter, after all, who actually scores if you get the all-important goal?

I have seen some marvellous movements in which the final touch was made by a player who could not help scoring from a position he had no hand in making. In real teamwork the object is surely to make things as easy as possible for the other members of your side, not to seek a personal triumph.

Cliff Bastin, 1936

My dad took me to my very first game at Highbury in 1938. A reserve game. I can remember sitting on a bar on the North Bank. There were quite a few thousand there because in those days nobody used to go to the away matches, really. They came to watch the reserves.

Frank Hummell

Oh, yes. Reserves games were very well attended. A crowd of two or three thousand was nothing. You have to remember, in the reserves you'd see people like Bremner, Cumner, Griffiths, who'd have walked into any other first team. Arsenal reserves could have played in the First Division.

Geoff Gilbert

You could count on 50,000 every week – going up to 60 or 65,000 – unless there was a snowstorm or something. Only bad weather kept people away.

Reg Lewis

I got locked out of Highbury once. When they played Sunderland. There was 73,000-odd in there and I was there one hour before the kick-off. And I got in when England played Italy and there was 73,000 then.

Tom Jales

That Sunderland game, we got locked out. A long time before the kick-off. We were stood in the street. We could hear all the cheers and we'd be thinking: *What the hell's going on in there?* In the end, it got so crowded out in the street, we just left.

Rose Jales

You had blokes with megaphones all round the edge of the pitch, directing people to where there was room to stand.

Sid Butler

In those robust days overcrowding was not so frowned upon, and Mr Chapman always declared that when 50 or 60 people were clamouring to be let out of the ground at least another 1,000 could be admitted who would either by persistence or cunning, gain a point of vantage. Before the installation of electric bells the chief steward had to force his way through the crowds to personally authorise the closing of each stile at the psychological moment, often a hazardous experience as torn clothes and trampled shoes testified.

S. Claude Stevens, *AFC Programme*, 9.1.71

I think they probably appreciated football more before the war because they didn't have a lot; the working man didn't have a lot of fun, really. It was either football or go in the pub and get drunk, wasn't it, on about half a crown? I think football was the biggest event in your life when you were a kid. You'd come home and talk about it, you'd remember the game. Every team had a character, you know, somebody you were going to look at. That would be the attraction. Now it's so one-sided, it's so biased they can't see the other side. You've always had sort of nutcases who can only see out of one eye, but it seems to me more than ever. I can go to football matches and appreciate the other side as well but I don't think a lot of people do nowadays. I don't know why. If you go to see a football game, you want to see your team win, naturally, but if the other side's better, that's it, you've seen a good game then, haven't you?

Charlie Robinson

When Arsenal got to the Cup final against Sheffield United, I wrote to the Arsenal, because when Lord Lonsdale unveiled the 'Arsenal' engine, Lord Lonsdale and Joe Hulme, at King's Cross – well, I was the fireman. And I said to Joe Hulme: *Joe – what about a ticket for the final?* Well, his words were: *Wait till we get there!* Well, of course, they got there and I wrote, I related the experience of the Arsenal team coming on the footplate and all that, and I think I sent my half a crown, and I got a ticket to go to Wembley.

And on that particular morning, we went down to get the Football Special, one of the Sheffield men, a supporter, come up to me and said: *Want to buy a ticket for the match?* I said: *How much?* He said: *Half a crown.* I gave him half a crown and got on the phone to my brother, where he worked, told him he's got a ticket for the final. Cor, you ought to have heard him! Made his day!

George Stinton

There I was at my allotment show two Saturdays ago with all these extraordinary characters presenting their carrots and their marrows. This little slice of Old England which is just disappearing. This little society, with all these people doing their stuff. And somebody said something like: *They're playing away today.* And I said: *Are you talking about the Arsenal?* And they said: *Yeah.* And I said: *Oh, that's my team I go and support them.* And suddenly about four of these old boys all popped up with: *Oh, when I was a boy . . .* The president of the club, a guy called Harold, he's about four foot nothing and he's so old but he's a brilliant little character, and the others, they started saying: *Oh, there used to be 60 or 65,000 down there when we used to go and we used to stand at the North Bank.* And they just started telling all these stories about what it was like and how they used to hand the kids down and all that. And I stood there and I thought: *I wish I'd been there to see all that, to see what it was like.*

Phillip Bloomfield

'A SHED UPON THE NORTH TERRACING'

It was always called the Laundry End because of Mayfield's Laundry at the back. They used to clear the chimneys at three o'clock on a Saturday afternoon, so just before the second half you might get the whole of that end blanketed in smoke or steam, whatever it was, like a fog!

Sid Butler

The documents for Contract No 2 for Alterations and Extension of Terracing at North and South Ends, and Substructure of new Stand on West Side of the Club Ground at Highbury – comprising Agreement and Counterpart, specification five drawings and Bills of Guarantee already signed by W.W.J. Cearns were produced. The seal of the Company was affixed to the Agreement and Counterpart and attested by Sir Samuel Hill-Wood and W.N. Edwards as Directors, and Mr Herbert Chapman as Secretary.

It was agreed that the Time Limit for the completion of the Contract entered into by W.W.J. Cearns be extended from 31 December 1931 to 18 January 1932.

AFC Board Minutes, 20.7.31

Mr C.W. Ferrier FRIBA attended the Meeting at the invitation of the Directors to discuss the delay in completing Contract No 2 of the Ground Scheme, which should have been finished on 16 January 1932. Mr Ferrier reminded the Board that the North and South Ends of the Ground were required to be substantially completed before the West Side was commenced. This was not done – in fact the Contractor was so far behind with the work that until mid-December i.e. five weeks from the end of the period of 26 weeks allowed by the Contract for the entire job – the West Side was not started and the side represents half the job. Mr Ferrier further stated that the Contractor having got so hopelessly behind with his time schedule it renders it obvious that the complaints Mr Ferrier made to Mr Cearns – of his inadequate organisation – were fully justified.

Mr Ferrier assured the Board that hitherto he had received no explanation from Mr Cearns for this delay in complying with the terms of the Contract. Mr Cearns had no grounds of justification for having broken the Contract, and in his opinion there was no reason why the Penalty Clause should not be put into operation. He had repeatedly asked Mr Cearns to give any specific reason for the delay – but without getting any reply.

AFC Board Minutes, 28.1.32

Bills settled with W. W. J. Cearns.

AFC Board Minutes, 31.8.32

Discussed roofing 'Northern End' but decided it should 'remain in abeyance'.

AFC Board Minutes, 17.10.34

Arsenal Football Club. League champions in 1930–31 and 1932–33. Cup winners in 1929–30, were raised to their high position under the guiding hand of Herbert Chapman, the greatest manager the game has ever known. Now Herbert Chapman is dead, and one of the most vital problems is to find a successor who will carry on his work.

The general public look on the Arsenal as the richest club in the country, able to withstand any kind of adversity. The facts are these: the Arsenal club MUST keep in the limelight at the top of the table or gain success in the Cup, to ensure that profit of many thousands of pounds each year – it has been estimated at £20,000 – which is essential to keep the club going. The Arsenal ground – with its new £50,000 stand – is the finest in the country, but the expenses entailed in keeping it up are enormous. Rates and taxes are well over £5,000 a year. There are also other heavy charges. As a going concern the club is a money-making machine unequalled in football. With a losing team and dwindling 'gates', the expenses of maintaining the ground would be a heavy burden. Some teams would be delighted with a tenth of the Arsenal profits, and would carry on comfortably. But not Arsenal.

The responsibility on the shoulders of the Arsenal team is a great one. I am told that there is a wonderful spirit among them to carry out the traditions of 'The Boss'. But it will not be easy. Many clubs have been jealous of Arsenal's rise. In their jealousy these clubs have forgotten what the Arsenal have done for the game. Arsenal put football on the social map. People talked about going to see them play as they would about the Varsity rugby match. They converted the crowds from rugby to soccer. Arsenal brought new moves to the field of play – or, at least, dished old ones out in a new way – and it is safe to say that had Mr Chapman lived, the next five years in football would have seen more changes than ever before.

Newspaper, January 1934

In following their policy of continually adding to and improving the amenities of the stadium for all classes of their supporters, the directors are laying out an extensive programme of works for the coming summer. Time is being taken by the forelock, and even before these lines are in print, signs of the builders' preliminary operations will already be making their appearance.

AFC Programme, 23.3.35

The roof over the North Terracing to be proceeded with as per sketch presented by Mr Ferrier at a cost approximately estimated at £2,000.

AFC Board Minutes, 23.2.35

Mr C.W. Ferrier FRIBA attended and produced the original and counterpart of the contract with Messrs Wilson Lovatt & Sons Ltd for the erection and completion of a shed upon the North Terracing.

AFC Board Minutes, 16.5.35

The reason they didn't put a roof on earlier, they wouldn't put one at the other end, they said the pitch would suffer – there'd be no air getting down the pitch, no through draught, you see.

Tom Jales

If you can remember the old North Bank, prior to the introduction of the refreshment facility at the back, had enormous doors which slid open. Those doors were open during the week so that you had a windfall of air going straight across the stadium. As far as light's concerned the sun comes from the other direction, therefore the North Bank should not shade the pitch, it's the other end that does that. But yes, it was a point in everybody's mind. However, since then of course technology as far as grass growing has changed hasn't it? We've got undersoil heating, we've got pitch irrigation, we've got all sorts of other methods. There's fantastic equipment now available, no longer does the man go along with his bucket, with his grass seed and do it by hand, it's all done in a very professional manner now, better technology's available. I know that the North Bank, when the cover was put on, it was part of the design so that the wind would still come across the pitch.

Ken Friar

In 1935, when we built the North Terrace cover, the clock was moved to the South Terrace. In the moving it fell and missed, by inches, our present clerk of works – George Elliott.

AFC Programme, 14.9.68

During the summer intensive work has been in progress to effect improvement in the stadium. The most visible result is the new covering which now stands behind the Laundry goal. This will be a boon to many on the wet Saturdays, a number of which, unfortunately, we are bound to anticipate during the season. The effect of other work done on various parts of the ground is not so visible, but it can be assured that constant progress has been made towards the realisation of our policy of making the Arsenal stadium into the finest ground in the country.

AFC Programme, 31.8.35

The new stand that will give cover to almost 14,000 bobites, I am able to state, will be quite ready for the first League match against Sunderland on 31 August. There will then be covered accommodation for about 40,000 spectators. In spite of its size, there will be only a very few restrictions to view in this new stand. On the front of it, picked out in red, will be three shields like those on the new West Stand.

'St Ivel', *Islington Gazette*, 9.8.35

Having spent a quarter of a million on accommodation in a few years, it must be a disturbing realisation at Highbury that the Arsenal ground is not big enough to be comfortable on big match days. One would have thought they could take a 75,000 crowd in their stride, but it is not working out that way.

The official return on Saturday was 68,000 and there did not seem much room for more. At the previous home game it was 70,000 and several people wrote to *The Times* (or was it the FA?) about it. Certainly lots of them wrote to me. The club answer is that the crowd packs badly. It generally is, but that never makes sense to me. If some hundreds or thousands cannot see after paying their money they are going to do their fighting best to get to the empty spaces – if they can. If they can't that is the business of the club, which has taken the customers' money in return for a view of the game in reasonable comfort. To ask the man who pays to turn himself into a sardine always struck me as rather impudent. He has to endure quite enough discomfort getting there, getting in and getting home. These observations are not meant to apply exclusively to the Arsenal, neither have they been inspired, in particular, by the crowd at the Sunderland match on Saturday. Most clubs give their best friends (the shilling supporter) a raw deal when the match comes along which compensates for the many which were not worth the entrance money. In no other department of the entertainment world would this be tolerated.

It was always Herbert Chapman's plan to put Arsenal in a position on the football map to command rich revenue from de luxe stands on the principle that in London you can ask the best prices for the best entertainment. 'You can ask more for your orchestra stalls at a West End theatre than you can at Wigan,' he once said. And the Chapman policy was carried on. I warned Herbert that it was dangerous to apply this to football, and I think I shall prove to be right. No club can put on West End shows for ever. There will be the lean times. And the club with the big banks may be better off than the club with the big stands. It is the shilling regular who counts in the long run. I'm all for covered accommodation, but not if it means carving more and more space from the shilling places – as at Highbury.

It has to be said for Arsenal that you do get your money's worth once you are in. The Sunderland match was a battle of giants without the unpleasantness too often associated with the meetings of these two clubs. True, a Sunderland player had one of those note-book cautions some of us have been perturbed about, but it was for 'talking' not kicking.

Newspaper, 18.9.37

'ONE MIGHTY ROAR'

Was Herbert Chapman ever flustered? Remembering the majestic way he and the teams he managed sailed through ups and downs, Cup tourneys and Championships, the question might well be asked. Yet Chapman, whose bust, sculpted by Jacob Epstein, can be seen in the splendid entrance hall at the Arsenal stadium, was never anxious to set himself on a pedestal, and would readily confess that his most embarrassing moment took place after an Arsenal home match, against Middlesbrough, had been abandoned through fog.

The players had stripped and were actually in their baths – thus making a restart impossible – when the light suddenly improved 'We want Chapman!' bellowed the crowd; and Herbert Chapman, armed with a megaphone, appeared in the front of the grandstand, far from happy! 'The referee', he began, rather self-consciously, a 'gentleman from Yorkshire . . . You come from Yorkshire', roared a voice, 'and there aren't any gentlemen there!' At this the crowd began to laugh. Gradually the laughter spread, until it was eddying about the vast stadium. The crisis was over. Still chuckling, the spectators filed out of the ground, leaving a much relieved Arsenal manager behind them!

Brian Glanville, *Arsenal*

First six years of my career I worked at Farringdon and then I went to Finsbury Park. I used to do early and late turn at Finsbury Park. And if they was at home on my late turn I always had the hump. We used to have one inspector there, old John Kirby — he'd come on at two o'clock like I did and he'd see I had the hump: *They at home are they?* And he'd say: *Go on then, I'll look out and when you get back you do the same for me.*

Tom Jales

I used to go to work with a bandage round my foot about Wednesday, hop along like this, you know. So I could get away Saturday. Then one Monday, I got to work and they said: *You've got to go and see the supervisor.* And he said: *And how's your foot.* I said: *Much better, thanks.* And he said: *And how was the football match you went to see?* Well, he'd seen a photo of me in the paper, Saturday night, going to the game! *Don't tell me lies*, he said: *Your photograph was in the evening paper!*

Rose Jales

We'd jump on a bus at the Angel, corner of Goswell Road. Number 4 or 4A. Open-topped ones — up Blackstock Road — and get off at Highbury Barn.

Tom Jales

I'll tell you what. You couldn't get on a bus. You had to hang on the back on the rail.

Rose Jales

On the old open-topped buses they used to have like a rubberised sort of thing, rolled up and strapped on the seat in front. And when you got on, if it was pouring with rain, you undid the strap and pulled it over to stop your knees getting wet. You'd have your mac on, but that would stop it falling in your lap.

Tom Jales

OUTSIDE BEGGING

It has been brought to the notice of the management that a great number of our patrons have been subjected to considerable annoyance through a practice of begging by small boys outside our ground before a match. The boys, holding some pennies (less than the requisite sum) in their hands, beg for the balance of the price of admission so that they can *see the Arsenal*. As this takes place outside the ground it is beyond the management's control, but they wish to bring to all our patrons' notice that this begging is done on an organised system, and that there is only too good ground for believing that the money so given is rarely devoted to the purpose mentioned. Patrons are earnestly requested not to yield to any misplaced generosity, and so to help us to quell an objectionable practice.

AFC Programme, 1.12.34

Down the bottom end where the Mayfield Laundry was, there was an alleyway that ran up the side of it and along the back of the ground. The coppers used to put their horses there them days. The kids would get up on the back of the horse, jump on to the top of the wall and people would help them down the other side — maybe one of their mums or dads would pay to come and he'd be there to help them get down. Nobody used to take no notice of them.

Ron Pottage

Well, my brother always sold programmes round there, practically all the family done it. Four brothers and a brother-in-law. I started when I was about ten. See, I come from a large family of ten children, and there's 20 years' difference in their ages. My dad died when I was 13, so my oldest brother was my father, if you know what I mean. So I used to get on his earhole and he'd say: *Alright. Come round and help me, I'll give you a couple of bob.* I used to get half a crown. Well, when I started work, as a vanboy on the railway, I only got 12/6. You'd go down there about three hours before kick-off to get your programmes. It was a fellow we used to call 'Admiral' Beattie run it. And it'd be half time before you finished, you know, paid in and got the few bob owing to you. So you'd just get in to see the second half. Unless you were lucky and sold out early.

Charlie Robinson

During the 30s, I used to play in the Mansions, Avenell Mansions, I was too young to go. Watch the crowds stream down the road with instructions from my mum to stay inside the railings. There used to be big gates they'd shut up to keep the football crowd out – stop them using the flats as a toilet. I used to help the caretaker shut the big gates up before the game. I was allowed to wander around outside the ground while the game was on. I used to collect cigarette cards and it was marvellous for that – everyone smoked and everyone threw their cigarette packs on the floor. It was a kid's paradise to go around the streets and collect cigarette cards, which were all the rage before the war. Then 20 minutes before the game ended they'd open the gates and out would come the first people and the stream would get bigger. I'd have strict instructions then to get back up the road and into the Mansions. And they'd all come swarming up the road towards me.

Frank Hummell

I've been coming down since 1933. As a young lad, in those days, we used to come down with our parents: really it was a cheap afternoon out. It was our game. There were crowds of 60,000, and you could come in and your dad could leave you at the top and they'd say: *Come on son, up you get.* And down you went, over their heads, till you got to the bottom. All the children were down at the bottom and parents didn't have to worry about where we were because when it was over you came back to meet them. It's hard to explain the atmosphere then. It was terrific.

Frank Martin

There was no segregation, all intermingled. It was lovely. All good-natured banter. All pulling each other's leg. You know, taking the mickey out of the opposing teams. Then with the children, when you got big crowds like that, they used to pass them down over their heads, roll them down. It was a fantastic sight – all the crowd would start going *Whoo-Whoo-Whoo*, and they'd be rolling the children down and they would get on to the edge of the pitch at the bottom. There wasn't a moat or anything, they come right down on to the dirt track around the pitch there.

Tom Jales

Match days always produce the fans of character – the extroverts who like to dress up, bang a big drum or parade on the perimeter track carrying large banners with lurid messages. One of those whom I used to find especially amusing was a supporter who followed us during the 1930s. If my memory serves me correct, he was a porter at Smithfield market. He owned an Aylesbury duck and he would tie a large red ribbon bow round its neck and bring it to all our Cup-ties. Then he would release it just as the players ran on the field. That well-fed, friendly bird became quite a mascot. He was a regular visitor for such a long while that I hope he died of natural causes. The RSPCA tried to apprehend this fan with the bird but somehow he – and his duck – always eluded them.

Bob Wall, *Arsenal From the Heart*

Jimmy Clayton lived and worked in the East End. He had to cut the chickens' throats for the Jewish people. He had a white duck. It'd come and strut around. He got wounded in the Second World War, very badly. We saw him a couple of times after, but never at football. Single man, he never married, he lived in a room down there on his own – we used to go down the slaughterhouse sometimes, if we were down Petticoat Lane or the Houndsditch Warehouse.

Rose Jales

Jimmy Clayton came from Burnley originally. He was only about 5′3″, 5′4″ and he always used to dress up in the red and white and take the white duck with him. Every match he went to, the duck went with him. There used to be a crowd of about 20 of us, always used to meet over there – didn't meet otherwise but over there. For ten to 12 years. We used to have another chap with us, name of Les Jessop who used to play in a band. And he used to wear his dress suit, come back from away matches and go straight to work. We went to Liverpool to see a Cup-tie and he came back with all the autographs on his dress shirt! (See plate 4.)

Tom Jales

Les Jessop, he was a character. He had one false tooth. And he'd turn round to one of the opposing team's supporters and say: *You're no good. You're no good. Look!* And he'd push his tooth right down. He was a comic. He had a tin whistle and a basket under his coat and he'd get one of these joke snakes coming out of it. We was up in Liverpool and we couldn't get on a tram, they were all full. And Les went and laid on the tram lines, so, of course, the tram had to stop. So we all jumped on but Les got up and the tram went. He got left! (See plate 5.)

Rose Jales

Bert Sadler. We was at Liverpool. Played a Cup-tie and beat them 2–0. The crowd all came down and he was over the barrier. And when he got home he was ill over it all and he died. You know, you got swaying in the crowd and he got pushed right on the crush barrier. He was standing just in front of us. The force of the crowd pushed him on to the barrier and, you know, they said he was alright but when he got home he was bad and he never recovered. He went to the hospital on the Monday to have X-rays but just never recovered.

Tom Jales

Owing to the alterations to the ground we find ourselves temporarily without our scoreboard, a deficiency which, although unavoidable, we greatly regret. These alterations are absolutely necessary and we hope that our supporters will acquiesce in a little temporary discomfort until the completion of the work has been effected, which will result in a better scoreboard and much better accommodation generally.

AFC Programme, 29.8.31

Arsenal's new motor noticeboard attracted a lot of interest.

Islington Gazette, 3.9.35

They used to have a little, you know, like the dodgems, a little car, a little electric car. They used to have one of them going round the asphalt track with the team changes on them. I would climb over and sit in the car and go round with them. Every home match! It had a long pole with a board on it with all the changes on.

Rose Jales

ARSENAL CROWD PELT PLAYER AND REFEREE
Arsenal 2, Blackpool 1
Some of the Arsenal crowd were in playful mood at Highbury yesterday – a mood which compelled the referee at one point to stop the game and address a section of barracking, orange-throwing spectators.

The sensation-moment of the game was a spot of bother just before half time between Arsenal centre-forward Drake and Blackpool right-back Blair. The pair finished a tackle with a vigorous scuffle until Referee Gamson dashed up. Drake showed him a torn pair of pants, and the referee played village blacksmith to Blair, looking at his 'hoofs' for broken studs and nails. He called the pair away, as though somebody was due for a holiday excursion to the dressing-room, but ended a long lecture with a seasonal gesture, making the lads shake hands while the wags yelled for mistletoe.

Shortly afterwards the crowd on the terraces joined the party and pelted Blair with oranges. Referee suspended play while he removed four oranges from Blackpool's bench. He addressed the crowd behind the goalmouth, but the answer was a lemon and abstract fruit like raspberries.

Newspaper, 27.12.37

Everton carried on with their exhibition soccer until the 38th minute. Then another wonder goal. Again it was Lawton, Stevenson had a hand in this too. He set Gillick going on the right wing. Gillick transferred to Lawton who, it seemed, could not possibly score with the middle once again blocked by that Arsenal barrier. But Lawton had a brainwave. He started to career to the left wing and with his body at right angles to the goal swung his left foot round at the ball to completely deceive Swindin and everybody on the ground. Goal! And, brilliant one though it was, nobody shouted. It came so unexpectedly! But the hand-clapping that followed seconds afterwards was deafening. Arsenal supporters can appreciate good work even though their side is losing.

Newspaper, 10.9.38

This is why you always got laughs in there. You was all intermingled, different supporters, all mixed up together. And one would say something: *Oh, you stupid so-and-so.* And everybody'd be laughing. It was fun to be there. Alright, you were disappointed if your team lost. It was a good afternoon. You didn't get much out of life: what else could you do of a Saturday afternoon? Go for a walk and look in shop windows. Possibly go to the cinema, up the Blue Hall, once a week. You had to queue up to get in there, too! (See plate 5.)

Rose Jales

The lads would all be together in their twos and threes. If there was swearing: *Hang on lads, there's ladies, here. Alright, sorry guv.* Like that. If something got a little bit out of hand, you'd say: *Come on, lads, break it up. It's a football match, you don't want none of that. Alright?* It'd be all over, wouldn't it?

Jack Hobb

If Arsenal were away, we'd look for another good game to go to in London. Like the Preston side in 1937, they were a great side to watch and they had a good Cup run. I can remember fighting to get into Spurs to see them in the sixth round after they'd knocked us out.

Sid Butler

The ones I used to like were Portsmouth. They had good supporters. All sailors. They had bells and singing: *Dear old Pompey.* And it sounded great.

Jack Hobb

Some of our worst days for thuggery at Highbury occurred when the old 'Islington Mob' clashed with the large contingent of sailors who used to follow Portsmouth on their away games in the middle 1930s. The sailors used to arrive with bottles of beer in each hand and position themselves on the South Terrace. The 'Islington Mob', a bunch of the toughest tearaways imaginable, would wait for them to finish their drinks. Then they would set upon them, with razor blades set into the peaks of their caps, knuckledusters and chains at the ready. The sailors, not to be outdone, would knock the bottom off the 'dead' bottles and wade into action, shouting 'The Navy's here' or words to that effect. On such days it was not uncommon to see a shuttle service of ambulances between the Royal Northern Hospital and Arsenal Stadium.

Bob Wall, *Arsenal From the Heart*

When I joined the ground staff, as an apprentice, we'd have to sweep the North Bank, the Laundry End it was called then, as well as the other stands, so I knew it very well!

If you're coming down from Finsbury Park or out of Arsenal Station, the turnstiles were right there, the first thing you came to – so that end was always full no matter what. It would be something to see from the pitch. Everyone packed in on the terrace and you'd watch the crowd sway down, this way and that – there weren't so many crash barriers – as more people tried to squeeze in from the back. But something like Hillsborough – it was terrible, that loss of life and the suffering – would just never have happened then.

They were all an Arsenal crowd with very few visiting supporters, so if you were a Bolton man, say, and found your way on to the North Bank you would have to take your chances. All you had to worry about was there'd be some leg pulling and cracks at your expense. They were sportsmen – if an opponent did something skilful, the cheers and the clapping would be almost as loud as if an Arsenal player had done it. They say a club gets the supporters it deserves, and that works both ways of course. Well Arsenal were clearly the best club and people were drawn to that, to the club's success.

Reg Lewis

At the end of the game great scenes of enthusiasm were witnessed, thousands of people swarming across the pitch. Amidst prolonged cheering Mr John McKenna, President of the Football League, presented to Alex James, the Arsenal captain, the League Championship Cup. In reply to a short speech of congratulations to Mr McKenna, James simply said: 'Thanks.'

Newspaper, 5.5.34

At the close the crowd invaded the pitch, overpowering the police who tried to hold them back. But all they wanted was to see Drake, Arsenal's record goalscorer, and when he appeared they cheered loudly and went away satisfied.

Newspaper, 4.5.35

The Arsenal remain the No.1 attraction. They have played to a million people at Highbury. In their away games they have been watched by over 750,000. They have in fact beaten their own wonderful gate-drawing records.

Picture the Highbury enclosure at a minute to five o'clock on Saturday. Arsenal had the game won, the Wolves were losing at Sunderland. Any minute the result of their rivals' game would come through. A win for Wolverhampton meant no Championship for north London. The men out there were forgotten for the moment, every eye was turned towards the scoreboard where the result would appear. Suddenly a great burst of cheering from those nearest the board. The Wolves had lost! The cheers swept round the ground until they became one mighty roar.

Then the final whistle. Arsenal had finished like champions with a five-goal victory.

There was no holding the crowd. From every side they poured on to the pitch. The players rushed for the safety of the dressing-rooms. All except Eddie Hapgood. In a moment he was swept up, found himself being tossed about on a mass of heads as the crowd shouldered him. Then the crowd clustered at the foot of the stand, yelling: 'We want Carr. We want Carr.' It was a fitting tribute in view of the great game the Arsenal youngster had played.

Police were powerless to stop the onward surge of the crowd, which became bigger every moment. Then came the best move of the afternoon, better even than the best Arsenal move of the game. The Arsenal band leader had struck up *Auld Lang Syne* and the crowd sang it, but they still went on jostling. Came that brilliant move. The strains of the National Anthem rang out over that pushing, shouting stream of humanity. Instantly the shouting died, the pushing ceased and hats were whipped off. The invaders stopped in their tracks, and as one great choir they all took up the song. That was their greatest thrill of the afternoon. The game that went before was suddenly a dim memory, even though it had meant so much.

Newspaper, 7.8.38

CHAPTER THREE

'Our Ground Has Been Requisitioned By the Public Authorities'

THE NORTH TERRACE, 1940–46

The outbreak of war in 1939 took no one by surprise. Discussions with the War Department and local authorities had been underway for nearly 18 months. Provisional plans for steps to be taken in the event of the unthinkable happening were already in place. Nonetheless, the sudden suspension of League fixtures after three unbeaten games at the start of the 1939–40 season and the immediate appropriation of Highbury for ARP, storage and first aid purposes amounted to a world turned upside down, as it was to be so often during the next seven years of war.

Forty-two of the 44 players on Arsenal's books in 1939 were to serve in the Forces, although many were able to turn out in Regional League competition during the course of the hostilities whenever leave permitted them a Saturday afternoon. Those who didn't – Cliff Bastin, for example, whose deafness meant he couldn't be called up – and other members of the Highbury staff were among those who worked on Air Raid Protection duties at the ground. In the meantime, the football club was forced to move north to White Hart Lane for the duration. Supporters – the old, the young and soldiers home on weekend passes – made the four-mile journey up Seven Sisters Road to watch an Arsenal side which included the likes of Stan Mortenson (top scorer in 1944–45!) and Stanley Matthews as regular guest players.

Highbury, meanwhile, was probably busier from day to day than it has ever been before or since: a hive of activity documented in the *Wardens Post* newsletter which was published from the ground during the early 1940s. Even the pitch was overworked, with two games on it a day – week in, week out – as a regular part of Islington ARP's physical training programme. The practice pitch behind the Clock End was used as a storage area for building materials. A barrage balloon wasn't enough to prevent its destruction by a 1,000 lb bomb in April 1940. Air raid shelter facilities in the West Stand accommodated as many as 1,500 local residents while the East Stand became a first aid centre and air raid warden's reporting post.

Iron bed-frames and other shelter furniture were kept on the Laundry End. When five incendiary bombs came through the roof on the night of 16 April 1941, the stored materials caught fire, melting the roof and setting the goalposts at the north end of the pitch alight. The night of 16 April was one of the heaviest of the blitz and fire-watchers were busy with the immediate danger threatening local residential property as dozens of other incendiaries fell in the streets around Highbury. The blaze at the Laundry End, unnoticed, was left to burn.

A claim against the damage – the first step towards the rehabilitation of the Laundry End – was in place with the War Damages Commission by early September, 1941. However, it would be 15 years before the terrace could offer a roof over spectators' heads again. For Highbury, like the nation, recovery and restoration was to prove a slower process, even, than the war itself. Arsenal though, and football in general, were to have an important part to play in the regeneration of a post-war way of life.

'WALK ALL THE WAY TO TOTTENHAM'

Letter was read from the town clerk of Islington asking if Arsenal were prepared to place the club buildings at the disposal of the council for shelter purposes under the air raids protection scheme. Resolved to reply that Arsenal will do anything possible and reasonable.

AFC Board Minutes, 13.4.38

Letter was read from Aerial Photographic Co. with regard to the company's property and camouflage in connection with air raid precautions. Resolved to reply thanking them for the suggestion but intimating that the directors had no desire to proceed with the matter at the moment.

AFC Board Minutes, 10.11.38

Agreed to erection of an air raid shelter on club property at Gillespie Road for the Mayfield Laundry.

AFC Board Minutes, 1.4.39

Cancel close-season game in Germany.

AFC Board Minutes, 13.4.39

Dear Sir or Madam
Season 1939–1940

As you are already aware, football was suspended by royal proclamation, war being declared, with the result that only two First League matches were able to be played at Highbury. Since then our ground has been requisitioned by the Public Authorities.

You will appreciate the difficulties that confront the Club, as the present revenues are comparatively insignificant and may even cease entirely in the event of the continuation of hostilities. On the other hand, there is a considerable expenditure on overheads which must still be met. In these circumstances, the directors, after most earnest consideration, have decided that season ticket holders shall be granted free admission to all Regional Matches played by the Arsenal on the Tottenham Hotspur Football Ground for the duration of the war, or until further notice, and when normal League football is resumed a new season ticket will be issued for the whole of the first season in exchange for the present ticket. No further change will be in order, and so far as possible the same seat or seats as those previously booked will be allotted.

It is to be hoped that the arrangement will commend itself to you, and I look forward to the time when all Arsenal supporters will be able to foregather on the Highbury ground as they had done in the past.

Yours faithully

sd. Geo. F. Allison

Secretary–Manager

Letter to season-ticket holders, 15.11.39

During the war we could get leave to come up to play – I was stationed in Shoeburyness, mainly, until the Normandy landings. That was at Tottenham's ground. The crowds were restricted then to 25,000 – some people would go along, I suppose, if they had a few days' leave and wanted to watch some football – but mostly, I would say, they were Arsenal supporters.

Reg Lewis

I went to football all through the war because I was in a reserved occupation, you see. I was a shunter then on the railway, troop trains and whatnot. I used to go all over London to see games. They all used to have guest players. Stanley Matthews, Stan Mortenson, they played for the Arsenal.

Tom Jales

I started to get the appetite for football towards the end of the war, when they were playing at Tottenham. So I used to walk all the way from Highbury to Tottenham and back every other week for the last season they were in the League South.

Frank Hummell

When we come home, as young men now, if we come home on leave, we'd say: *Where's our football?* And it was still there. We'd go up to Tottenham, or Chelsea or Fulham. It was still there.

Frank Martin

'ALL THE PLAYERS I LEARN ARE WARDENS'

When we arrived on the ground a practice game was in progress between some Arsenal players and local ARP wardens. Tom Whittaker was playing and he looked fine in his red shirt. He told me, while he was being complimented on his still youthful agility, that this was his first game since 1925. There's plenty of life in the old un's yet.

Eddie Hapgood was doing a bit of refereeing while Cliff Bastin, Bill Kirchen and Male were having great fun out there with the boys. Crayston was enjoying every minute.

After the game we all went into the dressing-room and between showers, baths, undressing and dressing we discussed *The Warden's Post* and the ARP services. All the players I learn are wardens and carry out their spells of duty with great care and with enthusiasm.

Cliff Bastin and Eddie Hapgood were particularly keen about the paper and expressed that its aims are worthy of support. I felt that every player would go to almost any inconvenience in order to help little kiddies, particularly at this Christmas tide.

Eddie Hapgood told us one or two amusing jokes.

The Warden's Post, 6.10.39

Many requests have come to me asking that this page be devoted one week to a comprehensive account of just what is being done at Arsenal Stadium since the first team play all their home matches at White Hart Lane. It all started when the Borough Council requisitioned the ground for the creation of a complete first aid post and a separate warden's post. An idea was in the air for providing physical training for Islington ARP workers, so it was decided to combine two schemes in one thus making Arsenal folk both wardens and PT instructors. This was put into practice with the result that an organisation has grown up far exceeding anything we had imagined in the early days of the war.

At that time all was haphazard and unformed. One day no less than 267 men came up for excercise in batches of 40 and 50; and each was provided with a strip and a bath, not to mention soap, towels, boots and shoes! The names of Arsenal players who are also wardens will be familiar to readers of this page who are doubtless cognisant of those who have left London. Thus Bryn Jones is in Cardiff, George Swindin at Leeds and George Drury in Nottingham.

Well, the PT went all right for a week or so but it was inevitable that a ball would be kicked sooner or later. That did it. Sometimes I have counted as many as 20 a side and no words could ever describe my feelings at the sight of 17 tough lads of the village all doing their best to have a crack at one or the other of Arsenal's many-thousand-pound stars! This could not go on for long and matches soon began to be arranged between teams from the different depots with our lads as referees. This led to the formation of a league which has since been extended to the whole borough, including teams from the police and the AFS. It is governed by a league committee and a higher league management committee. For my sins I am honorary secretary of both, aided and abetted by Norman Sidey and Billy Milne, joint secretary and chairman respectively.

In the visitors' dressing-room Punch McEwen reigns as uncrowned king. He is trainer, masseur, dresser, tactical adviser, guide, philosopher and friend to all the teeming hundreds who pass through the door. That brings me to the only snag. We have but one football pitch in the borough since Tuffnell Park has been taken over by the military; and each of the 210 matches on our programme has to be played on the Arsenal pitch. At the rate of two a day the turf is taking a terrible hammering but the depots take turns to send up volunteer squads to work on it whenever there is a respite.

And always around us the vast stands and wide terraces gape empty and forlorn save for a handful of critical (!!) spectators who suck oranges and smoke endless cigarettes. Perhaps the greatest fight we have here is against dirt. If universal untidiness is a legacy from the last war, then heaven help us after this one! Of course the lads come up for PT and general training in addition to the actual matches. The first squad of enthusiasts arrives at eight in the morning – a full hour before our night shift goes off duty! Sometimes we see a practice kick about on the College training ground which almost overlaps into a PT class; whilst on the stadium proper a dozen or more runners lap grimly round a full-dress football match. These boys are engaged in dull and monotonous work and if their laughter and chatter are any indication, our work here certainly brightens things up for them. The thought of that alone certainly makes it all worth while.

It must be remembered that all who come here do so on their off-duty days and only when the Arsenal players attend depots to take classes are the men allowed half an hour from work. Among them one meets fellows like Charlie Rush and Bob Cotton. Charlie has been with the Islington Borough Council for 18 years and in peacetime is a paper-presser at the Ashburton Grove Destructor. Now he's practically the greatest kidder in the ARP and one of the big noises at a depot containing more than 30 men. On his rare days off he as good as lives at the stadium and we still talk about the day he played centre-forward for the Arsenal ARPs when Tom Whittaker was hurt.

What great fellows they all are and what a fine spirit animates them all! And that's what goes on at Arsenal Stadium.

Marksman, *The Warden's Post*, January 1940

NIGHT PATROL

The midnight patrol of the night shift round the Arsenal Stadium is always rather weird to those of us who are so accustomed to the bustle and noise of the vast peacetime crowds. Tom Whittaker has discovered that a run round the ground about eight p.m. is a good time to spot lights from those back windows that are such a bane to all wardens who like to do their job as it should be done. From the top of Spion Kop for instance one can see the back windows of several streets in our sector so when a light is spotted, Tom stands and gives the signal when one of the others has found the right house and got the light well doused. Last week the moon was nearly full and the night clear. One could see both goals with ease and we paused to look back from the highest point. Memories came crowding in to each of us. What great matches and what great players are connected with that green stretch of turf that lay so sombre in the moonlight! In the almost overpowering silence the pitch seemed to be brooding over the past. There is a lot to be said for atmosphere, I myself could never get used to

Covent Garden Opera House as a glorified Palais de Danse, and the stadium at night takes on a personality all of its own peopled with shadows from the past.

'Doesn't it look queer from up here, so different from on the field,' Eddie Hapgood half whispered in my ear. 'It's a long time since I stood in the crowd although I used to follow Bristol City as a boy and if I thought I couldn't get to my place in the bobs before the teams came out I'd run my head off to get there in time.' 'Yes,' I answered: 'I was just the same. I remember the first match Charlie Buchan ever played here – the first match under the new offside rule and the Spurs beat us 1–0!' 'Ay,' said Tom, 'the crowd went mad with the speed of it and nobody thought any team would last the season out. I'd have been playing myself then but I'd just got back from Australia with a smashed-up knee so I was starting in as assistant-trainer.'

And so we went back over the years recalling incidents, goals, matches and above all, names: Jack, Butler, Dean, Blythe, Cresswell, and a score more from almost every club in the country. The wind blew colder and seemed to moan a little – and I swear shadows moved swiftly to and fro on the field below us. Suddenly high up in the great East Stand a light flickered and as quickly vanished. Our conversation stopped dead and we stood like statues. The light soon came again but lower down this time. 'Who's there?' we cried . . . but it was only the nightwatchman on his rounds so we returned to the post and were soon deep in an argument on the relative menace of incendiary or HE bombs.

The Warden's Post, 6.11.39

There can't be many men who can say they have used Highbury as a hotel – but during the war years I did just that every Saturday night. While I was based at RAF Henlow, I played as a guest for Arsenal in the War Competition, and, after the game each Saturday, I slept the night in the dressing-room – at the invitation of trainer Billy Milne. In the morning I would have a bath, get some breakfast and then report back to camp. I lived like a lord!

Bill Shankly, *AFC Programme*, 1.2.75

'16 APRIL 1941, LONDON TOOK A REAL PASTING'

In October 1940, a 1,000 lb bomb fell into the practice ground, where a barrage balloon was operating. Two RAF men were killed, the hut in which they were sitting was blown to pieces, and two of their comrades got up and walked away almost without a scratch.

Some months later, on 16 April, 1941, five incendiary bombs crashed through the roof and started a terrific fire which caused the roof over the terracing to crumble and collapse.

One of the brighter moments, according to Billy Milne, was on the night when the incendiary bombs set fire to the covered enclosure. As soon as the bombs landed he, together with the other wardens, hurried out to see what they could do to prevent the spread of the fire. Billy told me that his first sight of the incident showed the goalposts well and truly alight. As our goalposts had been specially ordered from a firm which had changed over to war work, Mr Allison had to hunt around for a spare set to be kept by for the great moment when the Arsenal ground would be thrown open for League football again!

Tom Whittaker, *Arsenal Story*, 14.4.41

We were evacuated for seven weeks and when we came back, I was going to school in Conewood Street. I don't know if that particular day I was going to school or coming back, the day after the North Bank was destroyed, but I remember walking on to the terraces, up over the mound where the turnstiles are. I looked across the North Bank to see what had happened the previous night. It was just a stinking, smouldering, smoking ruin. It was an ARP storage place and that stand was full of bunks. All the shelters that were built around the streets, brick shelters or underground shelters, they all used these iron bunks – three tiers – which had a canvas, sort of hessian, on. Simple metal frame and a bit of canvas. I can still remember the smell of them, of the canvas. We slept in bunks like that in the shelter in my flats. Anyway those bunks used to be stored on the North Bank because it was under cover. The incendiaries came through the roof – only made a hole about eight inches across, they were a foot or so long – phosphorus-type bombs. They didn't explode straight away, they just pierced the roof like they would any roof. And where they lay they would just smoulder, the phosphorus would just smoulder, and anything flammable would catch light. So they came through the roof on to the bunks which caught fire. So everything under the roof caught fire and melted it. If there hadn't been anything underneath, they would have just made holes in the roof and burnt out on the terracing. My brother was fire-watching that night. He's told me the North Bank was left to burn because they were so busy putting out firebombs on houses and stuff like that. He can't remember much more because he was so occupied with what was going on in our Mansions that night. April 16, 1941, London took a real pasting with firebombs, I've read about it since. Some of the worst fires of the Blitz happened that night. But that's my memory of walking in there and seeing that smouldering ruin the day after.

Frank Hummell

The manager reported that he had been in correspondence with the Islington Borough Council regarding the destruction of the North Stand by enemy action and that the question of claiming compensation under the War Damage Act had been placed in the hands of Messrs Corderoy and Sons who were undertaking the necessary action and submitting a claim to the district valuer.

AFC Board Minutes, 2.5.41

Reported to the Board that an offer made by T. W. Ward Ltd of Sheffield of £260 for the scrap metal of the North Stand had been accepted and that the War Damage Commission had approved the action.

AFC Board Minutes, 20.11.41

Board concerned that negotiations with War Damages Commission were stationary.

AFC Board Minutes, 6.11.45

Mr Binnie assured Board North Terrace would be restored to pre-war condition prior to the start of season 1946–47.

AFC Board Minutes, 6.12.45

The Board expressed concern that matters were not further advanced.

AFC Board Minutes, 2.1.46

Waiting for licence to commence restoration. Wilson Lovatt report no problems having men even though the work hasn't been assigned priority by ministry.

AFC Board Minutes, 23.1.46

Mr E.J. Drake attended for his promised interview with the Board, and outlined his career with the club – 13 years in all, and which culminated with an injury to his spine whilst playing in a Cup-tie at Reading on 24 February 1945. Drake is now unable to take part in any form of outdoor sport – and any manual work is also dangerous for him. Drake further expressed the hope that means might be found for him so that he need not sever his many years faithful and loyal service to the Club.

Drake withdrew and the Board discussed his case. Every possible sympathy was expressed towards him, and W. Allison was asked if he could ascertain if it were possible for Drake to be employed by the Contractors, Messrs Wilson Lovatt & Co., who are carrying out the restoration work on the ground. The idea being that Drake be given work by them in a supervisory capacity until such times as football gets running normally, i.e. August 1946, and it was agreed that if Mr Allison could make this arrangement whatever the remuneration to be paid Drake was short of £6 per week the Club should make it up.

AFC Board Minutes, 21.3.46

Binnie recommends that the question of negotiating a value payment or cost of work replacement of the North Terrace to be left until other points have been settled.

AFC Board Minutes, 31.31.46

CHAPTER FOUR

'A Different Enthusiasm'

THE NORTH TERRACE, 1947–56

> Britain's worst football tragedy occurred at the Bolton–Stoke FA Cup-tie yesterday. Thirty-three people, including one woman, were trampled to death or suffocated when two barriers suddenly collapsed under the weight of the crowd, 15 minutes after the start. At least 500 people were injured, four seriously.
>
> **Sunday Graphic**, 10.3.46

England returned to peacetime hungry for football. For a decade, games were watched by capacity crowds in all four divisions, gates often locked well before advertised kick-off times. Even at Highbury, where crowds of up to 73,000 had squeezed in to marvel at Bastin and James, the period immediately after the war saw an increase of the order of 20 per cent in the size of the average home gate. Whereas in the 30s attendances fluctuated significantly in response to the weather and the quality of the opposition, the late 40s and early 50s, when football itself – a noisy, colourful spectacle in an austere, straitened era – was the overwhelming attraction, saw 50,000 pack Highbury week after week.

The team, though still successful – two League Championhips and the 1950 FA Cup – were far from being the dominant force they had been in the domestic game before the war and fell away markedly after the last title victory in 1953. Thousands, however, continued to pour on to the North Terrace well into the 50s, braving the elements again to enjoy a new generation of heroes: Mercer, Lewis and the Brylcreem Boy, Dennis Compton.

The burning desire to *enjoy* during a period when there was so little fun to be had, coupled with the actual size of the crowds themselves, may help to explain the unique atmosphere – polite, friendly and responsible – for which the late 40s and early 50s are so distinctly remembered. The Bolton Disaster in the last months of wartime football was a reminder of the potential dangers posed by such huge numbers of spectators. Certainly, Arsenal and other clubs were quick to use it as a cautionary example when discussing crowd behaviour in the club programme or the press. It is perhaps significant that the Home Office inquiry into the disaster laid responsibility for it squarely on the shoulders of those fans who had forced their way through locked gates into a Burnden Park already stretched to its 65,000 capacity. No contemporary attention seems to have focused on the complete inadequacy, as we can see it 45 years on, of the crowd safety and control measures in place to deal with the kind of attendance which would become the norm over the next decade. Highbury's crowds, like any other after the war, were expected to look after themselves. In that different time supporters appear, by and large, to have done just that.

A feature of football between the wars had been the rise of the supporters' clubs which, as described by Rogan Taylor in his recent history, came into being primarily to raise funds for ground improvements (and occasionally transfer fees) on behalf of football clubs who might otherwise have found survival – let alone progress – impossible. As we have seen, Arsenal's development of Highbury during the 1930s was made possible by the unprecedented success achieved on the field. The crowds had streamed in to ensure a consistent level of gate receipts (and credibility with creditors) which would have made a traditional supporters' club of little or no relevance.

It was only after the Second World War that an Arsenal supporters' club was established. Founded by an East Stand season-ticket holder, Dick Jones, but drawing a significant proportion of its membership from the loyalists on the North Terrace, the new Supporters' Club had little in common with its pre-war counterparts elsewhere. Its purpose was very much to serve the supporters who comprised its membership and, only at one remove, the team which they supported. The organisation had little or nothing to do with Arsenal the football club. Most importantly, the ASC existed to facilitate away travel for the increasingly large number of fans who wanted to watch Arsenal around the country, rather than go to football elsewhere in London or spend time at home on alternate Saturdays. It sought to provide, too, an environment away from the terraces where supporters could socialise: games and sports facilities and bars were furnished just off Islington High Street and then, later, on the corner of St Thomas and Gillespie Roads behind the North Terrace itself.

These new developments – organised away travel and football as a social life away from the ground itself – were enormously important. For example, the Supporters' Club fostered a partisan spirit away from Highbury which saw a large group of supporters standing together and loudly announcing their allegiance to the Arsenal as opposed to anybody else. The team appeared to recognise and enjoy this first experience of the encouragement offered by a partisan element within the crowd. The roars of the crowd in the 30s had been orchestrated by the thrills of play at both ends. Here now, it seemed, was a new breed of supporter whose enthusiasm for football came draped in Arsenal favours. The rivalry with other teams' supporters was, of course, friendly and good-humoured. But this was a model of what the North Bank would become: a distinct crowd within a crowd – partisan, loyal and loud.

For the North Terrace to become the North Bank, a new roof was to be as important as the appearance of this new breed of supporters to stand underneath it. Although a claim against damage had been lodged with the War Damages Commission five months after the old roof had been destroyed, a new 'shed upon the north terracing' wasn't finally put in place until the start of season 1956–57. Despite the healthy gate receipts enjoyed after the resumption of League football in 1946, the war itself had made life difficult for Arsenal in economic terms. Just as the Great War had left Sir Henry Norris unable to recoup on his initial investment in a new home for Woolwich Arsenal, the massive debt incurred in turning Highbury into the Home of Football during the 30s was left hanging over the club when League football was suspended during the Second World War.

The 50,000 crowds of the late 40s and early 50s kept Arsenal's head above water but only slowly helped to pay off creditors who had provided the capital for a decade of investment in the 1930s. The nearly £30,000 Arsenal eventually received in compensation with regard to the fire on the Laundry End in 1941 was a long time coming. By the time it did, and Higgs Ltd had erected an exact replica of the original 30s roof on the North Terrace, the team was on its way into the doldrums. At the same time, change – within football and in the world at large – was just around the corner. Supporters, the players and the club were soon to be overtaken by a very different way of life, a sea-change that would be felt as profoundly within Britain's football grounds as anywhere.

'ALL WE EVER DID WAS WATCH FOOTBALL'

The crowds were always enormous. Arsenal were the draw team. They were the team to beat. Tremendous players and there was a charisma about the Arsenal. I got locked out of the ground the day Bryn Jones made his first appearance after the war. I got down there at one o'clock and I couldn't get near the ground. They reckon there were 20,000 people locked out – they closed the gates at half past twelve, quarter to one, which was two hours before the kick-off. I got halfway down St Thomas Road – all I could see was a sea of heads. But people were calmer then: there was no pushing and shoving. Hardly any policemen to be seen.

Geoff Gilbert

All that you did was that you posted your turnstile men to your turnstiles, you opened up all the areas and you sat back and waited for them to come in with the money. It was really like that. The whole thing was done visually because they were paying at the turnstile. You'd be amazed. There were peope here in those days who could look and tell you clearly how many there were here, and they were very accurate. When you could see two thirds of the person's body – these are not accurate figures but illustrate the point – they would say: *Well, you've got 40*. When you could see waist upwards, you'd got 50 and when you could see their heads you'd got 60. They got it right too! Don't forget we had lots and lots of staff that had been with us for 50 years, and grown up man and boy, many of them. They've seen all the gates over the years. People do become experts over a period of time, don't they?

Ken Friar

Football was a great outlet for people. I mean, very few people had televisions. All we ever did was watch football, or played it. After school was playing football. Saturdays was going down there, you know. By the time you got to senior school, 11 or 12, you had a school team Saturday mornings, get back and then go and watch the Arsenal.

John Platt

I'm not a psychologist but you also have to consider why people were coming to football in such massive numbers in the late 40s and early 50s. In those days we had an average crowd of 53,700. Why was that? You had a five-and-a-half-day working week, you'd had the war, people were getting over the war, they didn't have a lot of money in their pockets and it was their way of expressing themselves. They would finish work at one o'clock or whatever time they'd finish on Saturday morning, they'd come down here, they'd go into the pub and then have their pint by two o'clock. Quarter past two we were often shut and the gates were closed. It was *the* thing to do. It was a religion that everybody came down on a Saturday. I remember very clearly coming in here on a Saturday morning. I used to live locally and I would come in quite early in the morning. You'd come into this place on a Saturday morning at maybe eight o'clock and the buzz was unreal. There were already people queuing, sometimes overnight. It was an exciting time. There was an act, there were three of them, would come outside here, dressed in a dinner jacket, long-tailed dinner jacket, striped trousers and a coloured tie and they'd have banjos and they'd do a sand dance on this mat and they had a small Guinness bottle, turned up on its head and the guy would stand on his head on top of the bottle and they would go round and collect off the kids. It was a whole different way of life. In the 50s, there was a completely different way of life. And it was all good fun, no aggravation. We used to run this place on two men and a dog – and the dog was a Pekinese, you know. It was a very different era, and before I came it was probably similar back in the 30s. I think the gates probably peaked in the 50s because of the war.

Ken Friar

After the war I think you had the bigger average crowds. Before the war you had your record crowds like the 72,000 against Sunderland but it was up and down. After the war you were certain of 50 or 60,000 every week. But I can't remember any really bad crushes at Highbury. It was just one solid mass of people, packed together like sardines, but virtually no danger. A lot of pushing and shoving; if you were wise you'd know to stand somewhere that wasn't too dangerous, just like in recent years you knew where to stand to avoid the hooliganism.

Frank Hummell

If the North Bank moved you went with it. If the crowd moved forward, you moved forward. I don't know about other people, but me and my mates used to think sometimes: *Cor. This is a bit dodgy.* Sometimes you wanted the game to finish so it would ease up a bit. You was tight like that. You couldn't get your handkerchief out. Or you'd try and get a fag out. You couldn't. You couldn't have a fag.

Jack Hobb

After 11/2/50 vs Burnley FAC tie had been 'all ticket' the Board agreed in principle that the all-ticket match was not a satisfactory way of coping with the conditions as applicable to the stadium.

AFC Board Minutes, 16.2.50

The crowds then, you couldn't move and you couldn't breathe and getting out, going down those steps I used to think: *God if I fall that's it, you're dead aren't you?* I can remember my brother Jeffrey being passed down over the heads and he always used to sit on a little bench in front practically every game because he was little and he was just passed down.

Maureen Hewlitt

Tom Whittaker has asked me to say that owing to the very large crowds now assembling at the stadium for first-team home fixtures the danger to children has become a serious problem. The Board of Directors have decided, after consultation with the Metropolitan Police, to adopt a procedure which is already in operation at many other large grounds for the purpose of discouraging the attendance of boys at big matches. In future their half-price admission will be discontinued for Football League matches. The educational value to youngsters of watching the professional footballer in action is fully realised and it is felt that the boys will get this equally well at Football Combination games, so that the reduced (6d) admission at the schoolboys' turnstiles will continue in operation for reserve matches in future as it has done in the past.

AFC Programme, 11.10.47

I can remember my dad taking me to a reserve game, where Jimmy Logie was playing, and there was 29,000 there. At a reserve game, fifteen thousand was regular at reserve games and, if we were playing Chelsea or Tottenham, 20, 25,000, 30,000.

Steve Shaw

I remember when Arsenal were drawn against Spurs in the third round of the Cup in 1949. And everybody was saying: Well, you'll have to be there by Friday afternoon or you won't get in. I was there on the terraces at 12 o'clock with my sandwiches and lo and behold I could have walked in at one minute to three. The press had made such a hoo-ha about it, there were only 40,000 people there, 40,000 stayed away.

Geoff Gilbert

A constant cry from many of you these days is 'Why are there not more programmes for sale?' Early comers to the ground and late comers to the stands – all phone or write the same thing. The answer is twofold – firstly, for some inexplicable reason the demand is far greater than in pre-war days. Club statistics show that in 1939 only one person in four or five bought a programme so that we rarely sold more than 15,000 copies for any First Division match. It should be noted that our paper allocation today is based on these figures. Secondly the demand is now more in the nature of one in every two which means a need, considering the gates this season, of 25,000 to 30,000 copies each first-team match. This can be done on occasion but if attempted for all matches there will be little or no paper at all left for the last few weeks of the season. You write: 'But how can the spivs get plenty to print the cheap muck on sale outside the ground?' The answer is simple. We do not, and will not, deal in the black market.

AFC Programme, 6.12.47

Outside the Tube station was the best pitch, actually, but it was the hardest. You used to get knocked about. They'd knock you over, snatch 'em out of your hand. There was none of this queuing like there is now. The programmes were just a couple of bits of paper, really. You could flick 'em off. They were in bundles and I think there were 144 in a bundle. You'd do five of them, easy. I think the crowd's very sedate now, the way they queue up and ask for a programme. Then, you'd start up here and end up down there, they'd push you back. You'd have the programmes between your feet and you'd fall over them. I got pinched there once playing against Sunderland, just after the war. This copper come up and said: *Oy, I warned you once. You're nicked.* They marched me all the way up to the police station and up the Blackstock Road, two big coppers, and me saying: *Is that what I bleeding fought the war for is it?* – I can always remember that. Two biguns weren't they? All me money, all me programmes. Me brother came charging up and they let me out, but they pinched me for obstruction. I was outside the Arsenal station there, and they move you back away from the station, so you're right in the North Bank Entrance. To cut a long story short I got pinched and I go to Clerkenwell on the Monday or Tuesday. I lost a day's money, they put me in a cell till me case come up, and when the case come up, the magistrate laughed. He said: *Ah, couldn't sell 'em quick enough?* He charged me a nicker.

Charlie Robinson

In those days you had to be careful not to get caught on a programme, because you had the pirate programmes then. The Arsenal programme in the 40s had a crest on and cost two old pence. Now the pirate programme looked flash on the front but when you opened it, it was only two pages, back and front, and they were 2d, too. They used to sell them just outside the ground. Some people used to dive in and buy them but if you'd been at Arsenal you knew what the Arsenal programme looked like, so you wouldn't go and buy one.

Bill Needs

Two years ago when the time came for me to finish refereeing I turned my mind to thinking of a means of keeping in touch with football. I decided that I could not be a programme seller as I could never master the two wonderful words they cry – 'Gram Fishul!' I knew that I could not get in the police force so I turned my mind to becoming a steward, helped by my experience gained as an officer of the military police. So it was that I was appointed to assist in the packing of the crowd on the popular side.

It was no new experience to be on the Arsenal ground before a crowd. I had undergone that trial in the London Cup and in Combination games and had been shouted at by Arsenal fans for decisions against the Arsenal which, believe me, were just as hard for me to give as anybody in the crowd to accept. It was with some trepidation, therefore, on a sunny August afternoon that I first stood up behind one of the goals to observe the crowds coming in and I wondered where one started in that particular task.

At first it seemed so easy to see the crowd just moving into position and then things became rather more congested; people tended to stay on the terrace by the gangways and did not move to the centre. The first task I thought, was to try to get the new arrivals to form a moving 'snake' into the centre – which others might follow. This was done, but was not popular with those who had come early to stand by the gangways, but after a time it became accepted by the public in good part. I quickly learnt that I would have to put up with a good deal of banter from the crowd and was soon to learn that my name was 'Oscar'. No such name appears on my birth certificate, but I had been called many other names on this ground which did not allow for the usual qualifications of a birth certificate! It was surprising how quickly this name cottoned on and it is by this name that I am known today.

On my first appearance I was given a megaphone, but I soon found that this was a mistake. The only method of gaining the confidence of the people is by addressing them personally, and it was surprising how quickly they responded. When they found one was pointing to them as an individual and was anxious to place them in a spot which was vacant, they moved with alacrity.

Children were a problem. It was no easy matter to find a place for them where they could see, particularly as some of them were no more than two feet high! Then one has the children with adults; where the child has to be in front and the adult behind. With the assistance of a good uniformed steward and a policeman it is easy to place the people in the vacant spot, although it is not so easy to get people to move once they have made up their mind they are in a good enough place. It is essential that the gangways should be kept clear, although some people, having secured what seems to be a good view, will not always agree with this very necessary precaution. It is strange how so many people, having got in themselves, are quite unconcerned about those outside the turnstiles and will often clamour for the gates to be closed. This is very unthinking selfishness because if they themselves would only be advised by the stewards, many of those outside would be very soon comfortably housed on the inside.

However, the two years I have spent on this task have proved to be very enjoyable. I have made many friends with the spectators and look forward to the many individual chats I have each week. It is necessary to have an encyclopedic knowledge of the players and of the game. One is expected to know the progress of injured players and many other football statistics. One friend has, on occasions, been kind enough to provide me with a bottle of beer, which I have to drink in the open view of the crowd. Another one announces his arrival to the ground on the top of the terrace and then expects to be guided to his position just as an usher in a cinema would guide him to his place.

If only all the people would co-operate with the stewards – packing the crowd would be considerably easier and many more would secure a better view. It is surprising how one can see the 'gaps' from the front and the various ways in which one could help the spectators if only they would do as they are asked. To those friends who do help us I would say – 'Thank you very much for your co-operation.' To the others I would say – 'Give it a trial; you'll be surprised at the pleasant results.'

'OSCAR', *AFC Programme*, 1.4.50

Two weeks ago when we played Blackpool, a lot of spectators were seen to be climbing on walls and railings which were not built for this purpose. It happens frequently, but we mention this occasion particularly because one of the people concerned was seriously injured. Worse, an innocent passer-by, a boy of only 14, was also injured through no fault of his own.

There was quite sufficient room for everbody as the gates were closed well below the known capacity of the ground. These commando-minded people who feel an urge to climb to an advantage point inaccessible to the majority should respect the safety of others even if they are prepared to take the chance themselves.

Following this appeal, if there is no improvement, the management will take steps to remove these people from their perches and eject them from the ground.

AFC Programme, 5.10.49

Many visitors to Highbury, and indeed to other football grounds, have from time to time had occasion to be grateful to the men of the St John Ambulance Service, for these fine fellows do a lot of useful work behind the scenes, especially when the weather is warm and spectators have to stand for long periods.

Nowadays of course, the St John men who attend our games at Highbury have two first aid rooms in which they can treat their minor cases, and have the added advantage that they can call upon the hospital ambulance services when necessary. St John is one of the 'silent services' at the stadium; regrettably, none of us think much about them until we need them (rather like the water tap – we take it all for granted until one day we turn it on and no water appears) but they are always there, ready to do everything in their power to help you when you need them most.

AFC Programme, 21.3.53

We used to have 60,000 in the crowd and there'd be ten of us (St John's workers) down here.

Shirley Haxell

They always had quite a few St John's regulars, down in the corners, but you never saw policemen. There were hardly any policemen. In fact, we knew most of them. The largest police contingent at Highbury was the band. You got to recognise them and you'd say hello or, if they got in the way while you were watching: *Sit down! Get your hat off!*

Geoff Gilbert

In conclusion, now that 5 November is approaching, may I make a special appeal to all our members NOT to throw fireworks on the pitch at Highbury or on any other ground when visiting away matches. Apart from the possibility of damage to people's clothes, fireworks can cause considerable damage to the playing surface, and I do feel that if we can set a lead by not doing this ourselves, it may help to stamp out a little annoyance that must obviously be felt by those responsible for keeping the pitches in good condition. We all know that it is a great temptation to the young to throw a firework under a policeman's legs, but, at the same time, even the young must be proud of our pitch at Highbury, and must also realise that other clubs have the same feeling about theirs.

GunFlash 24, Oct 1951

The crowds didn't start dwindling until 54–55, when things got a bit mediocre, crowds of 40,000. Only the big, top games would get 60,000.

Bill Needs

They support their club through thick and thin, in all kinds of weather. We have only to recall the early part of this season. Arsenal were doing badly, were right down at the bottom of the table and showing little sign of improvement; still the good Highbury folk rolled up, making the attendances the envy of most club officials.

Charles Buchan, *GunFlash* 49, Feb 1955

Mr McInnes talks about 60 per cent of the football public being 'fanatics' who support the club through thick and thin, hoping for a revival. Take Arsenal for instance. When they were at the top of their form they were regularly getting gates of over 60,000 people. If Mr McInnes's figures are right Arsenal should get gates of over 36,000 when they are not doing well yet, looking at the figures printed in the newspapers (presumably correct), one sees that the last four home fixtures have produced attendances of well below that figure. It may be the weather, it may be the interest in other sports which are being broadcast on Saturday afternoons or it may be due to the general change in the sociological outlook on entertainment as a whole.

AFC Programme, 9.4.55

The first game back after the war was a midweek game against Blackburn. There wasn't a big crowd. But on the Saturday against Sunderland, we had 60,000 in the ground and we drew 2–2. It was so crowded that I was right at the back. The atmosphere was happy. I remember the beauty of them coming out on to the pitch – they really looked what they were. Tremendous atmosphere. It was magnificent. After the war people were happy, they'd come to enjoy the football – all intermingled, you came to a game and you stood where you stood. Segregation didn't exist. (See plate 16.)

Geoff Gilbert

Even the manager in those days used to talk about the North Bank, Tom Whittaker: *Don't forget! Always salute the North Bank.* We didn't go to the end like they do now. But we'd wave.

Dennis Evans

We had that terrible run at the start of the first season after the war, and we were playing Stoke City. There were 60,000 plus in the ground – no problems, you could have counted the number of policemen on one hand – and we won 1–0. When we scored, the cheer was so tremendous it was heard right up in Hornsey. It was Arsenal's first win at Highbury and Stoke were quite a good side – I think they were top of the table at the time. That was a wonderful atmosphere.

Geoff Gilbert

The game against Grimsby at the end of 47–48 when we'd already clinched the Championship. That was the biggest laugh I've ever had at a football match. Grimsby were already down and we didn't have to win. We were four up at half time. Last home game of the season, we won 8–0, Ronnie Rooke scored four. The match became hilarious. We had a penalty for the eighth goal and they didn't know who to give it to, so they gave it to Jimmy Logie who'd never taken a penalty before. It was just a very funny afternoon.

Frank Hummell

I remember standing on the North Bank for a Cup-tie against Sheffield Wednesday. It was the 90th minute and the ball came across. Reg Lewis nodded it in and we won 1–0. There was none of this falling over each other. They were being paid to score goals. The Arsenal players always used to shake hands with each other and run back to the centre circle.

Geoff Gilbert

Arsenal's Roar which undoubtedly is a very good second best to the famous Hampden Roar was probably not a little responsible for our win. It certainly gave a thrill to those of us sitting in the stands and the psychological effect on the players, even though it was unconscious, must have been terrific. We could almost put down in the records of goalscorers for this match, Arsenal 1 Sheffield Wednesday 0. Goalscorer, Arsenal supporters.

AFC Programme, 7.1.50

If a player committed a foul the referee would run backwards with the player. There was none of this calling players to them like errant schoolboys. You'd see him run alongside the player, you obviously couldn't hear what he was saying and that way the crowd was not incited.

Geoff Gilbert

During my whole career, Alex Forbes – I think – was sent off once and that was the only time I remember an Arsenal player being dismissed – we would never question referees' decisions or dream of threatening someone's livelihood with a tackle. If we scored, it was a handshake at most, and then back to the halfway line.

Reg Lewis

I remember a Cup game down here against Norwich. They had a right-back, Byrne was it? When Logie was playing. And you know Logie was a mate of Alex Forbes, weren't he? Logie's gone down through the middle and this right-back's come over and hooked him. Referee come over: *Right, I'm going to send him off.* Then Alex Forbes has come over and he's gone: *Leave him on, ref. I'll see to him.* So the ref's gone: *You and you, off!* Logie was the only one stayed on!

Ron Pottage

Whenever Arsenal played Newcastle there was a bit of a niggling thing. I think it went back to that Cup final when Newcastle beat us and the ball was already over the line, I don't know. But I remember one time. Tom Whittaker, the manager, came out on the pitch before a game against them and asked the crowds to behave themselves. You see, if they ever scored, people used to shout out: *No goal! It was over the line!* Other days, he'd come out with players they'd signed, like Cliff Holton, and introduce them to the crowd.

Jack Hobb

There wasn't a build-up in the papers like there is now. I used to read them and you'd just get a list of fixtures and, maybe, if someone was injured.

Chris Thompson

In 1953 we had to beat Burnley to win the Championship. The game was on a Friday night, before the Cup final, and it wasn't a full house. I don't know why. It was raining and the North Bank didn't have a roof on it then and, of course, there were no floodlights then, so it kicked off at half past five or six o'clock I think. Perhaps people couldn't get there from work. Anyway, we went into a 3–1 lead, then I think it was Elliott scored the second goal for Burnley and that was the longest 20 minutes I've known. Oh, that was a cliffhanger. We were really hanging on there.

Geoff Gilbert

We sat on the edge of our seats practically from the kick-off, because in the eighth minute Burnley took the lead through Stephenson. A minute later we had equalised. Alex Forbes, who was in one of his most audacious moods, scored with a tremendous shot. That was the signal for some of the most spirited attacking play I have ever seen from an Arsenal side and in next to no time we were 3–1 up. Doug Lishman, dashing into an open space, met a cross from Don Roper first time and sent the ball flashing into the net. Then the irrepressible little Jimmy Logie was on hand to round off another glorious all-out movement by the Arsenal half-backs and forwards.

So the scoreline remained until a quarter of an hour from the end, when Burnley got a second goal through Elliott. The Burnley players now turned on the heat as though determined to help their Lancashire friends, Preston, to pull off the Championship and Arsenal's defence came under enormous pressure. George

Swindin, in particular, played the game of his life. As always he was immensely courageous and he made at least two saves of elastic brilliance.

Every minute seemed an hour. The crowd, equally taut and restive, began to whistle imploringly at the referee. Burnley went on bombarding our goal. At any moment I felt they must equalise. When Holden fell in our area there was an agonising moment of suspense before the referee waved play on, and almost immediately Adamson drove in a vicious low shot which, incredibly, Swindin managed to beat out.

By now, our players were almost drained of stamina after their gruelling, all-out assault on a pitch churned into thick mud. At last came the final whistle and, under an appropriately red sky, they were lost to view, engulfed by thousands of jubilant Arsenal fans. When the shouting and tumult died away, the statisticians told us that we had finished .099 of a goal ahead of Preston. The title was ours!

Bob Wall, *Arsenal From the Heart*

Oh, yes. The Championship night in 1953. We'd been all the way to Preston the previous weekend and were so disappointed to lose 2–0. But we looked at all the papers and saw that we could win it, even if Preston won on the Wednesday night, which they did. It was very close at the top between Burnley, Preston and Arsenal. We could win on goal average if we beat Burnley that night. Well. One of my mates walked out. He went green. He couldn't stand it. He walked out and met us outside. We went to the pub on the corner of Gillespie Road, Brownswood Road. We were so happy. We didn't go in pubs much – working men's clubs after away matches – but not usually the pub after a home game. But we did celebrate that night. We kicked a Belisha beacon all the way up Blackstock Road, past the police station. When I think of hooligans today, I remember doing that! If I saw someone doing that now, I'd go crazy, wouldn't I?

Frank Hummell

ARSENAL 4 BLACKPOOL 1

17 DECEMBER, 1955

This match had a great deal to remember it by. To begin with, the last Saturday before Christmas is always regarded in football as a Christmas shopping day, and most clubs get their poorest gate of the season on that day. Our gate was 45,000; only one other First Division match exceeded 30,000, such was the magic of Stanley Matthews, although, of course, this was probably one of the best sides Blackpool have ever had. They were top of the table and we were sixteenth. We beat them 4–1 and the result was even more conclusive than the result suggests.

AFC Programme, 30.3.70

I remember that game for one reason. I'd played against Matthews eight or ten times before this game and I took every ball off him. I was so pleased. And it was down at the North Bank and they were attacking. Their left-winger, the South African, Perry, crosses the ball and I can see Con Sullivan's going to catch the ball. So before he caught it I start running and shouted for him to roll me out the ball. And as I got it, this whistle goes and I thought: *Thank God for that!* And I whacked it back in. Con's picking up his hat and gloves. Tommy Lawton's halfway up the tunnel, so was Matthews. And the ref says to me: *Sorry, Dennis. That's a goal.* I said: *What you talking about? You've blown up!* He said: *It wasn't me.*

Dennis Evans

The incident of the whistle blowing in the terraces, I witnessed very closely. It seemed that, according to the crowd, the ref was playing well over time and I can remember the crowd whistling for the ref to finish the game. I was standing next to a railway guard who was in uniform and he pulled out his whistle and gave a long blast on it, and I recall the incident of Dennis Evans very well. The spectators around the railway guard got very annoyed with him, some of them adopted a threatening attitude towards him, following him out. I left by another exit, so do not know what happened.

On arriving home, which is five minutes walk from the ground, I phoned the story to the *People*. The story was published and I received a cheque for £2.2s. It's an ill-wind that blows nobody any good.

A.E. Smith, *AFC Programme*, 22.8.70

It was not until the last few minutes of the game that any great thrill moved the crowd to vocal efforts. In the main they had to be content (and were content) to applaud the accurate (if somewhat slow-moving) play of the City, but to the spectator interested in football, this match had much to commend it. It was very pleasing to study the crowd's response to the game and to note the volume of clapping that followed each City move. A few spectators, bored with the seemingly slow progress of the match and lack of goalmouth thrills, started the 'slow hand-clap'. They were immediately shouted down by a large section of the crowd around them, and thereafter were very quiet.

C.H. Blatch, *GunFlash* 67, April 1955

Apart from Cup-ties it was virtually unknown to have away supporters at Highbury unless they were mixed up ones and twos in the crowd so you didn't know they existed. But Cup-ties they'd come and groups would walk round the pitch all dressed up in their colours. They'd walk around the running track and supporters would laugh at them. It was really jolly.

Frank Hummell

It was Cup-ties really, not so much the ordinary games. That is where the enthusiasm used to be.

Arthur Peakell

May I put forward, in the form of a postscript, my views on Mr Crossland's accusation that the average supporter has adopted a *win at all costs* attitude to the game. Since 1946 we Highbury regulars have witnessed more than our share of classic games, many of which have resulted in brilliant Arsenal victories. Yet, when the poetic artistry of these games has long been forgotten, the memory of two considerably less skilful, in fact, almost negative, football encounters will remain.

Wembley, 1952, when Arsenal's gallant ten men finally yielded to Newcastle after a display of team spirit that won more admiration than the victory of their opponents. Then, that summer evening, when Highbury seethed in the tension of a new League record – a seventh Championship – and the defeat of Burnley. Never a classic, this, but at the final whistle, players and spectators alike were too exhausted to care!

Here lies real soccer greatness: in the drama, fighting spirit, unorthodox success; all these, with the hope of an occasional 'classic', will command our attention on the rain-soaked, wind-swept terraces for many a season to come. The best of luck to all at Arsenal.

Ken Taylor, *AFC Programme*, 9.4.55

'LUCKY TO BE HOME'

The war finished and we all started coming home and this was us: The football. We'd queue to get in from here down to Holloway. And no bother if we were playing Tottenham, part of the family's Tottenham, but we would all come here together talking about different players. Did you see so and so last week? Lishman, Roper. Sometimes we'd queue for three solid hours. You'd go out with your cap on and everybody would know. *You off to football?* And your mum or your wife would say: *You want your brains seen to, you're going to get soaked!* But we didn't care. When we got in, the same thing, passing the kids down was still going on, it was all friendly. It was: We're all home. We're lucky to be home. And we're seeing our game. That was being home.

Frank Martin

When I came out of the army, 1946, there was six or seven of us, all been in the forces, used to meet at the bridge, Southgate Road Bridge in Hackney. We used to go for a drink in a pub called the 'Number Ones'. Go in there Saturday. I'd have a haircut and a shave, have a few drinks and get on the bus down to Highbury. You could bet the crowd would be 60, 62,000. Six of us went, we'd meet down the Shed End, we always went down there. Six of us and another couple of blokes, ten of us would have a sweep, who'd score the first goal. If you won it'd be a pound. You could do a lot with a pound then. You'd all be in there, arguing, but never any trouble. If a bloke came in with a little kid we'd pass the kid down over the barrier and the police would sit 'em down at the front where they wouldn't get squashed. I used to love it. Choc-a-block. Whoever won, they'd handclap them off. Alright, if we lost, I'd have the hump. That'd be me finished. I'd walk in and my mother would say: *Don't say nothing, the Arsenal's lost.*

Jack Hobb

You could see things on the terraces that you couldn't see higher up. You were that much closer. You could see the class of a player, especially the goalkeepers. Maybe some other teams' supporters were more fanatical. But we very rarely got on to our players' backs. We were different people from a different time. We had respect for each other and respect for the team. And standing on that banking there, we were part of Arsenal and were proud of that.

Geoff Gilbert

I first went to Highbury the first game after the war against Sunderland. I used to live in Chapel Market, catch the tram down Upper Street to Highbury Corner and then walked down the hill to the North Bank. I didn't know it as the North Bank then, of course. I was working for British Drug Houses as a vanboy, but I went down with the boys I knew from Chapel Market, Pete and Joe. My stepfather had a stall in the market and there were ice-cream parlours on the corners – they used to compete. Well, we used to go into the second one, the one nearest the Angel. We used to meet there, play football together in Leighton Street and go to Arsenal together. I was, what, 15?

Bill Needs

Couple of my mates used to come down on their bikes. You could leave them in a house there to be looked after. A little place down Riversdale Road, with a garden. They'd look after your bike for 6d.

Jack Hobb

My dad used to work in the gas-works at Greenwich. We'd get a coach over from the crossroads opposite the hospital. There was a little booking office and all the coaches were down the side there. You'd get on about half past one and get over there about quarter past two. You didn't need to worry what time you got there because if you were a kid they'd always let you through to the front.

Chris Thompson

You got in early because you wanted to make sure you got the best view. In those days, you never had a particular spot. You know, you couldn't in crowds of 60,000.

Bill Needs

The hour or so before the game started would be almost boring. There was no chanting, no singing, no real atmosphere build-up. It was quiet, really. It was like pulling the plug out of a bath when the teams came out.

Chris Thompson

You'd get in there, listen to the band, chat to your mates. If you'd got a paper, you'd read that. The clock was an attraction, you could look at the clock, especially before the game. Very few people could afford a watch. And when the game started, you always got a good view from the North Bank. You were all there mixed together with other supporters. Never any fighting that I saw. You'd argue, you know, but then at the end of the game, whichever team won, you'd just say: *Good luck!*

Bill Needs

In the old days they really did – everybody smoked and of course it was all men and there was this little sort of pool of smoke around the ground.

Maureen Hewlitt

You never got food or a drink in there, there was nothing like that. You took sweets or you'd go to a café. You know, across the way from North Bank there was a little café, wasn't there? Tucked into the corner there, by where there's a fish shop now. Over the years that became, like, the Arsenal café. She used to have all the photos up in there and everything.

Bill Needs

People were pushed and shoved around but they wouldn't get angry with each other. They'd say: *Hold it, mate. There's a kid here.* You'd call out to the ambulance people or the coppers and the kids would be passed down over the top. Of course, the crowd loved it when a woman had to be passed down as you can imagine. They didn't wear trousers in those days. Kids and women would often feel faint in the crush and they'd be passed down over the heads.

Frank Hummell

The main thing was the excitement and the involvement, the thrill of standing at an end of a ground, the team coming towards you. I have these vague memories and visions of two or three people and the ball going back and forth very quickly; wingers going past defenders and down to the touch-line; much wider play, with the forward line being five people rather than two strikers; people putting diagonal balls in from the halfway line, very different.

The sense, it's really strange, of huge numbers of people: not being able to get your feet on the ground because it's just enormous numbers, enormous crowds of people. In the wake of Hillsborough, people have a completely different concept of what that's about.

John Yudkin

'TO HELP NOT HINDER'

We all long for the time when it will again be possible for the rosettes of the opposition colours to flower plentifully amidst our crowd – and likewise see large patches of the red and white at our away games – but until then we can only give warm welcome to the few who are able to travel and to those exiles who make their homes amongst us. The old rosettes only seem to come out these days around Cup-tie time which seems rather a pity. Those friends of an evening made through a chaffing remark of: 'Down the Rams, Up the Reds!' or 'Up the Gunners, Down the Blades!' were great fun and I think a good thing for the game and everybody in general. (See plates 12 and 13.)

AFC Programme, 6.9.47

After the war, the number of people who used to go to away games really took off. Special trains, overnight coaches. The first time I went away with Arsenal was just before I did my National Service. I found my way to Villa Park by train for a game and stood on the terraces with a lot of older blokes who showed me the ropes, so to speak. I don't know how I managed it, I was only about 17 and on my own. Now that's really old compared to what kids do now because it's so well organised but there wasn't a supporters' club then.

Frank Hummell

The Board noted that the 'Arsenal Supporters' Club' had been formed and agreed that it would have no official connection with the Arsenal Football Club.

AFC Board Minutes, 12.10.49

I was one of the founder members of the Supporters' Club. They used to have a little stall outside where the headquarters are now. That's where I joined. Dick Jones was the first secretary. I used to know him through business. I was a buyer for a haberdashery firm and Dick Jones was a manufacturer's agent. It was him that got me interested in it. The first year, they got 9,000 members.

Arthur Peakell

When the Supporters' Club started, they had a building in Canonbury Park, you know, just down Upper St from Highbury Corner. They had facilities like table tennis and snooker but it never really took off there. Then they got that house on the corner of St Thomas Road, behind the North Bank. That made you go down the North Bank. Once they'd established that house, everybody would go down there and meet, talk about Arsenal. You'd meet other young lads, you know, so instead of three you became five and you'd all go in together.

Bill Needs

GUNFLASH, official magazine of the Gunners, takes away slightly the breath of one who was brought up in soccer when it was a terraces business and programmes, even bearing the names of the protagonists, were a luxury, by giving the Supporters' Club receipts of £4,274. Out of the financial statement for last season you extract the fact that such things as subscriptions, scarves, and badges accounted for £1,444 of this figure, and travel, mind you! – for a further £1,650.

In light of early personal experiences, it is easy to see the effect all this backroom propaganda has, not only on players but also on spectators . . . Conducted visits to the stadium . . . back numbers of the magazine and programmes . . . balloons with 'Up the Gunners' on them at threepence each . . . recreation rooms (for supporters, not players) . . . club-coloured ties . . . motor-cycle pennants . . . art plate photographs of the team . . . Well, well, . . . Roker Park and Hampden were never like this.

John Macadam, *Daily Express*, 8.8.50

Perhaps some of our members are readers of the *Daily Herald*. If so, they will probably have seen the remarks made in the 15 September issue by Tom Phillips concerning the Arsenal supporters. Mr Phillips – a journalist of note – has given it as his opinion (which he modestly states is good) that the Arsenal supporters are 'the worst in the country, if not in the world'. He freely admits he does not like our supporters – which feeling may possibly be reciprocated.

Mr Phillips goes on to say that we have had the gravy and that for 20 years we have 'bathed in the reflected glory of our great side'. He mixes his metaphors beautifully by continuing 'It was easy for them to stand around a bar counter and say, "Arsenal, the greatest side in the world!" I'm an Arsenal fan!' Arsenal fans, being reared on the best in the world, all stand around bar counters drinking expensive drinks – or at least, that would seem to be the imputation. Then Mr Phillips asserts that the Arsenal supporters are now 'scampering away from the ship which they fear is sinking. Watch them crawl back when Arsenal regain the heights – as they undoubtedly will once they weather the storm. It's the Arsenal supporters who should be on the carpet, not the team.'

As evidence of Mr Phillips's lack of knowledge, I would like to inform him that we have just signed Member No. 19,905, and at the present rate of enrolments will soon be signing No. 20,000. If that is 'scampering away' then my knowledge of English must be faulty. We of the Arsenal Football Supporters' Club stick very rigidly to our motto – To help, not hinder. We do NOT advise Mr Whittaker how to run the Arsenal nor how to pick the team. We do not interfere in any way whatever. We, as supporters, have been disappointed with the form shown by our team. But, Mr Phillips, this is the time when we go along and cheer them even louder.

GunFlash 45, 15.9.54

Arrangements have been made by the Executive Committee for a party of supporters to be at the station to welcome the supporters of clubs visiting the Arsenal. They take with them a large banner, suitably worded, and do what they can to help the visiting supporters in regard to showing them around London and getting them to the ground. No doubt many of you saw the photograph in the *Evening News* of the reception given by our club to the Birmingham City Supporters.

GunFlash 6, Feb 1950

My impression was that season ticket holders never used to go to away matches as much as terrace supporters.

Frank Hummell

Many of you will no doubt have seen reports in the national press of an incident which took place at the conclusion of the recent Cup-tie at Manchester, when an Arsenal supporter assaulted a police officer. The Executive Committee are most anxious that all members should be informed that the man in question was NOT a member of our club. Had he been a member, he would have been expelled immediately, as we are justly proud of the conduct of our members at the away matches and would not at any time tolerate such hooliganism.

GunFlash 18, March 1951

I would like to say how much I – and I am sure I am speaking for the rest of the players – appreciate the support that you are giving to us, especially at the away games. To come out on to the field and be greeted by your balloon barrage lets us know immediately that we have a lot of friends with us, and the wonderful display of red and white makes it easy for us to know where those friends are in the crowd.

Doug Lishman, *GunFlash* 33, Sept 1952

I'm an out-and-out Doncaster Rovers supporter. I last visited Highbury when the (Doncaster) Rovers played Arsenal in a Cup-tie and lost 4–0, 10 Jan 1953. In those days I was the Rovers supporters' cheerleader and at Highbury I met your leader, a chap with a very large black umbrella and we went round the ground together urging our supporters on. Those were the days.

E.J.G. Thompson, *AFC Programme*, 7.1.69

Now if you're talking about dirty games, we beat Doncaster Rovers in the Cup back in 1953. It was the dirtiest game I can remember. It was murderous. How we came out with a team I'll never know. They were kicking everything. You name it, they kicked it. I'll never forget that game.

Geoff Gilbert

One occasion, I remember the Supporters' Club had 47 coaches going to one game to Burnley in 1953 for a Cup-tie. I was on the Travel Committee.

Arthur Peakell

The time for the kick-off was approaching at Burnley and Mickey ('the Umbrella Man') was looking downcast as his usual request to the police for permission to walk round the touch-lines had not been granted. His non-appearance was disturbing our supporters, as we all had a little feeling in our minds that his usual run on to the pitch to greet Joe Mercer and Lionel Smith brought luck to the team. Mickey himself felt that somehow or other that straw hat must adorn the heads of Joe and Lionel for a few seconds before the kick-off.

It was here that Harry Drewett, known to all away followers as a great songster and cheerleader, stepped into the breach – this time in the new capacity of Diplomatic Courier of the AFSC. 'Operation Drewett' was immediately put into action and a path cleared through the crowd to the players' entrance. There stood the man who could say yes or no to our problems – the superintendent in charge of the police on the ground.

Drewett the Diplomat got to work and for ten long and anxious minutes the conference went on. The success of the Drewett venture was obvious to all when he called out to Mickey: 'I have done it! Come down here and meet the Guvnor.' So all is well. Mickey gets his hat on the boys' heads and Lionel does his usual war dance with him. Now we MUST win. And sure enough, we did!!

GunFlash 39, March 1953

Arsenal Supporters' Club provided an object lesson in the correct way to help a side at Burnley on Saturday. Three special train-loads made the journey and many others travelled in a fleet of motor-coaches. All told about 7,000 had come from London to Turf Moor. They certainly made themselves heard, and quite definitely were an important factor in their side's success. Notably eye-catching was the release of a mass of red and white balloons as Arsenal came on the field.

Graham Selkirk, *Sporting Record*, March 1953

Next comes the important question of where you are going to stand. I am assuming that you are not one of the people who can afford a seat, like a banker or a dentist. You have two alternatives. The first is to get right at the front. To do this for the big match on Saturday you will have to stop work and start queuing at midday on the preceding Thursday. But you will be sure to enjoy a good view of the game, and may even get the ball in your face. Your enjoyment will be spoiled, however, by selfish people who lean on you from the back. Or of course, you can take your time about getting to the ground and squeeze in at the back. Here you will see hardly anything at all, but can make yourself comfortable by leaning on the people in front.

Perhaps the best method of all is to take a short course at a good dramatic school. Then you can pretend to faint. This will get you handed over the heads of the crowd, which is great fun, and you will then be laid out on the touch-line, from where you can see the match in perfect comfort.

Wherever you stand, you will be entertained by a band in gorgeous uniforms which probably comes from the local gasworks. Their programme will always include *Colonel Bogey*. You know, Da-Da, and the same to you. At the conclusion of their performance they will march round the ground, led by one of the number who carries a large silver walking stick. Every so often he will hurl this walking stick into the air and catch it as it comes down. This is where you and the rest of the crowd cheer like mad, hoping that one day this will make him drop it.

A few minutes later you'll observe three men making their entrance in dark blazers and long shirts. One of these is your No. 1 target, the referee. He is the only one of the three not carrying a flag, although by the end of the match he may wish he had a white one. You can also distinguish the referee from his colleagues by the fact that he has the longest shorts and thinnest legs, and usually looks like a rather nervous solicitor.

Once things get started, he is fair game and may be insulted with any or all of the following standard phrases: 'Wake up, Ref.', 'Play the game, Ref.', 'What's the idea,

Ref.', and inevitably the most popular cry of all: 'Get some glasses, Ref'. If any referee is unsporting enough to turn up with glasses, the cry is amended to: 'Get some new glasses, Ref'. For advanced spectators, there are more subtle shouts, such as: 'Got this one down as a Two, Ref?' In other words, 'Have you forecast this as an away win?'

All these taunts are designed to express the conviction honestly held by practically the entire crowd that the referee is either a complete nit-wit without the vaguest idea of the rules of football, or an utter scoundrel who is in the pay of the opposing team. To be in a football crowd on one of the rare occasions when the referee falls flat in the mud is to be in the presence of sublime happiness. For linesmen the same insults can be used, plus advice about the disposal of the flag.

The game starts and your real job begins. It is fairly simple of course. For everything your team does you cheer. The activities of their opponents you either meet with silence, or, at the slighest opportunity, you vigorously express your displeasure. As in the case of the referee there are a number of approved epithets for hurling at members of the other side. These either refer to the individual's character (e.g. 'You filthy beast') or to any physical peculiarity (e.g. Banana bonce). In special cases you will naturally throw doubts about his ancestry. Should a member of the opposition kick the ball out of play at any time, you shout: 'Keep it on the island'. When one of your side does it, the cry is changed slightly to: 'Well cleared, Joe.'

You must, of course, also urge your team on with such stirring appeals as: 'Get stuck into 'im, George'. Needless to say, should anyone be unsporting enough to get stuck into George, you raise your voice in an indignant appeal to the Ref to: 'Send 'im orf!'

Cardew Robinson, *GunFlash* 65, August 1955

'EVERYTHING POSSIBLE IS BEING DONE'

Tom Whittaker has asked me to tell those of our regular supporters who have had trouble getting into the ground at recent matches that we at Arsenal are only too well aware of it, and are trying to legislate to prevent such complaints. Not only are the crowds bigger but the capacity of the stadium smaller owing to bomb damage that cannot yet be repaired. Our building licences have not let us get over all our difficulties with regard to entrances and exits but we do take notice of these complaints, and you can be assured that everything possible is being done to improve the comfort of our patrons' visits to Highbury.

AFC Programme, 4.10.47

Mr Binnie reported that after investigation he had learned that the club could claim a valuation payment now for the damage sustained to the North Terrace and rebuild when considered desirable. He estimated that against the pre-war price of £5,000 the cost of rebuilding the Stand now would be about £12,500, and he recommended the

Board to accept a valuation payment of this figure. The Board had discussion on the subject, and the matter was left for Mr Binnie to obtain an estimate to rebuild the North Terrace as it was before, and ascertain the difference in the suggested valuation figure. Mr Binnie promised to do this, and the Board would be informed in due course.

AFC Board Minutes, 19.9.50

Whilst on the subject of offered accommodation, most of you will remember the pre-war days when the North Terrace had a roof over it. This, of course, was destroyed by enemy fire-bombs during the last war and, until now, we have had so much other vital war damage work on hand that we have had to leave this until last. You may rest assured that the question of the uncovered 1s 3d accommodation has not been overlooked by the management. It has had to be a question of vital things first.

The question of licences and all the necessary formalities is now being investigated with a view to rebuilding the cover over the North Terrace as soon as possible. Many people have written complaining because we do not put a cover over the South Terrace and to this we can only reply that there is little hope indeed of the Club obtaining a licence for any such new work as this. Rest assured that the comfort of all grades and sections of spectators is constantly before the Directors and they will do all in their power to expedite the necessary works.

AFC Programme, 30.9.50

I would like to say a few words about the enormous success of the recent floodlit match at Highbury against Hapoel, Tel-Aviv. All our members who attended this match were unanimous in their opinion that here was something that had come to stay. Apart from the result of the game, the novelty of the occasion was one that was enjoyed by everybody, and I would strongly advise any of you who were unable to be there to be sure not to miss either the London Challenge Cup-tie against Hendon on Monday 8 October or the match against our popular friends from across the border – Glasgow Rangers – on Wednesday 17 October, both of which are being played at Highbury under floodlight.

GunFlash 24, Oct 1951

A letter was read from the Football Association stating that the Home Office were now rather concerned about floodlit matches and whether any form of emergency lighting had been considered to avoid danger of panic in the crowd should the main lighting fail for any reason.

The Board gave this letter consideration, and after discussion the secretary–manager was requested to obtain further information as to what would be acceptable as emergency lighting and what methods of installation would be suitable for Home Office approval.

AFC Board Minutes, 6.3.53

Despite the Football Association ruling to the effect that Cup-ties can be played with the aid of floodlights, there appears to have been some difference of opinion between clubs, and only a comparative few of today's ties will be 'lit up'.

It has been our opinion for a long time that the early sunset which causes us to kick-off at 2.15 p.m. at this time of the year could well be supplemented by floodlights in the second half so as to enable matches to begin at, say, three p.m. throughout the season.

One big factor is the inability of large numbers of spectators to get to the grounds in good time before the start. To obtain a midday meal and get to the ground well before the kick-off is a problem that many face and, not being able to overcome it, are forced to arrive at the turnstiles ten minutes or so before the game is due to start.

An example of this was our recent match against Wolverhampton Wanderers. The kick-off was at 2.15 p.m. and at 2.05 p.m. there was little indication that there would be a very large attendance. Yet in that ten minutes (and the following ten minutes) thousands of people descended upon the stadium and on entering the ground found difficulty in finding places to see, despite the fact that there was accommodation for an additional 6,000.

Much of the difficulty could, however, be obviated if League matches in November, December and January were able to commence at three p.m. and finish with the aid of floodlight. There need be no compulsion about the question and it would obviously have to be arranged after the mutual agreement of the two clubs.

AFC Programme, 7.1.56

Mr Binnie reported that he had received a letter from the War Damage Commission stating that a cheque for £48.17.9 which they had enclosed now completed the company's claim for War Damage. The Board agreed with Mr Binnie that this was not quite true as the North Terrace war damage had not yet been settled. The Board instructed Mr Binnie to contact the War Damage Commission immediately stating that the company did not agree that their war damage claim had all been met, and would Mr Binnie take up with them the North Terrace damage and report the result of his enquiries to the Board.

AFC Board Minutes, 1.7.52

The publication of our balance sheet last week showed two records. The first was the record gross receipts for last season which amounted to £200,877, and the second, the record profit of £62,129.

As is quite understandable, following the publication of these figures the question has been raised by a number of our fans as to the rebuilding of the cover over the North Terrace which was razed to the ground by enemy fire-bombs during the war. The position is that we are only too anxious to rebuild but we are unable to obtain the necessary permits and licences.

The whole structure involves the use of a high percentage of steel, and we regret to say that until the national situation in the supply of this metal eases there is little chance of us being able to put matters right. Rest assured that the cover will be put back as soon as possible to do so.

AFC Programme, 10.9.52

Mr Binnie reported to the Board on progress with regard to the replacement of the cover to the North Terrace which was destroyed by enemy action. He brought drawings and sketches to show the various schemes he had in mind. The chairman and his colleagues on the Board were unanimous in their opinion that the North Terrace should be covered in exactly the same way as it was before being destroyed by enemy action, and strongly stipulated that there was no need for any sketches or designs other than this, and Mr Binnie was instructed to proceed forthwith as requested and to contact the War Damage Commission immediately.

The Board were of the opinion that the club should be paid full value by the War Damage Commission on the cost of replacing, and Mr Binnie was requested to report his progress as soon as possible.

AFC Board Minutes, 23.9.54

Our regular spectators will be pleased to hear that we have, at last, been able to conclude our arrangements with the War Damage Commission and that the cover to the North Terrace, which was such a boon to the ground spectators before the war, will be available again next season. This will mean that we shall once again have covered accommodation for over 50,000.

Mr Binnie gave a further report to the Board on progress made in regard to the replacing of the cover to the North Terrace damaged by enemy action. Mr Binnie stated that, as already notified to us in correspondence, Messrs Higgs Ltd's tender of £24,726.17.0. (24,726 pounds and 17 shillings) had been accepted by the War Damage Commission.

AFC Board Minutes, 16.9.55

The secretary-manager reported that the preliminary work for the North Terrace cover had now commenced. The work this season would not interfere with the public on current match days.

AFC Board Minutes, 11.11.55

The progress chart in connection with the erection of the cover to the North Terrace was placed before the Board, and it was noted that the Club's architect had stated that work would be completed on or before 30 July next.

AFC Board Minutes, 27.4.56

It was so massive. The splendour. It was like a palace. It still seems to me it looks like the perfect ground. (See plate 33.)

Chris Thompson

The roof goes right over to the front and, I'm not sure if it is, but it feels like a lower roof than say the Kop at Liverpool or the Holte End at Villa which are quite high up and far back. In that sense it was in some ways a little bit more old-fashioned. I mean architecturally, in terms of structure, there was nothing innovative at all about it. When you're standing in the rest of the ground, or sitting in the stand looking at the North Bank, I've always been very conscious that it is a traditional terrace roof with trimmings. No other ground that I know of actually gave a trimming to the roof. I can't think of anywhere else you actually have the roof fascia coming round with emblems on the corners. That corrugated look is 'louvred vitroflex'. I mean, that is attention to detail which no other clubs gave. If you strip that away it would be like any other football terrace, but the fact that it's there is just another little indication this is different. This is a club which is different.

Simon Inglis

CHAPTER FIVE

The Beginning of 'The End'

THE NORTH TERRACE, 1957–70

During the late 50s, the national trend towards smaller attendances at football became evident at Highbury too. The rise in real incomes – and the increase in the number of consumer options available on which to spend them – had a part to play: the car and the television were, without question, the most obvious agents of change in the leisure market place of which football now found itself to be a part. The full-day Saturday holiday had become widespread. Taking the family out for the day before settling down to watch *Match of the Day* come Saturday evening had simply not been a choice available to the crowds that had flocked to football immediately after the war. On the field, Arsenal slipped into a period of unsuccessful mediocrity unfamiliar since the early 20s. On the big occasion the stadium still burst at the seams, as it did to enjoy the legendary final celebration of post-war football's values, the game against Manchester United's Busby Babes in February 1958. Our last glimpse of one of the most precocious and exciting sides of all time, the match can be taken to mark the end of an era. By the time Highbury was to witness such excitement again football and the North Terrace would have changed beyond all recognition.

The steady decrease in gate receipts (which it was hoped would prove to be a temporary phenomenon) was, at first, offset by increased admission charges paid by spectators with more income at their disposal and by the lifting of Entertainment Duty. Indeed, early on, it seemed much-needed ground improvements could be undertaken as a way of helping to entice the more selective customer back to football. As it transpired, however, the money was to be needed elsewhere. Real change on the terraces, when it came, was in response to very different pressures.

In 1961, Arsenal's 'life at the top' was brought to a keenly felt full-stop when neighbours Spurs pulled off the League and Cup double which had eluded even Arsenal's greatest side of the early 30s. Over the same 12 months the game saw, too, a radical realignment of the relationship between professional footballers and their employers. The first of two profound changes was the abolition of the 'retain and transfer' system, an archaic clause by which – even at the end of his agreed term of contract – a player's registration was retained by his club. A player could not leave one club and join another of his own volition, no matter what notice he served. Clubs 'owned' players to a degree, even then, unique in labour relations. After his eventual transfer to Arsenal from Newcastle United, George Eastham took the principle to the High Court and overturned the system that had led to a bitter and extended dispute with his former club on the expiry of his last contract. While Eastham 'freed' his fellow professionals, Jimmy Hill led the 2,000 members of the PFA through months of industrial dispute, eventually succeeding in abolishing the maximum wage – £20 a week in 1960. For the players, who you played for – and what they paid for it – became subjects open to negotiation. For the clubs, it was a rude awakening from the comfortable days of predictability in this important and potentially expensive area of their budgets. Ironically, Eastham himself led Highbury's first wages dispute the following year. With players in a new-found position of strength, the difficulties experienced as gates fell away became a matter of serious concern. This could be seen reflected in Arsenal's new bonus scheme, which rewarded players from week to week on a rising scale in line with attendances over 35,000.

Within a few years, footballers were earning incomes sufficient, in some cases, to support 'pop star' lifestyles. Where previously they had appeared to be comfortable, upstanding examples of the working men who packed the terraces, footballers became – at the very top, at least – well-paid young men rubbing shoulders with the rich and famous, apparently cut loose from their own – and their fans' – class blackgrounds. Football and footballers became a 'fashionable' proposition for working-class youth. Teenagers, it seemed, had come out of nowhere in the 50s. In 60s' London, they started coming to football – and coming on their own – in great numbers, drawn to the game as their parents had been, but also attracted by the aura of 'high living' those who played it seemed to possess. Most exciting of all, perhaps, was the prospect of the company of hundreds – even thousands – of their peers to be enjoyed in an accessible, unstructured environment.

In difficult financial circumstances for the clubs, Arsenal no less than any other, the importance of 'winning' became paramount, success the absolute arbiter of economic security. This, and the drift away from the game of more neutral casual supporters, helped develop a new culture among the smaller crowd which remained that was both more partisan and significantly more demanding than had been known previously. It was this culture which the new, 'unsupervised' young audience took on and shaped as its own. Football and football-supporting became a very conscious expression of identity. As several northern clubs like Liverpool and Leeds developed a style of play that reflected the new competitive spirit, their supporters offered an example to young fans at Highbury, and elsewhere. The chanting, the swaying and the passion of the Kop, once seen on television and among visiting fans from the North, took very little time to catch on at grounds around the country. The 'North Bank' already existed when this new culture, built around success and fashion, received a massive boost in the World Cup summer of 1966.

While the team struggled through the mid-60s, the North Bank became an exciting place to be. By the time Bertie Mee took charge and developed a competitive no-risk team policy that promised (and delivered) real success to the club once more, Arsenal had an End as loud, passionate and partisan as anybody's. When the Fairs Cup was won in 1970, the older supporters knew the triumph felt different to that they'd experienced as boys: there was a new edge, a new tension, a new sense of relief. Unaware of history, the new generation on the North Bank poured on to the pitch to lead the celebrations.

With the songs and the youth and the devotion to the Arsenal team, however, came a spot of bother. Fighting at football matches was nothing new – in Arsenal's case dating back as far as the club's Plumstead days! But violence on the terraces, when it occurred, had tended to be spontaneous, informal and sporadic. With young supporters now identifying themselves in groups larger, more abstract and – potentially – more powerful than those companies of family and friends which had been the basic units of the crowds of earlier years, when trouble flared now it was on a larger and far more visible scale. Liverpool and Everton fans had been dubbed 'Merseyside Maniacs' as early as the mid 50s: destruction of property and casual violence were part of the day out for a minority of the large numbers who followed those teams away. When Liverpool came to Highbury for an FA Cup-tie in February 1964, the scope and nature of the violence they brought with them to the terraces shocked most spectators. A small minority, however, were ready to be suitably impressed.

The 'taking' of the home end by Glasgow Rangers fans in 1967 established a precedent that the teenagers on the North Bank decided was not acceptable. In their eyes, protecting the terrace became as much a part of the lads' duty to the club as cheering on the team. By the time the press and learned gentlemen had found a vocabulary – 'animals', 'savages', 'thugs' – that set them apart from 'normal people', skinhead culture had arrived to mark the gangs of kids out even more clearly in their own and others' minds. A dark cloud was gathering over football which would break over the game and across the terraces into the early 1980s.

'THE GREATEST GAME EVER AT HIGHBURY'

That Man United game, it's one you look back on partly because it became famous after the event because of what it meant. But that particular day, everybody wanted to see them, this quite superb team with a lot of young players who were very clearly going to rule the roost. It wasn't that they'd been particularly built up in the press, but word has just got round. I had schoolfriends then who are Man United fans to this day because of that team. You just wanted to be there to see them.

Chris Thompson

There were two heroic phases. It will take a month of Sundays to forget them. The first came shortly after half time when in the bat of an eyelid – precisely two minutes and 30 seconds on the stop-watch – Herd and Bloomfield (twice) put the ball in Gregg's net three times to wipe out United's 3–0 lead at the interval. That set a spark to the gunpowder. It was admirable. But perhaps even more admirable was the

Manchester reply. Lesser sides would have wilted in the face of such a cruel blast. As if they were nonchalantly dismissing a troublesome fly they suddenly spun two more intricate, precision moves to leap again to 5–3. Here was their true pedigree, though Arsenal came once more to 4–5, leaving the end on a razor's edge.

The thermometer was doing a war dance. There was no breath left in anyone. The players came off arm in arm. They knew they had finally fashioned something of which to be proud. (See plate 17.)

The Times, 3.2.58

I always remember going to that Man United game before the air crash. I was standing where I used to stand, in the corner at that end, and Duncan Edwards came up, right near where I was standing. We had a full-back called Dennis Evans and, as Edwards came into the area, he hit him really hard. This was the first time I realised footballers did this kind of thing. And I heard Edwards say: *Oh, fucking get up!* Right in front of me. If I'd been up in the seats I wouldn't have heard a thing. And later in the game, they were both going for a 50/50 ball and you just knew Evans was going to do him. I think it was the captain, Dave Bowen, shouted and Evans pulled back and Edwards got the ball. If he'd gone through, he'd have injured him and Edwards wouldn't have gone to Munich. It happened right in front of me.

Laurence Marks

The Man United game was the greatest game ever at Highbury. I'm not knocking the games today, but there's been nothing like the atmosphere that day. I had the chance in that game of 'doing' Duncan Edwards because he 'did' my mate, Danny Clapton. Duncan kicked him and Danny went over on the cinder track and got scratched all the way down. Dunc was a big bloke, only 18/19, but I said to him: *Dunc, don't come through again.* I was shaking in my shoes saying it. Anyway, he did come through. He's beat one man, he's beat two and he pushed it too far. This is the time when players who want to do it go 'over the top' because the other fellow's got to stretch. I went to do him but instead I toe-ended the ball for a throw-in. I said: *It could have happened, Dunc.* And he smiled and said: *Yes it could, Dennis.* If I'd have done him, he wouldn't have been on that plane. I've never hurt another player but I wish I'd broken his leg. Great player. The atmosphere that day, there were 65,000 people in the ground, I'd say, and everyone was cheering. Not because of Arsenal, not because of Manchester United. Just cheering because of the game itself. Beautiful it was. No one left till five minutes after the game. They just stood cheering.

Dennis Evans

It all came down to that old chestnut: policing by consent. That's what it was. There was no way the numbers of police could have done anything to prevent people rioting if you had a 60,000 gate. But it was all good humoured and hoping that people were going to do as they were told. Nobody used to get out of their pram about football, you know. If the better team won, that was one of those things. I remember the game here against Manchester United, before the air disaster. Five–four was it, Arsenal lost? Three-nil down at half-time and then they got three quick goals. And they were

(Plate 1) 'Over the years there were some outstanding players.' The Arsenal team, 1922–23. Left to right: (standing) Voysey, Rutherford, Dunn, Boreham, Graham; (seated) Baker, White, Young, Bradshaw, Turnbull, Dr Paterson (Colorsport)

(Plate 2) 'A one-way man – his way!' Sir Henry Norris, who brought Arsenal to Highbury in 1913

(Plate 3) 'The Arsenal supporters, in a great variety of costumes, making a brave show.' Rose Brinkman (later Mrs Jales) at the centre, with Les Jessop on her left and her father, Patsy, below

(Plate 4) 'The Arsenal Duck was present.' Jimmy Clayton holds on to Rose Brinkman while someone else, it's assumed, was holding on to the duck!

(Plate 5) 'And everybody would be laughing.' Big-band drummer and Laundry End regular Les Jessop (bottom left) and friends head off to Anfield in 1936

(Plate 6) Bert Sadler

(Plate 7) 'Never anxious to put himself on a pedestal.' Herbert Chapman, who brought glory to Highbury in the 1930s (Colorsport)

(Plate 8) 'I would congratulate the police on their tactful and efficient handling of such a mammoth throng.' A corner of the then smaller Laundry End overflows before a Cup-tie against Aston Villa in 1926 (Hulton Deutsch)

(Plate 9) 'The great men of the day.' Alex James and Cliff Bastin (Colorsport)

(Plate 10) 'Ever on the lookout for improvements.' Ted Drake at the centre as a group of players crowd around an 'Enumerator', a device designed to count the huge numbers that poured through Highbury's turnstiles throughout the 30s (Hulton Deutsch)

(Plate 11) 'Only bad weather kept people away.' The Laundry End, packed for the first game of 1933–34. The clock, no roof and hardly a bare head in sight! The boards at the back of the terrace advertise the local Underground station, recently renamed Arsenal (Hulton Deutsch)

(Plates 12 and 13) 'A good thing for the game and everybody in general.' On the left, Dick Jones, the founder of the Arsenal Supporters' Club. On the right, club members arrive for a League game in Huddersfield in April 1955. Dave Stacey carries the giant rosette

(Plates 14 and 15) 'I went to football all through the war.' On the left, Reg Lewis, whose two goals beat Liverpool in the 1950 Cup final. On the right, Dennis Compton, 'The Brylcreem Boy' — Arsenal's first post-war superstar. Both men made their debuts before the war (the photos are from the late 30s) and survived to become heroes to a new generation after it (Colorsport)

(Plate 16) 'After the war, people were happy.' The 1947–48 Championship-winning team. Left to right: (back row) Forbes, Wade, Smith, Male, D. Compton, Mercer; (second row) Crayston, Lewis, Fields, Swindin, L. Compton, McPherson, Milne; (seated) Scott, Macaulay, Whittaker, Rooke, Barnes, Milne; (ground) Jones, Roper, Logie

good goals. Tommy Taylor, Dennis Viollet, people like that; Jimmy Bloomfield on the Arsenal side. The atmosphere was electric.

PC Roy Beasley, retd

You came out of there with your ears glowing and you'd seen a terrific game. What's happened since, of course, is 'win at all costs'. I'll be honest, I'd rather see 90 minutes of crap if we bang one in at the end than a real blinding game that we lose 5–4. Society, I think, has changed. That Man United game, you didn't feel flattened because we'd lost. Now it's all about winning. And I'm as bad as anyone.

Chris Thompson

'LACKING SOME VITAL FACTOR'

TAX ABOLITION

After a long fight the football authorities have succeeded at last in convincing the Chancellor of the Exchequer that the heavy burden of Entertainment Duty was an unfair drain on club resources and prevented the majority of clubs from holding their heads above water. Few foresaw a complete abolition (a 50 per cent reduction would have been most welcome) but no doubt the high cost of the machinery for the collection of the duty meant that it would be hardly worth while collecting the reduced revenue.

For many clubs it has meant the difference between solvency and bankruptcy and in any case it does mean that many of the smaller clubs will not have to transfer all their promising young players in order to balance the budget. It will, therefore, put these clubs on a footing which has always been a source of criticism in our game, for it has been rightly said by many people that every club should be capable of 'living' on its gate receipts. For the bigger clubs it will mean that their grounds can be put in order and the proper amenities provided for their supporters.

Go-ahead Arsenal are to splash out £20,000 next close season as another step in their plans to make Highbury one of the most modern and comfortable grounds in Britain. While other clubs discuss novelty money-raising ideas to boost their coffers the Gunners board gets ready to spend and makes moves to increase the comfort of their fans.

Secretary Bob Wall said this week 'We have all sorts of expansion and improvement plans before us. We are to start by rebuilding toilet facilities and other amenities in the ground this summer at a cost of £20,000.' The toilets have been up since the 1920s and are to be replaced. Only when Arsenal have brought all their amenities up to date will they start to think about expanding in other directions.

The fan is an even more important cog in the soccer set-up now the higher wages, bigger bonuses New Deal age is here and the local club are putting him first.

Islington Gazette, 1.12.61

In all the years I'm talking about from the 50s through to 76–77, I never once went to the toilet. I don't know why. In many games you couldn't get out. There was a café. I never used that either. Disgusting it was. Never used that. I mean it was really ridiculous when you think about it. £1 to stand on a slab of concrete in the rain? I mean it was madness. Cold. I mean, I've been to games when I couldn't see beyond the halfway line, when it's been abandoned at half time. Bob Wilson, one time didn't know the game had been abandoned, he was just still standing there. Where its been icy, where I've slipped over – conditions you wouldn't even think of going out in. I mean, if somebody asked you if you wanted to stand on this blank piece of concrete, in freezing cold and snow, you'd think they were raving mad. But this was a pilgrimage. The best thing was going up those steps and seeing the pitch. There didn't have to be anyone on it. Just the pitch.

Laurence Marks

I thought the facilities were abysmal, but I wouldn't have dreamt of moaning about it. That was part of it I thought. In fact they were improved as the years went on, not a great deal, but they obviously did make some sort of effort. I mean, when I started going there was a little green shed behind the North Bank where you could get alcohol, which I always enjoyed when I was old enough. I didn't think that necessarily had to go hand in hand with fighting, and I certainly don't think it had anything to do with it up the North Bank, not at all.

They took steps to improve things but I don't think people were bothered. I don't think it would have bothered people if they hadn't done that. I accepted it as being part of it, it was what it was like when I first went, and by ten or 15 years later it was still the same. Yeah we used to moan about the stink in the toilets, or my wife used to moan about having to queue up for ten minutes into the second half because there was only something like two ladies' toilets. But it wouldn't have stopped us going, and the lack of the food or the poor standard of it certainly wouldn't matter. No one I knew moaned about that.

Mick Essen

It had that little tea hut – you had a bit of cake, you know, it was lovely. It was a nice refuge as well in the late 60s or early 70s when the fists started flying. You'd go in there have a cup of tea and sticky bun whatever – Dundee cake. I mean on the North Bank, a pint of Whitbread tasted like water, and the pasty, *pastry pasty* we used to call it because there were never any meat in them, it was just like a bit of pastry. And later on they used to do those quarts, do you remember those quart things? Polystyrene cups for two quid, two pints of bitter or lager.

Steve Whitman

They never used to have the food outlets they've got now. If anything, all you'd eat would be fish and chips on the way home. We used to go to Manzie's in Chapel Street before the game. That amuses me now: Manzie's have got an executive box, haven't they? They've done alright out of us!

Tina Evans

Arsenal have taken another step in their plans for a complete Highbury sit-down. Workmen are putting the finishing touches to 5,400 new seats at a cost of £80,000. There used to be 15,000 standing positions under the West Stand but they have been displaced by the creation of 5,400 seats with room for 2,000 standing in front. This new seating will reduce Arsenal's ground capacity to 63,000. Yet it will mean that 17,000 fans can rest their legs next season. Arsenal's long-term policy is to get seating behind both goals.

Islington Gazette, 27.6.69

I believe the incidence of hooliganism will be halted when more seats are installed in football grounds. It is not easy to throw punches effectively or to strike someone with a bottle *and* get away with it when you are seated in a stand. A steward or policeman can easily remove the offender whereas, in a swaying mob of people, he has difficulty in detecting the culprit. Furthermore, you find far more emotion – and unhealthy emotion at that – generated by rival fans jostling shoulder to shoulder on the terraces.

The public seem to be realising this, too. Arsenal installed 5,500 more seats for the 1969–70 season. This was a direct result of repeated demands from our supporters.

Obviously, it is not only a question of people wanting to get away from the mob element. With higher standards of education and taste, you are bound to find more customers insisting on comfort in their leisure hours.

There will always be a hard core who would miss the atmosphere of the terraces, if crush barriers were replaced by tip-up seats. Yet, I am certain that, within the next quarter of a century, the vast majority of grounds will become all-seating stadia. The reason greater numbers of seats are not available today is the cost.

Bob Wall, *Arsenal from the Heart*

Of course then we had that bad period when you could more or less walk round and park a deckchair on the terraces, late 50s, or early 60s, when we really did have crumb players. The double act, Nutt and Tiddy. How we ever ended up with them I'll never know. Managers changing, we had no continuity. The crowds got to 17, 18,000 which was the rock bottom. I was one of them – you used to go and pick your place on the terrace. We were the Last of the Mohicans, the real hard core of Arsenal supporters.

Geoff Gilbert

As the years moved on people's incomes improved. They got the small family car. The wife went out to work and was at home on Saturday, maybe, her day off too. So there were other demands on families' time. Disposable income went up but there were more things to do with it. You had the advent of everyone having a television set whereas before, back in the early fifties, if you had a TV set you were quite well off. The car came along, as I've said. There were all sorts of other ways of spending your time. I think that people got more selective with their time and slowly, over that period – you also have to remember that between 1953 and 1970 we had a very lean 17–18 years – we lost public because of that.

Ken Friar

Young people, teenagers – there started being other things for them to do. At 15, 16, 17, there was so much more going on in the 60s. Even me, when I first met my husband, I was under 16 and he didn't like football. I started having to choose on Saturday afternoons when he wanted to take me out. I stopped going a lot. This happened to a lot of people. There was the big music explosion – you used to go in shops on Saturday afternoon, there'd be people in little booths with earphones on, dancing around, listening to music.

Tina Evans

We'd all go for a drink in the Gunners pub – that was our pub – before the game because you couldn't really get a drink inside then till they built that little bar. Of course, now you weren't having to get in that early. Crowds weren't that big – only crowds that were big were when you got Man United or Tottenham or Liverpool. But with crowds of 30,000 you could get in no problem.

Bill Needs

Every club is concerned chiefly about the falling attendances and now, we are quite sure, the attendances at League matches this season will, for the first time in the post-war period, fall short of pre-war. Simply, this must prove that the spectacle of our League matches, as a public entertainment, is lacking some vital factor.

AFC Programme, 3.4.65

That awful night in 65–66, when Billy Wright was being sacked, when there was only 4,554 for Leeds. We all came in the North Bank, Johnny Nash, Mick Sylvester, we all came in and we're going: *Mind the crowd! Mind the crowd!* And, of course, it was a bloody cold night and all, even though it was May, so we started building a little fire down the bottom there. 4.500! I never thought I'd see that.

Bill Needs

We have never been under any delusions – the hard core of Arsenal support is no more than 20,000, possibly because there are no fewer than 11 Football League clubs in the London area! Our 'big' attendances are derived from one (or more) of three circumstances, all readily understandable:

1. Arsenal playing well
2. Attractive opponents
3. Good weather

AFC Programme, 27.12.69

Some of the most remarkable crowd scenes in Arsenal's history occurred on Tuesday evening when Arsenal met Tottenham Hotspur at Highbury Stadium. A capacity crowd of 67,986 was admitted to the ground.

When the gates were shut almost three-quarters of an hour before the kick-off, more than 10,000 people were left outside milling in Avenell and Gillespie Roads and the surrounding streets. A police spokesman told the *North London Press* he had never known such scenes. 'Everything went very well and we didn't need to call in any extra men,' he said. Inside the stadium the ground was packed tight with spectators. More than 100 people were treated by St John's Ambulance Brigade for fainting or mild shock induced by the pressure of the crowd. The result of the game was a 4–4 draw and the receipts were £12,000.

North London Press, 18.10.63

We had one night here we played the Spurs and all those railings across the Clock End crushed to the ground through the pressure of people. We had over 100 patients out there, people coming in and out. The ambulances were coming in here, going out there, like a shuttle service. But everyone got done and serviced, we got through it.

Ron Pottage

The night I was locked out. It was a night game and everybody leaves it till the last minute. I was only about 13 and we were playing Tottenham. God, it was murder! The North Bank in Avenell Road, I tried to get to that turnstile. I was with my mate Dave and in the end we just didn't get there. I looked it up. There was 68,000 people. In the end, we're just walking back to the Arsenal station and: *Gooaal!* And the worst thing was I didn't know who'd scored.

Eddie Mason

I can run the last two minutes of that match through my mind like a film. It's more than 15 years ago, yet it might have been yesterday. It was almost the perfect game – tense, exciting, and in front of a full house.

Tottenham pasted us in the first half, and at 4–2 down at half time we were dead. Then somehow we got out of the grave and almost won. It was an evening game and it was obvious a long time before that there would be a big crowd. But quite how big it would be I don't think I realised until I was coming out of the tunnel into the glare of the floodlights: the place was packed to the rafters. Having a big crowd sets the scene for a match, it puts the players on edge, gees them up to play their hearts out. Tottenham were playing superb football. There was no doubt in my mind that they were the outstanding team in the country at that time.

But Billy Wright, our manager, gave a good half-time talk. He could have sworn and been angry – but he calmly said that we might as well lose 10–2 as 4–2, and to go out and try to win it back. Joe Baker scored early in the second half, and suddenly a strange feeling of anticipation swept through the team. Blanchflower and Mackay began to seem like ordinary players instead of world beaters, and we were gradually pushing them back. We knew a goal would come, it had to. What we didn't know was whether it would come in time. Then we got that corner, and I can visualise the ball floating across, with me realising that I had a good jump at it, and a chance, and the ball hitting the net. It's terribly hard to explain what it feels like to score such an important goal, in front of so many people, so close to the end.

Geoff Strong, *AFC Programme*, 15.10.63

Its funny about the 60s. I had to wait, till the 70s for the Fairs Cup to win anything but the crowd and Arsenal, they weren't a particularly great side, but they had some real good players (and some poor players), and when you went to games the atmosphere was superb. I mean my two uncles, early 60s, took me to that Spurs–Arsenal four-all draw. I don't know if you remember that? That was a knockout that night. My dad couldn't go and he was a bit reluctant about me going to that game on me own but my uncles always went up, so I went with them. We parked up and it was funny because one of me uncles is a right slouch and he goes: *Nah, it will be alright.* Me other uncle said: *I'll take Laird and we'll run.* And we got there and it was just absolutely mobbed. In those days you used to be able to say: *Got a child here!* And you'd push through, and we managed to get in. When we got back me uncle he'd been sitting in the car all night! Locked out! When we got in there I just remember that I've never been in a crowd like it before. I ended up halfway down the east side of the North Bank and got lucky cos I got put on a barrier. It was that mobbed but they lifted me up there. They got slaughtered that night because it was just after Spurs' Double year I think and we had a keeper called McKechnie. He weren't that clever, he was a bit heavy and that and I think he only played one game after this. Arsenal weren't doing that well that night – they were 4–2 down and one of the goals – McKay had pulled from just inside the halfway line, it was coming towards me and McKechnie thought it was going wide and the ball just had enough pace to go in the side of the net and that made it 4–2. But Arsenal came back. They had two corners in the last ten minutes. Geoff Strong got the equalising goal and that was near enough a couple of minutes from the end. I think Joe Baker got the other one. The atmosphere then was tremendous, nothing like it is now.

Laird Budge

'THE NORTH BANK, HIGHBURY'

The only communication which you'd have between supporters at the two ends of the ground – which you get regularly now – would be when they were playing games in the fog. People would shout out: *What's the score, Clock End?* Otherwise there was no identification of the two ends as different. Clock End or North Bank were hardly mentioned, you know. You were just a mass of people who stood in the same place every week.

Frank Hummell

I suppose you'd always got your loudest-shouting supporters on the North Bank, but not to the extent that you would go to the North Bank thinking it was any more special than any other part of the ground. I don't think people thought of football grounds in that way then. It seemed to me that the North Bank became more prevalent during the 60s while I was playing. That was when it became the North Bank versus the Kop, versus the Shed – all those rivalries. When I was a kid, I'd go on the North Bank partly because it was by the Tube station and, mainly, because the biggest crowd was there – and if you like to stand, being involved with the crowd is part of that. If I was meeting friends, we would always arrange to go on the North Bank, not because it was 'the North Bank' but simply because it was the best place to stand, for the atmosphere and for the view.

David Court

In the early 60s there was less of the chanting and all that, you got away supporters mixed in. But the North Bank always seemed where the most passionate supporters were, the heartbeat of the club.

Steve Kazmarek

When Arsenal were having their bad times and crowds were down to around 30,000, with a ground holding 70, it was only half full. You could walk round at half time if you wanted. I certainly don't remember the North Bank being like the 'home end'. I mean, by the Double year and the Anderlecht game, this tremendous bond down there existed by then but how long before, I don't know. If I had to put a date to it, I'd say when Leeds came back to the First Division, 64–65, that was when it started.

Chris Thompson

When we used to go, everybody was in their groups. Then it became more like, they'd get to the North Bank in their little groups but then they became one big group. One big shout. They all join in regardless of who they know, whereas in the 30s it was groups of 15 or 20.

Tom Jales

The young people who were going in the late 60s, the North Bank became where they would congregate. Previously if they'd gone, they might have gone with their dads. Then when they were older, they wanted to be with their friends and that's where they'd go. The North Bank, right bang in the middle, has been where the younger people went. That started in the 60s.

Tina Evans

I remember I went up to Darlington for a Cup game in 1965. They used to let us in the pub at ten o'clock then to get us off the streets. They were starting to get worried about fighting then. Well, I met up with these lads, 17 and 18, much younger than me but it didn't matter – we were all there for the same reason. I suppose I was their kind of character, you know, a bit of a tearaway myself! Johnny Nash, Micky Sylvester, Barry Baker (we called him Joe Baker) – who runs the Supporters' Club now. And we all started going up the North Bank together and that was when you started getting, say, all the Liverpool supporters going: *Liverpool! Liverpool!* and we'd be up there going: *Arsenal!* It got going between the two ends. It was great.

Bill Needs

I have supported Arsenal at both the Clock End and the North End of the stadium and they are as different as chalk and cheese. The Clock End is as quiet as the grave for most of the match, whereas at the North End we have thousands of supporters who are prepared to sing, chant and shout their encouragement. This has a marked impact on the team who always respond to our encouragement, and therefore play better when attacking the North End.

So if the supporters of the Clock End want to see the goals they have to shout for them as the North-enders do and with this added support maybe we can see Arsenal scoring freely at both ends of the stadium.

Dave Chesterton, *AFC Programme*, 6.12.66

I suppose it was 1966 I really got the bug. Before that I never stood on the North Bank. I stood on the East Bank, you know, in the enclosure. I can remember the game I did go to the North Bank, we beat Fulham 1–0. There were only 25,000 there, it was a horrible game, but the North Bank was singing: *We'll support you ever more.* It got our team going.

It was a lovely feeling. I don't want to talk in clichés or anything, but it was like an extended family. You had all the mates you wanted all around you and you was part of a group. It's a lovely feeling, a common cause, your team, and it's just a lovely glowing feeling.

Steve Whitman

The 60s, you just looked forward to whenever Arsenal was playing anybody big. You knew it was 50,000 up and that generates atmosphere. The North Bank was a bit more mixed in then. I mean, when you could get 5,000 away supporters up the North Bank that generated an excellent atmosphere but also, obviously, generated the other side of it. We saw a few scuffles up the North Bank, but it was never as bad as other grounds that I'd seen. I always remember a game once against Birmingham in the FA Cup and they had about 5,000 up the North Bank. It was funny because I'd gone out to the toilet and I'd come back and there'd just been a little bit of interspersing of the two lots of supporters and the law had come down the aisle to the right of the North Bank and split 'em off. And I was only walking down and I got thrown in with the Birmingham supporters. They had all the centre and I got thrown into that crowd. I had to stand there for ninety minutes with all these Brummies. Then they scored fairly late, didn't they? Furnell dropped it and they were all jumping around, with me standing there like a lemon.

Laird Budge

The first time I would have stood on the North Bank was when I was about 13. I had friends who lived in north London who were all Arsenal fans. It was a culture shock for me, coming from Birmingham and being a Holte Ender at Villa Park. The first thing was that in 68 I'd never really seen a Skinhead before. All my London friends were Skinheads. Not because they were identifying with the culture or were yobs or anything like that, they said they had to be Skinheads in order to survive at school. It was the thing to do. To go to a football match in the company of Skinheads when I was this middle-class schoolboy from Birmingham was quite something. I remember going to Highbury on a number of occasions during Easter holidays and being overwhelmed by the banter, that's what really struck me, the banter from the crowd, the ribbing that John Sammels would get, for example. There was a chap behind me who kept calling Bob MacNab *Bob MacKnob* and there was another guy I remember standing next to at one game who was covered head to foot with badges and had a duffel bag with Arsenal badges on. He was the archetypal anorak type. I remember I went to a couple of night matches and because the Holte End at Villa Park is larger and more open I remember being struck by how dark and sort of steamy it was in the North Bank. They're vivid memories, because I was quite young, quite small for my age: this combination of cockney banter and darkness and steaminess and the fact that you'd just emerged from this crowded Tube into this crowded built-up area and were funnelled into this very sort of claustrophobic atmosphere.

Simon Inglis

We're talking about the beginning of the hooligan era, you know, the Manchester United army going and terrorising the whole country and all the rest of it. I mean the North Bank then seemed a sort of really rough place where you wouldn't want to go. There was a cloud of smoke above the North Bank because so many people smoked, there was actually a thick cloud and you could see it from the Clock End, particularly at evening matches.

Anyway, once I went to the North Bank, it wasn't really like that at all. I mean, I went there because it was an exciting place to be because it was where the singing came from, and where all the excitement was, and where Johnny Radford used to run to if he'd scored a goal, and Charlie George and so forth. So it was a place to go.

Al Fresco

I am writing this letter on behalf of all the Arsenal supporters who stand on the North Bank end at all home matches. Some people think of us as a load of thugs, and the way the police act they have no two thoughts about us! The police just come pushing through the crowd and on many occasions punching their way through, grabbing youngsters for nothing. I'm fed up with what has been said about us. The truth is, that we are a loyal bunch of supporters who follow the team all over the country (and soon, Europe). The way our supporters sing and chant can only do Arsenal proud. So I say unto the police and to Arsenal itself – *Don't treat us as the thugs from behind the goal, treat us as supporters, then the 'North Bank' will treat the public, and police with the utmost respect.*

A. Green, *AFC Programme*, 12.4.69

Well I think that, the one game I can remember, perhaps because of the end result, was when Arsenal played Spurs in the semi-final of the League Cup in 69. It was nil–nil with a long way to go. What had happened was the first half had been all Arsenal. I mean it had been just noise and Spurs had been quiet, but as the game grew on and they knew they were going to have to go back for the second leg at White Hart Lane at nil–nil, then the Spurs supporters got louder and all the Arsenal got quieter. Then for about the last ten minutes the Arsenal really got hold of it, you know, really got behind our players. It must have been right on time, Radford got the goal. A lot of people in the seats were starting to move out and I felt that we lifted the players: *If you don't get anything now then it's not half going to be hard down there!* As it happens we went down there and drew one all.

Laird Budge

I think this 'end' thing – the North Bank, the Stretford End sort of thing – only really came in during the 60s. It was the 'in' thing. Before that, you just all used to go to the match. If you were a Tottenham fan, I'd be standing next to you. 'Ends' are a fairly recent phenomenon. The North Bank being the 'in' place to go is only the last 25 years or so.

Chris Thompson

'A MORE COMMITTED CROWD'

You were all in there for the same reason and it was so friendly. Everyone was friendly. And there was a lot more caring as well. You know, because I was young, the older men used to make way: *Come on, love. Come through.* Or: *Can you see?* Complete strangers. Much more caring. But that's just a change in society, not just football.

Tina Evans

Probably the first time I stood on the North Bank was for a Boxing Day game against Chelsea. I actually went on my own, I must have been 13 or 14. This was in the mid-50s and so my parents didn't need to worry about me going off. I got the Tube over from south London and got in early. I found myself a barrier right in the middle of the North Bank – the roof had been rebuilt by then – and watched the game from there. Kids were treated as something special then, it was the same at all the London grounds. If you couldn't see people would help you get to where you could, maybe standing in front of them. I can't for the life of me remember the score or anything, but Derek Tapscott – it was his sort of era – I remember he got a goal. Mid-50s, the crowds were very much bigger. It was a different sort of crowd, more knowledgeable in some respects because they were there to watch the football whereas later it became supporters against supporters more than cheering the team on. The whole thing was an interest in football rather than anything else, so perhaps people understood rather more about the game. Maybe that's just an older person looking back! A big difference was that you wouldn't only be Arsenal supporters in there. You'd be with neutrals and the supporters of the other side. The only thing I can liken it to was I went to a couple of internationals at Twickenham last year and we were sat there with Scots and French or whatever. Everyone was having a jib at each other but they were passing round the drinks. It was very much an event in that respect. It was great fun and I think that's something that people miss at football now because of the rivalry and segregation.

David Court

You'd only know where the away fans were if they scored. You might get a group of 20 or 30 standing together, and another group somewhere else. But they wouldn't all stand together in a big mass like they do now. Well, they have to now, don't they, with segregation? Which is unfortunate.

PC Roy Beasley, retd

I remember going to games 25 or 30 years ago. It was unimaginable that you'd segregate any part of the football ground. I remember watching Arsenal–Manchester United in about 63 or 64. It was an evening game, and I went on my own. I found myself standing with a lot of Manchester United supporters but it didn't matter. I've stood with Spurs supporters, Chelsea supporters. Funnily enough I remember once, I used to go on my own – I think because I was such an unpopular child! – and on one occasion I was watching Arsenal–Chelsea and I was standing in front of a lot of Chelsea supporters. I was in front of the barrier and they were behind the barrier, and Chelsea were winning. And there was an old drunk in front of me who was shouting abuse at Peter Bonetti, and everyone was laughing at him, both groups of supporters, laughing at him, and suddenly he got angry turned round and pushed me over, because I was the nearest person to him. These Chelsea supporters all jumped in and jumped to my aid, you know.

Laurence Marks

Before the mob encounters of the 60s and 70s and beyond, if there was a slight altercation (usually just between two people) the crowd would respectfully move away (a hole in the crowd!) and the punch-up would take its merry course. I remember my father saying, as one fight finished and one protagonist searched the floor: *He's looking for his teeth.*

Tony Pigden

Something that does strike me is that when we were playing in the 50s and early 60s, we had some very mediocre teams, but Arsenal the club had a style, Arsenal had class, they led football. Arsenal were the old school and they had a style about them, the Club had a style – not the team but Arsenal the football club, you know, the institution. I believe that has gone now, but in those days that was what it was. Even though the team wasn't right you supported the Club in the 50s.

John Platt

If you scored a goal you clapped! The kids'd swing their rattles round. You know, now, if Anders Limpar or Ian Wright get involved, like when Anders whacked that fellow Mark Pembridge, you automatically blame the other player don't you? It's not until later that you look at it rationally. That never used to be. People saw things in a slightly clearer light, less partisan. You'd appreciate things from the other side. I looked forward to seeing the Busby Babes. I wanted to see Duncan Edwards. And you wanted to see them play well. Now, if I see Glen Hoddle, I want to see him have a stinker. Gascoigne comes down, you want to see someone cripple him in the first minute. You didn't in those days. I don't think the bitter rivalries were the same, the mass hatred, that intensity. I know the mind plays tricks on you, but I seem to think that's a recent thing.

Chris Thompson

The first game I ever saw was against Wolves 67–68 I think we lost 2–0. I thought to myself I'd be better off supporting Wolves than Arsenal! That was the North Bank. I liked standing, even though I couldn't see much – the crowds were bigger even then. In them days you could walk around at half time under the West Stand. I must have been about ten. The atmosphere wasn't that great. Arsenal hadn't won anything for years, as you know, we'd just been living on past glories really.

Peter Hobb

I don't know if it was a different time when everybody smoked, or it was evening matches and it was cold. It was almost – there's a danger of getting carried away here – but the North Bank almost breathed. I can remember as a lad getting into the schoolboys' enclosure and you used to look up at this thing, it was like a bloody great mouth opening on to the pitch, with smoke coming out, you know. Sometimes it was just people's cold breath. As a little lad I remember wanting to go up there. I wanted to see what it's like, you know. It was a social thing, too, you know. You were up on the North Bank, one of the boys, and everybody smoked. It just sort of rolled on to the pitch. It was, in the 'modern' 60s, the nearest you could get at football to all the smoke they used to have on *Top of the Pops!*

John James

Where I stood, there was one of the supporting pillars in front, across the goal, really. So if people hadn't been before, they'd come to where we were and they'd see the pillar and they'd move, so it never really got crowded apart from really heavy games. The thing was, once the game started, you never noticed the pillar. You know, you're following the ball and you never really notice it.

John Platt

Before they put the seats in there, I used to stand on the west side and after that I moved to the corner of the North Bank. I didn't want to sit down. I was young and strong and I like to watch football standing. I stayed in that spot in the corner, on the Main Entrance side, for many years, two barriers up.

Alex Froso

The Clock End never had a roof did it, so I suppose the men stood at the Clock End and got drowned when it was pissing down with rain. I think the younger element were in the North Bank. When I was a kid it seemed the young kids were there and the Clock End was more the older supporters.

Just good fun weren't it? You used to enjoy going, you'd have a laugh, you'd get involved in the game. I mean, I remember this thing with the crowd swaying, there was a little bit of that going at one time. You know, when all the crowd rushes forward. It was just a laugh wasn't it? You'd go and you'd have a Saturday afternoon, a bit of fun, it was all wisecracks, always got a few comedians there, good to be involved with and all part of growing up, wasn't it?

Quite a few of us used to go. Mates from school. There was one kid, a friend of mine, Johnny Hoy, who lived in Avenell Road. He used to go quite a bit with us and his mum used to actually lodge some of the Arsenal players. He had a flat that overlooked the ground, the perfect place for an Arsenal supporter, there were quite a few of us who all got along there.

The Friday night out with the lads, you know, seriously late night down the West End, down a club or something. In the morning meet up Chapel Street, go in a café, have a cup of tea or whatever it was, up to the local pub, up to one of the Arsenal pubs. Sometimes we had a drink in a pub near the ground but most of the time we had a drink in local pubs and then up to the ground, I should think, about half two.

Frank Warren

I chose football because it was the only thing we had to do other than hanging about on the streets. We didn't get much pocket money or anything. You didn't spend your money on sweets or anything, you'd save it to get into Arsenal. Or we used to jib in. If it was a big crowd you could just get on the floor, under the turnstile and in, sort of thing. Or you'd know the geezer on the turnstile and he'd say: *Alright, over you go.* Everything was geared up to getting over football on the Saturday. Late 60s, we'd talk about the mob who lived up Ally Pally or the mob who lived down Highbury, we were going to meet up Saturday. Sometimes they'd come down to us. You know, going beyond football, Islington Boys Club all that, you and your mates would sort of stick together. And you'd meet people, like the Ally Pally. You'd never dream of going over Ally Pally if you hadn't met them at football: *Where you going tonight? Oh, we're going to Ally Pally, there's a do on.* And you'd all go up there. Same with the Con Club up in Finchley. Again, you wouldn't know nothing about that if you weren't over football, meeting different geezers. I could say 90 per cent of my mates are Arsenal supporters and people I've met over there. School mates and football mates were different, you know. School mates you spend days together, you become contented with each other's company whereas football mates are mates from choice.

Vidos Neophytou

Another thing about the late 60s: all kids liked football. That was the one thing you did on Saturday afternoon, or if you didn't go to the game, you listened to the results. In those days everybody went to football, so you all had your team. I think you'd find they were louder, more vociferous, in them days because you didn't have the segregation of supporters. You weren't shouting at the Clock End, down the other end of the pitch, you were shouting at a bloke who was 25 feet to the left or right of you, which made it even more fun. You always had that thin line of blue coppers and we never really wanted to go over and hit somebody on the nose but you were allowed to shout at him and say: *My team is better than your team,* you know, and shout louder than them.

Steve Whitman

Football in the 60s became fashionable as opposed to fun.

Chris Thompson

By the time we got to the Double side, football was very much about winning. When I first went it was all pretty cavalier, really, but after the 66 World Cup, winning was the thing. Like Leeds, who were a very cynical outfit who were going to win at all costs. Liverpool, too, were like that to an extent. And Arsenal, of course, followed suit. I think the crowd reflected that. It changed from the happy-go-lucky guy who'd applauded the opposition to a more committed crowd, with pressure on the fans whose whole weekend was living around the result. There became more and more urgency to win trophies whereas before you'd gone along not really expecting Arsenal to win but hoping they would. The crowd took a harder attitude towards football generally. The stakes were getting higher.

Steve Kazmarek

'OH, THERE'S ME DAD!'

The first game I went to was in 1962. I was eight and my dad took me to watch Arsenal play Bradford City in the Cup. We won 3–0. Mel Charles – he was the big hero then – he scored twice. I hadn't been all that interested in football before that but I'll never forget that. It's such a monumental change in your life, being in a crowd of that many people. I remember coming down the hill and seeing all those people. The smell of hot dogs. It was so exciting. When they scored, you thought: *There's something very important going on here!*

Steve Kazmarek

With me, as I say, I was too young to understand the tactics side of it but I mean I went to a game where there weren't even a goal but somebody would pick up the ball and the whole crowd just went up into a big crescendo like that. Without a goal being scored! I'd never known nothing like that. I didn't realise you could get 50,000 people in such a small space with a little green garden in the middle, you know. There are certain smells in there aren't there? I remember there used to be the hot chestnut man, I mean it's just the smell of it. You get a bit older and you're just going to see a game of football now.

Laird Budge

And I always remember when Arsenal played Oxford in about 1963. There was a freeze on then, with snow and everything, and it got cancelled. Then a replay and that got cancelled. Eventually they played it in the afternoon and I can always remember me dad took me to see it and I got the afternoon off school. I don't know what the excuse was at school. Arsenal won the game, and I shouldn't think there was a handful of people there, but to have the afternoon off school when you're a kid is like the ultimate thing.

Frank Warren

Mainly, in those days, the dads brought their sons. Now, the sons go off to football anyway when they're about 11 or 12. In those days they didn't. Your son went with you. If you went to football, you took him with you.

PC Jack Birt, retd

We used to stand on little fishing stools, because the crowds were bigger then. So we stood on our little stools behind the barrier so we could see.

John Platt

We always took a little box, beginning of the season and we left it there down in the corner, my brother's little box to stand on. We used to go and get it every week. No one ever pinched it. He'd bring it home at the end of the season.

Roger Hewlitt

Early 60s, Arsenal were playing Spurs and there was snow everywhere. They let the game go ahead. They left the snow on the pitch but around the pitch, they cleared it and they shifted it all behind the North Bank goal. They said to all the young kids – there was a 62,000 crowd – *you can't see, get on the snow and ice*. They started off and it was great – got a view and everything. But they were sitting on ice and by half time they were so cold – one of my brother's mates went off home in tears! But a lot of them stuck it out!

Peter Hobb

AN APPEAL TO THE BOYS!

In recent seasons it has become increasingly noticeable how autograph hunters have been besieging the playing pitch at Highbury, both before the kick-off and after the final whistle. The desire for obtaining the players' autographs is understandable, but have you boys ever paused to think of firstly, the possible damage that you do the pitch, and secondly, of the interference to the all-important pre-match loosening-up for the players? If you want the players' autographs, I am sure they will give them to you at the proper time and place, which is outside the ground, so I make an appeal to all the boys in our Club to set an example to other boys by keeping off the playing pitch AT ALL TIMES and endeavouring to persuade others to do the same. Never let it be said that the boys from YOUR school set a bad example to others!

GunFlash 109, August 1959

In view of incidents at other grounds this season, and in view of the increasing number of youngsters who climb on to our pitch at the end of the match, we feel that something must be done in order that we do not have a serious incident at Highbury. We have discussed the matter thoroughly with the police and have come to the conclusion that unless matters improve we shall have to consider detailing a number of policemen to parade on the track around the pitch throughout the match.

AFC Programme, 24.11.62

We rely very much upon the goodwill of our spectators but this has not been very evident in the recent past. Accordingly we have had to take some drastic steps. In future, therefore, any person who encroaches on to the field without authority is liable to be evicted from the stadium. We regret very much having to take this action but for the sake of the good name of the club we have been left with no alternative.

AFC Programme, 21.9.63

Yeah, you start down the front, because when you're a kid you want to get as near to that fence as you can. I can remember in those days climbing over the fence after a game. We used to run on the pitch. The fence would be a little dug out there, you'd get a foot on a seat and over you'd go, and I can remember running on the pitch when I was a kid. It was like a big thing to run on the Arsenal, to be on the Arsenal football pitch. When you're a kid it was a big fence, I'm talking about when I was a small kid! I can remember all the old stewards running around with their arms outstretched trying to stop us doing it.

Frank Warren

Most of our supporters will have read in the press that the Committee of London Clubs met last month to consider the minimum price of admission to League matches in London for season 1964–65 and that this minimum was fixed at 4s.

It is regrettable that increases have to be made but they are necessary to meet the every-day rising costs. At Arsenal Stadium it means that all match-day admission prices for League games will have to be increased but we are pleased to say that we have now been able to arrange a special enclosure for schoolchildren at 2s per head. This enclosure will be the North section of the East Enclosure which will accommodate approximately 1,000 children with a separate and direct entrance from Avenell Road. Two turnstiles will operate and will be located opposite the end of Elwood Street.

AFC Programme, 11.4.64

In our last programme of 1963–64 we announced that a special enclosure would be available for schoolchildren in the East Enclosure (north end) with turnstiles in Avenell Road, opposite Elwood Street. Representations have been made to us that some parents would like their children with them in the ground rather than have them in the special enclosure.

Any such children will be allowed through the pass door to join their parents. Parents are requested to enter the ground via the first 'adult' turnstile past the boys' entrance, going north. Unaccompanied children are restricted to the special enclosure because of the considerable damage they cause to our property when allowed to roam the stadium. Because of these arrangements there will be no transfer facilities from the north end of the ground to the East Stand in future.

AFC Programme, 29.8.64

My first game was September 1964 against Aston Villa. My dad took me. You went in the Schoolboys' Enclosure which was half price and the only way then to get on the North Bank was through a little connecting door if you were meeting your dad. Well, he only took me a couple of times, so I'd go with a mate and say to the bloke: *Oh, I'm meeting my dad on the other side and he'd let me through.* And I'd go: *Hello, dad –* waving to some imaginary person and I was there! I'm a tall bloke now, but I wasn't then, I was about ten. I think I saw bugger all for about three seasons. But I got the atmosphere! My dad would have had a fit if he'd known I was up the North Bank.

John James

Well I was a kid same as most kids with their dad. I suppose I was about six or seven. But I used to stand up, the old man had a season ticket. He was an Arsenal supporter, but in those days I suppose he was an Arsenal supporter when they was playing really well. Around that time those were the days of George Eastham, Joe Baker and they weren't very successful and they played I suppose pretty boring football. For a kid to go along, it was great fun. So we used to have a ticket up in the West Stand and I used to go there and I suppose when he thought I was old enough or whatever I used to go along and stand up. In those days you could walk round the ground, it weren't sectioned off. So what we used to do was to buy a ticket for the kids' enclosure, which used to be under the East Stand in those days, and then you used to climb through the fence and stand up, you know, bunk through and stand up in the North Bank. In those days (especially if you were skinny, and in those days I was a bit skinny) you could slip through the fence. Or sometimes they'd leave the gate open, you see.

Frank Warren

Five bob used to do us. It'd be 2/6 return on the train from Hatfield, tanner for a programme and two bob to get in the Schoolboys'. When you used to go in the Schoolboys', there was a gate through to the North Bank with a commissionaire who'd let you through to meet your dad. Well, all the boys who weren't with their dad, when the gate opened, it was: *Oh, there's me dad! There's me dad!* It was chaos. Nine times out of ten you managed to jib through on to the North Bank. But if you couldn't, well you'd stand there in the Schoolboys' looking up at the North Bank more than you were watching the game. We all used to play football together on Saturday morning, then meet up at Hatfield Station – the little buffet, there. The trains used to take longer in those days, we'd have to leave about one o'clock.

Lenny Brandon

As Arsenal supporters know, we allocated an area in front of the East Stand some years ago for the exclusive use of schoolboys at half-price admission. Previously we had no cheap price for boys for many years, because we did not feel that it was wise to encourage youngsters to come to our big games, on the ordinary terraces, where they could, and often did, get injured. Now, we find, a growing number of parents encourage youngsters to enter the cheap enclosure and tell them to ask to be 'passed out' to the North Terrace to join their parents. This destroys the principle we adopted for the protection of youngsters. We cannot continue to encourage schoolboys by offering a reduced admission price if they are to be subjected to the dangers of mixing with a large crowd of adults. If parents are to be so irresponsible as to allow their children to be subjected to these obvious dangers, then they will have to pay full price for them and accept full responsibility. With effect from the next home match, schoolboys taking advantage of the reduced price will have to remain in the special enclosure. No pass-out arrangements will be permitted.

AFC Programme, 25.1.69

I must have been about eight. Mid-60s. We all used to go there together. Our little neighbourhood, there were older brothers and we'd go with them, in a group. They'd dump us down into the Schoolboys' and we'd creep up on the North Bank. As time went on, we started going straight on to the North Bank, up the back shelf. All our little neighbourhood, Cornwallis Road, the Holloway boys, the Archway boys. We used to go over there 20-handed most of the time. Used to meet in the café up in Tollington Way in the morning and then walk up there. Get over there, have a sing-song: *Zigger-zagger!* All that. We used to get over there about one o'clock when we were kids. Meet all your mates, have a sing-song, a chat. The buzz of being over there was more than the football, really. It was seeing your mates, and all that. Being small you never got the chance to see a lot of the game! The crowds always seemed to be quite big. People would chat about players like they could see everything, but half the time you couldn't see what was going on, really!

Vidos Neophytou

'OUR LITTLE LADS'

You can call the average Leicester City fan what you like . . . but he is a toff compared to the characters that line the terraces in many other areas . . . Take Goodison Park where Everton have been putting on the magic in recent weeks. In front of spectators who, if they aren't the worst sports in the world, seem to be heading for that qualification. On Saturday hundreds of them jeered West Bromwich Albion and assaulted some of the players as they went for their coach after the game . . . This season, some six teams have been booed and jeered for long periods at either Goodison or Anfield. Bottles have been thrown at several players . . . and Teddy Boys have run out on to the pitch and played 'practice' matches in the goalmouth before the match at Preston when Everton were playing away. Everton fans have wrecked an excursion train and had free fights with other gangs following Liverpool. It makes you wonder . . . especially when you hear that similar things can happen elsewhere. Even in Regency Brighton. For there, on Saturday, Reading manager Harry Johnson was hit on the jaw by louts and two of his players were also struck as they left the field at the end of the game. It's a trend that is increasing. They even threw fireworks at a goalkeeper at Highbury on Saturday.

Leicester Mercury

The Disciplinary Committee at a meeting on 4 December received a report that 19 cases of misconduct by spectators had been dealt with during the current season. They decided to appeal to all clubs to take every precaution to prevent incidents involving spectators and to warn them through the medium of the club programme and/or loudspeaker system at their grounds that in addition to any action taken by the Football Association, the club will take the strongest possible action against any supporters who enter the field of play during a match.

Letter to AFC from FA, 26.12.61

The Chester Committee on Football which reported to the Government last May showed quite clearly the seriousness of the situation. They pointed out that between 1946 and 1960 there were 195 cases of disorderly behaviour by spectators brought to the attention of the Football Association – an average of 13 per season. In the next six seasons the average rose to 25 per season!

Harry Gee, Press Association, 29.10.68

These remarks are directed to the young hooligans who attend our matches and indulge in throwing all sorts of missiles and rubbish on to the pitch. Maybe the spate of misconduct in another part of the country has been the cause of bad conduct at Highbury, but whatever the reason we will not tolerate this type of bad behaviour which is likely, if not checked, to bring Arsenal Stadium into disrepute.

The goal occupied by the Liege goalkeeper last week was a disgrace and at the end of the match looked like a rubbish tip. At the match against West Ham there were quite a number of articles thrown on to the pitch.

AFC Programme, 23.11.63

It started early 60s. Like the Manchester United crowd who set about Lynn, pulled her shoes off. At the end of the game – we'd beaten them – they took her shoes off and threw them. She had to come home with newspaper round her feet and we tore her scarf in half and tied it round. She was only a youngster. That was when it started.

Tom Jales

Crowd misbehaviour was happening in the 1900s. People are people, and they're part of society and you can't change people. That behaviour was there all the time. I think it became more commonly known because it was more reported, wasn't it?

Ken Friar

I think how it started was they used to lay on special trains for them. They'd come down mob-handed. They used to wreck the trains and they'd all get down here and go in the pubs and have a few drinks and it would go on from there.

PC Jack Birt, retd

When George Best came into English football and Liverpool began to get popular, then we began to get trouble. I think the first time was when Tottenham supporters went berserk up at Sunderland in that famous Cup-tie and people saw the pitch invasion on television. Then the first nastiness we had was when Arsenal played Liverpool in 63. From then on, when George Best came in, you started to have problems. The element George Best drew, I think. I come from the era when I was brought up to respect people and respect things, to know that it was only a game at the end of the day and that I was lucky to be with a team that was so successful.

Geoff Gilbert

I think it started getting funny when Liverpool came back into the First Division. My father used to tell me there was always trouble when Portsmouth came before the war, so there's nothing new. But I'd stood there for five years and there was never any trouble. Then in 1964, Liverpool came down. Someone started throwing pennies down from the back and one hit a young kid and gashed his head. Blood started pouring out. The mood of the North Bank changed.

Laurence Marks

There was one game against Liverpool. I got down here early, about one o'clock, and they brought round some kids with their heads split open. What had happened, they'd let a load of Liverpool supporters in early to get them off the street because they were drunk, and they'd been chucking bottles over the top there that had hit people down the bottom. They was the only club who ever used to cause any bother, robbing the bakers' vans and throwing the rolls at one another and all that.

Ron Pottage

Violence both on and off the field at Highbury. Before the ball has even been kicked, a woman is assisted to the first aid bench after being hit by a flying bottle. Other missiles are collected in the foreground as police go in to calm the seething crowd. The fifth-round Cup-tie against Liverpool will be remembered by Arsenal fans for many a day.

Islington Gazette, 21.2.64

Early in the season, as you all know, the club and the local police had a little difficulty with one or two hot-headed Arsenal fans climbing over and running on to the pitch but I am very pleased to say that following action by the club, personal appeals by myself on the public address system, and the very helpful co-operation of the Metropolitan Police, the troubles died down and I think we can now say that we have a first-class set of supporters.

I take the opportunity of mentioning it at this time following the disgraceful conduct by the Liverpool supporters at the recent Cup-tie at Highbury. The throwing of empty bottles in the crowd at the Laundry End brought us near to very ugly incidents and, here again, the police and stewards are to be congratulated for their timely intervention. Factors which the public did not know about are perhaps even worse. There was a great deal of damage done to the Club's equipment in public lavatories and the bars and the way in which some people conducted themselves in the public lavatories was no less than thoroughly disgusting. Our staff, who had to clear it all up on the Monday, have never seen such a frightful mess.

Give yourselves a pat on the back. When we go to some other places in England, and when some other supporters come here, we realise what a good bunch of chaps you are and we are grateful for your level-headed and continued support.

Bob Wall, *AFC Programme*, 29.2.64

Things started to change in the mid-to-late 60s. It was insidious. There certainly wasn't one day when everything was fine and the next day it wasn't. Because it happened slowly, it crept on you. Hardly anybody was ever arrested at football in the 50s but then gradually you'd have a few arrested at each game and then it would get more and more. But because it was only a few each time, you know, it crept up. We had a few bad ones but generally we didn't do too bad here. During the 60s, generally, there was a more aggressive attitude. I don't mean physically aggressive – that was the hooligan element – but everybody was far more volatile, more outgoing. More baiting of the opposition. In the 50s you wanted Arsenal to win but it wasn't the end of the world, but during the 60s it got to where your Saturday was ruined if they lost. I don't really know why. Certainly, there were changes in playing styles and if it had something to do with a change in attitude on the pitch, everybody would pick up on it. You couldn't remain aloof. I mean, I'm quite a quiet reserved sort of person. Except at football. Now I certainly didn't start out like that. I think my football supporting has changed my character. I'm more aggressive than I was as a youngster and football's done that.

John Platt

Our supporters will remember, at the Chelsea match a few weeks ago, a supporter ran on the field behind the North goal and shouted at the referee and pushed him. He was immediately taken into custody and charged. He appeared at the North London Magistrates Court on the Monday morning, pleaded guilty, and was fined £5.

At the time it was thought and said, publicly, that this man was a Chelsea supporter and in order that the good name of Chelsea fans should not be affected we think it right to state, officially, in our programme, that the man concerned was not only an Arsenal supporter but a member of the Arsenal Football Supporters' Club.

It was gratifying, however, to receive a letter from him a few days later apologising to the referee and to the Club for bringing Arsenal's name into disgrace in this way. He is very contrite and has given us an assurance that in future he will express himself in an orderly fashion and from the terraces. He tells us that he, along with his son, both of whom are members of the Supporters' Club, follow the team regularly. He also tells us that his son has been a member of the Supporters' Club since he was three weeks old. This must almost be a record. We accept this supporter's assurances but, of course, with regret that he did not think about it earlier.

AFC Programme, 11.4.64

Supporters may be interested to know that at the West Ham United match on 20 November two persons were arrested in the ground for insulting behaviour, and when they appeared at the North London Police Court on the following Monday they were fined £10 each. We think this emphasises our intentions in this matter and the club, with the help of the police, will continue to take similar action.

AFC Programme, 4.12.65

At our last home League match v Leeds United, on 5 November, 12 individuals were evicted from the stadium before the match started, for throwing fireworks. It seemed to have the desired effect because there were no fireworks thrown on the pitch during the game.

However, the record was not so good in other respects. Nine persons, Leeds and Arsenal fans, were arrested during the afternoon for 'insulting behaviour'. One was fined £10, five were fined £5 and three cases were dismissed because of insufficient evidence.

Later, after the match, as some Leeds supporters were walking along the street to their motor-coach, they were set upon by a group of thugs – purporting to be Arsenal fans – who beat them up rather severely.

The Arsenal management will always take the severest steps against these people who seem to derive pleasure from making other people unhappy. Irrespective of whether they call themselves Arsenal supporters, we will hit as hard as we can against thuggism.

AFC Programme, 19.12.66

The trouble was to do with young boys, 16 to 19 years of age. They didn't have National Service to teach them how to behave, to train them – that's where it all came from. And those boys came to football to cause problems. I have seen Arsenal supporters who haven't watched the game – just swearing and throwing things. They were only a few, but a few made everything bad.

Alex Froso

I think what's true of football is what's been said of inner city 'theme' pubs now which is that, if you go to any of these big pubs in the centre of Coventry or the centre of Manchester or in London, you don't see anyone over 22–23 so there's no older generation to teach teenagers how to drink. And I wonder if that started to happen: that there was a lack of respect, that the youth became disconnected from the older supporters, you didn't see so many middle-aged blokes going to football any more. They were like a civilising influence.

Laurence Marks

I mean again, in those days, every tin of lager, every tin of light ale, whatever you was drinking watching the match, you were doing something you weren't supposed to. It was all good fun and whatever and that's where it was at I suppose. You were Jack the Lads and just made your way there. I mean, I don't even know why. I suppose like part of the old social system or whatever. Trying to learn to be a grown-up.

Frank Warren

I mean, I remember chanting with everyone else: *Come on the North Bank*, when it was all going off up there. Now, I'm the biggest coward going but you did want to see your boys give the others a leathering even though you wouldn't want to be involved yourself.

Chris Thompson

Remarkable scenes were witnessed in the evening during the return journey of the Glasgow Rangers' club brakes. Bottles had been thrown from one brake and a third vehicle was assailed with stones as it was passing. The occupants, all young men, dismounted, and marching back to where the stones were thrown, many carrying heavy iron bars, swords and bayonets, they attacked the people in a row of miners' houses, one old man being badly assaulted. The men spent nearly an hour skirmishing in the vicinity of wash-houses and outbuildings in search of those who threw the stones and eventually returned to the club brake and drove off.

Glasgow Mercury, 11.9.22

Then came the fateful Saturday, 5 August 1967, when we invited Rangers to play at Highbury in a pre-season friendly game. A group of their so-called supporters arrived outside the stadium early in the morning and created havoc in the local shops and stole milk from the front steps of local houses. Later in the afternoon there were scenes on the North Terrace the like of which we have never seen before. It is understandable that local shopkeepers and residents have asked us not to invite Rangers again.

AFC Programme, 22.9.73

There was an incident up the North Bank with Rangers. Their supporters were always down the North Bank and there was never much trouble because they were so drunk and old. I'm talking about 30-year-old men, very drunk and itching to fight. Our little lads, 14 and 15, weren't up to that so they'd walk into the North Bank and stand right along the back and they'd ask you if you wanted to have a go at them, but no one ever did. I remember one year when there was a fight, when the boys up there did try to have a go and I was petrified. I moved bloody quick, they started throwing potatoes with razor blades sticking out and we were all shoved in the middle bit. They were all on the back. They started throwing potatoes with razor blades and I thought: *No. this isn't for me.*

Mick Essen

A fortnight before the intense business of the League Championship begins Highbury had to put up with hooliganism and fighting on the terraces during the second half of this friendly which attracted a 34,586 crowd.

Most of the trouble came from the Gillespie Road end of the ground. Extra police, including plain-clothes men, entered the crowd to stop the quarrels and flying bottles.

The injured, some with blood streaming down their faces, were assisted by first-aid men, the alleged guilty parties were led elsewhere, and eight of them appear in North London Magistrates Court today.

Daily Telegraph, 7.8.67

The first fight I ever saw at Arsenal was at a friendly match against Glasgow Rangers which was diabolical, they were slinging bottles, really bad news, and that all happened in the North Bank. Glasgow Rangers supporters were in there, that was the first sign of seeing any hooliganism. I suppose I was about 16. I mean, you know, I come from a rough part of Islington anyway. You're not going to say you're not used to seeing it, but for football it was the first time I was ever in where it happened.

Frank Warren

One of the funniest times was when we played Rangers in a friendly. I took this friend of mine, Keith, who was a lot smaller than me. Rangers always took over the ground when we played them. I mean, I admired them for it. Anyway, there were these two drunken Scotsmen behind us and they were kicking the back of Keith's legs. I was frightened but I thought: *I've got to do something about this.* So I turned round and said: *What are you doing? Stop!* And I'll never forget this Rangers bloke going: *Sorry, mate. Here's tuppence for your mate, for hurting him.* And he gave us 2d. That was a long time ago. 1967.

Richard Stubbs

Most of our supporters will have read in the press or heard on radio that the club has decided to discontinue the sale of bottled or canned beer and bottled beverages generally in those bars which serve the standing sections in the stadium. It is regrettable that we should have to curtail certain supplies which spectators might prefer, but we feel sure that every sane-minded person will accept the situation in the interests of public safety.

Incidents such as the one which occurred on the North Terrace when we played Rangers recently cannot be tolerated and unless strong action is taken the terraces of football grounds will be occupied only by thugs; decent people will stay away. Although on this occasion the trouble was caused by a group of Rangers supporters, there was enough evidence from last season for us to know that it could happen again.

In view of the steps we have taken, it must now be regarded as an infringement of ground regulations if any spectator is found in possession of a beer bottle or can or any bottle containing a beverage, or even an empty bottle.

AFC Programme, 19.8.67

Back in 1967 I was employed as a GPO telegram messenger working shifts, including the occasional Saturday afternoon. It was my misfortune to be rostered to work on the afternoon of the Gunners v Chelsea fixture at Highbury. There was no way I was going to miss that game! My father telephoned my supervisor that morning to say I was ill in bed and would not be coming to work.

That afternoon, standing in the massive crowd on the North Bank, there was the usual banter between rival fans. There was no segregation in those halcyon days. I turned to see a Chelsea supporter being escorted out by a policeman, I showed my amusement by grinning from ear to ear and making a mocking gesture at the unfortunate fellow. The next moment it was my collar that was being felt as I too was ejected from the Bank, by two rather burly constables who each held one of my arms behind my back.

As I was led around the perimeter of the pitch, who should be sitting in the Lower East Stand but my Chelsea-supporting supervisor. From that day on I was known at work as a *long-haired lout*.

After being warned by the police as to my future conduct I was escorted through the marble halls into Avenell Road where almost immediately I was approached by a rather dapper middle-aged gentleman who asked me if I wanted a seat. Thinking he was a tout, I refused his offer having not two pennies to rub together. He proceeded to explain that he and his son were season-ticket holders in the upper tier of the East Stand and that his son was unable to attend the match due to illness. He offered me a chance, at no cost, to sit in the best seats in the ground (after having been thrown out of the four-shilling North Bank). I gladly accepted his offer and I can still picture myself up there with my Doc Marten boots and my woollen scarf tucked into my braces, surrounded by men in shirts and ties. I can still remember the score: 1–1, Radford the scorer.

Steve Whitman

I suppose that underlying threat, that danger, added to it all somewhere along the line, but I wouldn't say I enjoyed it. I remember in the 60s a walking-stick fight on the North Bank. Chelsea fans had blue and white walking-sticks and some of the Arsenal fans had sticks too and they whacked each other with them.

Steve Kazmarek

The modern idea of carrying walking-sticks, painted with the club's colours, is not offensive in itself, but, as we all know, they are frequently used as offensive weapons. Consequently we have decided to prohibit spectators from carrying them and, indeed, any form of banner or flag which might be used in this way. Anyone infringing this condition of admission (or any others for that matter) will be dealt with by the police.

It is disappointing that we should have to take such steps at Highbury, but we are determined that Arsenal Stadium shall not become a bear-garden where irresponsible youngsters can indulge in free fights. We have appealed to these people to behave themselves and they have not. They must now take the consequences if they force us to take action against them.

Bob Wall, *AFC Programme*, 5.8.67

I saw it building. I'm sort of thinking back now but I can remember on the pavement going away from Highbury there was outbreaks of fighting and it was, like, unusual, it was so unusual that the papers actually made a big thing of it. I can remember walking down Seven Sisters Road once. Going to Tottenham, we all used to meet at Manor House, I don't know if they still do that. And there were guys you looked at and you knew, were looked on as leaders. I can remember one of them doing something that I was quite shocked about. He was like walking down one side of the road and he stopped and pulled out an air rifle. I shouldn't think it was a real gun. He fired and it went straight through this newsagent's shop window.

Mick Essen

Soccer rowdies who bring violence and fear to Highbury are now really heading for 'bovver'. For a large squad of hand-picked detectives – nicknamed the Troubleshooters – has been formed to combat hooliganism on the terraces at Arsenal Stadium. Dressed in the right 'uniform' – including braces, skinhead hair-cuts and 'bovver' boots – they mingle with the crowds seeking out the trouble spots and the ring-leaders who incite the violence. The detectives, chosen as the type most at home in close contact with 'spotters', were concealed at vantage points around the ground. With high-powered binoculars the spotters continually scan the crowds on the lookout for a trouble flashpoint. When 'bovver' appears to be brewing or fans are seen to be armed, a radio message is sent over miniature radios to the detectives. The Troubleshooters – already near the scene – then move in before any real trouble can break out. In the past the problem has been to distinguish those responsible and get at them before they disappear in the crowd. The North Stand has sometimes been a 'bovver' headache for the police. Now the Troubleshooters are moving in. And louts who delight in violence and damage can suddenly find themselves arrested by tough bovver-booted blokes standing in their midst. First reports of the scheme have shown it a major step forward in defeating soccer hooliganism. A senior detective said: 'Our chaps are right in there with them in the thick of it if trouble starts.'

Islington Gazette, 4.9.70

'UP THE NORTH TERRACE'

When I arrived in 1963 – Bertie Mee got in touch with me and said: *Look will you come down and meet Billy Wright?* And I drove down, borrowed a friend's car and drove down from Loughborough College. I was driving around these streets thinking there can't be a football club anywhere round here. And then suddenly I turned right and it was like seeing something from outer space: these little houses and this huge thing at the bottom there with 'Arsenal', you know, and the flag flying. And I was almost scared. But if I was scared in the car . . . I got to the marble halls and waited there and I thought: *This is a football ground? This is a football club?* I was used to Nuneaton Borough and Bishop Auckland and that sort of business. Then Billy Wright said: *Come on, Bob, we'll go down the tunnel.* And we went down the tunnel, which is enclosed, and suddenly came out into open space. And I thought I'd gone into a cathedral. I actually went out – and it took my breath away. How could I ever have the nerve to play in front of this? That's what people don't realise – the adrenalin it takes and the bottle. Till my last game I was scared – every game, out of 365 games I played in first-team colours, I was scared. The bell would go and I'd go down that tunnel – and just before I stepped into daylight somebody threw a switch. It was a point of no return and there was no point getting scared: you were on your own and had to get on with it for good or bad.

Bob Wilson

When Bertie Mee was physio, nobody used to like getting injured. You used to train harder when you were injured than when you were fit. One of the sessions we used to have, you'd pair off and one runner would run all the way round the pitch while the other would run up and down the steps of the North Bank. You'd have to keep running up and down the terrace till your partner finished his lap of the track and then you'd change over. You'd always hope you weren't paired up with George Graham because he took so long coming round the pitch, whereas if you got Georgie Armstrong you knew he'd be back fairly quickly.

Jon Sammels

I remember why I stopped selling programmes down the Arsenal. They started charging us income tax. Before then it was just given you in your hand. I think it was about 1960.

Charlie Robinson

Do you remember the kids looking after cars in the 60s? A motorist would pull up and the kids would pounce: *Look after your car, Mister?* They'd generally give them 3d or 6d or say to them: *I'll see you when I come back.* The kid would probably go back in his house and come back later to collect his money. It wasn't a protection racket – they didn't smash the cars up – it was just: *Mind your car, Mister?* You know.

Steve Kazmarek

Claud Stevens has spent most of his life ordering Arsenal fans about. He'll be familiar to those lucky enough to reach the front on big-match days. Despite this exposure to millions of people over the years, he is a back-room boy at Highbury. One of the voluntary staff who shepherd the terraces into an orderly crowd. Stevens, 74, has been with Arsenal since 1913 and now bears the title Chief Steward of the Honorary Stewards' Corps. Last year the Club presented him with a porcelain cannon to commemorate his golden anniversary and colleagues gave him a gold wrist-watch.

He joined the Gunners when they moved here from Woolwich. He was a schoolteacher at Upper Hornsey Road School and lived in Stroud Green Road: 'A colleague helped the ground staff at Chelsea so I applied for a job with my local club. I became one of an eight-strong squad who sold programmes. The stadium consisted of mud terraces and a wooden stand in Avenell Road. Leslie Knighton introduced crowd-packers and over the years the corps has built up its ranks.' Stevens now supervises a staff of 100. They include schoolteachers, stock exchange workers, civil servants – and even shareholders in the Club. They are dedicated to their work and only leave through sickness or age.

Turning a motley mass of football supporters into an orderly crowd is an art. Patience, psychology and a thick skin are vital. 'We never use megaphones,' he says. 'The crowd doesn't like them so we rely on hand signals. It's like filling in a jigsaw puzzle – you look for the empty spaces.' How do you judge the density? 'If the steward on the touch-line can see people's chins then there's room for more,' is the answer. The record crowd Stevens has handled was in 1935 when more than 73,000 witnessed a League match against Sunderland. Capacity is now restricted to 68,000. The worst audience? 'The Cup game against Liverpool last season. It was the worst example of crowd behaviour I have ever seen,' he says.

Islington Gazette, 23.10.64

You walked up and down the edge of the pitch until they kicked off. Five minutes before the half-time whistle you got up and started walking around again, in case anybody rushed on. And then the same five minutes before the end of the game. In those days, the policeman's wages were not fantastic. I mean, today, they're quite good but back then you were only too pleased to get a few hours' overtime. I was only up in Highbury New Park. So I'd get on my bike, cycle home. I was indoors by half past five, having my tea.

PC Roy Beasley, retd

This is what we'd do on a Saturday: we'd go on a night duty on the Friday night, nick a drunk – Camden Town, they were all over the place; get up at half past nine, go to court; finish court at half past ten, 11; come home, have a little bit of grub; Arsenal in the afternoon, finish about half past five; back on night duty Saturday night. That was your Saturday doing football. Walk about with matchsticks under your eyes! 1958, 59, into the 60s, it was sheer enjoyment. We came here, we watched the football and we got paid for it. We got paid overtime! And never any trouble. There were three of us – one was a Spurs supporter, unfortunately – joined the police force together, went into Kentish Town nick together. We were there for 30 years. During that time, there was a lot of changes in the police force, but in the first days if you were on night duty, your duty here would be inside the ground. You paraded in here on the practice pitch, and then they'd say: *Behind the goals at the North Bank.* Or: *Up the North Terrace.* It was lovely. They used to really look after you, the supporters. You weren't a copper, really. You were just there. The only thing you did have to insist on: you didn't allow them to urinate in the aisles. That was the main thing. We'd sit behind the goal at the North Bank. There were two sets of seats with about four in each and that's where you were during the match when your duty was inside the ground. The stadium cleared in about half an hour. Once the stadium cleared, you were finished inside. That was it. The stations were Kentish Town, Holloway, Caledonian Road and Highbury. Roughly, I would say, 32 officers inside the ground for a full house. They were your night duty: You worked night duty the night before and then came and paraded here at half past 12, inside the ground. If you were late turn, outside the ground, you were paraded at half past one to do traffic points and the stations and that. And then, after the match, they'd carry back on to their shift. You used to do three weeks on night duty. So, if you were lucky, you'd get two home games and on the spare week you'd come and watch the reserves. If you got two homes, that was 12 hours' overtime and watch the football for free! When the boundaries changed, our nick changed from being in N Division, which took the Arsenal, to E Division. We lost it. We lost the Arsenal.

PC Jack Birt, retd

The way the police have been over the years is very much reflected in how the supporters have been. They've mirrored each other. In the 50s, the policing was very good natured. The copper would stand there and you could have a joke with him. If you wanted to pass a youngster down to the front they'd help.

John Platt

We were very tight-knit. You went on a relief and that's where you stayed. You covered everybody's backside, even down here. Sometimes a bloke would be late, he'd sleep in a bit and didn't get here till one o'clock. His name would still have come up. The only trouble we used to have was with the old peanut sellers, coming through the crowd with these little bags of peanuts, you know: *Pean-u-u-ts!* And you'd say: *Come here, you! What are you doing? Give everybody a bag! Now clear off!*

There was an old mate of ours, I shall never forget it. Ralph Gascoigne. The game was on telly and as the cameras came round, they panned on him and he was fast asleep. They said: *This is what this officer thinks of the match!*

PC Jack Birt, retd

During the past few years we have had the honour of being entertained on match days at Highbury by the Metropolitan Police Central Band, under the able direction of Mr Roger Barsotti, A.R.C.M.

The excellent music they provide before the matches helps to pass the time pleasantly, and we can always look forward to a display of marching at half time, led by the drum major. From the roars of the crowd it is obvious that they are all waiting for the day when he drops his mace (heaven forbid!!).

The band of approximately 45 players is drawn from the whole of the Metropolitan Police Force. Its director of music, Mr Roger Barsotti, is the only person in the band who is not a police officer. In 1946 he took up his appointment with the Metropolitan Police Central Band on his retirement from the position of bandmaster of the 2nd Battalion, The Queen's Royal Regiment. A former student of Kneller Hall, the band owes much to his hard work and capable wielding of the baton.

Of the musicians themselves – they are all amateurs and first learned their music in service bands, brass bands and orchestras before joining the police. Every one of them is foremost a policeman. Perhaps you have seen them walking the beat or patrolling the section. The 'home' or 'N' Division has three men in the band. They are trombone, side drum and vocalist.

The drum major, who so capably wields the mace, is an ex-member of the Royal Artillery and is a constable in the Metropolitan Police Mounted Branch, stationed at Walham Green. The Arsenal Stadium is the only regular engagement where he 'throws' his mace.

GunFlash, January 1954

I think people definitely envy us of our tradition, because that's something we cherish. Remember the guy in the old band who used to get the old stick and fling it up in front of the North Bank? At the time it used to be embarrassing. Your mates used to say Arsenal were the most boring, and it was true they used to be, but now I wish we still had that. Thinking about it, I think that was a touch of style. But at the time we were like the Bovril Northern Team of London. This whole band used to come out and the entertainment at half time was a geezer throwing a stick and catching it. People used to get genuinely excited about whether he was going to drop it. It was like a goal, and everybody said he dropped it once which I'm sure he did, but I can't remember him ever dropping it. He would have got slaughtered if he dropped it. And I miss that, but I definitely know people were envious of it. (See plate 18.)

Mark Burdis

The band used to come round with the bloke throwing the baton in the air. I think I only saw him drop it a couple of times. Everybody'd be going: *Whoo-oo-ah!* When he come down the North Bank, you could see him get really jittery! He'd get round the side and think: *Thank God for that!* It was great.

Steve Winfield

That police band, I'll tell you what – they were supposed to be a police band, but there was lots of them were civvies – they'd just stick a uniform on them. I remember meeting one of them, he was a civvie, playing in a band at a wedding reception in Southend. And there was the fellow with the mace. He retired down to Somerset and when the new bloke started, he went off round the pitch and he kept dropping his mace. We did have a laugh.

Ron Pottage

If someone's passed out in the crowd, you have to check three things: airway, breathing, circulation. Make sure the airway's clear so he can breathe. If he isn't breathing but his heart's beating, you've got to restore the breathing. If his heart's not beating, you have to do heart compression plus the breathing. But you've got to get him on solid ground for a start, get him laid out. That might have to be on the terrace. You'd have to get people cleared away or get the police to, and start doing it straight away. You've got three minutes. After four minutes – well, you know. You don't know what you're going to find when you get up there. A person's collapsed. Well, they might say it's alcoholic poisoning – which is a euphemism for being drunk. Well, if that's all it is, we're happy. You just make sure you turn his head to your colleague's side not yours!

Ron Pilcher

We used to get people come in here maybe with a broken arm and you'll bandage it up and they used to want to go and watch the rest of the game. Well, you couldn't force people to go to hospital.

Shirley Haxell

One chap came up to me once and his face was absolutely black, reddish-black. When we actually got him up to the first-aid room, it turned out it was all blood and mud. He'd got a football in the face which had splattered him with mud, he'd gone down with his hands to his face – he'd got a nose bleed, he had a broken nose – and it looked a horrible mess. Of course, once you got it cleaned up, there was nothing there – just a nick at the top of the nose. But when you first looked at him, you thought: *God, what have we got here?*

Stan Carroll

The trouble started during the 60s and I joined the St John's. They were doing this first aid thing at work and the bloke said: *Why don't you join the St John's?* And I said: *Yes, please.* And I'm in. And now you get a different perspective. I'm down the front now and people are looking at you. They're relying on you. Because the trouble was so bad then. I remember a West Ham game, I was carrying children out in my arms. I didn't see the game. The youngsters then, you know, in their 20s, they just had a different attitude. I remember I brought one young man in, he'd been cut all down one side, his face and everything, he was in a really bad way. I said, right you sit down there and the nurse will look after you. She's chatting to him, you know having a laugh and a joke, and suddenly she's jumped up and he's going: *I'll punch your so-and-so head in.* Now you tell me: why? I just don't know why.

Frank Martin

'A GENERAL RUMBLE OF DISCONTENT'

Anyone aware of the massive growth of the supporters' club movement could see it as a talisman – by definition, something having magical power – in the great changes which have begun, and will be continued, in pro football. A supporters' club's relationship with its parent League club is, at the moment, one of non-interference in policy; and the cautious separation of the two bodies is, in fact, enforced by legislation. My argument is that this situation, like so much else in the great balancing act which is football government, will not last another quarter century. The two will become one, with the holding of a season ticket – i.e. 'membership' – entitling a great number of supporters to a speech and a vote in their club management. It also entitles them, of course, to help carry the can when club affairs go awry!

The great post-war boom in football watching put the game on a false economy. And the forecastable falling away has put many clubs in trouble. Yet you could almost go so far as to say these troubles have been created almost entirely by mismanagement at Board level.

Which is why I have such faith in the arrival of supporters' clubs as another force. Their talisman-quality is this: that if the mood took one half of them to STOP watching pro football the League would tumble like a house of cards. The bowler hats would be out, and the bailiffs would be in. I have faith in the idea that a supporters' club, by its very nature, will eventually, and when it sees the necessity, become a powerful dissenting body. Liberal men and ideas are striking the front in all things in the world today. And in our little football enclave, the same will happen. Attacking the Establishment is an old pastime, and one well used by newspapermen. But in a game of the people, I fail to see the need for an Establishment at all.

In football, the big and the effective changes won't come from the top. They will start at club level. And one of the biggest single influences bringing them about will be you . . . the supporters' clubs.

Now go and riot! And good luck to you . . .

Stratton Smith, *Daily Sketch*, Sept 1957

All I can remember is that people were just generally unhappy, I mean we had some dreadful teams, there are no two ways about it. We hadn't won anything for all those years and nothing was happening. We seemed to be stagnant, you know, the absolute nadir of your footballing life. We're turning up there every week, we're finishing mid-way in the table every season, we don't look like we're going to win anything. It was just frustration. It's very difficult for a manager to identify with a crowd if he's not successful. It doesn't matter who the manager is. When the manager's been there a few years and you just don't see anything happening then the frustration boils over. Before Wright, Swindin had been an ex-player. He'd been brought up at Arsenal. We had a tradition of managers who'd been brought up with the Club. Whittaker, we'd had him, who'd been there since the 30s as trainer and physio and what have you, and then Swindin took over and so on. I mean Crayston was there as a manager for a while, an ex-player. There was that expectation. And suddenly we had this man from Wolves taking over as our manager and he wasn't part of our club. That was one of the feelings, that he wasn't an Arsenal man.

John Platt

The crowd got more and more critical as the time went on. I can't recall anyone liking

Billy Wright. I don't know why, really. All the people round us didn't like all this Beverley Sisters business, the razzmatazz. They thought: *This is football not showbusiness*. They used to come and sit up there in white mink coats over red dresses. That might have been something that upset people. They didn't use to shout out obscenities at the players or Billy Wright. But they would all be talking amongst themselves about what they didn't like. It was like a general rumble of discontent.

Tina Evans

I remember Billy Wright. I remember the Beverley Sisters up there, with their red tam o'shanters on. We were the laughing stock. It was the most embarrassing thing. Well, we got to the ground one day and there were people standing outside saying: *Don't go in. The club have got to do something about Billy Wright*. I don't know how many went in, but a lot of us turned round and went home. He got the sack soon after that.

Maureen Hewlitt

I remember the Wright Must Go season. It was bad enough going to Blackburn and losing 3–0 in the Cup. Then the Friday I read in the paper: *Baker and Eastham can go*. I cried. They were my heroes, you know. Putting them on the transfer list! With Billy Wright, even though I was only 14 or whatever, I knew we wouldn't win anything with him. I mean, 105 caps, he was a good player and a decent man. But we have to have him out: *Wright must go*. Saying that though, there was this incredible mixture. There was an intense loyalty that 65–66 season as well. There was a big game against Liverpool and this chant started: *The Arsenal! The Arsenal!* It was actually written about in the papers. We were having a terrible time. We lost 1–0. But I remember the crowd keeping that chant going. I mean, as supporters we don't have the chance to say: *Look we know you're a decent bloke and we don't want to do this to you. But we can see this team's crap and it's getting worse. Our lives are at stake here. So Wright must go.*

Richard Stubbs

So Billy Wright goes. Is this a victory for the handful of rowdy fans who screamed: 'Wright must go' outside Highbury Stadium, on the terraces and on railway platforms?

Since Wright took over in May 1962 – following George Allison, Tom Whittaker, Jack Crayston and George Swindin to become the club's fifth post-war manager – Arsenal have finished seventh, eighth, 13th and 14th – their lowest final League placing since 1930. In the FA Cup, they were knocked out in the fifth round in 1963 and 1964, in the fourth round in 1965 and in the third round this year.

The fans became angry, attendances slumped.

The 4,554 night attendance against Leeds on 5 May – when the Cup Winners' Cup final was being televised – was the lowest in Highbury history. The average home League gate of 29,000 last season was Arsenal's worst since the war. Fans carried banners saying, Wright must go! There were more and more demonstrations, inside the ground and out, by supporters who were disappointed at the club's lack of success and also because England stars George Eastham and Joe Baker were dropped and put up for transfer.

Daily Sketch, 14.6.66

I think crowds started becoming more aggressive, a feeling of: *I'm paying my money, I'm entitled to my say.* I think they started to be more critical, where before it'd been more with a joke and laugh. Where before men would come from work, meet their mates in a group, have a chat and a cigarette, a general social afternoon because it was the start of the weekend, they became more critical, expected more. More for their money, I suppose.

Tina Evans

Dear Mr Hill-Wood,

I am 21 years old and have been attending Arsenal for the greater part of my life.

I am one of those fortunate people that pay six shillings for the privilege of standing on your wonderful terrace. Make no mistake my glorious Chairman, my fellow cloth-cap workers and I (scrubby little fellows that we are) are truly honoured that you accept our presence at your magnificent stadium, but, your Honour, even dogs must have their bark and I should be most humbled if you would spare a few moments of your precious time to read the following meagre lines.

Lately, your Honour, I have been told that the volume of my bark does not meet the required limits for your ears or those of the team. Irrespective of how the team is playing I am told to bark to the full capacity that my lungs will allow.

Mr Chairman, the supporters that you see gathered before you on the terraces are not dogs, nor are they the cloth-cap workers of the 20s or 30s, whose lives revolved around the factory floor and the Saturday afternoon football match; they are intelligent human beings who are just as likely to patronise the opera after the football match as they are the greyhounds.

If Arsenal are playing well and they arouse my emotions, I will cheer just as loud as the next man, if not louder, but I certainly will not raise a cheer if the standard of play does not merit one.

Can one imagine a paragraph in the programme of a play, opera or ballet telling the audience to clap, irrespective of the standard of the performance?

Recently, my dear Chairman, I have read reports in the newspapers stating that Mr Bob Wall has proudly announced that the Arsenal management have decided to 'cage-up their supporters on the terraces'. Congratulations Mr Chairman, the trendy and very with-it Arsenal management are first again.

Why has the Arsenal management decided to take this action? Well, Mr Wall has been very vague about this but he did mention something about preventing people running on to the pitch.

What people, Mr Chairman, what people?

You know as well as I that only on very rare occasions does anybody trespass on the sacred Arsenal turf during the game. But what about after the match you say? Yes, I agree you do get a number of youngsters running on to the pitch but this has occurred from time immemorial and surely does not warrant such drastic action.

We are trying to prevent hooliganism, you say.

Well, Mr Chairman, the Arsenal crowd is one of the best behaved in the country and until we have any similar incidents to the one at Millwall, I think we should be treated as such. Every dog is capable of violence but we do not put down any dog until such violence is shown to necessitate this action.

Mr Chairman, strange as it may seem, I am writing this letter in the hope that it will aid British football, for I firmly believe that until a different attitude is taken to the man on the terrace, violence will increase. The man on the terrace should be welcomed at a football match and not merely tolerated.

Howard Kaye, *AFC Programme*, 1.11.67

Mr Wall would like it to be known that he was entirely misquoted. Indeed, he said that he would personally be very much against the erection of fences. What he did say, however, was that the club had in mind the building of a small dry moat around the perimeter of the track as much as anything to facilitate the movement of police, ambulancemen and chocolate sellers. This will also obviate the players having to climb down into awkward gulleys, which they have to do at the moment, if spectators are unable to throw the ball up to them. We certainly do not intend to emulate South America.

AFC Programme, 1.11.67

'THERE COULD NEVER BE ANYTHING BETTER THAN THIS FEELING'

One last plea on this, our Cup final night. Both the players and myself would like to hear the roar of encouragement which our players have faced abroad in this competition. The fantastic vocal support which Ajax gave their players in Amsterdam was almost unnerving. Believe us all, it really does make a tremendous difference. Give us all the help you can tonight, and I hope we will do the rest for you. (See plate 19.)

Bertie Mee, *AFC Programme*, 28.4.70

As all of you must know we have been, in our opinion, very fair about admission prices for Cup matches over the years. We never increase the prices for any rounds of the League or FA Cup, unlike a number of other clubs up and down the country, but we felt that participation in the semi-finals and final ties of the European Fairs Cup (comparable, surely, in popularity with FA Cup) justified an increase in admission prices similar to what you all experience in the FA Cup.

We were not unmindful of the fact that the chap who stands on the terraces every week inevitably cannot afford such a big increase as those who can afford to sit in the stand and so the directors decided that the standing accommodation should be 10s and not 12s 6d. as is charged for the FA Cup final. We feel that all fair-minded supporters will understand the motivation behind these decisions and we hope that those who have written asking for an explanation will accept this as a reply to their letter.

AFC Programme, 28.4.70

Night games with a big crowd have a special atmosphere. I don't know, maybe people come out of themselves more in the dark.

Steve Kazmarek

Of an evening it looks a bit satanic, Highbury, do you know what I mean? It's strange if you've never been into London, and there's old Victorian houses and you're walking down there and you're looking at everything ain't you? Amazingly, where Arsenal is, you go round the corner and there it is, like, and it was always dark. I think they've brightened it up a little bit now. It looked like a dark old stand and everything. When you got in there the lights went on and the grass looked a different green and it did have that sort of atmosphere of apprehension.

It becomes like a closed-in thing. When it's daylight you just walk in there but at night, I found with the evening games it was a totally different atmosphere. It tends to put a little bit more of a buzz in the game. I don't know why it does but it seems to. We used to stand up the North Bank and keep looking at the clock and you sort of end up willing them to come out.

Laird Budge

The dimming of the lights when play was about to start for evening matches gave the atmosphere of curtain-up at the theatre.

Steve Thomas

Those Anderlecht lads were class players – that centre-forward, Jan Mulder, a real star – and we came out there, we were 3–1 down, and the noise, it was nearly frightening even though you were on the home side. I thought: *God! This is unreal.*

Bob Wilson

I don't know if it's to do with success but before, during the 60s, I never knew any different. But that Anderlecht game, that was when I started being aware of the fans' real fervour, you know.

Eddie Mason

First time I stood on the North Bank was Fairs Cup final night. I'd been before – I used to go with my dad, who used to have a seat. I don't really know why I ended up there that night. We left early, got to the ground and I can remember going up those stairs – you know, the entrance opposite the Tube – those massive stairs. I was 13 then and it was awesome. We got in there and there was a feeling there that everyone knew we were going to win, even though we were 3–1 down. We went in on the right-hand side and me dad sat me on a bar there just under the roof. Night games, I think, are lovely – you can't beat it. And that night – every time a goal went in, you was on the ground, you know. So many happy people. It was just great. I remember, after, Bob Wilson didn't want to go off. It was jam-packed, like nothing I'd ever witnessed. And being there first time that night, you couldn't wish for better. That'll live with me for ever that atmosphere. I don't think you could ever match that again.

Steve Winfield

There was Frank McLintock coming up to the North Bank and that was tremendous. I mean the crowd needs a bit of a kick up the backside now and again, you know, they get a little bit sort of quiet and not sure, especially big games, a bit nervous. They feel it as much as the team. That was a tremendous gesture when you think of it. He came up and said: *We want you. We're looking to you.* It was that clear. I thought that was fantastic.

Mick Essen

The final of the Fairs Cup in 1970 was the first time for a lot of us. Arsenal hadn't won anything for 17 years, so the majority of the crowd that night had never seen Arsenal win a trophy. The only thing they won in the 60s was *Quizball!* To win that, it was a very special night. The North Bank was packed, it was tense because an away goal for them and that would have been it. And the euphoria in the second half when the goals went in! Lots of the crowd ran on at the end. Frank McLintock and Charlie George were up on people's shoulders. It was very special.

Steve Kazmarek

We was all in there for the Fairs Cup final. That was a great night. We all jumped on to the pitch and kissed the ground. And no one stopped you! Not like today. Like a load of bloody idiots we were!

Bill Needs

The goal I scored in the Fairs Cup final clinched it. Once that goal went in, I think everybody knew that, if we didn't do anything silly, we'd got it. That was a fantastic night for everybody. You saw some of the old boys who'd been watching Arsenal for years, they were crying. The whole thing was lovely. The game. The crowd. There were 53,000 there I think. There was so much goodwill. And relief that at last we'd won something, you know. I think it gave the players and the fans the belief that Arsenal could win things. And it went on from there. The next year they did the Double, didn't they? But I remember thinking after that game: *If I'm at Arsenal for the next ten years, there could never be anything better than this feeling.* For the Club and for the supporters, everyone who'd been here for years, the supporter who'd seen us struggling for years.

Jon Sammels

The most amazing scenes ever witnessed at Highbury erupted on Tuesday night when Arsenal won the European Fairs Cup to break a spell of 17 years without taking a major honour. Several thousand dancing, singing, cheering fans surged on to the pitch after the final whistle, breaking through powerless police cordons. They swarmed round the main stand and chaired Arsenal captain Frank McLintock round the pitch after he had collected the Cup from Sir Stanley Rous, president of FIFA, world soccer's governing body. They hugged and kissed players and made off with their shirts. Then the ecstatic fans gathered in front of the directors' box chanting 'Bertie Mee' until the Arsenal manager appeared with his assistant Don Howe, skipper McLintock and the Cup to acknowledge a victory salute. The fantastic scenes inside the stadium continued for a full 25 minutes after the game had ended with Arsenal 3–0 second-leg winners to triumph 4–3 aggregate. Most of the 51,612 crowd remained to pay tribute to their heroes.

Then there was dancing in the streets of Highbury as the overjoyed thousands milled out of the ground. About 500 fans thronged outside the windows of the Arsenal dressing-room in Avenell Road and chanted the names of their champions. Arsenal secretary, Bob Wall, who has been with the Club for 42 years, said afterwards: 'I've witnessed many wonderful occasions here in the past, particularly in the pre-war days, but I must say I've never seen anything quite like these scenes at Highbury before.' Two hundred police were on duty at the ground to keep fans in order, but there was little trouble – the celebrations were boisterous but well-behaved. There were no arrests and no serious injuries. However, one man collapsed and died of a heart attack during the game. A police spokesman said, 'Local support was very strong and obviously the fans were delighted their team won. Naturally, we made allowances for this.'

Islington Gazette, 1.5.70

Night games are always better than Saturday games. I mean the question I was thinking myself was: *What's one game that I would pick out, out of a thousand?* It would have to be Anderlecht, you know what I mean? It was a night game and it was just unbelievable, just out of this world, and I don't think that could have been the same on a Saturday you know.

I think because it's dark there's that feeling that everything is closer in. It may be colder and everybody gets closer together without realising they're doing so. Sound seems to act in a different way, it seems to reverberate round and hold in there and that sort of thing.

How can you describe it? From a supporting point of view I'd never experienced anything like it. I'd been at Wembley when we lost to Swindon and we lost to Leeds the year before. I was at Wembley for both of those and that Swindon game was probably the total despair of my football life. We hadn't won anything, you know, since 53. All the time I'd been watching we hadn't won anything and suddenly there I was, not just a British champ, this was a European championship. We were 3–1 down, you know, and suddenly it was as if there was an inevitability about the night, after we got the first goal we just kind of, you knew, the whole ground knew. It's almost as if Anderlecht knew as well. I mean nobody thought: *We're not going to do it.* It was just unbelievable. You didn't want it to finish. I mean normally if you're in a two-leg affair and you're one up, five minutes from the end, you're waiting for the whistle. This game you just didn't want it to end. It had to go on and on, you know. This was our moment. I've never experienced anything like it.

John Platt

CHAPTER SIX

'Hello! Hello! We are the North Bank Boys'

THE NORTH BANK, 1971–86

Had one tried to imagine life on Arsenal's North Bank during the 70s and early 80s while following football in the pages of the popular press, the picture would have been one of a life-threatening fortnightly excursion into the Badlands of the Wild West. The image – which certainly helped to frighten away a proportion of Arsenal's casual and family support – was one of innocent people trampled underfoot by vast hordes of young hooligans bent on destruction. Certainly, like everyone else, Arsenal had a problem with the behaviour of a minority of spectators on the terraces. The 'crisis' reached its nadir in May 1982. However, the situation in general – and at Highbury – was exacerbated by a widespread lack of any sense of proportion. The Government, the football authorities and the media, always ready themselves to bluster at some length on the subject, never saw fit to ask the North Bank regular how he or she perceived the scale and significance of the problem of crowd violence.

In many ways the 70s – traditionally seen as the worst of times on the terraces – were to prove the best of times on the North Bank. Highbury watched the triumphant rise and ignoble fall of two great sides during the period: the Double team of the early 70s and the exciting, if erratic, 1979 FA Cup-winning team which Terry Neill built around the talents of Liam Brady. The North Bank, by now, was the chosen home for Arsenal's most colourful, vocal and partisan supporters, having developed a distinct sense of identity within the stadium and beyond: passionate, loud and fiercely devoted to their team. Furthermore, the team's swings between excellence and mediocrity – Frank McLintock giving way to Jeff Blockley, Frank Stapleton being replaced by John Hawley – gave Arsenal's crowd an edge of scepticism and irony unique to the Highbury terraces.

The North Bank was an exciting and entertaining place to watch your football from and the majority of Arsenal's standing spectators continued to do so, having their own perspective to apply to the shock-horror headlines. The club itself took a commendably positive role, through a pro-active policy on safety and the development of excellent working relationships with the police, to ensure the security of its customers. The North Bank was a very big terrace and the numbers wanting to be involved in violence were very small. If you didn't want to be part of all that, only in very rare instances did trouble on the terraces interfere with your Saturday afternoon. Although there were significant developments in the culture of football violence during the late 70s – a worrying increase in the level of organisation and forward planning, for example, most notoriously exemplified during the visit of West Ham United in 1982 – it is important to recognise that the fighting remained, for the majority of the fans, a marginal (albeit regular) part of what life on the North Bank was all about. If violence was relevant to the general behaviour of the huge numbers of fans who stood at the home end, it was only in so far as it was an extreme and unacceptable manifestation of the exciting and committed atmosphere that made them choose to stand there in the first place.

For the most part, especially as football was now a pastime consciously chosen from a range of options available to ordinary men and women that would have staggered their parents and grandparents, the Arsenal loyalists on the North Bank helped themselves and the team to some of the times of their lives. During seasons of achievement, their numbers would be swelled by casual support: average gates of 27,000 in 75–76 grew to 36,000 in 78–79 (when the FA Cup was won) and fell back to 24,000 in 82–83. In the dark days of the mid-70s, and again in the early 80s, the North Bank diehards would still be there: wisecracks and sarcasm when expecting the worst, and as loud a crowd as anywhere when hoping for the best.

One profound change in attitude, which had very firmly taken root by the early 70s, was the sense that success was always to be enjoyed at the expense of someone else. In a world where winning was everything, opponents doing badly became as much a part of the fun as your own team doing well. This shift in values was, if anything, as important in keeping less committed supporters away from the ground as the threat of physical violence. It was a trend that led many older supporters to question the nature of their own commitment to their club. There is a danger here of romanticising a particular event with the benefit of hindsight, but, without doubt, the visit of Moscow Spartak in the UEFA Cup in 1982 left a profound impression on everybody who witnessed it. As they watched their team being beaten 5–2, completely overwhelmed by football of a precision and sophistication that took the breath away, the North Bank – the whole Arsenal crowd – responded with cheers and applause. Here was a genuinely enthusiastic appreciation of great football being enjoyed with an objectivity that Highbury hadn't heard or seen for over 25 years. It was a remarkable night, evidence of a rational strain being woven into the backdrop of passion spread out across the North Bank, while Arsenal headed towards the late 80s and, unforeseen, a second Golden Age.

'THERE WOULD BE NO CLUB WITHOUT YOU'

The North Bank was like the extra player. They keep the team going. They do their bit: they suck the ball in, intimidate the opposition, they give the referee stick if he's not giving us our decisions, you know.

Steve Kazmarek

Even now around Highbury, you'll find a genuine affection for the players who did the Double. I think the North Bank knew that for that one season those lads dedicated themselves and sacrificed themselves for Arsenal Football Club. They knew the things that were said about us were unfair. There were times, especially in the later part of that season, when we were being willed to get that goal, against Stoke, against Newcastle. It was the crowd, when we were desperate, only 20 minutes left – the clock's right there! – that willed us through. (See plate 35.)

Bob Wilson

The Double year on the North Bank sticks out. It was the 'in' place to go. It was lively, all the noise. You jump and hug the guy next to you. It was like: *this is where you should be*. It was your spiritual home. Now I sit in the East Stand, I've moved on from that and I honestly don't miss it. But at that time, it was like the youth club, if you like, or the disco. It was the place to be. Where you could express yourself without feeling a prat, basically.

Chris Thompson

In the Double season, one of their early games was against Everton. They beat them very well, 6–2, and a group of people who'd been standing around me for two to three seasons started hugging me: *It doesn't matter who you are you must be an Arsenal supporter, I want to kiss you! I want to hug you!* I thought it was very untypically North Bank that. I realised that it was something that hardly ever happened at Highbury.

Laurence Marks

There were definitely things that would happen in the North Bank that wouldn't happen anywhere else. I used to regularly grab strangers if we scored or be crushed by some huge great lunatic: *Fucking great mate! I love you!* You know, you'd never seen them before and it didn't matter.

Phillip Bloomfield

Up the back I'd say I was standing there from just before I left school, when I started going out of an evening as well as going to school, and started making a wider circle of friends, aged 15 maybe 14 through till, well, a couple of years after we'd done the Double I was still standing on the shelf, so maybe 18. After that there was a period when I was going out with a girl, we were going to get married actually, so I had to start off somewhere where the pushing and shoving weren't so bad. Although the police didn't like it, it was actually a lot of fun. It was harmless enough. I realise like with what's happened recently that sounds a bit iffy but it wasn't as bad, you know, it wasn't that bad then. It was more innocent. It all sounds very dodgy what I'm saying, but it *was* fairly harmless. I never saw anyone get hurt, because it wasn't like a sort of domino effect. There were crush barriers there. It only went a little way, it wasn't that bad. At the time I must admit I thought of it as part of the fun, it was all part of the atmosphere and I enjoyed it a lot.

I was saying, with this girl I had to start thinking that this pushing and shoving was all very well but not everyone enjoyed it. I didn't think she would, so I started having to find somewhere where we could stand, where we could still get optimum enjoyment and an atmosphere but perhaps not the pushing as well, so I graduated down. I moved into the middle then and we found a spot. There was pushing and shoving, 15,000 people standing shoulder to shoulder, you're going to get a little bit of swaying and that, but not so much. But at the top, as I said, at the top they were a bit loopy. I don't know if I was but I pretended I was, you know.

Mick Essen

I did watch one game from the roof, as it happens. The 1–0 home game against Stoke when we did the Double. It wasn't even that packed out that day, but if you climbed up by that door at the back, you could climb up and get on to the roof. There was two of us and we went right down to the front. As I remember, we couldn't see the North Bank goal. Once you got up there, there was no going back – it was bleeding frightening, like. They didn't try and get us down or nothing, weren't even waiting for us when we come down. They must have just thought: *Oh, let them get on with it.* (See plate 38.)

Lenny Brandon

I think you got a feeling on the North Bank about how the game was going, even how it was going to go. During the Double season, the North Bank was a big factor. They were great that year. I was up there for the game against Newcastle, Charlie scored, the atmosphere was great, people were there every week. Very, very good support.

Steve Winfield

What is it that makes me prefer standing? Maybe it's just habit. When I was first taken to the ground, I was taken by a guy called Robert Farrens – he's an actor, but in the 60s he was a pop singer, Bobby Shafto – a friend of the family. And he said: *Come on, we've got to go to football.* And I went: *Oh no!* All the herberts at my school had tried to get me to go and see Millwall and I wasn't having any of that. I came from the darkest reaches of Catford and the herberts at school went to football for one reason, and one reason only. But Bob finally managed to get me to come to Highbury and I came shaking in my boots, thinking: *I'm going to get my head kicked in.* Get down to the North Bank, go up the steps and walk in. I couldn't believe it. Forty-five thousand people, this arena, this mass of energy. I was totally overcome. It sounds a bit wanky but it was a really emotional experience at that age: seeing that expanse of grass and all that noise. It was just fucking incredible. And being stuck in the middle of the North Bank, being part of all that, I was thrilled and at the same time I was terrified. That was the Double season.

Phillip Bloomfield

There was Little Ollie, he sits up in the seats now but he's no bigger than he was 20 years ago. He was always scallywagging about, nicking peanuts off the cross-eyed peanut seller. There was another young bloke called Holloway. No harm in the geezer, all his hampsteads were rotten, all falling out. He was just a right nuisance, always tagging along. As you were coming down by the Plimsoll Arms, the peanut seller was always outside there before the game and then he'd come through the North Bank selling. And Little Ollie would have them off him.

Lenny Brandon

The peanut man, he was a character himself, always ducking and diving, keeping away from the police.

Steve Winfield

So, once again the much-maligned North Bank has put the rest of us to shame! Whilst the team struggled to find its true form against an underrated Stoke City side, the patrons of the North Bank sang: *Good Old Arsenal, We're Proud to say that Name* and *Arsenal, We'll Support You Evermore*. At the same time, the inhabitants of the West Stand loudly slow-handclapped the efforts of players who, only three months before, had brought the club its greatest hour of glory and who had been hailed (quite rightly) as heroes!

Say what you like about the lads who pack the North Bank, you've got to admit that they are the true *supporters*, and many of those who watch from the comfort of the stands have, by their own action, identified themselves as mere *'spectators'*, who will only pay their money as long as Arsenal are winning.

A.P. Fox, *AFC Programme*, 11.9.71

The first game I went to see was in 1972–73. I was sitting in the East Stand Upper and I didn't like it one little bit. We beat Crystal Palace. Alan Ball curled a free kick round the wall into the North Bank goal. All the people around me were just standing up and clapping and I just looked at the North Bank and thought: *That's where I want to be.* My dad said: *You won't be able to see.* But I didn't care. They were just going mad in there, and all the noise. Next game, I was down there.

Paul Hobb

One of the best atmospheres was a game against Leeds in the early 70s. Leeds were just animals then and Mick Jones and Bob Wilson went to collect the ball, and Jones just whacked him into the back of the net. They were already winning 1–0. And the chanting was going: *Arsenal! Leeds **Arsenal!*** And we came back and equalised and then Radford got the winner. We hated Leeds so much and then Jones done that. It was one of the best atmospheres.

Eddie Mason

My uncle took me – he's six years older than me – early 70s, maybe 71–72 something like that and then I just stood there ever since. I mean, like most people, I had a spot I'd go to every week, every home game. In the old days it used to be down behind the goal, quite low down, so you'd actually watch most of the match through the net. Then I graduated up a little bit. I used to try and get up the back and be really in and see what it was like in with that lot. but you can never get in there. If you didn't get to the ground early enough and I don't tend to arrive at one o'clock for games, then you'd end up down the front. It became our spot. When I was going with friends, if I didn't meet them on the way I'd meet them there. Like most people, you'd meet your friends in the ground if you didn't meet them travelling. It became a spot where I always stood, recognised all the people around me.

Al Fresco

After we stopped going in the Schoolboys', we always used to meet the third light in under the North Bank. So even if you lost touch with people for a while, they would know we'd be under the third light in, everybody'd be there.

Lenny Brandon

The first game I ever stood on the North Bank was against Leeds in 1973. It was on a Saturday afternoon and there was a big crowd, 45, 47,000 and I think it was nil–nil. The thing is, I don't think it was a very good game, I don't really remember anything about it. What I remember was the atmosphere, it was so overwhelming it was unbelievable. I was just under the roof at the back as you come in from Gillespie Road. It was electrifying – I'd been in the seats with my dad for three or four years – and this was just different! Very loud. Very vocal. And I felt safe, even though there was a hooligan element about in those days, I felt safe.

Jim Smith

In my opinion the decline in attendances is due to the following reasons (in order of priority):
(1) Too much football. Competitions such as the Texaco Cup, Watney Cup, Anglo-Italian Competition, and even the League Cup should be dumped. Football played after the close of the season proper is dross on the market and destroys the anticipation of the new season's kick-off.
(2) Television. There is no doubt there is too much football on television. The fringe supporter is these days of the opinion that he need not attend a match because he has a fair selection on both Saturday night and Sunday afternoon; I have often heard it said, 'Oh I shan't go this afternoon, it will be on the box tonight.'
(3) Crowd behaviour. You will observe I refer to crowd behaviour and not crowd violence as in the main I can only speak for Highbury (although I have on the odd occasion seen vicious acts of behaviour at other grounds). The average chap, whether he sits in the stand or stands behind the goal, goes to football to see the game and does not wish to listen to a whole series of chanted obscenities, again we are fairly free of this at Highbury, but it does happen there.

I fear this type of behaviour is preventing numbers of fathers taking young sons to football, and I fear that unless affairs improve we are in danger of losing a whole generation of decent spectators; perhaps this is laying it on a bit thick, but you know what I mean.

(4) Prices. This comes low on the list of priorities, because I think that with inflation a chap is just as likely to pay eight bob this year as six bob last year, but this question of course has reference to paragraph 1 and whilst a supporter looking at the pennies will pay eight bob for one match a week there is a very good chance he will not pay 16 bob for two, bearing in mind the not insubstantial rise in fares etc.

(5) Player behaviour. Spectators are fed up with watching temperamental players. Again we are fairly free of this apart from 'you know who', but players must be made to accept decisions, near misses etc. philosophically and not to adopt histrionic attitudes when decisions go against them

J.W. Crotty, AFC Programme, 14.10.72

I've been over there when the opposition has had hardly anybody turn up and the atmosphere, even in them good old days, hasn't been brilliant. You see they've got nobody to jibe at have they really? Its always best when there's been an opposition over there.

Jim Smith

I would go there, go to that very spot when we had that awful 75–76 season. We were struggling against relegation, crowds of 17,000 and so forth, and it used to make me cross that I couldn't get to my spot when we had a big game and suddenly the crowd was 35 or 40,000. It still makes me cry, pushing past people moaning: *Where the fucking hell were you against Norwich or against Middlesbrough! I didn't see you then!*

Al Fresco

In fact, when you've got a successful time, you come and you're like: *You've got to win this. You've got to win this!* Whereas when we're not playing well the true supporters are here and, even if they're not playing well, they'll still have a laugh and a joke. I mean I see it many times sitting up in the seats now, people not even watching the game, they're enjoying themselves talking about what they did last night, where they're going tonight: *He's no good! He should buy!* They've picked the team three times, it hasn't done any good, but they've picked the team. The worst times on the pitch are some of the best times on the terraces.

Paul Johnson

The good thing as a kid was, as well, you can play Birmingham City, Saturday, 18,000, but you can always get a good atmosphere on a certain section of the North Bank. You always felt this was important at that age. It could be a crappy game, low crowd, but the back and middle would always have that atmosphere, people jump up and down, do you know what I mean? Something that does stick in my head, the smell of Victor aftershave. You know the green bottled aftershave? I always stood in the same place. I swear there was a time, a couple of seasons, there was a distinct smell of Victor aftershave. You got used to it, you could never suss where it was from. I'm not saying it for a bet! There was a smell of Victor, that green bottle stuff.

Mark Burdis

The North Bank has been Arsenal. Even in the bad times, the years of Alan Ball, Brian Kidd, Jimmy Rimmer, that part of the ground, we went crazy when they scored. To be honest, they were good times then for support and atmosphere. I can't see a lot of youngsters putting up with that today, the North Bank and all. When a team's doing bad that's when the true supporters come out. Week in, week out, there were the same people on the North Bank then, really giving them a cheer.

Steve Winfield

I would like to thank the Arsenal crowd for helping us the way they did in the Everton game. All the boys in the dressing-room afterwards thought you were tremendous. Of course it helps. It makes a world of difference. Keep it up, and thanks again.

Malcolm Macdonald, *AFC Programme*, 18.9.76

The first time I went to Highbury I must have been about 15. Some of my school-friends were regulars on the North Bank. One particular guy. Martin Shevrill, he used to go everywhere with Arsenal, still goes as far as I know, and I went with him. I guess I really started supporting Arsenal 70–71 when they did the Double. I watched that on TV. No one else in my family was interested in football, I was the only one, so they couldn't really understand what was happening. It was pretty strange really. I was at a south London school so the nearest clubs were Millwall and Crystal Palace, but there were a few Arsenal fans there even though north London did seem a long way off at that time. We used the Tube, the Victoria Line to Finsbury Park. To be honest, I don't remember all that much about the atmosphere. I went to watch football and I enjoyed that, watching players like Trevor Ross and Alan Ball. Those players really stuck in my mind. Trevor Ross especially. The crowd favourites then were Malcolm Macdonald and the goalkeeper, Jimmy Rimmer. I didn't pay that much attention to the crowd but I always felt comfortable there. I was never ill at ease at all. Once I joined Arsenal, I was part of the Club and watched the games from inside the club, as it were. But the guys I used to go with still watched from the North Bank. I remember offering them tickets to sit down and they didn't want them. They wanted to stand on the North Bank.

Paul Davis

After listening to the sickening obscenities from both camps in last week's Merseyside Derby, it was a pleasure to sit in at Highbury.

Granted that the match provided nothing to get worked up about, it was still nice not to hear filth and four-letter words. And to see tiny tots all decked out in red and white, hand in hand with their dads who were themselves prepared to watch both sides and even applaud the other lot.

Amazing! You would never get that at Old Trafford, maybe not at Stamford Bridge, nor even at Anfield which once housed the most fair-minded and humorous crowd of all.

Daily Express, 12.12.77

It was tense because of a minority of people who were there to cause trouble rather than watch the game. The average football supporter is amazingly tolerant of the police. You know, they're told: *You're going to go in single file here. You're going to wait behind for ten minutes.* Although there's good reasons for all that, it doesn't always get explained properly to the fans. The public in general are very tolerant. Even the ones who go there looking for trouble – they're generally criminals outside football as well so they have a lot of dealings with the police outside football. They have a rapport with the police, so even if they're getting nicked or pulled out it's not like you come in the next week and don't speak to him.

PC Alan Smith

The thing was, even on a cold day, once you got in there the temperature was a lot higher. Because of the fact that a lot of people were sort of breathing out at the same time. You'd freeze walking to the ground, your hands had been like ice and that, but get in there and it wasn't cold, certainly wasn't by the time the team scored and you all started jumping up and down. You'd come out and sweat would be pouring off you. You'd go out and catch your death of cold, it'd be like minus ten out.

Mick Essen

It was Arsenal against Bolton, I think it was 1978, and it was on *Match of the Day*. It was possibly the most boring game ever played anywhere. Bolton spent the whole time passing back to the keeper from the halfway line and playing the offside. Eventually we won with a last-minute goal from Stapleton which TV cameras later proved was offside and the North Bank spent the whole time singing: *Boring Boring Bolton* and all the rest of it. Anyway, the next day the *News of the World* printed a picture of the North Bank and at that time I was going with this group of friends but I was the truest supporter because I went to the away games and they didn't. One of them was a Chelsea fan but he used to come with us just to go to a match and another one was a West Ham fan and the other two were fair-weather supporters. They had the picture of the North Bank with the headline *Stop This Filth* and they were complaining about the language we'd used to describe Bolton. They had a picture, with the goalkeeper and all the rest of it and I picked out my friend who was a Chelsea supporter and the two fair-weather supporters and the friend of mine who's the West Ham supporter who used to come with us, and I was the only one who was obscured by a flag. I was absolutely sickened because there I was, I was the true supporter and I didn't get in the picture of the North Bank. I was really choked about that.

Al Fresco

Another story, not to do with Arsenal, to do with the North Bank. I remember when Arsenal were playing Orient we come up here. West Brom were playing Ipswich in the semi-final and I remember I went round to where the station is, them turnstiles. We was hanging round there and for some reason this geezer come out. He was a turnstile geezer and he said we could go through. I went: *Oh thanks mate.* He must have thought we were West Brom supporters, I went in there and that was something else. It's weird because it was packed with West Brom supporters and if it had been packed with Arsenal supporters it's a different feeling. These West Brom fans were, like, farting, they were disgusting, honestly, they were like animals. Different clubs have got different supporters. To me that's the loudest I've ever heard the North Bank, honestly. The thing about the North Bank is when you're in there it sounds deafening, but when you're in the Clock End the North Bank isn't all that. I suppose it's dynamics of sound. But that's the loudest it's ever been. I must admit it was, definitely. All half-pissed, like Arsenal supporters when they go to away games! When you're at home you just got people coming from work, but here you had like 17,000. Even the kids were pissed I'm sure. These nutters from Birmingham, going mad and it was deafening you know. Honestly, I was a West Brom supporter for the day.

Mark Burdis

My cousin took me, he was a regular Arsenal supporter, older than me. I'd just got back from holiday. He knew I was an Arsenal supporter so he asked me if I wanted to go. It was such an event for me. I think we must have got there late because the North Bank was already packed when we got in there. You have to bear in mind that crowds were bigger in those days. It was a really sunny day, first game of the season and Leeds was obviously a big game anyway. The whole thing was so exciting even though I couldn't even tell what the score was. I mean, once my cousin took me down off his shoulders it was just a mass of bodies in there. But it didn't matter, I was so excited, my heart was pumping and the noise was just thrilling me. It was so loud and all the colour, I remember them singing: *Supermac*. We were right up the back, in the middle, where all the noise was and he knew I couldn't see so he put me up on his shoulders. But then he'd have to put me down because his shoulders were hurting!

Paul Jerrams

Arsenal–Sheffield Wednesday, 1979, first replay FA Cup. It was 1–1 (0–0 first match and we brought them back to Highbury) and they went 1–0 up early on. I think we blew the ball away when they had a chance in the second half, which trickled past the post, it should have gone in. I think we blew the ball away. We scored in something like the 93rd minute – Brady of course. Still my favourite all-time player, Brady. I think we willed the ball in, no two ways about it. Then there was a goal that Malcolm Macdonald scored in the 79 FA Cup from a corner against Wolves that put us through 2–1. I think if ever Arsenal are mediocre in the first half and kicking towards the Clock End or they're 1–0 down, you look to the North Bank to lift the team. We had a situation against Coventry years ago where we sang: *Terry Neill and his Red and White Army* for 20 minutes until the team scored. That is true.

Al Fresco

School fixtures clashed with the Arsenal, so I always turned them down. That's how much I loved going to football. I'd rather watch it than play it. Once I got into the routine, I knew where Highbury was and that, I started going on my own. I was only ten. My mum was quite lenient with me, really. She let me go even though she was a bit worried about the trouble, which was worse in the 70s than it is now. I spent my pocket-money going. I missed a few games when my mum was skint. But as I got older I just got more and more into it. I went in the Schoolboys' only when I couldn't afford the North Bank. If I had the money, I'd go on the North Bank. The atmosphere and the singing was much better, I felt more involved in there. I used to climb up those railings as you come in on the Avenell Road side and watch from there before the police made you get down.

Paul Jerrams

When you were playing at Highbury, that was what told you whether the ground was full or not. If you looked up at the North Bank and they were packed right up at the back, you knew there was no space in the whole ground. You knew you were playing in front of 60,000, which we'd get while I was playing. We were a Cup team more than a League team. We never really got in a challenge for the League in the period I was there. We were always fourth or fifth. One season I think we were actually on top at Christmas but petered out. I think that on a week-to-week basis it's when your supporters believe you can win the League they really start getting behind you. A lot of the time we were playing not meangingless games, but never meaning we were going to win the League, so it was difficult. We got to three consecutive Cup finals. The semi-finals are on a neutral ground and the final's at Wembley so I can't ever remember celebrating anything great in front of the North Bank, which is a pity. Now, under George Graham, I was at the ground when the team clinched the League Championship in 1991 and it's great to celebrate something like that on your own ground. Unfortunately, I never had that experience. Yes, we won Cup-ties, League games, derby matches against Spurs, but it's not the same as picking up a trophy in front of your own supporters.

Liam Brady

I remember before one of the Cup finals, we played Nottingham Forest last home game of the season. Drew 0–0. It was useless. But everyone on the North Bank seemed to have a flag. It was fantastic. And in the paper the next day it said: *Nothing remarkable about this game at all except for the massed flag-waving on the North Bank!* It made the Kop look simple. I've never seen so many flags in my life. They didn't have proper handles or nothing, just sort of plastic bits you held. They said: *Terry Neill's Red and White Army.* They sold them down on the corner of Gillespie Road. They couldn't have a stick because they wouldn't let you in. It was just unbelievable – I've never seen the North Bank look so good in my life.

Peter Hobb

Now a final word to all our supporters. Thank you, once again, for the tremendous support you have given us over the years. You are very much a part of the club. There would be no club without you and that is something of which we are always aware. Make no mistake about that.

AFC Programme, 29.8.81

We were playing Wolves, 81–82 season and it was winter, it was freezing, it was snowing. Most sensible people huddled under the shed. Me and my friends stood in our same spot, freezing to death, snow falling on our heads. Just because it was our spot. I think that's what you're proud of. When people knock you and say: *You must be mad, going there in the winter when it's cold and the way you're treated.* And you say: *Well, there's nothing going to put me off. Nothing.*

Paul Jerrams

I suppose, it just became a way of life. I'd make great efforts to get to games where maybe I shouldn't have bothered to. I was away at university and I'd come back for the game. It just seemed, whatever the eventual result was, you had to be there because they certainly wouldn't win without you. Also the standard of reporting is so poor, so biased, and the standard of commentating – I'm talking pre-Capital Gold which I think is actually a reasonable commentary – on what was then Radio 2, was so biased against Arsenal, that it was awful not to be there. At least if you're at a game you know what's going on, you know how well or how badly someone's playing, you know how well the opposition's doing. And you're not fooled by this sort of pro-Liverpool, pro-Man United, pro-Tottenham Radio 2 commentary from people like, whatever his name is, Peter Jones and the other wanker, you know who I mean, who just dominated it for years. You know, Liverpool could have the ball on the edge of their own area and there could be three Arsenal players bearing down on the player but Liverpool would be dominating the match according to them, and I couldn't stick that. The worst thing was no commentary, which was even worse, or no information because they wanted to cover Middlesbrough against Ipswich. You might not even get the score. You might blink and miss it. So you just had to be there whenever possible.

Al Fresco

The North Bank did used to make a lot of noise and I can remember games when it was only the North Bank shouting, getting behind the team. It's a traditional thing that the management would say to the captain: *We'll kick into the North Bank in the second half.* If there's any decision, the North Bank are going to influence the decision, we'd maybe get a penalty or two. That's always done, we'd always kick into the North Bank second half.

Paul Davis

The game we beat Villa here when they won the League in 81 was a really good-natured afternoon. Villa had the whole of the South Bank. It was like a carnival, almost.

PC Alan Smith

My next memory which springs to mind, is when Arsenal played Aston Villa, I think the year was 1980 or early 80s. Arsenal won the match 2–0, it was the last game of the season, and Aston Villa had to beat us to win the Championship, or rely on Ipswich losing, and obviously Ipswich lost; but the atmosphere was just electric, and of course we had an incentive as well, if we won, we was Europe bound. There was 57,000 in the ground that day; and Villa had the whole of the Clock End. It was like two separate seas, one of claret and blue, and one of red and white from the North Bank. One special memory, I remember, was that it was so packed, that your feet weren't touching the floor, and I'll always remember this old boy, he wouldn't stop shouting: *COME ON YOU RIP-ROARING GUNNERS*, the crowd got so fed up with it, that they lifted him up shoulder high, and passed him down all the way to the front, it was hilarious, it was so packed that he was just going down easily off everybody's heads. Great stuff. Great memories.

David Sartori

One of my most vivid memories of the North Bank is the last game of the 80–81 season when Villa won the League. They had all the balloons on the pitch beforehand and Pele came round. Well, first off, they had all the balloons in a big net and this Skinhead ran on the pitch, the police were chasing him and the North Bank were cheering him on, and threw himself into the middle of the balloons. Then Pele was running round the ground waving to the crowd and obviously not looking behind him. Everyone was singing: *Sign him up, sign him up!* And as he was running round, this other Skinhead leapt on behind him and was running round acknowledging the cheers with Pele completely oblivious to what was going on.

Andrew Allerton

At that time there seemed to be a lot of drifters, towards the end of Terry Neill's reign. I think people were getting fed up with it, to be quite honest, and when he actually left it couldn't have come a day too soon. When he did go, people started coming back. There was a lot of Greeks and Cypriots used to go to Highbury, and during his last six weeks in charge, they left, but then they started to come back. Funny enough, I know a guy over there called Stavros and he would not go there from maybe a year before Terry Neill left because of the teams he picked and the way they played.

Jim Smith

People mutter at the Arsenal. They don't slag the team off like they do at Spurs, but they lose interest. They'd like a little action and there have been periods where the Arsenal have been a sporadic sort of team to watch. You go out of loyalty, but you lose interest and you start: *Where did you go last night?* And: *What's on telly tomorrow?*

Maurice Gran

Sometimes when the game was boring even the pigeons took themselves away. They'd sit along the top of the North Bank and you'd sit looking at the pigeons, and you, oh, you'd be looking at the middle distance, the game would be going on, and you'd be thinking: *What's for dinner tonight?* Or *Have we got any sweets?* You drift off in the game sometimes.

Steve Whitman

Sometimes there'll be conversations that go on and the football's like a backdrop. It's like being in the pub. There's some entertainment going on over there but you're still having a chat. The reading books thing was around 1980. It was amazing because it was the antithesis of what you think football's about. Somebody brought a book along and we suddenly got into this routine: one book, six people and we took parts and read it. Sometimes it was more interesting looking this way and reading the book than looking that way and watching Arsenal. It just took off. Every week someone brought their favourite book and we extended it to European games so the book related to the country of the team we were playing. I remember the *Decameron* for Juventus. And there was Strindberg's *Miss Julie* (IFK Gothenburg). But the ones I'll never forget were *Death of a Salesman* and *Moby Dick*. I took *Moby Dick*. One of the blokes always had a stutter and in those two books he just became the characters. And he's never had the stutter since. It was such an important – I mean, I can't remember what the match was – but it was like Tony threw away his crutches and suddenly he could walk – talk – properly.

Richard Stubbs

We were playing Watford on a Bank Holiday Monday. It was in that dismal run of games after Howe left. And the crowd, well, they'd wanted Howe to go but because of the way he went, they'd decided they wanted him back again. Talbot had just gone and he was playing for Watford. We went two down pretty quickly. They were all over us, we looked a complete shambles and the North Bank started cheering every touch that Watford had – just completely and utterly disaffected from the team.

Nick Hornby

Back in the early 80s we had a real song-and-dance team, in the days of Mariner and Woodcock, and our season would end regularly in January and February. Arsenal have always had quite a funny crowd, quite vicious at times. Well, those days, there was nothing to do but laugh. It was quite funny to be there. George Graham changed all that. People's expectations now are higher and so they don't laugh about things so much, they take it more seriously.

Andrew Allerton

We hadn't been playing too well leading up to this game – Villa in 1982, so I scored against the European Cup holders! Few of the chaps were out the night before and we were going up the following day. I said: *If the cameras are there tomorrow, I'll go on!* So I've taken up a bag with all the kit in, the ball, boots, the lot. So we've got in there. The TV cameras weren't there but I said: *Oh, bollocks! I'll still do it, anyway, just for the laugh.* We got right in the bottom right-hand corner by the corner flag. The game started and I started stripping off. Got changed. Everybody around me's going: *What's he up to?* I've put the boots on, tied them up. So I've said to my mate who's holding the ball: *When the ball goes out at the far end, I'll jump over and you throw our ball on.* The ball's gone for a corner down the Clock End, Villa were attacking that end, and I've gone: *Now!* I jumped on to the pitch. Me mate's thrown the ball on and it's come over my head so I'm running on to it. It was like a wave as more and more people realised what was happening. The feeling was unbelievable, as it happens, the old adrenalin was going. The noise just sort of went across the North Bank in a wave. Rimmer was standing on the near post, he was in goal for Villa then. All I was thinking was: *If I miss this, I'm going to look a right cunt. It's fucking got to go in.* Anyway, it's all happened so quick, Rimmer's hardly had time to move and I've whacked it in. I've laid down like Charlie George did after he scored at Wembley in 71. The plods have come on, two of 'em, and we're just walking off and Rimmer's come up and give me the ball back and said: *You'll probably need that.* The North Bank's started going: *Sign him up! Sign him up!* As we got about halfway round, Terry Neill's in the dugout and he's looking at me daggers, like, because Villa have equalised from the corner! And the crowd's reaction has suddenly changed to: *Now look what you've gone and fucking done!*

Lenny Brandon

If we get beat by a better team, I'll clap the other team off. Very few times I've done that, though! Spartak Moscow was one. Do you remember that? They done us 5–2. That team, I thought, was absolutely outstanding.

Peter Hobb

Moscow Spartak, the moment when they scored the third goal and the whole ground just erupted in applause for them, I suppose that one incident stands out. Despite all the rivalries and everything, at that one moment the whole ground was united in their appreciation of an opposing team, an appreciation of football. I mean there we were, we thought we were going to get through, what were we, 3–2 down from the first leg? We played really well, we actually took the lead, and Don Howe had been on telly that night saying we only needed a 1–0 win, but when they broke away and just tore us apart with this third goal, I found I was cheering spontaneously and everybody else around me was, and, I don't know, if the North Bank should be remembered for one thing maybe it's that.

Al Fresco

I mean, we were really like pissed off at 1–0 and 2–0, but they got a standing ovation at the end. Arsenal went off and left the Russian team on there and they stood there and just got this ovation. It was just a brilliant exhibition of football.

Roger Hewlitt

I came very close to chucking it in because I found the atmosphere so foul. It changed when we played Moscow Spartak in the Fairs Cup and lost 5–2. I don't know whether you remember that game but I remember up to that period the crowds getting increasingly unpleasant and very racist and very anti-semitic, and I thought: *I'm not going to pay money and hear all this, I'll go and watch Barnet or I'll go and watch rugby or I'll go shopping, I'm just not going to do it anymore.* I've got such a strong memory of that game because normally when the other team wins people don't like it, but it was an education that night. And I felt that after that the supporters, it's been getting on for ten years now, have never been as narrow minded and parochial as they were before.

Maurice Gran

Saturday, the whole day was focused around going to football. Anything else I had to do was just an inconvenience. We used to stand just above the trench halfway up, just by that little fence. You were high enough up you could see over people's heads and have a good view of the game. At the same time, about five yards to your right was the core of the choir, right in with the atmosphere. You got the best of both worlds, really. We all knew where we were going to go, so whoever was there first would save the spot. We got to know all the people who stood around us, so there was no problem getting into your space. You don't know them personally, but you say *hello* and they know where you stand. It was like that for the best part of ten years.

David Court Jnr

That view was really beautiful. That's a feeling that's never left me from when I first went to Highbury. The first match I went to was Bristol Rovers in the Littlewoods Cup. We won 4–0 and Charlie Nicholas scored twice, a beautiful lob that Merson would have been proud of. The place went mad. But I remember walking in for the game. I went in the big entrance in Gillespie Road where it says: *Arsenal. Home of Football.* And I walked up the steps and as you get to the top, the crest of the terrace, and you look out over the pitch – the pitch was immaculate. I thought it was one of the most beautiful things I'd ever seen. It just got me right there. And I used to get that feeling every time. Especially first match of the season, like, you've had three months off and you go back in: *I'm home. I'm home.*

Stewart O'Brien

'NO OTHER TECHNOLOGY AVAILABLE'

None of us realised how dangerous it was. I don't imagine it was so dangerous in the 30s – there wasn't so much movement in the crowd. But I remember the first time I was on the North Bank and Arsenal scored and I went down about 15 steps. I was terrified on the way down but it was like watching air-stewardesses on a plane – nobody else was frightened, so I thought: *this is great.* And that's how it was all the time, really, and if three or four people had gone down you'd have been in trouble. I think there were times when I felt there were too many people in the ground. At the time I just thought I was being a wimp but looking back on it I think there were – and they were relying on far too much to get away with it. There were spots that just weren't safe – like those steps at the back. I was attracted to all that but I think if I'd known how dangerous it was, I wouldn't have had quite so much fun as I did.

Nick Hornby

Every football supporter must have been shocked by the disaster at Ibrox earlier this season and we feel sure that everybody attending this match today will want to do everything he can to avoid a similar situation at Arsenal Stadium.

We appeal to you, therefore, to take your time when leaving the stadium and to avoid any action which could contribute to a situation where spectators might be injured. Obviously this refers particularly to the end of the game and it is at this time that we would like you to remember what happened at Ibrox and to act accordingly.

AFC Programme, 20.2.71

There did used to be a crush getting out of that really small exit, Avenell Road side, and then the really sheer drop down those stairs. I think they changed that after the Ibrox disaster. There were times you just got carried down those terraces. Your feet never touched the ground. If someone went down you'd be in trouble. Do you remember the game against Derby in the early 70s, the barrier collapsed. I think that was the biggest crowd I've ever been in and that was frightening really. And the barrier went and you think: *Where's the next barrier going to go?*

Peter Hobb

There was one match I remember we went to, Arsenal–Derby 72, a Cup replay which was played in the afternoon. My feet never touched the ground from the moment I got to the top of the stairs. There was actually a barrier that collapsed that afternoon. I think there was a lot of jiggery-pokery going on, a lot of people going in double, and a lot of money changing hands, and I reckon there was probably about 70 to 80,000 people there. I was watching the turnstiles down there, it was very naughty. There was a period at Highbury where the turnstiles were very dodgy. There were definitely more than 63,000 in there.

Maurice Gran

When we played Derby County during the Miners' Strike. The tragic thing about that, and no one will ever believe it really was true: that was marked to come out the following day, that barrier. All barriers were regularly tested and that one was due for replacement, but no one expected that crowd. There was probably 80,000 people here that day, 12,000 left, I think there were 68,000 people inside the stadium. Well there was a lot of trouble you may remember up there in Derby, wasn't there? A big kerfuffle on the field. People came to the confrontation. One did get concerned. We had all sorts of methods of keeping in touch, but it was a visual check. There was no other technology available to us at the time.

Ken Friar

I remember that Derby game during the power cuts. That was the biggest crowd of the season and a barrier went. That seemed to be happening quite a lot around that time but you didn't think at Arsenal, well, it was happening at Micky Mouse grounds, wasn't it? But there was so many in that day. You could always tell when there was too many in, but I never really got frightened at Arsenal.

Lenny Brandon

I remember one night when I was a bit concerned, not over any trouble, but it was a night when there was too many people in there. I thought: *There's a real danger here that people are going to start passing out, and there's not enough space for them to be carried down to the front.* It was against Man City in the League Cup about 78. And once a bit earlier than that when we beat Chelsea 2–1, well, my old man never got in that night. I was working with him at the time I think. When I saw him the next morning he hadn't got in. He'd been queuing right back to Finsbury Park Station and he hadn't got in. I thought: *This is crowded.* I'm used to standing at the back over the years, and then in the middle, when it's like pushed all forward. But the thing about that is that you can actually sort of brace yourself against the barrier when you are pushed. You got used to it and it was alright, you would have a bit of room, a foot in front of you, but there wasn't that night. If there had been pushing that night then what would happen was your chest would take it, the brunt of it if you was in front of a barrier. I wouldn't say I was frightened, but I was concerned. I mean I'm not going to faint but other people might. The temperature goes up about 20-odd degrees when it gets as full as that. It's very very hot in there, really hot even when it's an icy night outside. Even in the gangway people were standing, although God knows how they could see because it's like down the steps isn't it, and yet it was so full that people were standing in there. If there was like a roar they'd jump up to see what was going on.

Mick Essen

Then, in the 80s, I used to like standing in the middle, you know, and you're a bit above it. There's a big step up and the bar. I used to stand up there. Even though I used to get squashed on the bar, I used to enjoy that – they used to push you and even though it hurt I used to find it enjoyable. I know that's ridiculous. But it's a sort of scary thrill, if you know what I mean. We'd wait for the charge then all go: *Aargh!* with the pain and then laugh afterwards.

Paul Jerrams

It's weird how people are gluttons for punishment. You get pushed, shoved, people farting in your face, burping, smelling of drink. It used to be fashionable for everyone to push. I think they got it from the Kop. There was no need for it, really, but you used to go: *Cor!* And you'd push as well!

Mark Burdis

I was at a meeting, early 80s, a meeting in Leicester, British Diabetic Association.

There was an Arsenal game on the Saturday afternoon, a Cup-tie against Manchester City in fact, and the meeting finished in Leicester at half past 12 and the kick-off was at three o'clock. I worked out that if I got the one-twenty-something train, it got to King's Cross at two fifty something. I used to ride a motor-bike then, so I left my motor-bike at King's Cross and got the train, left the meeting about 15 minutes earlier than I should. But there were rail works between Watford and King's Cross. It got to King's Cross about eight minutes past three and I was sitting on this train desperately praying that it would move in and wondering if I could jump out and run down the line. In the event I jumped out of the train about 10 yards before it had actually come to a complete halt, jumped out and the door swung to and clouted me behind my Achilles tendon, and I was sort of doubled up, hobbled to my motor-bike and went up to the ground and got there about twenty minutes past three and stood in the North Bank for the remaining 25 minutes. At half time it was still nil all. I started feeling a bit faint, not very well and thought: *That's funny, my shoe feels wet.* I took my shoe off and there was a sort of half a pint of blood. The train door had clouted my Achilles tendon, not just bruising it inside but gashing it quite badly on the outside. I hobbled down to the St John's Ambulance and they looked at my Achilles tendon and said: *This is a hospital job, better take you up to the local hospital. Where's that? It's the Whittington.* I'm working there as a consultant, so when I arrived in casualty I gave a false name. It was actually while I was working there as a consultant, it must have been 80 or 81.

John Yudkin

We'd watch from here, the control room, and we'll have people in the four corners of the ground. If there's any problem, they're brought here. On a big game, we'd have 30–35 volunteers working.

Shirley Haxell

You could always reckon on Chelsea, West Ham, Manchester United, Liverpool – you knew you were going to have bother of some sort. Or if it was a grudge match, you know, with points at stake. In those days, you used to get an advance warning from the police, to expect trouble. When I first started about 15 years ago there weren't so many here. But then all of a sudden – I think the Brigade just decided we needed more. I suppose we realised we were sometimes being overwhelmed with casualties. We used to have two or three in each corner – but it went up to half a dozen.

Stan Carroll

It's changed a great deal since I first came, because once upon a time you opened the doors and let them all in and shut the doors, played and sent them all home and that was the end of it. It's changed dramatically since then because there are so many other things involved now. We have electronic enumerators showing how people are coming in, for instance. The pattern in behaviour in attendances has altered enormously. In the 40s and 50s by two o'clock on a match day we were often shut. By two o'clock now on a match with an attendance of 44,000 you might have 5,000 in. All the rest will come in in the last hour. We know on a very busy day, if we were anything like closing down, we can monitor the attendance per minute as it's coming through. We've got a flow rate, we can predict what's going to happen, we can predict what time we're likely to shut down if we think we're going to. Then we will predict that attendance close down. If it's say, at 2.23 which it was for one match, half past one we're on the phone to all the local stations, London Transport, British Rail. They're getting signs made up at Hammersmith and at Euston and Victoria whatever, and at a given time they will say the gates are now closed. So if the gates close at 2.23 those signs are out there stopping anybody else coming. You have to warn London Transport because if you do close down and people do get shut out: one, we need extra police in the street outside to move the crowds away; two, there are fewer trains programmed through from three o'clock until nearly five, one every 15 minutes. We now need trains backed up so they've got to be brought in. Programme sellers need to be moved around from place to place where the crowds are going to be. We've always invested in technology, probably one of the only clubs to do so, and we've got quite a sophisticated set-up. There's closed-circuit cameras everywhere. We know what's going on, we can tell where the crowds are coming. We can monitor, because of our enumerator, the various areas. It's far more sophisticated than people might think. A lot of this has been in place since the early 80s.

Ken Friar

Highbury is one of the few grounds that won't need drastic improvements in the light of the Popplewell report on ground safety.

Says Arsenal managing director Ken Friar: 'Apart from minor works we have a completely clean bill of health. We have a 100 per cent safety certificate from our local authority, the GLC – and our safety procedures have the full approval of the local fire service and the police. If the fire brigade or police come up with an idea to improve ground safety, we implement it.'

The Club's most recent measure was to change the siting of some terrace exits so fans could get out quickly in case of emergency.

Even before the Safety of Sports Grounds Act was introduced, Arsenal employed a firm of civil engineers to check the stadium and detail exactly what work needed to be done.

AFC Programme, 3.3.86

'BUCKETS OF BEER'

I used to like the old scoreboards as well, with A,B,C and the score, you know. Nine times out of ten they cocked it up. Number would drop in and then he'd pull it out, because it was the wrong one.

Steve Winfield

The toilets were disgusting. The thing with them, when it was a big crowd, was getting out to go. It was half time, wasn't it? Little trough, weren't even painted in them days at the back there.

Steve Winfield

The old J Bar, they used to have about three people working in there and all the thousands trying to get in. There used to be an old girl who worked in there, all the young kids used to know her. She used to look after you a little bit. Throw a few pies your way and that. To the left end in there, you used to get a lot of older geezers, drinkers who weren't really interested in the football. Why they couldn't just have had a drink down the road, I don't know.

Lenny Brandon

I don't know what year we put the facilities right across the back there. I was worried at the time, when we put the facilities in, I was very concerned about it because the finishing was in corrugated-type metal, it wasn't the old wavy stuff, it was angled metal very attractive, like a plastic leatherette-type finish absolutely made for graffiti, absolutely tailor-made for it. And I was thinking: *Oh my God! What have we done here?* Because once you get graffiti on to that type of surface you never get it out. I remember doing a piece at the time and saying: *Well, this is yours—we put this in for you, the North Bank, etc.* There wasn't a mark on it, they did respect what was theirs. I think that it's worth recording that. They certainly sold drinks up there, yes, and then we put a lot of other things in as well. It was a risk but what we felt was that we would like to give them better facilities, even though it reduced the capacity.

Ken Friar

Going to different grounds, Villa Park always impressed me. Before they put the roof on it and lowered it, you went in the top of the Holte End and you got vertigo, because you looked down. And the same thing happened, to some extent, with the North Bank until they put that canteen in. It was the depth of it, like Santa's Grotto or something, you could never work out whether it went on forever or there were people there – it was just a dark bit. The irony of it was that when they put all that in, the ban on beer came in. They opened it originally selling buckets of beer – two-pint buckets! And then suddenly, within a year, they had to turn it into a hamburger joint and sell Slush Puppy or whatever it is they sell up there now.

John James

I'd never dream of getting a drink or anything then. They had this little place down the back and it was just a nightmare getting down there. That's before they built this new stuff. And obviously when I was younger I didn't used to drink beer so I didn't often use the toilets. It's only when you've had a couple of drinks that you need to go at half time. The catering more recently was better, obviously. There was an outlet on both sides and an outlet in the middle. I think the middle had toilets as well. I remember I felt sad when they put all that in because they took away a lot of the terrace, cut the capacity by about 3,000. Before it was there, we used to kick the corrugated iron at the back. It used to make a loud, loud noise. Couldn't do that no more because since they built that, the police used to stand at the back of the supporters keeping an eye on everybody.

Paul Jerrams

'A GOOD FIRM'

Frankly, I'm sickened by the attitude of some youngsters today, even though I've worked all my life with wonderful kids on our Gang Show productions.

My remedy to soccer hooliganism will horrify some people – I'd birch them. Yes, it's time we matched toughness with toughness. Discipline went out of the window the day psychiatry came in. Don't get me wrong, psychiatrists do a fine job but there are too many 'do-gooders' around these days who do no good at all.

We must give our magistrates stronger powers. Only one thing scares hooligans – pain.

Ralph Reader, *AFC Programme*, 8.11.75

Arsenal had a couple of old boys who were a bit handy, like. They weren't the singers. In the 70s Arsenal did have a couple of blokes that 'led' Arsenal, not in the singing but when all the trouble was there. And obviously because you got up there all the time you learn about these people. There was a bloke called Putney, and Johnny Hoy. They were looked on as who you could go and see at Arsenal if there's any problem. They would be the fellows that were in there to sort it. I mean you always used to find all the herberts that wanted a bit of trouble, when we were playing at home against Liverpool or Chelsea, they were always talking about going to Euston after the game and things like that. I think that was mainly people that are very close, that lived in the area of Highbury, around that way, Dalston and places like that, more so than the outlying-district people coming in.

Laird Budge

I think the police had it sewn up even then.

Steve Winfield

I'd never been to a football match before I came to work here. The first game I ever did here was Coventry City in the fourth round of the Cup in 1977. The day was very much like it is now. You turn up and get paraded several hours before kick-off; you have something to eat, and then go on and do your specific task: if you're outside, you're searching the fans going in, if you're inside, you wait till the turnstiles open and then look after the crowd inside. For the first year, you filled in where there was a space. If someone was missing you would do their job, wherever that was. But after that first year you get what's called a fixed post. At the start of the season, you're assigned to a job – in those days it was North Bank rowdyism or South Bank rowdyism – you'd do that, and you'd be in the same place every week. So you'd get to know the fans, that was the idea of it. I was assigned to the North Bank for three or four seasons between 1979 and 1983. Well, the gates open at one. You'd get the first rush of fans. They'd all run in to find their own special space. The first hour was easy, just people coming in and slowly filling up. After two o'clock it would get a lot busier. Most games were relatively quiet but if you had someone like Man United, Spurs, West Ham, Chelsea, you had to be looking out for the groups of away supporters in the North Bank. It was the done thing then, that the away support would try and infiltrate into the home end. They'd come in in ones and twos and slowly build up a little crowd in the corner. Suddenly it would go up: Arsenal singing *Arsenal* and there'd be an answering call on the other side, *United* or *Spurs*, or whatever. For a while they had policemen on the turnstiles talking to people who weren't showing colours and you could tell by their accents. Or they'd try that thing of asking supporters to name the Arsenal team. If they didn't know it, they were the away fans. It didn't work very well because football supporters know who plays for a club like the Arsenal.

It was just a matter of you trying to spot them and either get them out and walk them down to the South Bank, or get them ringed by police before trouble could start. Some games they'd get maybe 400 up in one corner. But if you get two groups coming at each other, a few hundred, it's only the ten or 12 at the front who are going to fight to start with. And the rest are edging back because they don't want to be the first to run in. So the crowd would part, then come together and you could see fighting in the middle of it. It would only be 20 or 30 at the front who were actually doing the fighting. We would generally be in there and separating it before hell could break loose. During my time, they opened the big sterile areas between the fans – that was in vogue for a while, keeping a section of the terrace clear between say, the Arsenal and the Tottenham fans. Grounds are getting pushed for space now, so they can't afford to do that. Anyway, I don't think there was anything to prove they worked. The normal supporters could see trouble starting as easily as us. You could see people going: *Come on kids, this way. The fight's going to start now!* They'd move to one side. They knew it was going to go off. And the fans didn't generally attack people with kids or anything. It was more their own equivalent on the opposing side.

It's surprising how many people you can get to know on the North Bank by standing at the one point every week. Whether they're normal people just there to watch the game or they're hooligans, just by seeing them come in every week. You start off with a sort of nod to each other and then it doesn't take long before you're speaking to them. Of all the games you do, 99 per cent of them, all you've got to do is watch the game, or watch the crowd. There are minor things – lost property, things like that – but even 15 years ago there wasn't fighting on the North Bank every week. There might be one or two you had to escort out but, on the whole, it wasn't 'Rourke's Drift' every week!

PC Alan Smith

Maybe it was going on before, but it was in the early 70s I sensed the violence and the tribal stuff coming in. And you started to see it happening.

Jon Sammels

I think the media have a lot to answer for, interviewing hooligans as they come out of court! If they hadn't glamorised it all, built up myths, it would have gone away sooner.

Chris Thompson

I remember some rival fans of Chelsea and Man United and Tottenham getting in, but nothing major. We never had thousands of our supporters on the pitch because they had been chased out, things like that. I just don't remember anything major. A hole normally grew in the middle, people swopping punches or kicks or whatever and then the police coming in and perhaps escorting them down the track into the club. Perhaps I'm wrong, my memory's perhaps not that good, but I don't really remember anything much. If anything, it's a funny excitement, if you know (and you can tell) when someone near you is not an Arsenal supporter. You just sense it. And it's just that little bit of excitement: *What's going to happen here?* You never really thought anything nasty was going to happen. You might get a thump but you never thought you was going to be stabbed or a bottle over your head.

Paul Johnson

There were always plans and things. People used to hear rumours, you know, about Rotherham supporters who were going to try and take the North Bank when they played them in the Cup! I remember one game when I was a kid, a dozen Arsenal supporters walked in chanting: *Tranmere! Tranmere!* or whoever it was and the North Bank ran out. And I thought: *Oh, no! There's Tranmere supporters in the North Bank.* That was just Arsenal supporters messing about but there was a big phobia about it, a paranoia – and it was part of the fun. There'd be rumours about it happening all over London – there's going to be a fight at King's Cross or at Euston. They were meeting a train at Paddington. It was all bullshit, most of it. But I mean, there was a fight inside Highbury every single Saturday I went between about 68 and 75 or 76.

Nick Hornby

Yeah it was a bush telegraph. You always knew that Tottenham were going to come in at the right-hand side of the North Bank perhaps – meeting at two o'clock. Then they were going to throw confetti up in the air, and then it was all going to be off. That sort of stuff. Playing Manchester United one season, a group of our *well-known people*, shall we say, were in the north-west corner. They was shouting out: *United United*. So the first thing the police do is get them all together, escort them along the cinder track into the Clock End. At this stage we don't know who they are or anything, but as they're going round the track, people are going: *Here, that's so and so. They're only Arsenal supporters!* We're going: *What's going on here?* Fifty, 60 perhaps, it was a good firm, got sorted round the track, and put in the Clock End. Police think they've done a nice job, washed their hands of it, and walk away. Two minutes into the game, *bosh*, it's all gone off at the Clock End. Arsenal's actually got in the Man United end, and everyone's just laughing about it. I couldn't believe it. It was brilliant really. I mean, the police thought they'd done a good job putting rival supporters from the North Bank into the Clock End, and of course they hadn't. They'd put the wrong supporters in there. I mean they have got some front these people, really have.

Paul Johnson

They'd just get in there and whack people, you know what I mean? If it was persistent they'd just hoik you out, they'd go in there and break it up by matching aggression with aggression really. That was like an unwritten law up there, and you had to do something a bit grief-full to get thrown out. I had a mate thrown out three times once, against Chelsea. He was shouting a lot, and he was standing right near a copper and he was effing and blinding and this, and the copper came and took him out. This was before the game. And he went out, come back in. That was the days of wearing the old trilbies and pork pie hats, and the copper spotted him by the hat and took him out again. He went outside threw his hat away and his jacket and he got in for a third time. He still got thrown out again. I mean, in those days they were always looking for faces but, again, it added to the atmosphere.

Laird Budge

At one stage, mid-70s, it was bad over there. They definitely had one of the hardest firms. Nobody really liked to come to Highbury unless they were crowded up. Our little crowd weren't really trouble so much as walking down the street singing and dancing and that, shouting abuse at the other supporters. But we weren't running in looking for trouble. The ones who were, some from round here, some from other parts of London, they'd just be there looking for a fight. There were a lot of people like that, I mean, I was with some of them, being brought up in North London, you feel the need to be in with them, with what was going on. But the real leaders, the troublemakers, they never used to hang about in the groups. They come with their own little crowd, get involved with the trouble and at the end of it, disappear. They used to hang about after the games looking for trouble. I did go through a little phase when I used to knock about with these guys but only for a short while, you know, looking for other groups of supporters to have a punch up. But for me, I'm glad to say, that came and went very quickly.

Vidos Neophytou

If you got in the North Bank early, you'd hear all the rumours: *They're over there. They're down there.* And I suppose everybody was brave until you got within 20 yards of them. That's when, you know, you've been Billy Bigshit up the front and they're all pushing from the back and you want to slip off out the way! Going away, the aim was always to 'take' their end. If you could get a scarf, an opposition scarf, then you'd wear that to school on Monday. I remember Johnny Hoy and a bloke called 'the Postman', they were leaders, sort of thing. You'd tag along behind them. I mean it used to be just continuous, didn't it, people getting thrown out? Policemen all round the side of the pitch. And the Old Bill, they used to just pull geezers out for singing wrong, didn't they? It would get them out of the way, wouldn't it? They wouldn't have to get involved in anything then. If they can get someone on a silly nick, that's them for the afternoon. I do remember once having a knife pulled on me, against Chelsea. The crowd was running backwards and forwards. I wasn't involved in anything but suddenly I was surrounded by geezers I didn't know and one of them had this knife. I couldn't say nothing because I don't know who they were – I couldn't say: *I'm Arsenal. I'm with you.* Because I don't know if they were. I just had to swallow and I was away. But, you know, most people would run away. If you had 100 geezers chasing three geezers, if the three turned round you can guarantee the 100 would run the other way! I've never subscribed to the view that people just go to football for the trouble. You have to have football in you. All the people I used to know who liked a fight, they didn't go to Arsenal for the fight. They went for the football. They were Arsenal fans.

Lenny Brandon

It was good really. In the middle of the North Bank, well, for a big game word would go round to get there nice and early and it wasn't very often we got moved. One or two of my mates got into trouble being a bit over-enthusiastic. But me, well I don't mind to stand and watch it but I wasn't going to get involved. I was a bit of a coward, really! I love Arsenal and that but that was going a bit far. I was more one who would follow and be one of the Jack the Lads! I suppose a lot of it was a charisma thing. You wanted to show off to your mates. Everyone did it.

Steve Winfield

Despite the reluctance of Arsenal, we plan to build a moat around the Highbury pitch in 1975 to combat the growing menace of a crowd invasion. The directors and officials of English League clubs, but a decade ago, would have raised their hands in horror at the thought of having to take deterrent action against their spectators. Spectators, but a decade ago, would hardly have thought of encroaching on the field of play! Today, however, in the light of the events of last season at Newcastle and Manchester every responsible official of a football club has to think in terms of top security. Why? Football crowds are no different from other demonstrators and, when their ire is raised, they act similarly. Spectators react to what they like and we love them for it. But they also react to what they don't like and we must not hate them for it! The anodyne is good football and sportsmanship but we don't always get it. Therefore, as responsible promoters of the spectacle of football, we officials of clubs have to make sure that if spectators get out of hand we can ensure that they are prevented from (a) doing damage and (b) breaking the rules of the leagues and associations to which we are affiliated.

Long ago in South America, where this problem first raised its ugly head, the clubs decided to erect wire fences but there are many objections to this simple (on the face of it) solution. Not only does the fence obscure vision but in addition we have the situation where British people abhor any scheme which smacks of the 'concentration camp'. What is more important in these days of vandalism is the possibility of a situation arising on the terraces when innocent people might want to spill on the pitch (with police approval and help) in order to avoid a major hazard. For this reason many thinking people in football had come to the conclusion that fences are 'out' and dry moats are 'in'. It is not good enough to say – 'We have a fine set of supporters, it can't happen to us.' It can always happen to 'us'.

Bob Wall, *Islington Gazette*, 28.6.74

There was a lot of inter-rivalry, different factions. When they started to ban away fans from the North Bank, it took away the common enemy. When you used to get the Liverpool fans up there, say, it would be great – we were us, they were the enemy. And then suddenly all that went and a lot of the atmosphere went. I mean, everybody goes on about the fights and violence has always been part of football – that's led us to where we are today – but a lot of it wasn't about fights. The police made it a confrontational situation by keeping us apart.

John James

I found the policing at Highbury very good. I've never had a problem with the police – at other grounds, yes, but never at Highbury. I've found you could talk to them, they were good humoured. I don't think there were so many uniformed police after about 76 onwards. You had more plain-clothes police. I used to always go to the Boxing Day games. I went over in 79 against Chelsea. Halfway through the game there was trouble. There were a lot of Chelsea in the North Bank and all of a sudden these police came from nowhere. They were plain-clothes. I don't know if they had a tip-off. It made me feel safer seeing the swift way they dealt with it. I was very impressed. And I remember an occasion in the early 80s, a mate of mine shouted an obscenity at Kevin Keegan, when he was with Southampton I think, and this bloke came up to him and tapped him on the shoulder and said: *Just watch your language will you?* We knew there and then he was a plain-clothes policeman but the guy didn't take it any further and nor did my mate. (See plate 21.)

Jim Smith

When we first moved to these flats it was lovely, then all of sudden for about five or six years it got really violent, nasty, you know. Some of them would jump on the roof, on that balcony. You'd have about 100 of them all trying to get on the roof, if it was Manchester United or Liverpool or them sort of teams, even Leeds. Trying to watch the game – they didn't have the South Bank Complex then – we used to be able to see the game, stand on the loo and you could see three-quarters of the field and the far goal. I suppose if they got on the roof they could probably see a bit more. We're lucky they got security gates after about five years, and we've had no problems since. They used it as a public urinal. That's the only thing we got against the Arsenal, they should have Portaloos here for people queuing up. You can't blame the man. He's got to go, a man's got to do what a man's got to do. There's nothing there for women at all is there? It's unreasonable.

Charlie Robinson

I do remember one Boxing Day against Spurs, 1979, and there were loads of fights going on and you know how you'd get those big holes appear in the crowd with herberts having a go at each other. I remember at one point this big circle opened up and there was this one bloke standing in the middle wearing an anorak, with his hands in his pockets. Suddenly this fist just appeared from the side and hit him. Smack! on the hooter. And it was cartoon time, it was like *Tom and Jerry* or something. He just went over and we all fell about. They took him out, he was in a terrible state, really, claret all over the place. Then about half hour later they walked him down again, the St John's, and he got back in the crowd.

Phillip Bloomfield

At Highbury we tried to surmount this problem by having a caged-in area where we could detain troublemakers until they could be dealt with later. But a roving TV camera at one of our matches spotted the 'cage' and it was quite properly pointed out that to detain people in this manner was illegal, so we had to get rid of our cage.

Terry Neill, *Revelations of a Football Manager*

And we're quite friendly with a guy called Bob Bevan who's a football after-dinner speaker and he was, back then (we first met him about 12 years ago), trying to get a scheme started to get the players to do more. I think a lot of us feel very strongly that the players don't do enough when there's trouble, whatever it is, at the ground. They may do from behind the scenes. But they don't publicise, if they don't like what's going on, if they don't like physical violence or racism and so on, then they've got to come out and say so. The players stay extraordinarily quiet.

Maurice Gran

I just think it is part of social behaviour. It could have been anywhere. The fact that it revolved round a football match was just one of those things. It could have been somebody from the Angel, a gang from the Angel, having a fight with a gang from Highbury. It's a particular age group where it happens. Sixteen up to about 20, 21. Maybe some of those people haven't grown out of it. There certainly was that time when it all happened, and it was the same people every week who went for it and did it. The majority of them were people who I think if you could stand up man to man with them they'd run a mile. But there was that 'pack' thing wasn't there? If it hadn't been football, I mean, it's happening in cricket, it's happening in boxing. It's that element you get, like happened in Leicester. Tony Simpson was boxing for the World Title, there was a lot of trouble there and a CS gas canister went off. Now the thing was, you shouldn't sell drink at boxing matches, but the fellow never bought the gas canister at the boxing match, didn't get pissed when he bought the canister. He'd made up his mind to go and buy that, I'm sure he never bought it that day over the counter anywhere. He's had that for a while, he's decided to come along and use it. And if you've got a lunatic who wants to do a thing like that, what are you going to do? Nobody can legislate for that. Like at football, there were some serious stabbings weren't there? A few people got killed in those days. That was the time when you think to yourself: *My kids are not going to stand up on the terrace.*

Frank Warren

As the 70s went on and then the 80s, I'd say it reached its peak. It was getting more organised, you know, weapons starting coming out whereas before if you'd had a fight the worst weapon anyone could hit you with was like the end of their boots, which certainly hurt but it was unlikely to kill you. It was unlikely to leave scars six inches down your face. But it started getting very nasty and it was almost like a competition to see who'd do the worst things. You'd get like West Ham fans arranged like – what did they call them? – the Inter City Firm, you know, who go up on their own. They pay extra and go on an Inter City train. I don't know, others are more qualified than me to say but, I think, the thing about the Arsenal was like, it was always a good laugh. We'd all get off the train at an away game, and we'd all be singing and that. I'm sure other team's supporters say the same, but I thought it was a lot more innocent. There were some right nutcases, but it was mostly like a bunch of kids. Fighting's not all that innocent anyway, but there are degrees aren't there? It was like handbags at 20 paces. There were geezers there who were quite tough and there were minor fights. But there was none of this organised stuff.

Mick Essen

'THEY TURNED THE NORTH BANK INTO THE FALKLANDS'

Whenever we played a top London club, Tottenham, West Ham or Chelsea, I always expected some trouble. There was always certain areas of the North Bank where a wise supporter like me knew not to stand. I knew enough about the behaviour of football fans to know where trouble would start. It worked for me, I never got in any trouble. Like the West Ham game. You remember with the smoke bomb and all that? Well, I'd been expecting it. I was up the Clock End very pleased with myself that I was watching it from the other end. Most football supporters are intelligent enough to know what's going on. If you want trouble you know where to get it. If you don't want it, unless you're a little bit naïve, you know how to avoid it. I certainly did. I do believe that the violence is organised, fans do organise where they're going to be, so you can get to hear about it. I know whenever West Ham or Tottenham have been expected, a lot of fans would come down from the Clock End to protect the North Bank. It's like an army, stood in the North Bank because someone's going to try and smash it up, and they're going to protect it. The Clock End was always more renowned for trouble anyway. It always seemed to be the west side the away fans came in, from the Gillespie Road turnstiles, and they all used to stand up there in the corner. So when trouble started it would spread across. That's why they built those fences, it would happen often. It would spread across because the aim of the away fans was to get into the middle of the North Bank. Once that was achieved, they could say they'd toppled the North Bank, they were in the middle, singing.

Paul Jerrams

I remember when West Ham turned the North Bank into the Falklands War and I hated that. That a supporter was killed outside. It was like the Falklands, the gas being spread around.

Richard Stubbs

The first time I went on the North Bank was that West Ham game when they invaded the North Bank. I went with a friend and an older guy with his kids. There were seven of us. So the first experience of the North Bank, as soon as the players came out, was running for our lives and getting on the pitch to get out of the trouble! I was 13 or something and dad was off somewhere else so I went with them – there was this older guy, mum and dad were happy for me to go with them. And the North Bank was the place to be, wasn't it? Where all the singing and the atmosphere was. We came up on the train from Potters Bar to Finsbury Park. Got in the ground and realised there was a bit of an atmosphere – it was a time when if it was a local derby you almost expected there to be trouble, sort of thing. The older guy we were with thought the best place to stand would be right in the middle, in front of the hard-core so that if anything happened we'd be protected. From about half past two onwards there were West Ham fans trying to get in either side and you could see that there was fighting. I always remember someone saying: *Oh, that's just a decoy. There's something else going to happen.* And then as soon as the players ran out, everybody was applauding and they started the game – I suddenly heard this sort of crack behind us, a cracking noise. I looked around and there was just smoke everywhere and suddenly there was like thousands of them came in from behind, they'd thrown a smoke bomb into the middle. My friend grabbed me and dragged me on to the pitch. There was lots of people getting on to the pitch to get out of trouble. Probably one of the most frightening experiences you could wish to have, being caught up in the middle of that lot. The first time I'd been to football without my dad, I mean, it looks like good fun when you see it on the telly but when you're actually in the middle of it, you don't really want to be part of it. It was a frightening experience. Even before the game, you know, the ICF had this reputation and you could see little bits of fighting going on. One or two people were going: *Come on, let's go and join in.* But I think the majority of people were fairly unnerved by it. It was quite eerie really. I remember standing on the pitch and because it was such a confusing thing that had happened, hearing all the ICF chants, it was the weirdest thing. And I really didn't know what was going on but I remember seeing a documentary a couple of years later about West Ham and the ICF and hearing the same chants, it brought it all back to me. It was the eeriest feeling, having been caught up in the middle of that. There had been quite a lot of police in trying to stop the fighting at the side but then when it all kicked off in the middle, well, I was just rushing through the crowd to get on to the pitch. I think the players got taken off and me and my friend were on the pitch, looking around for the guy with his kids. We eventually found them. They'd got on to the pitch as well. His daughter was very upset about everything, she was about the same age as me. We decided what the best thing to do was. They were leading people round to the other end, but we thought: *We might as well get back in the North Bank.* And we did, by which time the police had got things fairly well under control. It was OK after that. In fact we went back to where we started. A bit stupid really. I think they tried to get in again towards the end of the game but there weren't so many that time and the police jumped on it fairly quickly. So many people had got out, it wasn't so packed in there and I have this memory of looking across the terrace and trying to work out who was who, whether there were still West Ham fans in there. You were looking over your shoulder thinking something was going to happen again. With the fighting up at the side there were maybe 50 or 100 people fighting – it was just a little scuffle, but it seemed fairly major to me. I talked to school friends who were there as well and when the teams came out they applauded and couldn't understand why nobody else did. They reckoned there were several hundred West Ham up at the back. I don't know. When the smoke bomb went off and it was all behind me, I couldn't really see. I just remember the confusion.

David Court Jnr

What was frightening about it was that we knew they were trying to get in, we knew that there was going to be a rumble. But what was frightening was the confusion with the smoke bomb, you get this sudden roar and nobody knew what was going on. It was just absolute chaos. That was what was frightening – that you really didn't know what was going on. They came in with a flag – people forget the flag. It wasn't just smoke bombs, they came in with a flag. It was like a cavalry charge, like the *Red Badge of Courage* or something. There was the smoke bomb and this huge roar as they came piling in on the Avenell Road side and there was the flag and absolute confusion. The North Bank wasn't as split up with fences then, it was just one great big terrace, and it was frightening because it was like a military invasion, you know. It was like something out of a war. It wasn't your normal couple of people slugging it out ten yards away. It really was frightening, even though I got off without any personal injury and the person I was with got off without any personal injury and the people around me. We ended up and watched the rest of the match down the Clock End, but it was frightening because it was your worst fears personified. I mean, it was how it must have been at Heysel, or Hillsborough, – well, no, Hillsborough's different – but it must have been like that at Heysel.

What they did, what the ICF did, was the sort of activity that eventually led to Heysel. But it's like saying: *Why go out for a walk after midnight?* Somebody's got to because otherwise you let these people win. *Why walk home at night, late at night?* You've got to do it because otherwise everywhere is a no-go area. I mean, I don't want to build myself up as being particularly brave or anything because I'm not, but the North Bank was where I stood to watch the Arsenal. If I had to unfortunately share it with several thousand West Ham fans, and maybe not dance about too much when we score, then, maybe that's a compromise I have to make. But they're not going to shift me off. Although, actually, when they smoke bombed us, they did shift me off because I was marched down to the Clock End. I did seriously think: *Why am I coming here? Why am I doing this?* But there you are, I was back on the North Bank two weeks later.

Al Fresco

We introduced fencing up there, purely because there was so much movement with so many people, the police felt that we should stop that sway. A lot of it came about when we played West Ham some years ago and somebody threw a smoke bomb or something. That caused a lot of problems, and that really caused the introduction of those fences. One tries to anticipate some things, but there are other things one can't anticipate. That afternoon was one of them. You'd have machine-guns on four corners if you were going to anticipate everything. We had to react to that, we changed the method, we put fences in up there to stop that lateral movement rushing across the terraces, because people would have got hurt.

Ken Friar

None of what we have today would have been possible without the fantastic support of which we are so very proud. Through good times and bad, we have sustained a high level of attendance which is vital to our very existence. It is to YOU, our supporters, that I make this appeal, not only in the name of Arsenal, but for football in general.

In May, the most horrific sights ever to be witnessed at a place of sport, received worldwide media coverage and, of course, I refer to the final of the European Cup in Brussels.

The tragic loss of life left the world in shock and the sympathies of each and every sane thinking person are extended to those near and dear to the bereaved.

After the sickening scenes in Brussels, words will no longer do. Only deeds will provide the sincerity of purpose.

Government has since introduced further legislation that may go some way towards reducing the problem. It can only be totally cured by society itself and with your help and co-operation, it can be done. If the damage to the game is to be repaired, then it is for clubs such as ourselves – and that means you too – to grasp the initiative.

When a few mindless fans misbehave, then *all* football supporters become tarred with the same brush. Generalisation can often be unfair and in the case of almost all of our supporters, this is indeed so. Never has there been a more important time for Arsenal to take a lead. We have been first in many things in the past and as we start this centenary season afresh, let us ensure that we maintain a trouble-free stadium – a place where youngsters and families can come in safety.

Let us not hear the foul and abusive and, sometimes racist, chanting that is the hallmark of the sick in mind. Let us be proud of what we have and take pride in what we want Highbury to be once more – the 'Home of Football'.

Peter Hill-Wood, *AFC Programme*, 20.8.85

Do you know, I don't really remember the North Bank being trouble. I remember the Clock End more. Up there, they were good as gold, really. We'd have a laugh up the North Bank. The worst afternoon down here wasn't an Arsenal game. Everton played Southampton in a Cup-tie here and you've never seen so much gore. They had the Stanley knives out. Oh, my godfathers! There must have been 60 or 70 of them we treated and we patched them up, send them off for a stitch if they'd go or others would say: *Just patch it up for now, I must see the match.* I think there was a pitch invasion, too. They all come out the North Bank towards this end. That was the worst.

Ron Pilcher

The tenth FA Cup semi-final at Highbury on Saturday could be the last there. Thousands of supporters invaded the pitch, which is unprotected by high terrace fencing, after Everton's late winning goal and again when the match finished. There were 75 arrests.

Arthur McMullen, the FA vice-chairman, who was present, said there would be an FA inquiry into the incident by early June at the latest. 'We will have to ask if police were in sufficient numbers,' he said. 'We cannot and would not instruct Arsenal to erect fences. That is for them to decide. But we can consider whether Highbury should be allowed a future semi-final if there are no fences,' he said.

Ken Friar, the Arsenal secretary, said, 'No one said anything about fences last week. I expect no comeback.'

The Times, 16.4.84

Having supported Arsenal at home and away for several years, and seen many away games through fences like caged animals, we feel the need to express our anxiety. We were horrified to hear of the scenes that took place at the FA Cup semi-final. It now seems that the FA will ask the club to erect perimeter fences if we wish to host future semi-finals. Please do not.

We believe our supporters at Highbury can pride themselves on their behaviour and that we should not allow the mindlessness of certain away supporters to ruin our enjoyment. Surely the loss of revenue from a few games which do not involve Arsenal is a small price to pay to remain one of the most civilised clubs in the game?

Adam Rose/Malcolm Dick, *AFC Programme*, 7.5.84

A lot of people have a go at the Arsenal but they were the only directors who said: *We will not have barriers. We will not force our supporters to be like animals.* And they lost money from it. They wouldn't give them semi-finals. But they stood up for something. I love them for that. No barriers.

Richard Stubbs

Well you don't normally get problems within your own family, and the North Bank is part of the family of Arsenal isn't it? I'm not suggesting for one minute it's purely the visitors – if there is going to be any aggravation between Arsenal and the visitors then it won't be any one side causing it, we might provoke it, they might provoke it. But visitors, if they weren't here, then I don't think the North Bank's going to start fighting among each other. So bearing in mind the visitors are kept to one end then it could probably only happen down there. If they were moved to the North Bank it probably would happen down there.

Ken Friar

I think by and large the Arsenal North Bank was very well behaved. It rarely had a pitch invasion, the first major pitch invasion Arsenal weren't playing. I think things have improved a lot. I mean I give them credit, they haven't got any fences up, they have improved. Even when it was very bad there was not a lot of spillage on to the pitch. Remember, standing on the North Bank was one of the privileged positions of the Football League, you were never behind the barbed wire, you were never behind a fence.

Laurence Marks

'I'LL GO SOMEWHERE ELSE'

I moved to the Clock End. Derby games, all the Tottenham fans used to congregate in the corner of the North Bank. I don't know why it was like that, I don't know why in them days they didn't think of segregation. I remember once I was standing and I was looking at the Tottenham fans and looking at the Arsenal fans, and there was a gap. Even as a kid, I was going: *This is mad. They are going to be kicking the shit out of each other.* Then after a while, not that you ever got involved in fights, but, once they started the segregation, the away fans went in the Clock End, and all the 13-year-olds went to the Clock End because it was really cool, you know, just to be there. Not that you even went up to the fence or anything, just you were there, you know: *Who's having it?*

Mark Burdis

I stopped going when all the trouble started. My mate said: *I'm not going. It's getting too rough.* And I said: *Yeah. We can't run like we used to.* I always had it in my mind that there was a little crowd that used to go round all the football grounds and cause trouble. I just said to myself. *I'm too old for this lark.* The boys would come home and say: *Bit of trouble down there.* I get worried if they go and there's trouble.

Jack Hobb

What I thought about the North Bank, by the time we left it – asides from the fact it wasn't safe – were you actually going to leave there at twenty to five intact? – was you felt it's them and us now. I always felt, when I stood on the North Bank, those players could have been standing on the North Bank as well, if they weren't playing. I knew Charlie had. Then it got to the 70s, and it started getting to the point you were crammed into a shitty area, where there wasn't any difference if we got there an hour earlier, you couldn't get to the toilets even if you had wanted to go, if you were there with a woman or kids you had difficulty . . . with swearing, telling them to be quiet. It wasn't a nice place to be in and I thought to myself: *I'm not going to stop coming to the Arsenal but what I'll do, I'll go somewhere else.* That's what we did, we sat in the lower East Stand and then, of course, it became so expensive to stand on the North Bank it wasn't any bargain. I also think that the reason people stood on the North Bank was not only the atmosphere but because that's where you'd been put.

Laurence Marks

One suggested answer is to abolish terracing and make all-seat stadiums. Jimmy Hill tried that at Coventry but it failed. The relative affluence of the modern football fan – whether he is unemployed or not, it seems to me – has meant that many of them can afford to pay £5 or so for a stand ticket. Many of the incidents involving Chelsea fans in the 1984–85 season took place in the stands, not on the terraces.

Terry Neill, *Revelations of a Football Manager*

In 79, we became season-ticket holders and moved into the seats primarily to ensure Cup tickets. We'd got to three consecutive FA Cup finals and we wanted to avoid the scramble. One year my brother hadn't got a ticket and another year I had to pay over the top for one. I suppose we were mid-20s then. The atmosphere's not the same up there, it's not as committed. They're older, they're more impatient even though most of them have come from the North Bank at some point. You sort of grow up into it, I suppose.

Steve Kazmarek

This season, for the first time in the history of the club, we will have sold ground season-tickets. The number that we are selling corresponds with the number of ground tickets available should Arsenal participate in the FA Cup final. We have, therefore, guaranteed ground season-ticket holders the opportunity of purchasing an FA Cup final ground ticket, providing our allocation is not reduced by the FA.

AFC Programme, 2.9.80

Well, it came about because the allocation of Cup final tickets was a real problem, it's always been very small. Even when Wembley held 100,000, I think when I first came here we used to get 11,000 as a competitor, which was clearly not enough. We used to have a system whereby people stuck coupons on to a form collected from the programme. I remember seeing one with one gap, he'd got his 23 and there's one missing for his 24, and he wrote on it *went to Bar Mitzvah*. And there was another one with one missing and he said *see letter attached*. The letter attached said that on the way to the ground he had been stopped by police in a murder enquiry. He gave us all the details of the Detective Inspector's name, the station and the name of the murdered person! What we tried to do was issue enough ground season tickets to ensure that the number of season tickets that we had would meet the number of tickets that we got from Wembley. That's how the original idea started, to award loyalty by saying: *These guys are loyal to us, we'll be loyal to them.* But of course it's changed again now because of the reduction in Wembley's capacity.

Ken Friar

We felt that we wanted to make our young supporters more involved with the Club – and this was the best way to do it. When youngsters join Junior Gunners, we like to think they feel closer to the Club, and the players. We hope that youngsters will enjoy coming to Arsenal, and will remain Arsenal fans for the rest of their lives.

We want to get back to the days when dads and uncles came to matches with their youngsters – and there was a family atmosphere at grounds. We'd also like to be sure parents can let their youngsters come to football matches on their own, knowing they can watch the game in perfect safety; which is why we made a special enclosure for the Junior Gunners, in front of the West Stand.

Debbie Wakeford, *AFC Programme*, 10.9.83

Arsenal FC are now proud to announce their intention to launch 'the Junior Gunners', a new and exciting club for both boys and girls under the age of 16.

Full membership of the club costs £5 and each member will receive:

A membership card.

A membership certificate.

A silk scarf.

A sew-on patch.

A pen.

A metal badge.

A colour photograph of your favourite player.

A newsletter which is sent to you four times a year.

Reduced admission to First Division matches.

Free admission to all Football Combination and Youth matches played at Highbury.

Organised tours of the stadium.

A chance to lead out the first team before a first-team match at Highbury.

All souvenir items carry our distinctive Junior Gunners' emblem and are exclusive to Junior Gunners' members.

AFC Programme, 7.5.83

It's a natural progression. You start off as a kid, you stand with your mates in a group on the North Bank – or the Kop or the Stretford End or the Shelf or wherever. That's what you do. You get older and things change. You might sit a few times or you go and stand somewhere that's a little less boisterous. Then you get older, 50 or 60, you want to sit down. It's natural, isn't it?

Phillip Bloomfield

I used to go with my mates from school, you know, fourth year, fifth year, sixth form. Coming from Finchley there was a lot of us supported Arsenal. Half a dozen of us would go down the Arsenal. I used to live in North Finchley and my mates used to live in East Finchley. We used to catch the bus. I mean, I didn't have any money – I was only at school – so I couldn't afford to get on and off the bus. This was years before travel cards were invented. I used to catch the bus and they'd be waiting at the stop and, so they knew which bus to get on, I had to wave my scarf out the window. If they didn't see a scarf waving out the window they were to let that bus go and wait for the next one. It did actually work. I still see them. I still play football with them, but they don't come to the Arsenal. Suburbia I suppose isn't it? I mean a lot of people my age, I suppose, stop going to football when they get married or have a family. That's the standard thing.

Al Fresco

The last eight years or so, I've been standing on the North Bank in the corner. Down in the Avenell Road corner. Comfortable. Friendly and family. Lots of kids. What made me go back up there was the hooliganism down the Clock End. The match that really did it, I was with my son. Manchester United. They were all over the terracing. I hardly saw any of the match because of all the trouble. You'd suddenly be pushed and shoved and you didn't know why. People would be running to get away and the holes would develop in the terraces. Fists would be flying. A lot of it was they'd be full of drink. I just said: *This is it. I'm not standing here anymore. I'm going down the North Bank.* This would be about 1985. I got to know a few people down there. Kids were starting to come back there. There was no pushing and shoving. We enjoyed all the noise of the North Bank, the songs and the banter. Alright, you got the bad language but hardly any trouble – just once against Spurs a couple of years ago – and families started coming, putting their kids on the barriers. I met the crowd I go with now and five of us have got bonds.

Frank Hummell

CHAPTER SEVEN

'Born is the King of Highbury'

THE NORTH BANK AND ITS HEROES

The Laundry End, the North Terrace and the North Bank all had their heroes. Nippers waited outside the Main Entrance for hours to catch a glimpse of Alex James or Dennis Compton, much as kids do today in the hope of getting an autograph from Paul Merson or Anders Limpar. Every player in a red shirt is our representative: the active agent of the will of the thousands on the terraces. On the players' shoulders rest all our hopes and fears come Saturday afternoon. It's a grave responsibility! And the vast majority, of course, live up more or less to our expectations. But heroic status has been reserved for those few who, for whatever reason, delighted or inspired – as well as satisfied – those that passed through the turnstiles every other week. While each individual spectator has his or her own favourites, the heroes have managed to touch us thousands at a time: Drake, Mercer, Brady, O'Leary. They are rare and absolutely essential.

While much of what makes heroes heroes has remained the same, the quality of the terrace fans' relations with those heroes has changed in many ways. In the old days, the little 'uns could tag along with wee Alex to his confectioner's shop at the top of St Thomas Road, their dads could play dominos with 'Big' Les Compton at his pub in Hanley Road, their mums might ride home on the Tube with Joe Baker. In the early 1990s, you'll be lucky to catch sight of one of today's stars once they've slipped away to the Home Counties in the Merc. Although they're as patient and good natured with authograph hunters at the gates as their predecessors were, the new generation live in a very different world from that lived in by the thousands who cheered them every weekend from the North Bank.

The maximum wage – an inaccurate and unjust reflection of the players' contribution to the balance sheet – served to keep the Laundry End's heroes within reach. With earnings perhaps twice or three times as high as the average spectators', the pre-60s' footballer's life was comfortable, though not extravagant – and only for as long as he could kick a ball for money. Any player with sense sorted out a 'day job' to help secure his future. Nobody, until the market found a level it would bear well after the abolition of the maximum wage in 1961, could get rich by playing football. By the late 60s, however, players at top clubs were at least able to support lifestyles which had started to set them apart from the fans on the terrace.

Charlie George, probably the North Bank's greatest-ever hero, is a very interesting example of this change in relations. He stands at the end of one era, in many respects, and on the doorstep of the next. None of the Double side became wealthy as a result of their endeavour. Charlie least of all: as a youngster, he was on the bottom rung of Arsenal's service-related bonus ladder. Nonetheless, top players already seemed a breed sufficiently apart for the ordinariness of George's Islington upbringing to be part of his appeal to the fans on the North Bank. This feeling of Charlie as 'one of the boys' would simply not have been relevant, say, to Hoxton-bred Joe Wade, 20 years previously. (Wade, in fact, made good in his own way and married a director's daughter. George, ever the romantic, married his childhood sweetheart.) Part of what made Charlie so important to the North Bank was the feeling that, in terms of the life you lived, you could be him and he could be you. There were obviously other aspects of this remarkable young footballer's demeanour, not least his playing style, to compound his enormous appeal but his background as a local boy was the cornerstone of his unique relationship with The End.

The teenagers who sang: *Born is the king of Highbury* about the young George were responsible for another change of values that, 20 years on, would have important implications for the game. Supporters of older generations had felt their attachment to be to the Club and to the idea of Arsenal. The 'fashion' of football in the 60s, however, and the 'pop star' mantle of George Best which Charlie – among others – took on, gave the North Bank's new heroes a stature in their own right, distinct from and occasionally as opposed to the Club, which the older fans were quick to recognise as something new. With agents still a phenomenon of the distant future, players weren't yet in a position to exploit this new status in any meaningful way. When Charlie George retired, having left Highbury for Derby, Southampton and Hong Kong, he took on a pub in the New Forest. But the million-pound transfer, and all that followed, was just around the corner. Once Trevor Francis's sale to Forest had broken that barrier, the steady rise in incomes – for top-flight professionals at least – became a breathtaking charge. With percentages of transfers, signing-on fees and a wage to match, it became possible during the 80s for players to earn enough in a career to be able to live off the game forever. With the right advice, it could be argued, Charlie George would have retired a millionaire today. And, although the North Bank would still have loved him, they might not have been able to relish in the same way that sense of Charlie as one of their own.

Liam Brady, Arsenal's greatest post-war talent, was one of a new generation able to take advantage of the fresh horizons opening up to players of the modern era. He remains one of the few unqualified success stories in the now long-running adventure saga of the English Club Footballer Abroad. Before moving to Italy, of course, Brady had held the North Bank – and the rest of Highbury, too – in the palm of his hand. He personified all the virtues by which every Arsenal crowd has defined its heroes.

Firstly, Brady was a product of the Club's youth system. It is ironic that Arsenal's least successful period, the late 50s and early 60s under George Swindin and then Billy Wright, should have proved to have been the seedbed for all the glory that has followed. In turning round a situation in which the Club had traditionally bought its greatest talents, the two managers — Wright especially — suffered endless heartache at the time. Thirty years on, they deserve the credit for having been the architects of Arsenal's future. The scouting and youth-development schemes they established, so ably developed since by those who followed them, bore fruit a decade later with a Double side built around eight home-grown players. While it had taken the crowd a decade to come to terms with this new approach, the continuing success of the youth policy has now become a source of great pride for supporters and the Club alike. Restless at first during the 60s, frustrated by the success of expensive stars at other clubs while Arsenal's youngsters struggled, the North Bank of recent years was happy to wait patiently as the next crop of young talent was prepared at London Colney.

Liam Brady was also as exciting a ball-player as Highbury had seen since Alex James. His flair for the unexpected, the gift of beating men with the same facility as he could pass short or long, meant Brady could be relied on to provide that something extra: the single moment of skill that made an afternoon memorable and worthwhile. Apart from anything else, the Irishman was idolised as a reminder that football was a *beautiful* game.

The importance of the flair players on the North Bank cannot be over-estimated. In recent times, especially, Arsenal's reputation has been one for hard work and indomitable team spirit. Even though evidence of effort is looked for, too, in the supporters' assessment of every Arsenal player, the team's reputation has only served to sharpen the terrace's hunger for the talents of a Marinello, a Petrovic, a Nicholas, or a Limpar. There is a traditional conflict of values at the Club, reflected on the North Bank too, when faced with the problem of accommodating precocious individual talent in a team pattern built around the virtue of graft. Of course, effort is a third quality in players that endears them to the crowd. The North Bank recognised, in the likes of Wilf Copping, Leslie Compton, Frank McLintock and, more recently, Tony Adams, an absolute commitment to the Arsenal cause which mirrored the commitment of the supporters themselves. But, confronted with the flair versus graft paradox, the North Bank's attitude has often been in conflict with the policy of the Arsenal management. The terrace fan will always be willing to give the gifted individual the benefit of the doubt, in return for the occasional moment of illumination during the course of a grey afternoon. Inevitably, the management's sense of priority will always favour the value of hard work. Perhaps Liam Brady's stature, both on the North Bank and in the dressing-room, lay in his capacity to resolve the contradiction. 'Chippy' was never either lazy or dull.

Part of the challenge faced by every player at a well-supported club is that of being able to sustain a degree of quiet, inner concentration in the glare of public and very outspoken scrutiny. Most successful pros can describe the process of getting used to playing in front of a big home crowd. For many, the roars of the North Bank are an important motivating factor. For all, the sense of a crowd being 'on your side' is of real benefit. The hero's 'grave responsibility' brings with it the self-belief that the home end's approval can inspire. Just how important that approval is may be difficult to define once the approval has been earned. A more clear-cut impression of its significance is got by examining the impact a hostile crowd can have on a player on the receiving end of 'stick'. Perhaps it is in the nature of a team game, watched by thousands of anxious spectators, that the shortcomings of the whole will be simplified – mythologised – into the perceived failings of a single individual. Alongside the history of heroes from Jock Rutherford down to Ian Wright runs a less glorious theme: the sad story of the talents – Horace Cope, Bryn Jones, Don Roper, Jon Sammels and the rest – who, under the East Stand's eyes and in the North Bank's hearts, could never get it right.

'ONE OF US'

For the teenagers, the spirit of the new Arsenal is Charlie George – long-haired, loping, impertinent and often brilliant.

In Islington, he is the fourth-form pin-up. They cut his pictures out of magazines to stick on bedroom walls.

There are *I love Charlie* badges, and it is said he has had more to do with ending the Skinhead cult than any other sociological factor. (See plate 26.)

The Sun, 5.5.71

For me, Charlie was one of us. He acknowledged we were there and that was enough. I mean I remember one game when he completely mishit a shot and as he picked himself up he winked at us as if to say: *I missed. I'm a prat.* He recognised we were there. We were up on the North Bank, he was out on the pitch but, basically, he was playing for us. I met him once on the train and got his autograph. I mean, I was saying to you about hippies on the North Bank. Well, Charlie was the archetypal hippie, hair down to his shoulders – I suppose he made the rest of us acceptable! There was no question of him being worried about being with the public, with fans. He might tell people to piss off but he was one of us. I remember him headbutting Keegan once and looking round at the North Bank as if to say: *Well, no one saw, did they?*

John James

I know that when Charlie George was going there, he felt a good time on the North Bank was actually getting into a fight. I remember once at a Peterborough Cup game, away, he went into a bakers and stole a tray full of cream buns. He had a great time throwing them at people.

Maurice Gran

I just think Charlie George, I don't think anyone will ever take his place. There's a special relationship he had because he'd actually been up here and everyone thought: *He might have been standing next to me a couple of years ago.* Bollocks, I know. The fact is he would have stopped going up there when he started playing for the Youth Team. But it was a nice thought.

Mick Essen

Early 60s I used to go over there. I must have been about 12. My brother-in-law took me first, there was a group of them used to stand on the Clock End. Well, you're either Spurs or Arsenal if you live in this area. Then as I got a bit older, I weaned my way up on the North Bank. When you were younger you'd stand in the Schoolboys', as it was then, or on the South Bank because it wasn't so rough. You know, as you 'graduate' you want to stand on the North Bank.

The players whose names we used to chant: George Eastham I thought was a fantastic player, Joe Baker, Alan Skirton, and a player I used to like called Joe Haverty, a little left-winger, Irishman, he used to knock the ball and skip over the tackles.

As you grow up, you're playing, you go to secondary school, play for the district and read your write-ups in the *Islington Gazette* – I don't think you ever realise one day you're going to be playing actually for Arsenal. When I achieved it, it was something you just couldn't put into words. When I was 13, George Male was the scout then and he asked me to go and train. I think it was Mondays and Thursdays, a lot of kids from different areas, John Barnwell used to train the kids when I was there, with Dennis Evans and Alex Forbes. Unfortunately, at school, when I was about 15, they asked me to leave Holloway, I was slung out or whatever you want to call it, and I had to go to another school, Hugh Myddleton in Clerkenwell. I always remember the careers officer coming round and asking you what you want to do and I just said: *It's no good looking at me – I'm going to Arsenal.* Once I'd trained over there, that's what I was going to do. Once I'd set my mind on it, that was it.

I joined them in 66. At 17 we used to play Youth Team games on the pitch – that was a buzz in itself. But I was never in awe of it or anything. But I mean, Arsenal, to me, is a football club on its own – *the* Arsenal – and if you've watched them from the terraces and then you're lucky enough to pull on the shirt – well, the adrenalian when you step over that line and there's 17,000 on the North Bank and they're chanting your name. If you don't get a buzz from that there's something wrong with you. I played in a lot of great stadiums but playing at home in a big game, and supporters chanting your name, there's nothing like that. And I was fortunate, I suppose, because in a lot of their eyes I couldn't do anything wrong – that stood me in good stead. Other people might say: *Oh, he's a right so and so.* But with the North Bank I could do no wrong.

I always got a tremendous amount of pleasure out of the sort of affection, the rapport, you build up, I suppose, through standing on the North Bank as a kid and knowing the majority of my pals were still standing there when I was playing. It's hard to describe the feeling you get when people are chanting your name.

When I went to Derby, I can remember playing up there for Arsenal, giving the V-sign to them, total, absolute abuse – we drew 2–2, I scored both goals. I gave them total abuse but when I signed up I just built up a rapport straight away with their fans as well. Always had a laugh and a joke, if you scored a goal showed the people on the terraces who are paying your wages a bit of affection. I mean people who score goals and run straight back to the halfway line they might as well be fucking dead! I think you've got to give something back to the people on the terraces. If I scored at the North Bank I knew what I was going to do – turn round and run to them.

First time I came back to Highbury with Derby, we'd just been knocked out of the European Cup – scored four goals against Real Madrid and still lost! – and I knew all my mates were all Arsenal and my family were there. This bloke come running out of the North Bank with a bouquet of flowers and I thought: *Fucking hell!* You get a lump in your throat. That's appreciation for you. I still got a chant off the Arsenal supporters. That was something else.

From when I used to play and the people before me, the money just seems to have gone sky high. They've got to get money into the Club and charge supporters to pay for the players' wages. It's always nice to earn a few quid. Good luck to them. I don't begrudge anyone earning good money. But it has escalated out of all proportion. I wonder whether it's good for the game – a lot of clubs could go by the wayside.

I go over the Arsenal now and I like to see players with a bit of flair. Arsenal's my first love. It'll always be my love. I'm just an Arsenal supporter, basically. When I was at Derby, I'd always ask how the Arsenal got on. I fell out with the manager at Arsenal and when they had a bad time, after I'd left I'd think: *Good! Good!* But after a while that eases and you want them to do well. Once you've been an Arsenal player, you're an Arsenal man. And the supporters are the same. You walk in there and the hairs prick up on the back of your neck. Arsenal, it's an institution. So I sit in my seat now and when Arsenal score, I'm up on my feet, thinking: *Lovely!* You want them to win.

Charlie George

The greatest goal at Highbury I saw was scored by Charlie George against Newcastle during the Double year. It was nil–nil with about 20 minutes to go. The stern Newcastle defence was not giving much away when Charlie George collected the ball outside the area. He rifled in a shot which bounced back off a defender's leg, he collected the rebound, ran past the defenders and hit a screamer which gave McFaul no chance. A marvellous goal from a very talented player.

Colin Wood, *AFC Programme*, 1.1.74

Probably one of the most important goals I scored was against Newcastle. We weren't playing particularly well and we only won 1–0. I played a one-two off a defender and hit it into the corner. Well, the atmosphere, we hadn't played well but we needed the win and I've gone to the crowd at the North Bank, at the same time as being pleased, I was drained. We knew we needed that win.

Charlie George

I tell you, the great appeal of going to football is going up those stairs and seeing the pitch. There doesn't have to be anyone on it, just the pitch, and you thought: *I'd like to play on that.* I thought: *That's what I want to do.* A story I often tell and I'm sure he's told you himself, when we were at school, Charlie George was always getting thrown out of class and stuck in the corridor. We always used to stand round in the playground talking about our ambitions and he said his ambition was to play for Arsenal and score the winning goal in a Cup final that is one of the thousand best. And he did it. He's one in a thousand people who scored one of the best goals, and he's done it and that was the undoing of him. It should have happened to him later.

He did it in his first full season at Arsenal, I mean, you've scored the winning Cup final goal that won you the Double and you're the local boy. You're the boy who five seasons earlier was standing on the North Bank. That's scary.

Maurice Gran

The players would come out looking like: *I've got an Arsenal shirt on.* And when we were playing our Sunday football with the Boys Brigade or the Scouts, in our own minds – one day – we'll have that shirt on.

Frank Martin

In those pre-television days of the late 20s and early 1930s we gazed with the same starry-eyed wonder at the great men of the day.

I can remember on one occasion when Eddie Hapgood stooped down to gather a ball out of the guttering at the Avenell Road end at Highbury, how I put my hand forward to touch his shirt. Back with my gang after the weekend I related my experience. They all gathered round to touch my hand where it made contact with Eddie and, of course, for the next week or so I always had to play left-back. (See plate 1.)

Doug Wilson, *GunFlash*, 1956

Oh, Jock Rutherford. He had a shop down here when he was playing and then he had an off-licence when he packed up. But he could, well, he was a great big tall, gangling bloke and he'd be coming down the wing – he'd flick up the ball and knock it past the full-back with his heel and then run round the bloke. And talk about a swerve on the ball – this wasn't with the beach balls they've got now, no, a great, heavy leather ball – he'd take a corner on the left with his right foot and the ball would curl round the penalty spot in an arc. And he could do the same thing from the right with his left foot.

Ron Pottage

Our great victory, therefore, was all the more welcome and inspiring and I am certain that our supporters would be delighted to see Dr Paterson again wearing the red jersey. It was typical of this great little sportsman that he should come to the rescue of his old club in the hour of need and I cannot write too highly of his splendid action. Dr 'Pat' had not played serious football for some considerable time, and it was only to be expected that the great crowd of 50,000 people should give him a rousing and encouraging welcome. And right well he played. It was obvious that he was not in perfect physical condition but he wisely avoided too much scampering about and his centres nearly always reached the desired spot. There was all the old evidence of the brain aiding the boot and the crowd roared its delight once when the Doctor literally sent the opposing half-back running the wrong way by a clever feint and rapid turn goalwards. It was the touch of the old master and I am only voicing the general opinion when I say that regret is general at the enforced absence from the game of such a brilliant player.

AFC Programme, 20.2.26

I'll tell you one now. Alex James. The crowd just loved him. He was a marvel. He'd just move his foot and opposing players would go by him. It was fantastic, the things he did. And his old long shorts. Thirty, 40-yard passes through to Joe Hulme. Joe Hulme was the fastest thing on two legs then. Down the wing he'd go. Straight across. Bastin. Wallop. They wouldn't chant. Just everybody saying: *Go on Alex, Go on Alex.*

Tom Jales

Alex James, in my time, was a legend – you know, how he could send defenders the wrong way. We always had our heroes. I used to keep pictures and that. And Wilf Copping. I had a picture of the seven Arsenal players who played for England against Italy at Highbury. That was a bruising game. But Wilf Copping, he was a tough man, never used to shave before a match and all this, and they said he was the only one who really enjoyed that game. He was a real tough character – and he was a favourite because of that.

George Williams

Oh, Joe Hulme. He could go. He was a flyer. Never kicked a football till he was 18 years old. Rugby and running before that! He was so quick off the mark that they'd all stand there waiting for this offside lark, made it easy for him. *Whoof!* He'd be gone past the half-back, the back and right to the byline, pull it back and there was Bastin, he'd be waiting on that far corner of the penalty area and Joe'd pull them right back away from the goalkeeper. Bastin'd run in, either foot, *wallop!* Marvellous. (See plate 9.)

Ron Pottage

Ted Drake was my hero when I was a boy. Centre-forward, foot or head, he didn't mind, as long as he scored goals. I've seen him with plasters all over his head but he played on. All my mates, when we were young, Ted Drake was our man. And Cliff Bastin. He was clever. He was clever with his feet, Boy Bastin.

Jack Hobb

Dennis Compton was the player with real charisma. To give you an idea of his drawing power: when he made his first appearance for Arsenal in 1947 after his knee operation, we played Chelsea reserves and there were 29,000 people turned up for that game. He had something, it was intangible – you knew something was going to happen. They used to call him the Brylcreem Boy because he used to advertise Brylcreem – he put bums on seats as the expression goes. He was probably the first football 'superstar' in this country. And the flying winger, the most exasperating player, but what a crowd-pleaser: Ian McPherson. Flight Lieutenant Ian McPherson. I can remember him one game against Huddersfield in 1947–48 when we won the Championship. He was a double DFC. He started at one end of the field, went through the whole Huddersfield team, got in front of the goal and scooped the ball over the bar! It was more difficult to miss than score. But that was him.

Geoff Gilbert

That first season after the war we all thought we were going to go down. A lot of the old team were past it, some of them hadn't come back. We bought in Ronnie Rooke and Joe Mercer who were both getting on themselves but they saved us, really. We were bottom when they came and we finished up a creditable 13th. We had this winger, Dr O'Flanagan, and I remember one goal he scored – I've read about it since and it's been a bit exaggerated – it was a free kick just outside the box. He picked the ball up, cleaned it all off on his jersey and whacked it into the top corner. Won us the match.

Frank Hummell

Which Arsenal player do you remember most? – the answer would have to be Joe Mercer. Joe would be the first to admit that he was not built with an athlete specifically in mind, his legs in particular, but what a player, and what a captain. If we were a goal down, you didn't have to ask who the captain was. Joe, a great man, and a great humorist off the field, was hard on it; a good leader has to be. I remember Cliff Holton telling me of the first game he played for Arsenal, away from home; he missed a possible scoring chance (only a half-chance, Cliff swears), and a few seconds later Joe ran alongside him and said quietly: *If that's the best you can do, I'll have to come up and have a go myself.*

AFC Programme, 8.1.74

A very personal memory is seeing Ian Ure run out in his first Arsenal appearance. I had gone to see Arsenal play Dundee in a friendly – we had no fixture that day, due to yet another early FA Cup exit. I had my arm in a sling due to a broken wrist but Ian Ure took my autograph book through the team coach window after the game and collected ALL the Dundee players' autographs. They were Scottish Champions at that time. I wrote to thank him, and we became pen pals. He sent me a couple of programmes etc. He was the first real footballer I 'knew', so when Arsenal signed him it was a dream come true for me.

I met him again years later when I went to Hennef Sports School to see Arsenal training while on a pre-season tour of Germany. I met all the other players of course (August 68) and enjoyed their company for a couple of days. So when we won the Double a short while later I was extra delighted as I'd met all the players who made up the team. Except for Ian of course – who sadly left just before the wheel of fortune turned.

Steve Thomas

It's always been a different thing for Arsenal fans. I mean, the other night I was at a book launch thing at Waterstone's with Eamon Dunphy and he gave this extravagantly emotional performance – he burst into tears in the middle of it – about the death of football, about George Best and how that age is dead. And I had to get up and I said: *Well, all that's a bit beyond me because I've been watching Arsenal for 25 years and while you were watching Best and Charlton and Law, I was watching Peter Storey and Ian Ure.* I mean, in 1968 my hero was Bobby Gould!

Nick Hornby

Charlie George had it, that identification thing. Prior to him I don't think there was – there were good players but there wasn't an identification. Apart from Charlie George there wasn't with the Double side, there wasn't that identification. I was thinking of Baker, I was thinking of Eastham, they were probably the players of that era, the 60s, but they never really generated that absolute devotion.

John Platt

They've had a thing with their goalies – they did with George Swindin, Jack Kelsey. And after Jack, I guess I was the next one they had a close feeling for. Then Pat, they just thought it was wonderful that they could rub Tottenham's nose in it, you know. And then John Lukic became a folk hero, really.

Bob Wilson

Before Wilson, after Kelsey, we had McKechnie, McLelland, Burns, Furnell – put all four of them together and you wouldn't end up with a goalkeeper. But that McKechnie, I'm not being hard on him but he was a lump – he got a lot of stick. Even Wilson when he first come in got stick. I don't know what it was with keepers up there, whether they were always looking at Kelsey. But Wilson won them over eventually. I think that was because of his bravery rather than anything else. He used to show that he was committed and that drew them round in the end.

Laird Budge

Goalkeepers are the closest to the fans and they're often the difference between winning and losing. It's a shame, really, that Arsenal have never really had any 'characters' as goalkeepers. I'm not saying they're not nice blokes, and you don't really want the kind of 'character' who comes out flapping at crosses. I do remember one night when Bob Wilson and Bob MacNab had a flaming argument. I mean Bob Wilson comes across as being quite a middle-class type of person, certainly not your f-ing and blinding type. They had a flaming argument over nothing and the whole ground went quiet – you could hear it all from the back of the North Bank. The last two people you'd expect to be arguing like that!

Andrew Allerton

Bob Wilson retired in 74. I remember that it was a very emotional night against QPR. It was a Monday night, Liam Brady come on as substitute and he got an equaliser. I can remember Wilson led the team out, although he wasn't the captain. The crowd was singing his name throughout the game, they were sorry to lose him.

Jim Smith

I really couldn't think of moving on. They'd started to break up the Double team, there were rumours that they were going to buy Phil Parkes or whatever. I didn't ever want to hear people saying: *Oh, he used to be a good goalkeeper.* When I packed in on 30 April 1974, my greatest reward was – we were playing QPR, there was nothing on it, crowds had dropped off to 30–32,000 – that for my last game, 40-something thousand came. In my opinion, they came because they knew it was my last game. That's a real respect, no amount of money could buy you that sort of thing.

Bob Wilson

I look forward to running towards the North Bank end today because it will bring back so many wonderful memories of my four very happy years with Arsenal. I believe no ex-Arsenal player ever completely shakes off the atmosphere of the place. I believe I did the business during my four years here. I missed only one game in that time and established what I can only describe as an unforgettable relationship with the fans. It was difficult to play badly at home because I knew the fans were always behind me. And that is one hell of a good feeling for any footballer.

I remember one nightmare match when I handed West Bromwich Albion their winner through a terrible blunder. Arsenal were in the middle of their worst run of defeats – seven in a row. Malcolm Macdonald headed us in front after ten minutes but David Cross equalised before half time. In the second half I chased a ball out towards the corner flag, won it but then tried to pass the ball upfield instead of dribbling to the safety of my area. The ball went straight to Cross who scored again. I did not know where to look. But to my amazement the fans started singing: *Don't worry Jimmy.* I have never known anything like it. They could have hung me out to dry for such a boob.

Jimmy Rimmer, *AFC Programme*, 8.3.77

We were having this terrible run but went 1–0 up against West Brom, who had a really poor side, and we thought: *At least we'll win this.* Then they equalised and we thought: *At least we'll get a point.* And then Rimmer just sort of palmed the ball out to Regis who passed to Tony Brown who scored. We just couldn't believe it and the North Bank actually turned on Rimmer. That's the first time I can remember the crowd turning on the keeper.

Andrew Allerton

But we had a lot of characters over at Arsenal, we had Terry Mancini, for what he was worth. I can remember him scoring against Wolves one night, it was pouring, there was about 18,000 there and he scored his one and only goal at the Clock End, it was a header from the corner. He ran all the way up the corner flag, done a jig around the corner flag and ran almost all the way up to the North Bank. They took to him, they knew he was lacking skill but they took to him.

Jim Smith

When they used to come down to take a corner kick, George Armstrong say, I could shout out to them, shout their name and they'd look up. Now, in a seat, nobody knows you. You're not there any more. You're just another chair.

Alex Froso

Alan Ball used to always have a thing, he'd stand and warm up in that bottom right-hand corner, and he'd talk to the people who were in that area all the time and he got a rapport with them people. And that don't take nothing does it?

Laird Budge

I saw many great players from my corner of the North Bank. But the greatest of them all was Liam Brady. He had something special. To me, when he had the ball at his feet it was like somebody playing a violin. One of my customers asked me once, a lady customer: *Why do you like football so much?* I told her that, for me, watching Brady with the ball at his feet was like me having a woman in bed. When he left, I couldn't understand why the Club didn't give him what he wanted. But we don't run the Club. The big people make the decisions and we are the followers, we have to follow them. But it was a disappointment. (See plate 22.)

Alex Froso

I never went out of my way to become popular by my actions, other than playing. That's all changed now. Players now will stand there and applaud the North Bank after a game. When I was playing, I think they knew – even though I didn't go out of my way – there was a respect there because they were really behind me and appreciated me.

Liam Brady

I never had any idols as a child, pop stars or anything like that, but my main man was Frank Stapleton. I was totally smitten. I only kept the programmes that had pictures of Frank Stapleton in. When he went to Man United, it was a bit of a problem because I decided I was going to be a Man United fan. Then I realised I really couldn't be. I realised that it wasn't really Frank Stapleton. It was just his face I particularly liked in the team. Really, what it was was Arsenal.

Emma Young

Players are aware of who the favourites are, of who the fans really like. Personally, as long as the crowd are on my side I don't care. I know there'll be players who are more popular with the crowd than others. That's a natural thing. It doesn't affect me if the crowd likes Charlie Nicholas more than it likes me! As long as they like me as well! It's interesting, if the crowd's going through the players, chanting their names, the players do listen out for their names, whatever they might say! It's natural.

Paul Davis

'YOU WANT SOMETHING TO TAKE HOME'

It's the atmosphere, isn't it? When a ground's full, it's electric, your performance is better. The adrenalin flows.

Liam Brady

Getting the crowd behind you is a very big bonus, I think. Well it's a known fact. They're going to help you. Everything you do's going to be right! You're not going to tell me that a player can't hear that.

Guy Thomson

So now I know what those fellows are feeling as they run out on to the pitch. And on each occasion I relive them again. What are the feelings? The first is pride. The Arsenal is a club apart. It is the one which every other wants to beat and the one to which all players would like to belong. It is an honour to wear the red shirt. The second feeling is responsibility. The club has set a high standard of play and behaviour and it is up to every man to maintain it. The third is the thrill of playing on one of the Meccas of soccer and on a ground where everything humanly possible is done to achieve perfect conditions. And the fourth is comradeship with the fans. They say that the Arsenal has a cosmopolitan crowd. Nonsense. It has the most fervid supporters in soccer, as jealous of the Club's reputation as anyone. A player cannot help giving of his best with that sort of backing.

Bernard Joy, *GunFlash* 6, February 1950

When you're playing towards the North Bank, it gives you such a fillip. But it's a pressure, too. Think how nervous we felt going out in front of 60,000 people every week. I used to be a bag of nerves in the dressing-room. If things weren't right I'd lose my temper. Joe Mercer used to vomit. One or two, no names, used to have a smoke in the toilet. And I was one of them!

Dennis Evans

Talking of memories, it probably sounds strange that one which gives me as much pleasure as almost any other should involve the moment that my playing career ended. There I was . . . being stretchered off the Highbury turf with a broken leg one April afternoon in 1955. At the ripe old age of 39, I knew that it was all over, I would never be able to come back. And yet, as I lay there, knowing that I was no longer going to be able to play the game I loved, the marvellous ovation I was given by the crowd so moved me that I forgot the pain and felt only happiness. I always got on well with the fans and as the cheering echoed around the stadium I even managed a smile and a wave as I was carried off. It was a great moment for me.

Joe Mercer, *AFC Programme*, 26.12.74

You only hear the crowd roar if you're not involved in that part of the game – if you're a left-back and we're attacking down our right wing, down by the corner flag, yes, I can hear the crowd then. Or if you do something and it's finished, like you've had a shot at goal. But I'd never hear the crowd if we were defending.

Dennis Evans

You come up playing for the youths and the reserves, in front of small crowds and then start playing for the first team with 60,000 people. That becomes like a drug. You don't want to play in front of fewer than that. The energy that comes from the amount of people who are there. The buzz, the noise – you go back to playing a reserve game, and you can hear what people are saying, the crowd becomes individuals. There is no feeling like playing in front of a big crowd. That is something I'll always remember and always miss, I think. The energy, the adrenalin. I never needed to be geed up to play then. I would play better in the big games, with the big crowds. To run out in front of 60,000 people, the majority of them shouting for you – some people can freeze on that, but it brought out the best in me. You can forget most of the games but you never forget that feeling. And the North Bank was where a lot of that was generated because while I was playing in the 60s the crowd became more competitive and that was the side the noise came from.

David Court

The thing about the North Bank from my point of view was, well, a relationship is the only thing you can describe it as. I arrived at Arsenal in 1962 as the school-teacher and the amateur. Ian McKechnie dropped out of the side and I had six games. I did OK but they bought Jim Furnell. They persisted with 'Fingers' Furnell and there was I, five years later, still a reserve player. I think the management and the crowd thought I was part of the furniture. People knew I had a style – this head-first crazy style – I don't think they thought though, that it was going to be good enough for the First Division. So it was difficult when I first came in for Jim Furnell, after he made a complete muck-up in a Cup-tie against Birmingham and I came in for the replay. I did OK but it was very hit and miss, I could sense the crowd wasn't really on my side, but then I was in a losing side. It all changed very quickly at the beginning of the next season, when I started my solid run. We started at Tottenham and won, and we were top after seven or eight games, 68–69. A relationship got established very quickly. My emergence from a confidence point of view, I would say the North Bank played almost as big a part in that as the coaching staff. I mean, you expect your friends and family to be loyal but you know the guy who pays his money every week and sees you every week is really the ultimate test. I suppose because of the Loughborough PE background, I used to try and analyse what you have to do to establish yourself. I remember distinctly playing against West Ham one day, I think we drew 3–3 at Highbury and, looking at the programme afterwards, I saw the name Wilson in goal for Arsenal and I looked at the other side and saw Hurst, Peters, Moore. I remember sitting in the dressing-room and thinking: *I played better than any of them and they won the World Cup.* That was overcoming a real psychological barrier as a player. The other real psychological barrier for a player is that affinity with the crowd where you know – as a goalkeeper, consistency is the ultimate aim – you know that the guy who pays his own two pennyworth every Saturday, when you have your moment of a catastrophe (and you know you're going to make an error at some point!) you need him to turn to his mate and say: *Bugger me! I never saw him do that before.* I soon had a sense of that, that they were with you, and then it became more personal than that. I used to do little things, rolling my sleeves up, spitting on my hands, to gee myself up and I had a style of play. It's important to have a style if you're to build a relationship with the crowd. It might not be a beautiful footballing touch – in my case it wasn't a goalkeeping style like Pat Jennings or Jack Kelsey, it was a 100 per cent committed crazy style – but with me they knew if it was one-against-one or the ball bounced between two people, head-first I was in there. And they loved that. Once I'd established myself, I'd come out and turn right and almost as soon as I hit daylight they'd be chanting my name. I would sometimes wait halfway before I saluted them – it's good to hear – don't rush it, milk it! At first I was shocked to hear it and then I realised they were going to do it for me every time. There was a joy in the security of knowing – they're the first to know if a player's had a game below par – even if I had an off day, losing to Stoke 5–0 as we did in the Double year, at the next game they'd be there chanting your name, probably even louder than if you'd won the week before. It was strange, really, that I had this thing with the North Bank. I mean my background was so different to the majority of footballers. That was the other joy for me. My dad was Borough Engineer of Chesterfield, I grew up in this big house and turned up at Highbury in my college scarf and duffel coat and here I was with a relationship with a crowd that made me feel like I was one of them.

Bob Wilson

Some days when the crowd got behind you, you could reach out and touch it. It felt like nothing could stop you. The adrenalin and the power of the crowd does something to the spirit. It's a bit ethereal I think. The crowd don't initiate it, but if they sense the team believing in itself, they pick that up and it becomes a whole. In that respect, they become a part of the team. I always found when I scored a goal, there was a split second when you're almost anticipating the cheers of the crowd. That's like the full stop. In a way, it's as if the crowd's exhilaration is more spontaneous than that of the players. And I think the supporters' feelings when a goal goes in are as intense as that of the player who's scored it.

David Court

Ian Wright's got it. I mean he goes into the crowd when he scores and he's celebrating as much as you're celebrating.

Laird Budge

When you score, especially if it's your favourite player, you feel so happy for him. It just sort of bursts out of you. You sort of let it all go.

Julie Wheeler

There's a terror that you'll make a mistake, a silly mistake like everyone does, a mishit or you clear air, there's that tension. But if you get a good touch early on, the crowd responds to you. The crowd lifts you. You really feel about nine foot tall if something goes right and they clap you. You get a response and suddenly you feel like you can do anything.

Charlie Nicholas

Alex James. I used to stand outside the dressing-room till he came out. My cousin and I would stand there and would not move. He always used to walk right up to Finsbury Park – he had a confectioners' shop up there – we'd walk up with him, chatting away. He was always last out!

Rose Jales

They pester the players, annoy the police, drive the commissionaires to despair and obstruct the public. In comment they are nothing if not outspoken, I have heard myself referred to as 'Garn, 'e ain't nobody, only a director' and 'ain't a player, 'e's the man wot draws the white lines on the pitch.' One day last week I spent the whole day at Highbury and the same little bunch were waiting as I left in the afternoon as were there in the early morning. It was hot and a breeze kept the gritty dust stirring but the three little girls (yes, we have football girl kids now!) looked as fresh as paint. I remember the hours I waited in the rain outside the Winter Garden Theatre for Dorothy Dickson's autograph and a long cold afternoon when I waited to see Dixie Dean and Charlie Buchan in their street clothes! To some extent one can understand and appreciate the enthusiasm of the young, but to the plagued player the autograph hunter, of whatever age, is something of a nightmare. Accepting the fact that it is the penalty of fame, it can be very vexing at times.

AFC Programme, 13.9.47

I can remember coming off the North Bank to collect autographs. Jimmy Bloomfield was captain at the time. The late Bloomfield was a big-headed sod. A group of us begged for his autograph as he walked from the ground past the turnstiles in Avenell Road, we walked with him for a good 50–70 yards but he would not budge. Eventually I piped up: *If your handwriting is as good as your football, you must be very good.* He stopped dead in his tracks. Turned around and asked who had said that. I replied that I had. He immediately signed my autograph book and continued on his way. This must have been sometime around 1960–61.

Peter Leslie

I was absolutely mad about Jack Kelsey and I can remember standing there and thinking: *Now, do I want him in the first half and us scoring down the other end? Or having us score this way in the second half but seeing him right down the other end?*

Maureen Hewlitt

My school satchel, ruler, notebooks, etc. now all started to bear the names of the Gunners. Looking back, maybe they weren't as great as I imagined but they were like gods to me.

Steve Thomas

I used to get the letters and all that business: *Can I have your tie-ups?* You know. And I got a lot of letters when I left. Lovely letters – made me cry, you know – from genuine Arsenal supporters saying they were sorry.

Jon Sammels

Shoot! magazine was running a competition for football fan of the year. I think they still do it every year. When I was 15, the season Charlie Nicholas joined us, I entered this competition. I had to write down why I'm so loyal, where I go and all this. They picked me out as one of the monthly winners, who go into the grand final, to represent Arsenal. I won prizes from *Shoot!* and Braun. An electric shaver I didn't quite need at 15 but I've used it since! Sports bag, football kit, I had my picture in the programme. *Shoot!* had a thing with me and Charlie Nicholas, a picture and a story, you know. The grand final was at the Café Royal in the West End, nice and posh. I had dinner with Charlie who was my hero at the time. I didn't win but it was a really proud night. I took my sister as a guest because she was in love with Charlie Nicholas. It wasn't a very nice meal. There was wine and being young I got quite drunk. Frank Bough and Bobby Robson were on the stage and they interviewed me in front of hundreds of people. I was quite nervous but I think the wine helped. I was really chuffed. Charlie was great. I'd got to know him anyway. When he first joined Arsenal, he told me I was the first fan he'd recognised because I pestered him so much for autographs and pictures. He knew me by name: *Hello, Paul*, kind of thing, in the end. He was nice. He even offered me and my sister a lift home after it but we got the Tube, much to my sister's disgust! I'm not one of those who looks for the limelight. I just said: *No, we've got our return tickets, thanks.* My sister nearly beat me up afterwards. Now I've got older I don't have that personal interest in players. I'm just interested in them for football. I think that changed in the period between leaving school and going to work, becoming an adult, I suppose. If I see a player in the street I like to say hello but the difference is I don't chase them up the road for an autograph. I suppose the personal thing used to make you feel a bit closer to what was happening in a game but I think it's something that most fans grow out of. I know one fan who's in his 30s who still behaves like that but I don't really care for that no more. As a 15–16-year-old, though, it was a great thrill, you know.

Paul Jerrams

We used to run round to the Clock End. We worked out that if you didn't go out, if you went round under the East Stand, you could meet the players. They come out this door and we'd go round there and meet them, have photos taken and that. We'd wait for an hour, hour and a half. They talk to us. Alan Smith I always talk to him and Paul Merson. They're all really friendly, like you know them.

Julie Wheeler

There wasn't that sense of them and us. Well, there was and there wasn't. You can take it both ways, I think. Alex James had a sweet shop just round the corner from Rock Street. My dad would go in there and buy some sweets, during the week, and you'd see Alex James, the great Alex James. I mean, this man was God. I think it was respect for the players, no one would have called out: *You're a wanker* then.

Maurice Gran

Buffalo Systems Ltd
The Old Dairy
Broadfield Road
Sheffield S8 0XQ
UK
+44 (0) 114 258 0611

All our products are made with care under close supervision in our
factory in the United Kingdom.

Buffalo
S y s t e m s

How to get the most out of your Buffalo Clothing System

Buffalo System clothing is suitable for most outdoor activities. Instructors and professional users who spend long periods of inactivity use **Buffalo** simply to keep warm.

Several designs of shirt, jackets, trousers and salopettes are available, some of which are activity specific. Please do ask for advice.

With a single layer **Buffalo System** Shirt you should be comfortable from October to April when active and generating body heat.

When active, your body produces more heat than is needed to sustain life. To get rid of this excess heat, your body sweats. **IT IS VERY IMPORTANT TO WEAR THE SHIRT NEXT TO YOUR SKIN.** This ensures that perspiration has a chance to escape away from your body instead of being trapped next to the skin in a base layer. It is worth remembering that water conducts heat away from the body many times faster than still air.

Even a very light thermal base layer will hold sweat, in the form of water, for quite a long time until it dries.

Temperature control is achieved by opening or closing the zip closures and balancing ventilation with insulation. Do not worry about cold air coming into contact with your bare skin, this is all part of the **Buffalo** experience.

When wearing a **Buffalo System** Shirt next to your skin, you will find upon ceasing activity, that the sweat on your skin will dry very quickly. When your skin is dry you will not chill.

If you are at rest for any length of time (the actual time is dependent upon climatic conditions), your body will naturally start to lose heat and you will need to put on a second layer in the form of one of our JACKETS.

Your **Buffalo System** Shirt has been designed to be a close fit to ensure maximum performance. The looser the fit, the less performance you get.

We also produce a range of **Buffalo System** Sleeping Bags which can be used in conjunction with our clothing to give a durable, versatile and cost-effective system. Windproof garments are also available.

Washing

For washing your Buffalo clothing, we recommend a washing machine setting for woollens or 40° wash. We recommend non-biological powder.

Of course, in the 30s, they were well paid compared to everybody else but there was a limit to the pay, a maximum wage, wasn't there? I think players mixed more with ordinary people than they do now. We hero-worshipped them of course. Alex James, when I was at school, we used to make up stories about what he could do with a ball – pure fantasy a lot of it. And when he was on a radio show one night, we reckoned he probably had the audience moving the wrong way!

George Williams

I used to know Leslie Compton. When he was a player he had a pub up Hornsey Road, the Hanley Arms. Then he moved up to Highgate Village, the Prince of Wales. Used to go up there to the domino club, Tuesday and Thursday nights.

Arthur Peakell

My mother was in the rag trade in the East End and there was an East End lad who was the driver for the firm who lived in a two up two down in Leytonstone somewhere. It turned out that Vic Groves had grown up in his street and he was a close buddy of his. I went to meet Vic Groves and Leslie Groves and got shown round their sitting-room and all its battle honours. It was a wonderful feeling. It was an amazing sense of meeting royalty, it was an incredible sense of excitement. There was much less of the pop-star image. Even in those days pop stars were being paid inordinately large sums and professional footballers were being paid relatively tiny amounts.

John Yudkin

Players were more accessible in those days. I can remember playing at West Ham and meeting my wife in the West End later, I got on the Tube at Upton Park with George Eastham and Joe Baker. We were sitting there talking to the supporters and signing autographs. We used to meet people, socially, at the local pub in Southgate and most of the supporters who came in there were North Bank people. The supporters we met tended to be the ones who stood rather than the ones who sat. We had quite close links with some supporters. Even went to the occasional wedding reception!

David Court

Footballers were always slightly different to the average guy, they were doing what everybody else wanted to do. You might see them down the pub or whatever, but they were still slightly apart from you because they had a gift that you didn't and they were doing something that you wanted desperately to do. The pop-star type of footballer really developed from Best, he was probably the first. Bobby Charlton, Bobby Moore, you know, they were more of a clean-cut old-fashioned type of idol. I think footballers will always be regarded as slightly a breed apart from the supporter, but once the real Best-type came in and they started going to the night-clubs and they were always in the papers, that was when it all changed. Certainly, my attitude towards those that were with other teams changed. I became far more antagonistic.

But I was quite happy when Arsenal went out and got them. When Arsenal bought Peter Marinello, I didn't know anything about Peter Marinello but suddenly we had this guy with the long hair who was going to do the business for us. There was a rival to George Best. My club had to have what all the other top clubs had, had to have somebody like that, you know.

John Platt

I think we know more about them as people now, from the papers, you know. In the old days, you didn't know anything. I mean, everybody likes a bit of a gossip, don't they?

Maureen Hewlitt

In the 60s, you used to want to touch the players to see if they were real. They were figures then. Nowadays you can go and watch them train, mix with them a little bit – that breaks down that myth. Back then, they were 'groomed' – you could always pick out a pro footballer, they were always well turned out. It's just moved on now. They used to have to look like they were Arsenal players. Graham sort of brought it back in, with the blazers and that. Of course, people like Merson will never look the part anyway! In the old days you could pick out a player.

Laird Budge

I think players are less accessible now. Over the last 15 years or so it's become more difficult for fans to meet and talk to players. Because there's a lot more pressure on players to do well and there's more commercial things and presentations and stuff to do with people, players do perhaps want to keep out of the way a little bit more. While fans are still keen to meet the player and chat about the game, you know, the players aren't so keen on that. They want to relax and get away from it a bit more. I think now players wouldn't want to be stopped in the street to talk about last week's game, where in the past, maybe, they wouldn't have minded.

Paul Davis

You tend to find the bigger the superstar – I never ever saw Charlie Nicholas turn anyone away from an autograph. I mean the Club's attitude and the players' attitude was totally different. I sent off for a sheet of autographs about 1980 I got a letter back: *Dear Colin*, it read, got me name wrong, you know, *you will appreciate, they've got to do their training* and all this. When Charlie went up to Aberdeen, a little while after, one of the magazines printed a double-page spread on him. He's the one that really got Jenny hooked. He was a big superstar and flashy in the nicest possible way, he did good things that made you sort of drool. I wrote this letter: *Would you sign this picture for her, please?* He was her first big hero. Within three days a letter came back *To Jenny lots of love Charlie Nicholas*, couple of kisses on it. We haven't had too many like that.

Chris Thompson

Charlie Nicholas had a good rapport with the North Bank. They like those players – a bit flamboyant, you're not quite sure what they're going to do. The sort of players

Arsenal, traditionally, aren't supposed to have. The papers tell us we're machine-like and boring. Players like that give us something to rival the best.

Steve Kazmarek

Without the North Bank, the tension between a talented player and the management would be broken earlier. Charlie George would have left sooner, Nicholas would've – George Graham couldn't afford to alienate the crowd in his first season by dropping or selling Nicholas. You can see the same thing happening with Limpar. It was very important for those players to be valued by one end of the ground.

Nick Hornby

My time on the North Bank, while I was at school, Charlie Nicholas was the big thing. He was just God to lads of my age who supported the Arsenal. There was something about Charlie. I mean, he was never overly successful on the pitch. But, you know, the little bits he did do were just incredible. I think the charisma of the bloke carried the crowd along. They absolutely loved him even when he wasn't playing that well. He almost had a showbiz air about him. I remember when he first joined, everyone was willing him so much to do well. Every time he got the ball the whole atmosphere of the place would rise. And, you know, the very special things he did, you were hoping he was going to do that every time he got the ball, you thought that something might happen. His general personality really came across to everybody, I think.

David Court Jnr

When we played Spurs, 84, Charlie Nicholas was playing. He scored to make it 3–2. Best goal I ever saw Charlie score. Up the North Bank, he beat about three players, keeper come out and he slid it in from an angle. That was unbelievable. That was a great game all round. Best game I saw Charlie play. He always used to score against Tottenham.

Peter Hobb

I stood in the hard core at Celtic when I was a boy. I think a lot of people would say, to sum me up, I've got a lot of street cred because I came through that way. I had a hard upbringing and I hung about with the boys. Basically, that stands you in good stead I think. I've never been a guy who had an ego problem, believing fantasies about myself. I've got my own beliefs and I'm very easily satisfied. Me being satisfied is giving a bit of entertainment when I'm playing on a Saturday, or watching a bit of entertainment on a Saturday from great players I've played with at Arsenal and Celtic. I appreciate that as much as a normal punter does. My father used to take me to what we call the Celtic End here and sit me on the barrier, as early as six or seven. I was fortunate because I watched the Lisbon Lions here. I saw greatness and success and entertainment. That's what I've had with the supporter: *I think I look for the same things they look for.*

Between the ages of seven to 15 it was a dream. Just a dream that was so far in the distance you thought you would never get to it. It was like that for me. I mean, I saw Dalglish before he left Celtic. I bumped into him and was terrified to ask him for his autograph. I used to see all the Celtic people at functions and I'd never ask for their autographs. I was petrified of the people. I was in awe. And even at 15, I still had that. Even now, I mean, Dalglish I get on very well with but I'm still in awe.

I signed as a schoolboy when I was 15. Within two years I was in first-team football, when Billy MacNeill was here. When I look back now, I think my first ever game is the one I'll always remember. The tension in your body, you don't have a clue what people are saying to you: you're just in a dream, a total daze. You just go out and it just happens. I had good fortune: I scored two goals and we won 4−0. When I look back now I remember the help I got from the older players. The buzz you get when you run out and look up at all those people who are what you were.

My first game at Arsenal, I was aware of a new crowd. I suddenly started feeling pressure, to be honest, as we were going down the tunnel. The boys were great towards me, the players. Graham Rix said to me: *Right, man, let's go.* I just intended to enjoy it and hopefully get the result. As we were going down the tunnel, one of the Arsenal staff said: *Just hang back. We're going to introduce you separately.* I had to come out as an individual. That's something I'd never particularly enjoyed. It was a tremendous feeling standing there and getting such an ovation but I also felt embarrassed by it. All I really wanted to be was part of that team. Again, I've got great memories of that game, the tremendous response I got from the fans. I don't know what it was, because I had a pretty average game, so I don't know what it was. Within ten or 15 minutes I thought: *Hang on!* I felt like I hadn't really moved clubs. I had the same affection there as I got at Celtic and for that alone I'm ever so grateful. I always had the highest esteem for the crowd at Arsenal and the people who run the Club. I had my differences about some of the football things but the crowd were absolutely magnificent.

It is hard leaving. I left Celtic in the close season so there wasn't a *See you, boys* or nothing. And then when I left Arsenal and I had a day to go in and say goodbye to people who I'd got really close to. You know, it breaks you. It takes a strong man to leave. I was aware of how the crowd here at Celtic felt when I left because I was on the terraces when Dalglish left and he was my hero. The reaction when he left was one of numbness. When I came back here as a player with Arsenal I had to take some stick from the crowd − I just had to accept that. I could understand their feelings.

Charlie Nicholas

The Paul Davis testimonial against Celtic. I mean, Charlie Nicholas had never got the chance to say goodbye to the fans. At the end of that game, he takes his shirt off and where did he run to? He comes to the North Bank and throws his shirt into the crowd. The whole place just went up: *Born is the King of Highbury! Charlie! Charlie!*

Stewart O'Brien

You get some people who like the workhorses. The David Hilliers and John Jensens. I've got nothing against those players. You need them. But you also need a bit of class, a bit of sparkle. That's what you go to football for. If I had my way, Charlie Nicholas would still be here! Alright, he never done it every game but when he done it, boy, did he do it! There'd be games that we didn't even win, he'd do a couple of things

(Plate 17) 'Something of which to be proud.' Arsenal v Manchester United, 1 February 1958. Dennis Evans (centre) and goalkeeper Kelsey defend as Taylor and Viollet (far right) attack the Arsenal goal (Hulton Deutsch)

(Plate 18) 'People envy us our tradition.' The Metropolitan Police Band, conducted by Roger Barsotti with vocalist PC Alex Morgan far left (Colorsport)

(Plate 19) 'The only thing they won in the 60s was Quizball!*' The quiet man, Bertie Mee, who brought glory back to Highbury for the first time in two decades with the Fairs Cup in 1970 and the Double in 1971 (Doug Poole)*

(Plate 20) 'Making sure that we can control what goes on inside the ground.' North Bank supporters wait to be searched as they enter the Avenell Road turnstiles (Doug Poole)

(Plate 21) 'I found the policing at Highbury very good.' An enthusiastic young supporter is helped away from trouble on the North Bank

(Plate 22) 'The greatest of them all.' Liam Brady, Arsenal's outstanding post-war talent, in action against Spurs at Highbury

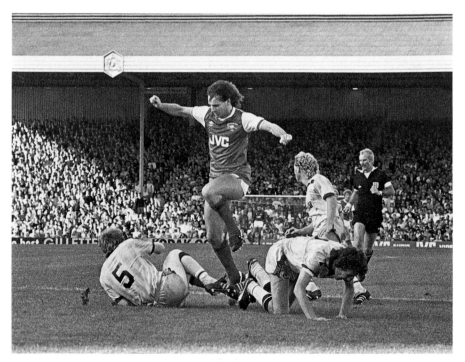

(Plate 23) 'Someone who can do the unexpected.' The North Bank looks on as Charlie Nicholas picks a way through the Coventry defence (Doug Poole)

(Plate 24) 'You were put on the spot very quickly, weren't you?' Dissent on the North Bank during 1991–92

(Plate 25) 'Raising £16.5 million for the North Bank is a monumental process.' Laying foundations for the future during the summer of 1992

(Plate 26) 'Long-haired, loping, impertinent and often brilliant.' The essential North Bank hero, Charlie George

(Plate 27) 'Expecting more.' George Graham, architect of Arsenal's second Golden Age

(Plate 28) '100 per cent Arsenal.' David O'Leary, who played a record number of games for Arsenal during 20 years at Highbury, with the Charity Shield in 1991 (Doug Poole)

(Plate 29) 'A cultured player.' Paul Davis, another one-club man, affording style and continuity to Arsenal's midfield for over a decade, with the Littlewoods Cup in 1987 (Doug Poole)

(Plate 30) 'I used to feel really a part of it all.' The last game played in front of the North Bank, Arsenal v Southampton, 2 May 1922 (Bill Smith)

(Plates 31 and 32) 'How can it be done?' Two of the men responsible for building Highbury's future, Managing Director Ken Friar and Vice-Chairman David Dein (left)

that meant I went home happy. He had that whole North Bank in the palm of his hand. Even after he left.

Peter Hobb

The Paul Davis testimonial I was dreading, to be honest. It's the only time I've been back. The boys kept telling me: *You'll be cruising.* But I'd come back to Celtic when I was with Arsenal and I got real bad stick. I wondered how the Arsenal punters would react to me and, obviously, my mind was focused on the North Bank. I don't usually go out for a warm up, but that night I went out on purpose just to see if I'd feel something in the air – I didn't really get much feedback. I got clapped when I came out but then when I was waiting on kick-off time, I made the gesture, I clapped them without going over-strong about it. But gradually they were giving it to me and giving it to me. At the end of the night, it summed it up, I went over and gave them my Celtic jersey because, well, a lot of my mates, Celtic fans who drink in my pub who were there, they couldn't believe the reception I got having left a big club like that. They knew what had happened to me here. If anybody can look back on my career and have something to say about me, if they want to say I left here and went to Arsenal for four years and I failed, I would say: *Remember Paul Davis's testimonial, you ask those people on the North Bank how they would respond to that.* For someone who wasn't really a big success as a team player, I take tremendous pride from what I had with the fans I gave my Celtic jersey to.

Charlie Nicholas

You pay your money and you want to go home with something, don't you?

Laird Budge

We've always had an idol on the North Bank, haven't we? First it was Charlie George then it was Brady. Then Charlie Nicholas. And now it's Anders.

Paul Hobb

I remember when Peter Marinello come down. On his debut, he beats three men and scored at Man United. Brilliant. His next game was home to Chelsea. Sixty-two thousand in and five minutes before the game these two blokes come and stood in front of us. We thought they were Irish at first, there's a lot of Irish at Arsenal, but it turned out they were Hibernian supporters. They'd come all the way down from Edinburgh to see him play. They said he was the best player they'd ever had and they wanted to come and see him. From Edinburgh!

Peter Hobb

I think the first one was Charlie George, because he was a North Bank boy. I mean, there was a lot of people who said he was a yobbo, but he just happened to be brilliant at football. I think there was all that identification stuff, and on his day he could be brilliant and really take the mickey out of people. That's what the thing was with

Charlie George and Charlie Nicholas, when they were having a good game, when they were joining in for 90 minutes, they could reduce the opposition to just thinking: *Well, we'd rather not be here.* There are people who like that. I mean, I like that, I like to see, like, that famous clip they always have of George Best where he just danced around seven of them. Well, you don't often see that being done. And I think Charlie George could do that and Nicholas did it a few times and Brady could do it.

Roger Hewlitt

With the crowd, I was straight in there. I played well on my debut. I'd take people on, I'd go past people. People knew what I was about from the very beginning. I think the North Bank have always had their favourite players. Charlie George was prior to me. It was never a pressure. That's an incentive, a spur.

Liam Brady

Fucking Petrovic! That man was genius. He was a replacement for Brady. Never given the opportunity and then they sold him! That last game, I mean, the North Bank were just screaming his name: *Petrovic! Petrovic!* We knew it'd be the last time we'd see him. Certain players like that, the magical ones, I'm not saying the rest of the ground doesn't see it but the North Bank's got that raw passion. They see that magic and they just scream in ecstasy.

Phillip Bloomfield

It's part of being an Arsenal fan and part of being on the North Bank – the frustration that the people you actually want to see aren't playing half the time. I mean, it's happened throughout my life at Highbury. I remember shouting for Charlie George to come off the bench, 73–74, Charlie Nicholas on the bench. Petrovic. You know, Eric Cantona – if he was at Arsenal, he'd be on the bench for home games and wouldn't be in the squad for away games!

Nick Hornby

The style of my play, if I'm having an off day and my touch is out, I'm not the kind of player who can run around and kick people and really put the effort in that people can say: *Well, we appreciate that.* My game is effective when I have the ball so, although I probably could have worked harder at that other side of the game, I think the punter would always rather see the side that's an attraction to them, me getting the ball and doing something with it.

When I first came to Arsenal, Graham Rix had told me about the North Bank. Even though he had his differences with them towards the end of his career, Graham had a tremendous opinion of them. He also had a tremendous opinion of Vladimir Petrovic and he told me how the North Bank had responded to Petrovic, how they couldn't believe it when he left. So I knew what type of players they liked. The really skilful players were the ones they took to. Like Charlie George, or Merson and Limpar now. They love them. I can look back now and say maybe the style didn't suit but I think the crowd were always understanding of that. The North Bank have a special focus on what they want to see and that can never be taken away from them.

I think the North Bank as a unit will always be too strong an opinion for Arsenal never to have a player like that in the side. I'm sure the directors and the management are aware of the type of player the North Bank likes to see. I'm glad to see Paul Merson doing so well there now, so consistently. I hope he's still there doing it in two or three years' time, to prove that the North Bank have one of their guys there long-term.

Charlie Nicholas

I think the North Bank's very sophisticated. It's always known who's pulling his weight in the team. And it values different things in different people. Any set of supporters who can value Nicholas and Adams equally – there's two different things going on.

Nick Hornby

The North Bank likes the kind of player who can take the roof off. Charlie George, Brady, Merson, Limpar. Someone who can do the unexpected, Charlie Nicholas. You've got nothing on and suddenly it's a goal.

And then you've got the real Arsenal lads, like Tony Adams, someone who'll die for Arsenal. Like David O'Leary. He only has to come on for two minutes and he'll get a bigger cheer than if Ian Wright's just scored five goals! (See plate 23.)

Guy Thompson

I think the North Bank loves people who are like them: 100 per cent Arsenal. People like David O'Leary and Tony Adams. Players who'll give 100 per cent for the Arsenal, you know, who do it for them. (See plate 28.)

David Court Jnr

I think I like effort even more than skill. Maybe that's because I've never played.

Maureen Hewlitt

It took two or three seasons. It was a gradual thing, you know. My style of play is a bit conservative on the running around side of things and I tried to work on that, running around a bit more, doing a bit more tackling. I think the crowd noticed that and appreciated that. The management and coaching staff wanted me to do that and it was when I started doing it, I realised the crowd really liked this, this was what they wanted, and that pushed me to do it even more.

Paul Davis

They look for a player who gives 100 per cent. I've heard people go: *He's shit. Get rid of him. He's not trying.* That's what you hear: *Work, you bastard, work. Earn your money. You shouldn't be wearing an Arsenal shirt.* I feel that myself. If you put an Arsenal shirt on me, whether I'm shit or not, I'd run and run and run. You'd never give up. And if you see a player not working, no one wants him in the team.

Paul Jerrams

Well, I think lack of ability they have difficulty with after a while because they can't understand why the manager keeps picking him. But lack of effort – and I think this has always been the case – lack of effort on the field, to somebody who is standing there watching somebody doing what they would dearly love to be able to do, is an absolute killer.

John Platt

It is easy enough now to say that Arsenal should have infused earlier in the season young blood like Cliff Holton, Ben Marden, Arthur Milton and David Bowen, who have done well in recent matches. But how could they? While Arsenal were in the running for the Championship and still in the Cup they could not afford experiments. This blooding of youngsters is a ticklish business. However promising a man may look in the reserves, you cannot know whether he will survive the extra speed, cleverer positioning and the tense atmosphere of the senior side. He may be all right in the friendly surroundings of a home game, but lack fight to be a success away from home. Irreparable harm may be done by putting a man in the first team too soon. Confidence may be lost and it may never be regained. On the other hand, there is the danger that he might be kept so long in the reserves that he can absorb no more and he begins to go backwards.

The grooming of an Arsenal youngster takes a matter of years. He cannot be rushed into the senior side before he is ready. But there was no second team during the war years because the ground had been commandeered by the Civil Defence. All the youngsters, therefore, are post-war products, acquired since Highbury was in use again, after 1946.

The number of star players who have been transferred to Arsenal makes us overlook at times the fine footballers who have been produced. Before the war, players were groomed in the 'A' team or the Margate nursery or were put out to selected amateur sides. Here are a few produced through those channels – Reg Lewis, Dennis and Leslie Compton, George Marks, George Male, Alf Fields, Horace Cumner, Eddie Carr and George Curtis. (See plate 34.)

Bernard Joy, *AFC Programme*, 7.4.51

The present-day fantastic prices asked in the transfer market for ready-made players (in many cases not as well 'made' as would be expected by the price) seems to have created a minor tidal wave of reaction by the number of very young players who have been introduced into first-class football since the start of the season. One can, of course, see the logic in giving trials to promising youngsters rather than paying a lot of money for (in many cases) only half-proven established men; but surely there can be only one boy in many thousands who warrants introduction into League football at the age of 17 or under.

It is not so much the physical strain, although in all conscience that is bad enough in some circles, but it is not a difficult matter to imagine the mental effect on a youngster if he had a bad day on his first outing in front of forty or fifty thousand critical spectators. The average spectator is fair minded and patient about the youngster who is trying to make the grade but there are those who are hypercritical and none too reticent about voicing their forceful opinions aloud. Contrary to the common belief, many a player can and does hear the remarks shouted at him in the course of the game, and while the experienced man ignores it and carries on, happy in the knowledge that 90 per cent of the voiced criticism is expressed in the heat of the moment and quite often is the result of an inability to appreciate the real facts, the untried youngster can be permanently affected by such things.

AFC Programme, 10.11.51

They look to Arsenal to bring them through which other clubs don't. I think Arsenal probably followed slightly on the back of the Busby Babes who were probably the first to actually bring a whole load of them through, but Arsenal did develop very quickly after that, which manifested itself in the Double side and has done, as well, with the two recent Championships, It did take a while because, no matter how good youngsters are, you can't bring two, three or four of them into a side – they may do very well for a while but if it's in a period like it was in the middle 60s and you're not winning anything, you think: *This isn't right, it's not working.* It did take a while for them to understand it, but then we got to the League Cup final and we got to another one and although we lost them, there were signs that things were happening. They did adapt to it and now I think they look to it, you know.

John Platt

In the early 60s the crowd wasn't used to seeing young players come through. Now supporters are proud of youngsters who have come through. Back then, they needed to be educated to expect them and be patient with them. I'm sure that contributed to some young players disappearing from the scene. Tommy Coakley would be an example. He was a hustling little player who looked like he might be a right-sided version of George Armstrong and comparisons were made. Well, of course, Geordie was a one-off and the crowd loved him but Tommy, I don't know if he might have become a good player, but he ended up only playing half a dozen times.

David Court

O'Leary, to me, is everything about Arsenal. That bloke, he is Mr Arsenal. He's just been there ever since I can remember.

Stewart O'Brien

For all the time I supported the Arsenal, my favourite has been Spider O'Leary – an Arsenal man through and through. And I think the biggest compliment he paid Arsenal was come 79, 80, 81, when he and Mark Lawrenson were probably the best defensive partnership in the country, regulars for the Republic. Now Brady had gone to Juventus, for big money, Stapleton had gone to United – a lot of Arsenal supporters never forgave him for that as you know – and I'm sure O'Leary could have gone, but he was the one who remained behind. You go and see him today, if he actually makes the bench when he's just running up and down the track, he gets tremendous applause. He's thought of very highly at Highbury.

Jim Smith

Every footballer wants to be popular with the supporters. I grew up with Arsenal. The supporters saw me develop and I think I always had a special relationship with the whole of the crowd, I would say, but particularly with the diehards who were on the North Bank. When I went abroad, I think the crowd understood. I didn't go to another English club as if to say: *Arsenal aren't good enough.* They respected my decision to go. When I came back with West Ham I didn't have a problem with them, I got a good reception. First time you go back it's difficult. But you're a professional footballer. It's in your mind: *This is where I grew up.* But you adapt.

Liam Brady

That Man United game, it was in the Cup. I got there late and United were already three up. I got in and Stapleton scored the fourth. Into the North Bank. It was devastating. I mean, I'm sure it was right for him, to go to Man United and they were paying his wages. But here was a bloke you'd seen developing as a boy, you know, part of that Irish connection, to become such an important member of the team. And he's scoring against us. It's like a cancer or something, one of your body's own cells trying to do you in. It was terrible.

Phillip Bloomfield

I think the crowd wants a successful side. If the team's doing well and there are a couple of youngsters in it, great. But if the team's not doing well and there are youngsters, it's not great. The side's got to be doing well. Now the team's successful and we've got youngsters coming through, I think it's easier for the crowd to handle that.

Paul Davis

They're thrilled to see a new face and know it's come from their own and they're prepared to give that player twice the length of time they would a bought player. When you are the home-grown player – the rumour starts with the youth team games – and supporters know they've come through and they're an Arsenal man, there is that added patience to really see if they can make it. All our successful teams have had as many home-grown as bought. That is something peculiar to the Arsenal and long may it exist.

Bob Wilson

It's great. You grow up with them. You see them play in the youth team at London Colney, then the reserves and then the first team. It's like they are part of my family.

Alex Froso

'A DOUBLE-EDGED THING'

Mistakes were inevitable with the turf in such a treacherous state. I think it was, then, an ungracious action on the part of a small section of the crowd who took it into their heads to barrack Cope. The barracking took a mild form, it is true, but I have no doubt it had a disturbing effect on our left-back. He did nothing flagrantly wrong; his trouble was that in meeting the sodden ball he frequently sliced it – a palpable case of mistiming and, in the prevailing conditions, excusable. Cope, when he blunders, is as conscious of the fact as any other member of the team. Spectators should realise that allowances must be made on a day like last Saturday.

AFC Programme 6.4.28

BRYN JONES CRITICISED AT HIGHBURY
UNITED'S CLEVER LEADER
Arsenal 2 Manchester United 1
Judged by this affair at Highbury, there are some supporters as well as players getting tired of the football season. The attendance figure was down to 30,000, and among those present were many severely critical of the efforts of the players. An Arsenal victory didn't satisfy them. There were players too showing signs of that tired feeling.

Starting 'on the wrong leg', Bryn Jones was 'got at' by a section of the crowd, and thereafter was obviously so worried and anxious lest he should do something wrong that he could do little that was right.

Newspaper, 15.4.39

Once they came back to Highbury it was alright they got going again. One player, he was the record buy before the war, Bryn Jones, and he didn't fit in too well. And then the war came and when he came back he was older now. And he started to click. He started to play well – but he was that much older, so it didn't last too long.

Tom Jales

There wasn't the same 'tribal' thing then of everybody liking a player. People tended to have their individual favourites, although there might be one player who nobody liked – who didn't fit in.

Tina Evans

The first unpopular player we had – I say unpopular, he used to get some stick but if he was around today he'd be a world beater – was Don Roper. He came from Southampton and he never quite . . . we used to be on the terraces and be nearly crying: he'd beat a man then he wouldn't do the right thing. He'd be slow. But I remember one game against Blackpool in the late 40s when Wally Barnes was injured and had to play on the wing. Roper filled in at left-back and marked Stanley Matthews out of the game.

Geoff Gilbert

There is still a section of the Highbury crowd who cry in parrot fashion, 'Get rid of it' to a player who is trying to work an opening for a colleague or for a shot at goal. They evidently forget that the player is striving to do his best in the interests of the side. It makes me wonder why so many onlookers try to teach the players their jobs. I can only think it is because they are so keen to see their favourites on the winning end.

Some of them are still inclined to jeer at players who are not doing as well as they expect. I remember the caustic remarks made in one game against Don Roper. True, he was having a thin time. Nobody knew this better than Don himself. The harder he tried the more things went wrong. But that does not excuse the crowd for their behaviour. A player going through a bad spell needs encouragement, not jeers.

Charles Buchan, *GunFlash* 49, February 1955

In between, the youngster had to listen to some of the knowledgeable ones among the spectators – Arsenal spectators – who saw all the faults, but never the virtues of the big fellow. 'Lawton's too slow! Lawton's not there again! Lawton's trying to do too much! Lawton's not doing enough.' Yes, he heard them all, and he didn't like what he heard. He couldn't understand why Arsenal supporters, of all people, should be so free with their criticism and so grudging with their praise, if any.

Harold Mayes, *GunFlash* 53, June 1955

Bill Dodgin. I can remember him doing a Lee Dixon in the sixth round of the Cup in 1956, putting a 35-yard back pass over Jack Kelsey's head, but that was into the Clock End. I think it was a Cup-tie. They lost 3–1 and those around mumbled how useless Dodgin was.

Peter Leslie, 3.3.56

John Barnwell's confidence was destroyed in front of the North Bank. I think maybe, Jon Sammels would say the same. And there have been others. There are always going to be lads who are going to be the butt of the crowd.

Bob Wilson

Jon Sammels is leaving Arsenal – the club he was mad about as a kid in Ipswich – because of barracking by a section of the Highbury crowd. And manager Bertie Mee has reluctantly put the former England under-23 player on the transfer list. The 26-year-old Sammels has received the full treatment from the boo-boys before but the matter came to a head in the European Fairs Cup quarter-final first leg against Cologne on March when he had to be withdrawn at half time. Since then, Sammels has played twice as substitute in away matches.

Islington Gazette 14.5.71

Yes I liked Sammels, he was a bit unlucky. I think it revolved around his style of playing. He didn't get stuck in, he was a player who looked lazy without being lazy. I mean one of the greatest players of the 60s was John White, brilliant footballer, stick he used to get from the Tottenham crowd was unbelievable, because he didn't get stuck in and I think Sammels was the same, you know. As I say, they don't like people who don't appear to be giving their all for the Club, and if you've got a particular style of play, if your style is a laid back style of play, you suffer. I mean, George Graham used to get a bit of stick as well if he weren't banging the goals in. George was a great player, the icing on the cake when you were on top, 1–0 up he started turning it on and you'd win 3–0 and he'd do the business. You were one-nil down, you wanted fire – that was the feeling. I mean, it may not be necessarily the case but that was the feeling the supporters had and some were suffering for it. He was a good footballer, I liked Jon Sammels

John Platt

My first home game was against Burnley. I scored the winner at the North Bank. I was nervous but more excited than anything, really, to be doing something I'd always dreamed about doing: playing at Arsenal in the first team. That's something every North Bank fan would love to do and I just felt so lucky to be able to do that. I mean, Charlie George used to stand up there, didn't he? And maybe it meant something more to a local boy than me. But there was no keener Arsenal fan than me as a kid even though I didn't live anywhere near the ground. That first game meant so much to me.

I had a hard job when I first came in because, in a lot of ways, I took George Eastham's place. It was hard for me to replace the king, you know. To all the supporters, he was the man. But I definitely felt I won them over. Like any footballer, when the crowd's with you, everybody there, you can give that little bit extra. The feedback I got was they liked me, they were pleased I was out there in a red shirt. One of the problems was that if there were 30 or 40,000 people out there, I wanted to please 40,000 people and you can't do that!

I think that's what disappointed me so much about what happened in the end. I made my debut at 17, I played in the England youth team which won the mini-World Cup, played at Wembley at 17. Maybe I had it all happen too soon. When people talked about the young players at Arsenal, Peter Storey, Peter Simpson, George Armstrong, I was always the one that was mentioned: *Oh, yes. He's going to play for England.* I can remember playing at Arsenal and the North Bank chanting: *Sammels for England!* They used to have little songs for me. And then a year later? It's something I've never really been able to understand, to analyse why it happened. It happened. There was nothing I could do about it. I'm not bitter about it. I'm just sad that from being a player I think they did like, it just all changed.

Looking back now, I would probably have to say I was unprofessional about it. In hindsight, I would never have let it affect me the way it did. I was so hurt by it. At first, you think: *I'll show them.* But when it keeps going on and on. At the end, I didn't want to play at home. It's very unprofessional but when it's happening to you, you get rocked by it. If I could have taken a step back from it, but I think it got on my mind and it snowballed. It affected the way I played. I just didn't want to be out there. If I'd been Bertie Mee I wouldn't have played me. You've got to think of the team. It did affect me and I wasn't playing well. At Highbury anyway.

Again, you look for reasons why it happened. At one time I asked for a transfer from the Club because I didn't think they were looking after the young lads like they should have been. It came out in the papers and it came over as if I was trying to be bigger than the Club. Now that's not me, but it's how it came over. I was supposed to be earning X number of pounds – I wish I had been! I eventually re-signed and people saw these figures and thought: *No wonder he's bloody signed!* I wasn't earning anything like that, but we had got a loyalty-bonus scheme worked out. At the end of each season, you'd get 12½ per cent of all your bonuses again for every year you'd been at the Club. I know I wasn't greedy but maybe that had something to do with it. Maybe that bounced back on me.

Perhaps I could have understood it if the team had been struggling. But we were up there, you know. Even if I'd been playing badly, I'd have expected the crowd to give me the benefit of the doubt. I think what didn't help me was I broke my ankle pre-season 70–71. I was out for about three months and missed all the pre-season training. The team was doing well. I remember sitting there watching, thinking: *I'm going to have a job getting back in here.* And I did! But I got back in, results kept going well; but then we had a little spell, lost a couple of games, and maybe the crowd thought: *We were winning when he wasn't in the team.* Maybe it's him. There was a lot of competition for places and maybe they thought they wanted someone else in. At one time, I thought it was because they wanted Charlie in but then Charlie was playing regularly. I don't know why it happened, I was the forgotten man a bit. When people talk about me and Arsenal now, they talk about the way I left, the treatment from the crowd and all that. People forget about the nine other years.

I think what happens with that kind of thing, someone starts saying something and it snowballs. By the end I was getting stick from the North Bank but I think a lot of it started from the stands. That affected my game, perhaps, and the North Bank picked up on that, naturally they wouldn't know why I wasn't doing it. At the end of the day it was my fault. I wasn't mentally strong enough to handle it.

I knew I was going to leave after we beat Leicester in the Cup. I'd arranged it with Bertie Mee. It had got to the stage where I actually gave the crowd a V-sign. That's not like me, you know. Bertie had me in the office the next day, not to dust me down, but I said: *Look, I'm sorry I did that.* And he said: *I can understand why you did it. I'm not saying it's right but I can understand it.* I was sorry I'd done it but it was just pent up, sort of. Everything came out. I was having to keep it all in. I couldn't go to the other lads. I tried to be chirpy and one of the lads – I knew what they were going to achieve and I knew I wasn't going to be part of it. I've told myself it doesn't matter, but it still hurts even now.

Maybe I was spoilt and had it all too soon; couldn't handle it when these people who I thought loved me, didn't. When something means that much to you, the same as it does to the supporters, and you see it slipping away from you, I defy anybody not to be affected by it.

The nice thing about when I left was the Club didn't want me to leave – the directors and the management – and I got a lot of nice letters from supporters saying they didn't want me to leave. A lot of them did, of course. But a lot of them didn't.

I never really wanted to play for another club but I was so emotional about it I had to get away. I signed for Leicester because of Jimmy Bloomfield who I knew from when I first joined Arsenal. Coming back to Highbury, I can remember Jimmy's team talk: *Now you know how important this game is to Jon and myself.* And we went out and lost 3–0! But it's strange. Went back, that first game, and the North Bank were there chanting my name and you think: *Well, what's going on here?*

Jon Sammels

I think the North Bank is very loyal to the managers. I remember when Don Howe was going, they stuck by him, really. But when Arsenal supporters get to the point when someone has to go, that's it. But I think they're loyal on the whole. Players are different. They're more immediate. They're out there doing it and if they're not doing it, you want to know why or you want to do something about it. Paul Davis is a prime example. I can remember on the North Bank coating him off and then two seasons later, he couldn't put a foot wrong.

Mark Burdis

Paul is a measured player, a cultured player. A lot of the work he does, the passes he makes, wouldn't be appreciated by everybody watching because they wouldn't understand. The pass he really wants to make he might prepare with a pass before that. (See plate 29.)

Liam Brady

Thinking about Paul Davis, I think that was maybe why he had a hard time with the crowd when he first came in. If you play that way – I wouldn't just kick a ball, if I pass the ball I want to know there's someone on the end of it who's got a chance of dealing with it, rather than just go: *Get on the end of that* – like Paul does, I think maybe it's harder for a crowd to see what that lad's doing than if you're rushing around all over the place, crashing your tackles in. That's easy to see. With hindsight, there's a lot of things I would have done different in my time at Arsenal. But one thing I'm pleased about is I never said: *Right, I'm going to abandon the way I think football should be played and do something different.* Even when I was taking stick, having a bad time, I wouldn't hide and when I got the ball I wouldn't just crash it.

Jon Sammels

I had a tough time from the crowd, I would say, the first couple of years. I never put it down to racism. I put it down to my style of play, the way the team was playing and the position the Club were in. We weren't having a great time. There were a lot of players who weren't performing. I think the crowd expects a lot of hard running around, a lot of tackling, particularly from young players just coming into the side. My game wasn't particularly based on that so for the first couple of years I had a hard time. You'd make a mistake in a game and you could feel the crowd ready to start having a moan at you. You can feel it. Then you make another mistake and it grows. So that halfway through the game, you've made four or five mistakes, the crowd are really on top of you. As a youngster it's hard. You're coming into the side, you need confidence. You need people to be behind you and you want your own crowd to be behind you. It's difficult. And if you're getting a hard time from the crowd you need players around you to give you some support. I really didn't get that support. They were having a bad time, too, so it was difficult for them to give the young players the support they needed. So it was doubly difficult. I remember for a while feeling it was nicer to play away from Highbury.

I felt I actually played better away from home for a long time. I was 17, 18. It taught me a lot. I think it hindered me to start with so I like to think I could help young players coming through now.

Paul Davis

Obviously there's players that the crowd as a whole don't like, but there'll always be a group of people who, well, like I remember there was a group of lads who stood in front of us: the Perry Groves Fan Club. They'd turn up every week with the t-shirts and everything. It became almost like a joke, in the end. Even if people don't like a player they still have an affection for them. Perry was the prime example. People pretended not to like him, but they liked him really! Because he was Arsenal that made things OK in the end.

David Court Jnr

With Perry Groves, I've loved that thing where, as long as the man doesn't cross touch-line, he's a hero. When he's warming up everyone's going berserk and then the moment he gets on the pitch, they'd go: *Oh, fuck off Groves!* That was great. That afternoon at QPR last year with all those songs: *We all Live in a Perry Groves World, Perry For England* and then *Perry For Arsenal*, and he was waving and laughing. It's one of my favourite memories of the last couple of years.

Nick Hornby

The North Bank, as long as I've been going, to their credit – occasionally they boo when a name comes over the tannoy – but really they're true and true.

Steve Winfield

I mean, it must have an effect. If you're sitting in the dressing-room and they call the team out before the game and 15,000 people boo when they say your name. How's the guy going to feel? A lot of the people are like sheep. They hear someone slagging off a player and they do it, too, rather than think for themselves.

Paul Hobb

There's always one player they have to criticise. You know, Sammels or Chapman, or Groves – Jimmy Carter at the moment. And at the same time, they're too forgiving of their heroes. I mean, you just have to look at Charlie Nicholas's record for Arsenal – but he could do no wrong. The North Bank has to have a hero.

Andrew Allerton

I know we pay to watch, and we deserve to see quality football and that. But I don't see the point slagging a player off and making him edgy, thinking: *I better do something good or they'll slag me off.* I mean, it must affect them. It's the same in any line of work, isn't it? If someone has a go at you, you think: *Fuck it. I don't need this.*

Guy Thompson

If anyone has a go at any of the players we turn round and have a go at them. I think it's really out of order, if they support the team, to have a go at one player.

Julie Wheeler

The little cancerous growth, the hate thing, starts up in the seats and then it starts to spread. I think the last ones to really turn against you are those who when you run out give you that boost to your confidence and you acknowledge them in return. The North Bank is the first to boost you and the last to leave you.

Bob Wilson

CHAPTER EIGHT

'We Hate Tottenham and We Hate Tottenham'

THE RIVALRY WITH SPURS

Local derbies are famously passionate occasions. For the clubs involved, they represent guaranteed capacity gates in all but the most extraordinary circumstances. For the players, they offer an opportunity to restore pride and reputation in a single 90 minutes should the rest of a season have brought little or no reward. For the supporters, especially those living within a few miles of the ground, the outcome of a derby game has an effect – keenly felt and out of all proportion – on their work and social lives in the weeks until the next clash, as they rub shoulders day-to-day with supporters of the opposing team. Much of your identity as a supporter of the one team is defined in negative terms by you not being a supporter of the other. The local derby is the most intense, if not the most crucial, of the season's fixtures. A victory can be enjoyed for years, entering the private arcana of the rivals involved. A particularly ignominious defeat can hang around supporters' necks for even longer.

The above are general virtues of a rivalry, with neighbours or near-neighbours, with which all football fans – in Sheffield, Bristol, Manchester – are familiar. Arsenal–Spurs games, however, tend to be fired by a bitterness all their own. This may be due, in part, to the peculiarly harsh and unforgiving edge that north Londoners enjoy in their sense of humour. This is the natural home of the wind-up, after all, and the appetite for mockery is not tempered, in the metropolitan sprawl, by any sense of regional solidarity or fellow-feeling. There is little hint of celebration, of a local occasion to be proud of, here. The games – and the rivalry between supporters – are unremittingly competitive, and victory is the only satisfactory outcome.

The two clubs didn't get off to the best of starts as neighbours. When Henry Norris settled on Highbury as the new home for Woolwich Arsenal, some of the most outspoken opposition his plans faced came from the Tottenham Hotspur Football Club, four miles up Seven Sisters Road. Spurs were, understandably, concerned that a new stadium so close to White Hart Lane – on which they had recently lavished improvements to the tune of £50,000 – might offer a real threat to their gate receipts. In fact, Norris's judgment that this densely residential area of the city would happily support two teams was proved right. The season after Arsenal's move to north

London saw Tottenham's average attendances actually rise by some 20 per cent, while the recent arrivals attracted over 20,000 'new' spectators to Highbury. And all this without the benefit of a new 'local derby' because while Spurs, elected to the League only five years previously, were enjoying life at the top, the Arsenal had brought their Second Division status with them from Plumstead. It would be interesting to know what proportion of those who visited Highbury during its first season were spectators from the other end of Seven Sisters Road, 'slumming it' on weekends Tottenham played away.

If Arsenal's move across the river had been cause for concern at White Hart Lane, Norris threw fat on the fire in 1919 when he successfully plotted his Club's return to the First Division at the expense of neighbours Spurs. In the last season before the Great War, Tottenham had finished bottom of the First Division. Arsenal themselves had only managed a moderate fifth in the Second. The first season after the war should have seen the first north London derby. Quite what brand of political negotiation Norris – now Sir Henry – used to lobby a majority of the League's chairmen sufficient to elect Arsenal back into Division One only he and the League president, John McKenna, will ever know. That Spurs were relegated was, of course, their own responsibility. But that Arsenal, thanks to their chairman's manipulation of the corridors and 'smoke-filled rooms', should be the team to replace them was a bitter pill.

Subsequent relations between the clubs during the 1920s inevitably smouldered with ill feeling. Spurs fans had been outraged by the events of 1919. Arsenal supporters, one can imagine, resented their neighbours' dominance of a decade on the playing field, much as they would again during the 1960s. Matters had already come to a head by 1922, with players and spectators involved in clashes of such violence – during a game at White Hart Lane on 23 September – that the incidents were referred to an FA inquiry. Come the end of season 1927–28, Spurs fans were convinced that a jealous Arsenal (unlike Tottenham, yet to win a major trophy) had thrown games in order to ensure their team's relegation to the Second Division, where they languished for all but two of the remaining years before the Second World War.

Tension eased by only intermittent confrontation, relations had improved to the degree that Tottenham proved memorably friendly hosts when Arsenal were forced to use White Hart Lane for matches during the war. When League football resumed in the late 40s, in keeping with the spirit of the times, the old rivalry was apparently conducted on the friendliest of terms or, at least, the friendliest ever. Incredible as it may seem, during the 50s, Arsenal and Spurs supporters spent whole derby games in each others' company.

The 60s, though, saw a return to old ways. Starting with Spurs' League and Cup double in 1961, fans on the North Bank had to suffer a decade in the shadow of their neighbours, during which Arsenal achieved a higher League placing than their neighbours only once. Balance was only really restored when Arsenal, in turn, completed their Double in 1971. For the players involved, emulating their local rivals may have been of only poetic significance. For Arsenal's fans, the importance of that achievement was paramount. The victory which clinched the League Championship being won at White Hart Lane was the icing on the cake. Spurs diehards muttered: *They're dancing on our graves*, as the North Bank streamed on to Tottenham's pitch at the final whistle, on the night of 3 May.

By now, the rivalry had been deepened on two fronts. For the lads on the North Bank, 'running' the Park Lane at away games and defending the home end at Highbury were confrontations as physical and critical as the games themselves. The clash now, too, had come to be seen as one between two clearly defined sets of values. Spurs were big-spending, erratic and flamboyant, both on the pitch and behind the scenes, while Arsenal's home-grown traditional virtues were despised by Tottenham fans who relished their neighbours' 'lucky', 'boring' reputation.

In more recent years, too, a new theme was to be woven into relations between the two sets of supporters which, increasingly, became something of which many fans on the North Bank could only feel ashamed. The Arsenal–Spurs rivalry, until the 70s at least, did not seem to have been darkened by the sectarian divisions which have soured the Glasgow, Edinburgh and, to a lesser extent, the Liverpool and Manchester derbies over the course of the century. Both clubs, settled in north London, have drawn equally on the large and local Jewish community for a significant proportion of their audiences. It must be said, there is a casual, familiar strain of anti-semitism which informs north London life in a wider context. But, during the 70s, in the wake of the appearance of the proto-nationalist culture of the Skinheads on the North Bank – and exacerbated by street and terrace activity by the National Front and the British Movement, especially after the far right's collapse at the ballot box during the 1979 election – Spurs fans became identified as a target for violent anti-semitic abuse. The fatuousness of this attitude, given the common background from which both clubs drew support, betrayed a level of ignorance that is difficult to reconcile with Arsenal fans; justifiable pride in the contrasting lack of abuse directed, over the years, at black players and spectators at Highbury. It should be remembered, too, that it wasn't only the North Bank that found songs about 'gassing yiddos' acceptable.

The anti-semitic stuff was a shameful, ugly episode which still informs the rivalry between the fans to a degree. Arsenal supporters still habitually refer to their Spurs counterparts as 'the Yids'. Spurs supporters, for their part, have taken on the vocabulary of abuse as a means of undermining it: Star of David flags, for example, are a regular sight in the Tottenham crowd. This – and the efforts of the Club, the police and, significantly, fans themselves to make it clear on the North Bank, and elsewhere, that anti-semitism would not be tolerated – helped to mitigate the problem over the past two or three years. This consciously sectarian strain imposed on the Arsenal–Spurs rivalry has, however, entered the language to a great extent and the vocabulary, at least, of anti-semitism – even in today's more tolerant crowd – continues to reflect the stark hatred that is part of the tradition of north London's derby games.

⚽

We argue with Spurs supporters round here all the time because we're the best club. Not being biased or nothing, but we've won so many trophies compared to them. We just sling all these things back in their faces, they soon calm down. There was this one, he was getting on my nerves. We were doing an experiment in school and he was going on about the North Bank being pulled down and everything. So I went: *What's that out the window?* And I poured all these chemicals and walked away, saying: *Oh, it doesn't matter.* And suddenly his experiment blew up – I was so happy with myself.

Julie Wheeler

Intense rivalry has existed between Arsenal and our neighbours, Spurs, since the days before the First World War when our Club moved its home from Woolwich to Highbury.

Indeed, in the 1920s, I can remember there were pitched battles in the streets between rival factions of supporters. The knives used to come out, literally. So did iron bars. The violence actually spread to the field. Once at White Hart Lane three players had their names taken and one was sent off. These unruly scenes attracted a lot of correspondence in the newspapers and passions became so inflamed that, at one point in the controversy, the then chairman of Arsenal intervened.

Bob Wall, *Arsenal From the Heart*

Probably 45,000 people were on the ground to watch a struggle that was always rather too keen to produce much good football, and over-zealous partisans did not improve matters by hurling execrations whenever a player suffered hurt or the referee did not act in the way desired.

Daily Telegraph, 30.9.22

Such was the curtain to a match which might have been enjoyable and wasn't. Who was to blame for the fact? If you expect me to answer 'the Arsenal', you will be disappointed. I write of what I saw, and I think the real primary fault lay with a section of the spectators. The Arsenal players were not immaculate in the second half, but on their behalf, I must add that they were subjected, earlier in the game, to comments which were unfair and provocative.

I am afraid some of the Spurs supporters are so ardent in their loyalty to the team that they rather childishly resent their players being at all unceremoniously treated. We all admire the Tottenham type of football, but it is unreasonable to expect all other teams, many of them not so clever as the Spurs, to adopt the same classical methods. The Arsenal were quite entitled to go in for spoiling tactics. They went in for these tactics as soon as the match began, and at once some spectators began to howl at them as if they were assassins. Can you wonder that the men from Highbury got a little rattled and out of hand?

Daily News, 30.9.22

Our match at White Hart Lane last week has been the dominant topic at least in London football circles. Much has been written about all the incidents in a strenuous game and much more has been said, the views varying according to the pebbles of partisanship through which the game was viewed. Accusations of roughness have been levelled against some of the Arsenal players, but we can derive a full measure of satisfaction from a perusal of the written views of many reputable critics, whose opinions are given elsewhere in this issue. The blindness of partisanship has much to answer for, and much as I deplore recriminations, I am bound to say that I know no crowd more devoted to their team than that which swears allegiance to the 'Spurs'. The old adage that the King can do no wrong is fully exemplified in the halo of virtues which the Tottenham crowd places around their favourites, but it is, to say the least of it, regrettable that these self-same 'virtues' in other players are regarded as 'vices' deserving of instant condemnation.

We must emphatically deny the accusation of foul play. That there was robust shoulder charging we frankly admit and that this, when indulged in by the Arsenal backs, was not palatable to the partisan spectators was evident, for their shouting and general behaviour left no ground for doubt while the throwing of cinder and other material at Blyth might possibly be characterised as a little harmless amusement, to add force to the vocal abuse. I feel bound to record in fairness to ourselves, the fact that things were thrown at Blyth in the first half and in the second half a hefty missile was hurled at Bradshaw and was handed to the referee. I have played football long enough – for some time with the best class professional – and I know the mental make-up of the footballer. I do not blame either the Tottenham players or our own for anything unpleasant which happened last Saturday, so much as I place the onus upon the unthinking and rabid enthusiasts, whose common sense seems to be entirely warped by the fury of the partisan fever which overwhelms them.

AFC Programme, 30.9.22

BIG FOOTBALL SENSATION
THREAT TO CLOSE THE TOTTENHAM GROUND CROWD CONDEMNED
PLAYERS SUSPENDED AND CENSURED

Smith, the Tottenham right half-back, who has been capped for England, was suspended for a month for using bad language to Graham, the Arsenal player. Graham was censured for retaliating instead of reporting the offensive expression to the referee. Dunn, the Arsenal goalkeeper, was censured for rushing out of goal to protest to the referee against the Tottenham goal.

But the finding of the Commission which will cause most comment is that which deals with the Tottenham spectators. 'These are warned that a repetition of their conduct at this match will result in the closing of the ground.' The Commission was satisfied that the spectators 'interfered with the proper conduct of the match'.

Daily News, 7.10.22

I come now to the last finding of the Commissioners, in which they say they are 'satisfied that the spectators interfered with the proper conduct of the match', and we are warned, if you please, that a repetition of such conduct will result in the closing of the ground.

What a finding! The conduct of the spectators was most exemplary, and there is not a scintilla of trustworthy evidence in support of this astounding decision, which has been received locally with contempt and derision.

W.H. Prescott, MP, Tottenham, 21.10.22

⚽

The attention of our supporters is drawn to the fact that we have made arrangements with Newcastle United to play the League match which had to be postponed on 2 March owing to our Cup-tie with Aston Villa, at Highbury next Tuesday afternoon, We had hoped to offer the fixture as an Easter Monday attraction to our followers and Newcastle were quite agreeable to the suggestion. When, however, the matter came before the Football League for consideration Tottenham Hotspur raised an objection on the score that their 'gate' on Monday would be affected. We then made a proposal that the match should be played on Monday morning instead of the afternoon but again the Tottenham management made a successful protest. How a morning game at Highbury could possibly have an adverse influence on an afternoon match at White Hart Lane we quite fail to appreciate. Our view of the matter is that there are enough enthusiasts in London to fill both grounds on a Bank Holiday even if two matches were played at the same hour.

AFC Programme, 30.3.29

There were extraordinary scenes at White Hart Lane this afternoon, where 57,246 people – a record for the ground – saw Tottenham Hotspur and the Arsenal meet for the first time in five years. A big crowd rushed the gates when the ground was closed an hour before the start and mounted police were temporarily powerless to stop them. Several people were hurt in an earlier rush when the gates were opened. A crowd of nearly 60,000 people, some of whom had been waiting since three a.m., was outside when the gates were unexpectedly opened soon after noon – more than three hours before the kick-off. Immediately, there was a mad rush for the two-shilling stand. A number of people, including several women, were knocked down, and police and ambulancemen had to deal with many minor casualties. In a quarter of an hour the gates of the stand were closed, and a notice 'Stand full' was put on. On the steps leading up to the main stand a crowd of several thousands swayed and struggled. Those behind pushed forward, and those in front pushed back. Women screamed, and several were handed out over the heads of the crowd.

Thousands of people continued to pour into the district by every possible means of transport and on foot until, an hour-and-a-half before the kick-off, the Tottenham High Road was a mass of slow-moving traffic. Special police were summoned to deal with it. Confusion was made worse by a series of accidents, the worst of which involved a boy who was knocked by a motor-cycle. At half past two, when the gates were closed, there was still a big crowd outside and more people were still pouring into the district. The crowds rushed the main gates as they were being closed and forced them open again in spite of the mounted police. The gates were eventually closed and locked. Mounted police guarded the entrances.

Evening News, 16.9.33

I used to go to Tottenham every other week. But of course, you went over there, you didn't say you were an Arsenal man. It was a bitter rivalry. I never got in any trouble with them. I used to know quite a lot of Tottenham supporters. And quite a few Arsenal supporters used to go over to Tottenham.

George Stinton

I used to stand up in the top corner of the Laundry End and I'll tell you what. You'd see the same people every week, the same crowd. And then the next week, down at Tottenham, you'd see all the same people. If you liked football, you went – it didn't matter so much who it was. You'd all be mixed in together, swear at each other and row and then go up the pub together after.

Ron Pottage

Today's visit of Tottenham Hotspur is, of course, one of the events of the season and in extending a warm welcome to our great London rivals I express the hope of all of you who are looking on: may the game prove worthy of the occasion. Time was when these local 'derbies' were not fought out in the best of tempers; the excitement of the crowd has often reacted on the players with the result that an unwarrantable excess of zeal has been shown. But of recent years there has been a marked improvement in this respect and this afternoon we are looking forward to a keen match, with the play clean and sportsmanlike.

AFC Programme, 26.11.27

Arsenal Stadium was requisitioned as an air-raid shelter and first-aid post and the practice ground used as a barrage-balloon site. So the Tottenham club immediately said: 'If you don't mind sharing with us, why not come and play at White Hart Lane? You can use the pitch one week and we'll play here the next.' They proved wonderfully hospitable hosts and, although I was away on army servce, I know that out of that gesture developed a very real comradeship between the clubs. I think, too, it made the two sets of supporters understand each other a great deal better. In October 1951, Arsenal made a presentation to Spurs to commemorate the great help given to us in wartime by everyone at White Hart Lane. This bronze plaque now hangs on the wall of the Spurs boardroom as a permanent testimony to that period.

Bob Wall, *Arsenal From the Heart*

The thing was, in the 50s, people used to do a five-and-a-half-day working week. Work till one o'clock, over to Highbury, meat pie and a cup of tea for lunch. And because there were no motorways and people had less money, you got no away supporters there. People would go to Tottenham one week and Arsenal the other.

Steve Shaw

The Arsenal–Tottenham game always used to be terrific over here, huge crowds but there'd be no problem, you could have your rosette on. No, you went to see your team and that's it, you'd be standing alongside them.

Charlie Robinson

The Tottenham supporters when they came tended to go to one end but not for any particular reason. There was no segregation.

Geoff Gilbert

And now for what is surely the highlight of the season to all Arsenal supporters – the return match against our friends at Tottenham on Saturday 23 December. Let us be quite honest about it and admit, quite openly, that this is the match of matches that we want to win. Personally, if we don't win it I shall have to disappear for a while! But whatever happens may it be a jolly good game and may the better team win. As far as our Club is concerned, we must give all the support and encouragement we can to our team, and this can only be done by standing together in one great block and letting the team know that we are there 100 per cent behind them. You will all no doubt remember where we stood at Tottenham for the first Cup semi-final against Chelsea last season – on the centre line, on the opposite side of the ground from the players' entrance. So let's get there early and bring every Arsenal supporter we know with us, whether they are members of our Club or not. We must also have plenty of colour so that Tottenham can see the greatest display of red and white that they have ever seen!

GunFlash 15, December 1950

There are a couple of clubs in this country of which you may have heard – maybe heard a little too much. Their names: Arsenal and Tottenham. Now if ever you want to represent hate or enmity or Cain and Abel in mortal combat you couldn't do better than draw or paint an Arsenal supporter and a Spurs supporter having a quiet chat.

Nowhere else in England can footer rivalry be as intense and hot-headed as it is in north London. Imagine my surprise, bewilderment, astonishment, and complete state of flummox when, on going to a dance for both sets of supporters, I found good-natured chaff – no more – and such a high standard of camaraderie and sportsmanship as I did not believe could exist outside a public school after-the-cricket-match celebration. I found Arsenal and Spurs supporters hobnobbing on the best of friendly terms. Spurs supporters openly admitted that the best team won (which reminds me that here, in my usual pedantic fashion, I corrected someone with 'You mean the better team won', to which he replied, 'They were better 'n that, guv – they was the best!' And Arsenal supporters telling them that it had been a good, clean game and their turn would come next time.

This was indeed a revelation. And it seems to me from what I saw that if we can get more and more supporters' clubs and can get mixing together in this atmosphere of mutual jollity and mutual praise, then we shall have gone a very long way indeed to solving one of soccer's worst features: the intense and almost unbearable dislike of one group of fans for another.

Ralph Finn, *Sport Magazine*, November 1952

You'd talk about football all the time in school. There was the rivalry with Spurs fans. It was very important even then. Probably even more so at school because Tottenham were the glamour side then. There seemed to be more Tottenham fans around, as is the way when a side's doing well. They had the glamour of Greaves and always seemed to be spending money whereas Arsenal were a bit in their shadow. They usually beat us!

Steve Kazmarek

When I was a kid, nine or ten, I went to Arsenal. All my best friends were Spurs supporters, this was the year that Spurs won the Double. I was going alternate weeks with them to watch Spurs, who were far more exciting, and the other weeks to go and watch the Arsenal. Being a lone Arsenal supporter, it was like asking friends to come into my house and you just knew that whatever they were going to see was not going to be as half as good as what they watched in their own house the week before. Of course, by the time that Arsenal were really good which, I suppose, was the day after they lost to Swindon, you really wished you still knew those people, the same people who had really rubbed your face in it.

Laurence Marks

One of the strangest afternoons at Highbury was when Spurs were playing Wolves in the FA Cup semi-final. We were at home, some nothing game. And Spurs were a goal up until right at the end. Wolves got a penalty. Everybody was listening on the radio and they went: *Shh!* And Hibbitt scored and this almighty roar went up. You'd think we'd won the league! Our game was on *Match of the Day* that night and the commentator goes: *I don't know what the cheering's about but it's nothing to do with this game.*

Paul Hobb

I've always been: *The bigger the game, the more I feel* – I don't know if it's responsibility or a kick up the backside. Instant motivation. I've always been like that. The bigger the arena, the bigger the contribution I'm going to make to the game. And, looking back, most Tottenham games were like that. I was always ready mentally for them. Sometimes it was a struggle, to be honest, mentally. If I had a bad week getting slagged off in the press then had to go off away from home like Sunderland, or somewhere, on the Saturday, I'd be thinking: *I don't really need this.* But Tottenham was never like that. I knew what it meant to the fans to beat them.

Charlie Nicholas

The basics are the same: you want to win for your supporters. I don't think there's any other games where you're conscious that you're playing today for your supporters. In a derby game, you go out there and you know you're playing for your supporters. The games become very, very competitive and that's common to north London, Turin and Glasgow. Obviously, in Turin you're playing in front of 90,000 people so it's that much more intense but, basically, wherever you're involved, that's the special derby. I mean, I've come up to Glasgow now and there's no match more intense than Celtic–Rangers

— maybe not for all the right reasons — but it's the same thing, everybody wants to be able to stick their chest out at the end of the game and say: *We're the best.*

Liam Brady

Couple of times with Tottenham, I think things got out of hand at one stage.

Steve Winfield

Charges were laid against 17 people, eight of them teenagers, at Highbury Corner Magistrates Court on Monday as a result of incidents at the Arsenal–Spurs football match at Highbury last Saturday. Police said about 200 people were ejected from the ground when fighting broke out between Arsenal and Spurs supporters in Highbury's North Stand and the violence continued after the match.

Islington Gazette, 9.4.76

I remember Tottenham on Boxing Day 1979. They was all congregated up on the west side of the North Bank — this was the days before them fences were put in — and a massive fight, a massive surge, they came right into the middle of the North Bank. At Tottenham now, I'd wear my scarf. Not that I wear a scarf anymore, but if I have a special Arsenal shirt, I'll wear that at Tottenham now. Even though there's still a tension between Arsenal and Tottenham which won't go, obviously, because of the geography of it, I don't think it's so vicious. The hatred's not so bad. I mean in the 80s I remember an Arsenal–Tottenham game when a girl, older than me, tried to rough handle me. That says it all, doesn't it? We'd just beaten them — like we always do — and she put her leg out, tried to trip me up, and pushed me. I ignored it, but I thought: *Women are trying to do it as well!*

Paul Jerrams

They give you half of an end at Ipswich or they used to, half of a terrace. We were on one side and for some reason I was right up near the fence, near all the Ipswich lot. We were segregated and it was the first game of the season and you're always a bit wound up the first game and the last game. And someone stood up with a scarf, it didn't say *Ipswich*, it said *Tottenham Hotspur* and everybody went mad. Funny isn't it? So there I was, getting crushed against the barrier. Everybody went mad purely because they held up the Tottenham scarf.

If you want me to give a theory on it, I'll give a theory on it. In this country we don't have a masculine adolescent sort of rite of passage. I mean, if you're Christian or whatever, you don't have a barmitzvah or things like that, you don't have a year in the bush or anything, and, without wishing to make too much out of it, to some extent football and things like it, maybe music and possibly certain fashions, take the place of it. You develop an identity within a group in those teenage years. You develop your own identity as part of a large cultural group. I consider everybody as an individual — I would certainly consider myself as an individual — but, to some extent, you become classifiable in a limited way, because you're an Arsenal supporter, because you're a football supporter, or because you're a punk-music fan or because you're a heavy-metal fan or because you're a dance-music fan or whatever. To some extent, football supporting has played that role, that it's what young men do, it's what teenage boys do, it's one of the things they do through adolescence. It's one of the things they do when they're growing up and so you go along with it. I don't believe in violence, I don't believe in fighting with people just because they support Tottenham and you support Arsenal – I mean, loads of people I know support Tottenham, I work with them and the rest of it and always have done – but you can go to a level that just sort of stands back from violence. You can go to a level of verbal abuse, build up on the adrenalin of it: we beat them (as usual), you can sort of have a go about it – *2–0 we beat the scum 2–0*, or *silent Spurs* and stuff like that. And that's exciting and you do it because you gain an identity through doing that, you gain a positive identity through being a supporter.

Al Fresco

Vicious anti-Jewish propaganda being sold at Arsenal home matches is to be investigated by police. Arsenal chiefs are to have talks with senior officers about the sale of abusive material outside the ground. And an MP has raised the matter with the Government's sports minister. The material – badges saying 'I Hate Tottenham Yids', and a record acclaiming Arsenal but abusing Jewish people was on sale at Arsenal's home match against Everton two weeks ago. It is not the first time it has turned up at Highbury, and it has been claimed that the extreme right-wing British Movement is behind it. Arsenal is anxious to stamp the material out.

Islington Gazette 5.12.80

We want our stadium to be a safe and pleasant place for our supporters, and away fans, to visit. In co-operation with our stewards and the police, we're doing everything we can to achieve that aim.

So, we were shocked and angry that our Littlewoods Cup semi-final first leg against Tottenham was marred by repeated violently abusive anti-semitic chants – and we also had to remove provocative and offensive banners. The people who chanted those obscenities and brought those banners to the ground are a disgrace and an embarrassment to our club, and to our huge majority of well-behaved supporters. We don't want you in our stadium.

AFC Programme, 21.2.87

There was a year or two that was disappointing in my eyes when it seemed that racism might take control. Not take over, but people used to get off on doing racist chants. Jews not blacks. The Spurs thing I'm talking about.

Richard Stubbs

Arsenal have got as many Jewish fans as Tottenham have, probably more. It's just this blinkered ignorance that's existed for years. You've got clubs like Everton and

Chelsea who are racists, but this anti-semitic thing seems peculiar to Arsenal and I'd like to see it come to an end. It's really out of order.

Stewart O'Brien

I'm Jewish so I notice. There was one time this bloke asked me for a cigarette so I gave him one. They started singing: *One man went to gas, went to gas a yiddo.* This bloke I'd given a fag to started singing it. I just turned round and said: *If you're going to sing that song, I'll have my cigarette back, thank you.* He goes: *What?* I said: *My grandparents died in that. It's not funny.* And he sort of went: *Oh!* There was this silence. He'd just never thought about it.

Natasha Horbacki

We've had conversation about it with people and they've gone: *Oh, we didn't know.* And we'd say: *You didn't know? How can you not know?* But the North Bank over the last few seasons was getting much better. They didn't sing that kind of thing because the actual majority would sing back if it started: *You're just a bunch of wankers.* Which made me really proud. There was a majority voice against that which wouldn't have happened three seasons before.

Emma Young

I don't think it's really got anything to do with them being Jewish. I mean, they used to hate it when we'd go: *Yiddos! Yiddos!* So they've sort of adopted it: *We are the Yiddos!* They love it now. Big Star of David flags, and that.

Lenny Brandon

We've been very lucky. I mean, if you have any liberal leanings, football can make life very difficult with the incidence of racism, sexism and anti-semitism. We tend to forget that racism in the form of anti-semitism is still pretty endemic at Highbury. Nobody 'means' it. I don't think there are so many Jewish supporters at Arsenal and the Tottenham supporters have taken it on board, sort of thing. It's just stupid, like the colour of shirts or something – but all the same. I've always felt proud that, for example, when the Highbury crowd were having a go at Michael Thomas (I argued with a lot of people about that, anyway!) they'd call him a cunt, he was lazy, he was an idle bastard but I don't remember anyone calling him a 'black' any of these things. I remember Plymouth coming up for a Cup match, they had all the Clock End, and they were all making monkey noises and the North Bank just went: *Aaaah! You wankers! You provincial wankers, you've never seen a good black player.* You know, that feeling on the North Bank that afternoon, I'm not saying it was anti-racist fury or anything it was just: *You lot are so uncool.*

Nick Hornby

You still get it at Tottenham games, don't you? It still gets you. You just hate them. I mean, I've got mates that are Yiddos I suppose but I don't think I've got a close mate who is. They're just all the same, aren't they? They're just horrible people. Even my youngest, he hates them. I help run a local team up in Hatfield and we've got a couple of Yiddos play for us. My little one really struggles to understand how I get on with them!

Lenny Brandon

I mean, you'll never agree with them, will you? You can start off polite and nice, you know, nod and: *Yes.* But it always ends in arguments.

Paul Hobb

Don't matter where you are in the League. You could be having the shittiest season, whatever, but if you beat them! Like when Terry Neill left, Don Howe's first game as caretaker manager was away to Spurs. We hadn't won for weeks, nothing. We went there hoping to keep the score down. Well, Charlie Nicholas played and scored twice. We ended up winning 4–2. That was it!

Peter Hobb

The only trouble I've ever seen at Highbury was last season when we beat Spurs 2–0. I was coming away and there was this big ruck behind one of the burger stalls. Loads of police piling in, you know. But that's understandable, isn't it? It's Arsenal v Spurs.

Guy Thomson

Although they might not admit it, I think when Hoddle was around, they would have liked to see him in an Arsenal shirt. Gascoigne? I admired him as a player but he was too much of a clown. Arsenal wouldn't want a clown like that. He was more suited to Tottenham than Arsenal. I think Arsenal are a more strait-laced club and I like that. It's the tradition, the organisation, the history. People might say it's old-fashioned but it's served us well. It works for Arsenal.

Paul Jerrams

I stood on the Shelf once by mistake. I got there at half time and didn't know my way around so I just went to the first turnstile. I got in there and had a look around and realised I was right in the middle of the hard-core Tottenham. And to make things worse, we were 2–0 up! So there I was, surrounded by all these herberts screaming: *Tottenham.* I straightaway became a Crystal Palace supporter! They got the goals back second half. Ardiles and someone else. And it was like the North Bank, all lads together screaming for their team. It was different, obviously, because it's just that strip and it's not covered but I would have to concede the passion and the feelings were the same.

Phillip Bloomfield

It's smaller than Glasgow. I've been to watch Liverpool and Manchester derbies and Arsenal–Spurs is every bit as exciting as them. But Celtic–Rangers is a different derby because of the hatred. Outside Celtic–Rangers, it's as good a derby as anywhere. But up here it's religious. And it's ignorance and religion. They think they know about religion up here but they don't. Part of it as well is the difference between the English and Scottish Premier Leagues. As far as Celtic fans are concerned, it's between us and Rangers. Aberdeen are a good team but in their eyes it's between us and them. Whereas with Arsenal it's between them and Tottenham and then Liverpool and Man United as well. It's a big, big difference.

Charlie Nicholas

If you'd asked me when I was at school, I just hated Spurs. I went to school with a lot of Tottenham supporters. They had quite a good team, won the Cup twice and we kept losing finals and so I just hated them with an absolute vengeance. Now, I really don't know too many Spurs fans. I suppose that must say something but, now, I don't really have that hatred. Except at games sometimes. On the North Bank, I think the hatred is as intense as it ever was. But in the past, when people used to look for the Spurs result, under George Graham expectations have changed and, certainly the last few years, people look for the Liverpool result. Liverpool, Leeds and Man United, you know. In football terms, the rivalry isn't as intense as it was.

Andrew Allerton

The best atmosphere I remember was at the Tottenham game we won 2–0. The ground was just packed, everybody cheering and shaking hands, turning round and saying: *We've scored! We've scored.* I just hate them!

Dawn Hicks

If ever I come home from work upset over business, I ask my daughter to put on the tape of when we beat Spurs 2–1 on their own ground in the Littlewoods Cup semi-final. That gives me great pleasure because I really hate Spurs.

Alex Froso

CHAPTER NINE

'To Urge our Boys on to Victory'

WORDS AND MUSIC ON THE NORTH BANK

We started in 1913 with the North London Silver Prize Band but after the Great War the Arsenal Band was formed under the conductorship of Mr J.H. Kitchenside. The Band did not reform in 1946 and we were without until we engaged the Band of the Metropolitan Police . . . opening with the first game of the season v. Huddersfield Town on 18 August, 1951.

AFC Programme, 2.10.73

The old standards hollered by the estimable Constable Alex Morgan, and the music played by a succession of Silver Bands at Highbury before games and at half time, are a part of all older supporters' memories of football from the North Bank. As such, they find their way into the story elsewhere in these pages. And the North Bank had already disappeared by the time live music returned to the pitch at Highbury, for the first time in 15 years, with the notorious – and raucously barracked – appearance of The Shamen during the Sky-televised game against Manchester City in the autumn of 1992.

The story of musical entertainment *for* the crowd aside, 80 years of songs *from* the crowd follow two very different tunes. The first is the long, well-meant and hopelessly out-of-touch search for a standardised club song. The Arsenal programme was already shopping in the late 20s and early 30s. The Supporters' Club took up the Grail after the war and almost, it appears, succeeded in getting *Anchors Aweigh* away (as it were!) for a few years during the 50s. In the face of the burgeoning creative talents of the North Bank in the 60s, however, all seemed lost for the cause of formality and standardisation until the unlikely coincidence of copyright law and Jimmy Hill hit upon the music and words for *Good Old Arsenal*, which still rings in the ears of the supporters who were around to enjoy the drowning-out of the Kop at Wembley in 1971.

Of course, the success of *Good Old Arsenal* owed much to the credibility bestowed on it by being taken up by the informal choir that now existed on the North Bank. Their massed clapping, chanting and singing routines, for which home ends everywhere had become famous, were something else altogether.

Small groups, it seems, were singing pub songs and Christmas carols on the Laundry End before the war. An essential part of Supporters' Club coach trips to away games in the 40s and 50s was the composition of new songs for the happy band gathered on the halfway line to have a stab at, as they released their red and white balloons across Fratton Park or Turf Moor. It was the early 60s, and televised coverage of the Kop – already a unified, disciplined and overwhelming orchestra of noise – which inspired the lads on the North Bank, and elsewhere, to take up the challenge.

In its time, the North Bank proved to be as loud, as irresistible and – albeit intermittently – as imaginative as any terrace in the country. It was perhaps at its finest with the impenetrable and relentless *Over and Over and Over Again* and the anarchic *Knees Up Mother Brown*, both of which can be claimed as Arsenal's own.

The North Bank's halcyon musical age of the 70s, however, gave way in the 80s to something more subdued, in keeping with the general change evident in Highbury's atmosphere. From time to time, an occasion would be risen to – like the week in 1988 when Manchester United and Everton, in the FA and Littlewoods Cups respectively, were soundly beaten in front of a packed and deafening terrace. But times had changed. Importantly, one of the effects of crowd segregation was to remove the rival visitors' choirs to the far end of the ground. Violent confrontation was avoided but the sting was drawn, too, from the battle for vocal supremacy. As a result, the more close-knit physical circumstances of away games have meant that the North Bank of recent years had often been best heard at grounds other than Highbury.

What hasn't been lost, though, is the sense of humour: *We All Live in a Perry Groves World* on the cult anti-hero's appearance on the touch-line, *Boring, Boring, Arsenal* hailing the Championship win in 1991 and *What a Waste of Money* to greet the arrival of Ian Wright. It may be said that the ironic detachment of a crowd sophisticated enough to enjoy stuff like that would have had no place in the fervent, partisan atmosphere of the North Bank choir's great days.

'CAN YOU HEAR THE NORTH BANK SING?'

There was no chanting – and no obscenities – I can recall. My mother was a bit, you know, puritanical. She wouldn't have let me go if there'd been any problems like that.

George Williams

Here's a bright idea from Mr Mitchell – a real war song for the Highbury boys, to the tune of *The Man Who Broke the Bank at Monte Carlo*.

As you walk along Gillespie Road
You can hear the nippers shout,

When the 'Reds', without a doubt
Have put their foes to rout.
The lads who grace the Highbury field
Will do or die, before they yield,
And prove themselves a credit to the nation.

Perhaps Mr Kitchenside and talented musicians will oblige with accompaniment.

AFC Programme, 12.9.25

The sparse attendance on Saturday did not in any way affect the success achieved by the community singing, so efficiently organised and carried out by the *Daily Express*. The conductor, Mr Thomas P. Ratcliff, received a lusty response from an enthusiastic choir, and the music provided by the band of HM Grenadier Guards, under the leadership of Lieut. George Miller, was highly appreciated and contributed its full quota to the success of the event.

AFC Programme, 29.1.27

Another reporter could not help wondering why a group of Arsenal supporters started singing *The Bonnie Banks of Loch Lomond* as he passed by into the stadium. 'They may have heard Alex James singing it sometimes,' he mused. Inside the stadium, 'all sorts of aural torture were in evidence – all the things taboo in Glasgow such as bugles, bells, rickety-racketees and mascots of every conceivable shape . . .'

John Harding, *Alex James*

On the occasion of the Leicester City match our band gave the first rendering of the *Up the Gunners* march which, we hope, is to take a permanent place in our musical programme as our club song. Today when it is played once more the lyric will be sung by Monte Rey. The march has been specially composed for Arsenal by Gilbert Stacey, and it will now be possible for copies, words and music, to be bought at all cafés and bars in the stadium at the price of 6d.

AFC Programme, 1938

After the game you could hardly speak from shouting. Not songs so much, just cheering, oohs and ahs.

Sid Butler

Forties, only time you used to get any singing was Christmas time, you know, Christmas morning when people would sing Christmas carols.

Bill Needs

You used to sing your own songs, in your little group. And there'd be other people singing other songs. It was a happy atmosphere: *What they singing over there?* You used to sing your little pub songs.

Jack Hobb

You cheered your team but it was all individuals. *Come on the Gunners*, or *Come on the Reds*. There was no chanting as such. There was cheering. The first time they had a song, I believe, was when they won the Cup in 1950 and the police band adopted *Anchors Aweigh*. That caught on to a degree.

Geoff Gilbert

Singing really started when we started going to away games on the coaches. Written by people in the Supporters' Club, we had our own songs, back in the early 50s.

Frank Hummell

About a year ago, with the permission of the Arsenal Football Club. we approached Mr Barsotti and asked him to play our club song prior to the teams coming out on to the field. He willingly acceded to our request and has certainly been doing his outmost to popularise the song ever since. We are again publishing the words of the song, and would ask you all to do your utmost to make yourselves heard at all future home matches, especially on the occasion of the Cup-tie against Aston Villa on 9 January.

GunFlash, January 1954.

Very soon the great red and white splash was making itself very much seen and heard, so much so that leading national sports writers made comment on same in their match accounts. And it was here, before the game actually started, that Pompey suffered their first defeat. The Arsenal supporters singing their song and the continual chanting of A-R-S-E-N-A-L was literally drowning the home crowd's famous *Pompey Chimes*.

The deafening roar which greeted Captain Joe and his men surpassed anything the Navy and Pomponians had done for the home team. Our boys were obviously warmed – realising that they were not alone – as they lined up to the unified strains of *Send Arsenal down the field* . . .

GunFlash 5, 10.12.49

I used to sit on a crash barrier and was held there by my brother. In those days scarves and rattles ruled. There was no singing or chanting. Just polite cheering. No swearing, no cursing. There was an attempt some time in the 50s to get the Laundry and Clock End to sing the Arsenal signature tune. The words were printed in the programme. I can remember the police band playing *Anchors Aweigh* when Arsenal took the field but cannot recollect the crowd singing the words.

Peter Leslie

To meet the popular demand of Arsenal supporters we print hereunder the words of the Arsenal song which used to be heard on the ground some years ago and which we shall be very happy to hear echoing and re-echoing from our stands in the future to urge our boys on to victory.

The song is sung to the tune of *Anchors Aweigh* which will be played by the Metropolitian Police Band on the occasion of every first-team match as their last tune before the kick-off – so let's hear all you budding singers and if you should lift the roof we shall be very happy to bear the cost of replacing it!

Send Arsenal up the field,
For one more goal,
No other team can fight,
Harder than the boys in red and white.
Never let their glory fade,
Long may it glow,
So let us all give out with,
Up the Gunners!
Up the Gunners!
G O A L!!

AFC Programme 11.11.63

The words that were written to the tune of *Anchors Aweigh*, I'm sorry that never took off. It could have been our song. It was a good song. I still remember it: *Send Arsenal down the field, for one more goal. Never let their glory fade.* And all that! That was written by somebody in the Supporters' Club. There was another one we liked that was to the tune of the *Eton Boating Song*. The whole coach would sing. And we'd try to get it going on the ground but it was hard. People weren't like that in those days, didn't like to sing out loud, weren't so outgoing as they are now.

Frank Hummell

Many supporters have suggested that the old Arsenal song to the tune of *Anchors Aweigh* was not quite what they wanted and at the suggestion of a number of supporters we are taking into use today, and for the future, a new song with very simple words to the tune of *Roll Out the Barrel*. The words are:

Roll on the Arsenal
Let's have a barrel of fun
Roll on the Arsenal
We've got them all on the run.

Win all our matches
Then we'll have nothing to fear,
One, two, three, four, five, six, seven
And the gang's all here.

Today the police band vocalist will sing them in order to give a lead to the spectators. We commend this new song to you and we hope that you will sing it at every match, and enjoy it.

AFC Programme, 4.12.65

On Bank Holiday Monday we played a special tune on the public address system and asked for spectators' views. You all left us in absolutely no doubt as to what you thought of it and you will be interested to know that of the reasonable number of replies we have received there were only two who like it. Most other people were quite scathing in their criticism. Needless to say, in view of the response, the composers have been told that it will not be used at Highbury.

AFC Programme, 16.9.67

Unfortunately, the present-day Arsenal fan does not appear to be interested in a club song. The old one lasted for 30–40 years but was suddenly considered to be 'square'. We then ran a public opinion poll though the Supporters' Club, and a new song was devised but nobody sang it so we gave up. It will have to be a very representative new song now if we are to look at it again!

AFC Programme, 6.9.69

THE VICTORY SONG

'Our Band' – the Metropolitan Police Band – is very proud of the Club's recent achievements and the Director of Music, Major Williams, and the Band Librarian, Lance Munday, have written a song entitled *We are the Champions* in honour of the team's success in winning the Fairs Cup. The words are printed below and during this afternoon the vocalist Alex Morgan will teach you the tune.

We are the Champions
We are the Champions
! ! ! ! ! (clap hands)
Fairs Cup Champions now
A-R-S-E-N-A-L
Come on let's take a bow
We are the Champions
! ! ! ! ! (clap hands)
Fairs Cup Champions now
Two-four-six-eight-ten-el-even,
No one can show us how

AFC Programme, 19.9.70

ITV has been forced to scrap a soccer song contest – because it fouled the copyright laws. And it seems millions of supporters are breaking the law every Saturday when they roar out their team's hymn during a match. Arsenal fans were challenged to write the words of a theme song for next month's Cup final. The lyrics were to be sung to the tune of Elgar's Pomp and Circumstance march – *Land of Hope and Glory*. But yesterday a spokesman for the organisers, London Weekend, said: 'We were told by the Elgar Trust that we were contravening copyright regulations. In the light of this news it's probable that soccer supporters break the law every time they sing to the tune of a popular song.'

London Weekend has now devised a Cup final song for Arsenal, to the tune of non-copyright *Rule Britannia*:

Good old Arsenal.
We're proud to say that name,
While we sing this song
We'll win the game.

Daily Sketch 12.4.71

There was a fantastic architectural felicity about the North Bank, which was the size of the roof. It helped make noise. The people weren't very different from anywhere else – the architecture of the North Bank made it special. There was this lovely feeling in the ground when it was full that you just wouldn't get anywhere else. It's a big ground with the feeling of a very small ground, I always thought.

Nick Hornby

The majority of the sound came from under the shed. The atmosphere was better because it kept the sound there. When you sung on the outside you lose it, it just goes up in the sky.

Paul Jerrams

I think men are a bit shy about singing and getting involved. Covered enclosures make it easier, lights go out, you can all sing and chant. Night games – it's all dark – even the people who are out in the open can actually take part in the singing and shouting so you tend to get a better atmosphere. You get blokes saying *Come on, so and so!* who in daylight, I think, would be too embarrassed to say that.

John James

It was around the mid-60s when the North Bank really started to emerge. I don't remember much singing and chanting before that. I remember one year there was all Spurs fans in the North Bank, they sort of took it over but, by the next year, the Arsenal fans in there were chanting back. You were starting to get televised football. You saw Liverpool and the Kop on *Match of the Day* and I think other clubs started to imitate that. It seemed that you'd watch the crowd. At big games, you'd hear the chanting and the counter-chanting. That seemed very important: *Were we winning that one?*

Steve Kazmarek

It was when Liverpool returned to the First Division that chanting really started, you know. We've got to be thankful to Liverpool, really, they brought a lot of new things in. Before them, people used to cheer and that but there was none of this singing like you get now. They were more fanatical than we were down here. We'd look to see what they were doing.

Bill Needs

That song: *I'd walk a million miles for one of your goals, Jon Sammels*. I can't remember there being songs much before that one was around. It must have been about 1964–65. I remember listening: *What are they saying?* It was great. But it's funny, I would get a little bit embarrassed by it. You didn't know how to reciprocate, you know.

Jon Sammels

Manager Bertie Mee certainly hit the nail on the head in the first programme of the season when he asked for more vocal support from the fans. As a regular spectator at the Clock End I am most disappointed at the lack of vocal support compared with the North Bank end of the ground. Even the North Bank 'choir' were shown up by the repertoire of the Liverpool supporters recently, but at least they make themselves heard at most matches at Highbury.

Graham Jones, *AFC Programme*, 16.9.67

I can remember standing there and Liverpool supporters singing: *You got your education from the Kop*. And a lot of us knew that was true, because when the singing started, songs like turning *The Mighty Quinn* into *The Mighty Jim Furnell* well, the North Bank had a certain amount of originality. But in our heart of hearts we knew Merseyside was making the music.

John James

Late 60s–70s there was much more singing than there is now. There was always someone starting: *Zigger-Zagger!* It's more in fits and starts now. Then it was non-stop. I suppose I was looking at it as a kid then, so the atmosphere was more exciting. There was more hoot then, and all, of course. I think the singing was like another competition, seeing if you could out-sing the opposition. You'd always get someone shout: *Give us an A!* And it was non-stop, singing players' names. Now it's not like that. We've got the same stars, but the atmosphere's not the same.

Vidos Neophytou

Arsenal suddenly have a choir. It may not know all the words, all the chants, but the confidence and cockiness is there, massed for everyone to hear and see. In the soccer song league, Arsenal are only just starting. The last time Arsenal won anything, football crowds did not sing. They clapped. It was that long ago. The thing that has carried Arsenal on over the last two decades is loyalty. Take Paddy Farrell. Every home game for 17 years, Paddy Farrell has stood on the Highbury terraces and hoped that some of the glamour and the brilliance of the 30s would return. He stood and hoped through wind, rain, sleet and cold feet. Now, on Saturday, he will wear his Arsenal rosette to Wembley. Even Paddy Farrell is learning to sing. He is sure his patience will be rewarded. Supporting Arsenal is fun again. 'It used to be like that in the early days,' says Paddy. 'I was a teenager then myself. Now I'm damned near a grandfather. I think they'll win. I think they owe it to me.' Arsenal supporters wear red and white, the same as Liverpool. They sing many of the same songs. But only now is there a communication, an instant spontaneous understanding developing between sections of the crowd. On Monday they drowned Tottenham. At Wembley on Saturday, they take on the much more formidable Kop choir. Underneath it all lies a belief that Arsenal can re-live all the glory that north London babies swallow with their cornflakes. There is a whole generation of supporters to whom success is new. They are the cheer leaders in the crowd participation that started in Liverpool and Manchester.

The *Sun* 5.5.71

The first time I went I remember thinking: *I wonder where they get all the songs from?* It feels good when you start off a song. I started off a song once. Yeah! 30,000 people singing along to me! I mean, you get some people trying to start it and everyone goes: *Aaargh!* It's nothing but you'd feel a right idiot. I remember one little Skinhead bloke. Four foot nothing, no hair. He always used to start singing and everybody'd just go: *Go away!* He'd end up singing on his own. I felt sorry for him, actually. The time I did it I think I was drunk. I think it was against Everton. We'd had a few beers earlier and then we'd gone down the Plimsoll Arms and I said: *I'm going to start a song!* You feel a bit more outgoing when you're drunk, don't you? And I just started one halfway through the game and everyone just joined in. I thought: *Yes!*

Guy Thomson

During my time on the North Bank, one character I will always remember is Barking Jim – the Craig Johnston look-a-like. He used to stand on the top-side with his mates and start all the singing. I particularly remember him starting: *He's bald, he's fat, he's gonna get the sack* to big Ron Atkinson when we beat Sheffield Wednesday 5–0 a couple of years back.

Edward Costello

There was a woman, I used to hear her everywhere. She used to go: *Come On You Reds*. Everywhere we hear her, everyone cheers because she's so famous now. When there's a quiet moment in the crowd, she starts. I admire her. She's so regular, you know. There was one man whose voice I recognised. He used to start off the North Bank. God knows where he used to stand but he used to scream at the top of his voice: *The-e Arse-nal-l!* And then, as if he was the leader, about 600 men would start to sing, you know. That always impressed me because I never had the courage to do that! I'd join in but I'd never start them off.

Paul Jerrams

You screamed from the minute you got in there till the minute you left, didn't you? I never had a voice at the end of the game. That was what was amazing. Being in that shed under the roof, you'd scream your head off and it would be just deafening in there. Incredible. You'd get rolls of it, like thunder rolling around.

Phillip Bloomfield

⊛

Highbury's never been a particularly vociferous ground. Partly it's that north Londoners don't think it's 'cool' to sing and chant. I mean, I lost count of the number of times we were outsung by the likes of Barnsley when they came down in the Cup.

Andrew Allerton

The chanting individuals who take on the Nuremburg Rally aura of a crowd acting in unison remain a very very tiny minority. I suppose when you see the Kop chanting and swaying and arms in the air and united, singing, that's where the biggest number of people acting as a homogeneous population, but at Arsenal, West Ham, Chelsea, Tottenham, I've never felt that it's more than about 10 per cent of the whole area.

John Yudkin

During that year I'd always sing, like at Wembley when we did the Double. We outsang the Liverpool supporters with *Good Old Arsenal* and *You'll Never Walk Alone*, funny enough, even though that was their song. And the Man United game a couple of years ago but then we'd just won the League and I'd had a couple of drinks during the day. But I don't tend now to sing.

Eddie Mason

When Dawn started coming, she didn't used to sing. I used to poke her in the ribs and go: *Sing!*

Julie Wheeler

It's going to sound like a real generalisation, but I think the North Bank will put up with a mediocre first half say, and then over half time we'll sort of collectively decide, without even saying anything, collectively decide *right, its five to four, its four o'clock we're going to try to lift the team*, and we'll give it ten or 15 minutes, but if there's no improvement during that time I think mostly we'll let it go these days. Maybe in the old days we would have kept it going a bit longer.

Al Fresco

I think the players want the fans to lift them and the fans want the players to lift them. It's like a catch-22 situation. Games are usually tight in the first half hour and that's when you really want the crowd to get behind you. I can understand if people aren't happy if even by the second half things aren't going well.

Paul Davis

I think it's moved on a little now, because you're paying a lot more money and you're looking for a lot more entertainment. In the old days I think that the crowd picked the team up. Now the team pick the crowd up, you know what I mean? If Arsenal start playing a little bit, then they sort of get behind them. Up till then it's all expectation, they're expecting it to happen but in them days you didn't, particularly if they were playing one of the top sides, the crowd really got behind them then and they lifted them. I think that's where the North Bank got its name, in the 60s and 70s rather than now, you know, into the 90s. I mean, other people might disagree with that. And a couple of times when I haven't been able to get into the North Bank for one reason and another, I sat in the East Stand. I think sometimes in the East Stand, the people in there, they're more the people that have moved out of the North Bank after the 70s and gone in there. Particularly on the North Bank side of the East Stand, I mean they're real fervent in there, more so than a lot of people.

Laird Budge

The last couple of seasons they were a bit quiet and they go a bit quiet when we're losing. (Of course, I never joined in the chanting anyway – well, you can't at my age!) But on the last day of the North Bank, that fellow who shouts: *Come on you rip-roaring reds!* Went round the whole North Bank after the game, calling that out.

Maureen Hewlitt

When they sing that song: *Let's go fucking mental*, I love that song. Because that's what you're there for. You're there to go mental.

Richard Stubbs

In the 50s there wasn't any organised clapping or chanting. That came in, in the 60s, especially when Brazil started to get more noticed in the World Cups and different sorts of clapping and chanting came in. I can remember clapping routines coming in – I don't know if you know the tune *Wipeout* by the Safaris. That was one of the first.

David Court

There was one song we used to sing: *And we'll all sing together, in aid of the AFC*. That's very vivid. But early 60s the atmosphere wasn't that great. There weren't many songs.

Eddie Mason

I think its growing up, really, growing up with the North Bank. You're old enough to get in with the boys and have a little sing song and enjoy yourself, and when you think it's gone past you a little bit, you move out. I think back in the 70s, there was some real wit with the songs in the charts. There's nothing now, it's just standard stuff whereas in the old days whatever the popular songs were, people just jokered it around and changed the words. I remember one I used to like – for a player that weren't that clever really – for Bobby Gould, we'd sing that old Eagles record *Viva Bobby Jo*, and changed it to: *Viva Bobby Gould*. It was a good song that people could latch on to, you know, and again a bit of thought went into them. I've always been impressed with, like Birmingham, they used to have *Keep right on to the end of the road*. And they used to really sing that and all and then you get the Geordies singing *Blaydon Races*. Arsenal never had one of them, not since *Good Old Arsenal*, in the 70s. I remember going to Tottenham when we won the League and they sung that for 45 minutes in the second half and it never stopped. It bowed out, didn't it, the *Good Old Arsenal* song?

Laird Budge

To the tune from the film the *Long and the Short and the Tall* they sang:

> *Fuck 'em all, fuck 'em all,*
> *Chelsea, West Ham, Liverpool,*
> *For we are the Arsenal and we are the Best,*
> *We are the North Bank so fuck all the rest.*

To the tune *The Halls of Montezuma* they sang:

> *We will fight fight fight for the Arsenal*
> *Till we win the Football League.*
> *To Hell with Liverpool,*
> *To Hell with Man City,*
> *We will fight fight fight for Arsenal*
> *Till we win the Football League.*

Another song was sung to the tune of the *Eton Boating Song*. It had two verses!

> *We will support the Arsenal,*
> *The greatest team of them all,*
> *And we will enjoying supporting,*
> *Whether they rise or fall,*
> *And we'll sing sing together in aid of the AFC*
> *And we'll sing sing together in aid of the AFC.*
>
> *Fulham can stay at the Cottage,*
> *Southampton can stay at the Dell,*
> *And as for Tottenham Hotspur,*
> *Well, they can go to Hell, to Hell,*
> *And we'll sing sing together in aid of the AFC*
> *And we'll sing sing together in aid of the AFC*

To the tune of *Mame* it was:

> *Sammy, Sammy, I'd walk a million miles for one of your goals, Jon Sammels.*

Then there was *Na Na Na Na , Na Na Na Na Na, Hey Hey Marinello*. That was to the tune of *Kiss Him Goodbye* by Steam.

And to the tune of the *Quartermaster's Stores*:

> *He's here, he's there, he's every fucking where,*
> *Charlie George,*
> *Charlie George.*

Peter Leslie

I was born under the North Bank stand . . . (to the tune *Wanderin' Star*)
Bertie Mee said to Billy Shankly . . .
Storey, Storey Hallelujah . . . (to the tune *Glory, Glory*)
Like West Ham they fade and die . . . (to the tune *Bubbles*)
The Dambusters (various versions)
Knees up Mother Brown
You'll Never Walk Alone
We went up to Wolves, we took the North Bank . . . (to the tune *Messing About on the Water*)
Tony Madden

When Marinello come, there was that Steam record: *Na Na Na Na, Hey Hey Marinello*.
Roll Out the Barrel – that was an Arsenal one. *When You're Smiling*. The Jim Reeves one,
Distant Drums, that became: *Distant Bums*. That was another one from a record wasn't it?
Lenny Brandon

I remember us singing: *We are the Champions*, that Chelsea game in 1971. How often
could we sing that with that pride, that sense of community? And again last season,
when we were losing to Chelsea and got a win out of it, and we sang that to remind
ourselves: *We are the Champions*. They are sublime moments.
Richard Stubbs

We hate Nottingham Forest,
We hate Liverpool too;
We hate West Ham United,
But Arsenal we love you
    Words, North Bank
    Music, Elgar.   ***Evening Standard***, 2.10.73

Quarter-final against Manchester City. We went up to Maine Road, City had a good
side then, got a draw – a nil–nil draw – thought the job had been done. The replay
was down here. Hudson came on as a sub in the second half and we won it in the end
– a penalty. Just before that penalty one of these chants went up – they stick in your
mind – it was a cold night, February, I think the game was – *It's fucking hot in here*.
The one and only time I ever heard that one. I don't know why it happened but there
it was, 57,000 there that night and it really was fucking hot.
Chris Thompson

My mate was saying about when he stood on the North Bank, his era was: *We've Got*
the Biggest Willie in the Land. About Willie Young, you know. And there was a mob from
the Plimsoll Arms used to turn up in the North Bank every Saturday and it was around
the time Cloughie and a few others had been saying: *Come on, lads. Don't swear*. This lot
sort of took it to heart and started singing: *Tottenham are cads. Hello. Hello. Tottenham*
are cads. Hello! And then when Shilton had been up to naughties and that Saturday, at
Arsenal, the whole North Bank was singing. *Does your Missus know you're here?*
Eddie Mason

With Shilton that time, it was disgusting, it really was, apart from continuous cries of: *Tina, Tina*, the more printable ones like: *Does your Missus know you're here?* it then degenerated into things like: *Does she take it in the mouth?* It was disgusting but the great thing about it was that he took it, that he didn't turn round and berate us and all the rest of it, that he accepted it all and did a sort of wave to us.

Al Fresco

I used to like when the FA Cup came around and they'd sing that: *We Shall Not Be Moved*. I think that was much more when Arsenal were more famous for the FA Cup. They don't sing it so much now. And when they sung the Letters of Arsenal slowly and when they got to E it was a great big E-EE-E! That was unique to Arsenal.

Paul Jerrams

I think songs now are all about players and results. Buy a new player and you'll get a new song. Or about a particular result. Or if there's something in the paper about someone – say if Terry Venables started going out with a bimbo or something, you'd have a song about it whenever Spurs came down. A couple of seasons ago the Double song started up again. I think it was because the Double video came out.

Guy Thomson

I was a ball-girl at the start of the season, the first four games, down in the corner of the North Bank at the West Stand. Every time I used to walk past, there was this little crowd that used to shout at me. I don't know where they got my name, maybe from the programme, but they started singing my name. It was really embarrassing. Then after I finished as a ball-girl and I was just standing there, they came and started talking to me. One time they saw me and started singing: *Julie, give us a wave*, and everybody sort of joined in. You know, they do that sometimes. They don't know what it's about but they sing it anyway. I just hid my head in my shirt!

Julie Wheeler

Even though we started the *Red Army* business, I don't think we tended to come up with the classics that you get at other places. It always worried me that we never had one song that was recognised as being ours. I mean, people talk about that one *Over and over and over again* which I don't know the words to, and probably you don't either, but we never had one that was ours like *You'll Never Walk Alone* or *Always Look on the Bright Side of Life* or *Blue Moon*. I always felt we should adopt something that would become ours.

My choice, for what it's worth, because I think it does say something about the psyche of an Arsenal supporter, would be *Blowing in the Wind*. There's an element of fatalism about that song which I think there is in the Arsenal crowd. *The answer, my friend, is blowing in the wind*. I think it would have suited us perfectly.

Al Fresco

'TAKE YOUR MASK OFF, DUXBURY'

Avoid barracking the referee and players, and don't be too partisan. Don't call ungentlemanly remarks to players; it does not add to the pleasure of your fellow spectators.

Herbert Chapman, *Athletic News*, 25.8.28

There was a couple of old boys there, they'd been going to Arsenal for 50 years in my imagination. They were always shooting their mouths off, you know, cheeky, sarcasm and that. Swearing, too!

Paul Jerrams

Cliff Holton had a shot like a donkey, he could break a crossbar from 30 yards and if he was going to have a shot, especially at the North Bank end, you could see him winding up and the crowd would go: *OoooOoOh!* They loved it. Whether it went in or not! Because he gave it effort.

Dennis Evans

Midweek reserve match on a foggy day (I don't think the match would have been started today): George Swindin coming back from injury was in goal and as most of the play was at the Clock End he gave us a running commentary. From time to time ghost-like figures appeared through the gloom to shouts of: *Here they come George.* At times there seemed to be only Swindin and the crowd behind the goal in the stadium. Someone remarked: *They have all gone home George and forgotten you.*

Beryl Brown

You do get the occasional clever football song. I don't know who writes it, who's getting a percentage, you know. You get some very funny supporters. A line we actually used, a line I heard at Arsenal, on the North Bank: I heard someone say, 30 years ago, when someone took a ball in the groin and was crawling in agony on the floor, the bloke next to me shouted out: *Don't hold 'em, count 'em!* I used that three decades later in a script.

Maurice Gran

Alex Forbes was built with rather hunched shoulders and was one day told: *If you took that sack of flour off your back – you could have got that pass.*

Beryl Brown

I used to stand out on the North Bank for reserve games in the 50s. I used to go as a kid to reserve games and I remember one day Arsenal were playing. There were about 10,000 there – you used to get crowds at the reserves then. There was one bloke down the front, every time this particular Charlton player kicked the ball, would shout out: *You're useless, Sid.* Or *You're bloody terrible.* Well on about the third attack, this Charlton player left his position and came on to the North Bank and had a row with this bloke.

Laurence Marks

You'd sit down behind the goals when they kicked off and the first thing you'd hear would be: *Mister! Take your helmet off! We can't see the game!* The person who used to get all the flak in those days was the referee. Never any of the players. The ref got the stick.

PC Jack Birt, retd

There was baiting of the referee, but even that was more good natured. Sort of: *Have you left your glasses at home?* That type of humour.

John Platt

Sometimes I swear at the referee, but not much. If it's really obvious, a bad decision – like you can see they've handballed it or something – I get up and I shake my fist at him.

Julie Wheeler

Of course there'd be swearing. Some people can't hold back from swearing – the tension and that. But not the 'bulk' swearing like you get over there now.

Tom Jales

Swearing was not something that was normally tolerated in the 50s, especially if you had a lot of young kids on there. I've known situations where someone might swear and people, nothing to do with the kids standing there, would say: *Oi! Watch your language.* And if there were females about, it certainly wasn't a thing to do.

David Court

As long ago as March 1965 we were receiving complaints from spectators that there was a clique of so-called supporters on the North Terrace who regularly congregated on the east side and indulged in foul language to the embarrassment of decent people. It has become so bad that a number of older supporters now refuse to come to the stadium and bring their women-folk (wives and daughters) because they are not only embarrassed but shocked that men can conduct themselves in such a digusting manner.

***AFC Programme**, 4.12.65*

We used to have a right old skylark about. I mean, you could in the 60s, you could have a good old eff and blind and no one would take any notice. Let's face it, that was part and parcel of letting off steam. The law wouldn't take much notice. It was a normal thing, been going on for years. They became 'naughty' words later, in the late 70s and 80s.

Bill Needs

We end this *Voice of Arsenal* with a special plea. PLEASE, PLEASE, North Bank, refrain from the foul language you used here in the game against Manchester United. You may think it is harmless. IT IS NOT. It keeps many spectators away from Highbury, and this is something the Club cannot afford. We do appreciate the way you support the boys whether they are winning or losing, but do have some regard for other people and most of all, for this great club. We shall be looking for your performance today – as well as the team's.

AFC Programme, 17.10.81

It's a sort of double-edged thing with the Club and the North Bank. They want them to shout but they don't always like what they shout.

Steve Kazmarek

We had a season where we did nothing but swear. All the time. Ludicrous. It was like kids. But it just became part of it. I think there was an alternative comedy character who did it. That's what initiated it. When we scored: *Shit. Wank. Piss. Bollocks!*

Richard Stubbs

There's a lot of that. Someone may shout out something and there's a swear word in the middle of it. You can see all round people are creased up laughing. You're not going to do anything about it. If someone's being deliberately offensive or obscene, yes, you've got to act, but not if a swear word's let go in a humorous situation. I mean, if you were told: *Everyone who swears, throw them out*, you'd have lost all your policemen within the first five minutes. Anything that is causing ordinary people on the terrace offence – anything racist, which is an absolute offence – then, yes, you act.

PC Alan Smith

My son learnt some very good swear words here at the Arsenal.

PC Roy Beasley, retd

There's someone who stands near us, I don't know who he is, anytime they're not playing well you hear his voice: *Come on girls! Pull together!*

Maureen Hewlitt

Yes, in a way, you're relaxing. You think: *Well we're not going to win this. But there again we weren't going to anyway!* And you meet people, you start talking, people start making cracks so you turn around and say: *Yeah, good.* So you might come out with one yourself to try and better it, you build up a rapport. I can remember one time when Pat Rice of all people put a shot into the crowd and a Scottish bloke standing next to me – he hadn't said a word all through the game, he was standing there arms folded, and when everyone else was going: *Aaaah* he stood there tight lipped – Rice took a pot shot from about 40 yards out and it blew into the North Bank. This bloke stood there and he finally opened his mouth and said: *I'll get it*, and that cracked me up. A bloke in front of me once referred to one of our players being as much use as an ashtray on a motorcycle. When I've got the hump now and I'm watching the team not doing alright now, they are the two cracks that I always come out with.

Mick Essen

There was this bloke with a real foghorn voice. Big bloke, with a very pock-marked face. Bloody awful game, everybody was moaning: *Why has he dropped Nicholas? Why isn't so-and-so playing.* And suddenly, this fellow yells out: *Bring back Brian Talbot.* That was his thing. He got a good laugh out of that. And that kid down the front: we were playing Man United and Mike Duxbury came down to take a corner. This kid yelled out: *Take your mask off, Duxbury!* That was hilarious. And Duxbury must have heard him.

Maureen Hewlitt

To me, the joy of it is it's funny at the time. It's not profound. It's just maybe 400 people who hear it, just a silly remark, probably one you've heard a million times, it's just funny for that.

Roger Hewlitt

The generous applause given to visiting goalkeepers. I especially remember David Platt being given an 'Arsenal' goalkeeper jersey when he took over in the Villa goal, and laughing with the crowd . . . April 91.

Steve Thomas

Arsenal were leading by about seven goals when the ball just crossed the line again, unseen by the officials. Opposing goalkeeper Johnny Mapson scooped it out, kicked the ball up the field then turned to the crowd and said *Well that was number 8 wasn't it?* He had the crowd behind him on his side for the rest of the game.

Beryl Brown

If you've got a keeper who's really outgoing, it's good. Hans Segers is quite a giggle. Steve Ogrizovic as well. Ogrizovic last year, he would run along his line and jump up. Everybody would whistle and go: *Whooah!* when he jumped. Then he ran along, went to jump and stopped. That's good, isn't it? After all, it's only a game for God's sake. Seaman talks back to the crowd quite a lot. He got hell when he first come here because of the business with John Lukic. But now he talks to people quite a lot. It's another 'bond' isn't it? You're not just coming to see a player do a job, it's like you're coming to see a friend of yours.

Guy Thomson

There's this bloke, big fat bloke with a really loud voice. He's always shouting at David Seaman and Seaman shouts back. Everybody can hear them. He goes: *Seaman, you have a woman's legs! Seaman, you have a woman's bottom!*

Julie Wheeler

I talked to Seaman once during the game. It was against Derby, do you remember? It was really windy and I shouted out: *When are you going to score?* And he heard me and turned round and said: *Second half.* And he hit the bar, second half, didn't he? Someone scored from the rebound. And I talked to Tony Adams. I shouted out: *Go on, Tony, get in there.* And he turned round and winked at me. I don't like it when people slag Arsenal players off. That game against Coventry, where Lee Dixon scored an own goal, and there was this bloke giving him right stick. Everyone could hear him and Dixon heard him. He was by the touch-line and sort of stopped. He definitely heard him. I said to this bloke: *Look, if you could do better, you'd be out there, wouldn't you? Just leave off.* The bloke told me where to go, which was a bit upsetting! But then he just sort of disappeared.

Guy Thomson

I loved against Wimbledon, the whole North Bank was on at Hans Seger about him being fat, going: *Have a diet coke!* Singing: *You're so fat, it's unbelievable.* And it got to where he went to take a goal-kick and he was laughing. He turned round and went: *Wait a minute!* He had to take the goal-kick but he was doubled over laughing. That was really funny.

Julie Wheeler

I entirely agree with the views expressed this season in the programme with regard to racist and obscene chanting. However, I have yet to see any criticism of the equally disturbing outbreak of 'sizeist' chanting. In games against Wimbledon and Manchester United this year, certain players from the visiting teams – namely Hans Segers and Neil Webb – were ridiculed for their apparent stoutness. This kind of behaviour is simply unacceptable to civilised Arsenal fans. Do supporters on the North Bank really think that cries of *You're so fat, it's unbelievable* are actually funny? Are these same people unaware of the fact that a number of their fellow Arsenal fans are a 'little bit on the tubby side'? I'm not visibly overweight myself but some of my friends are and they find chants of this nature upsetting. So I would like to take this opportunity to ask Arsenal fans to think before singing seemingly 'innocent' songs as others may find them offensive.

Eric Hoggers, *AFC Programme,* 22.3.92

In the 50s, people used to cheer and clap and that was it. Society's changed. There's less inhibition now. It's the players, too. Back then all you saw was a pat on the back. Look at Ian Wright now!

Tina Evans

CHAPTER TEN

'To Own an Arsenal Shirt Would Have Been Unheard of'

FASHION ON THE NORTH BANK

To suggest to the office worker in his collar and tie or the grandad in his cap and muffler, standing on the Laundry End in the 30s, that the clothes on his back had anything to do with anything would have been to make yourself a laughing stock. Beyond a mention of the suitability of a flat cap for headgear on a packed terrace, fashion was something that existed in the pages of glossy magazines and not on the terraces at Highbury. The majority of Arsenal's pre-war crowd hurried to the ground as soon as work finished at lunchtime on Saturday. People arrived dressed in their working clothes, sartorially unprepared for these first – and best – hours of the weekend. The great escape from the humdrum of daily working life was too hurried, and perhaps the wage-packet too small, to include a change of clothes. Club favours, when they came out for the big Cup-ties, were invariably home-made: a splash of colour against the browns and greys of everyday life.

After the war, it was the Supporters' Club rather than the Football Club which recognised a potential market for clothing and memorabilia in the team's colours. Ties, scarves and berets were all sold to raise funds for the ASC in its early days. At first, the terraces seemed, above all, to reflect the austerity of the times. But with the rise in incomes during the late 50s, the all-day Saturday holiday and the appearance of the teenager, the ground was laid for a revolution in football fashions.

Initially, at least, the young people on the North Bank brought their fashions from the street on to the terraces – most obviously the boots, jeans and braces of the late-60s' Skinheads' fashions into which the gib of your scarf or the set of your de-bobbed bobble hat could be incorporated to make their own statement. Over the course of the 60s and 70s, the football fan's clothes became reflective of the world of leisure rather than the world of work. Arsenal, like other leading clubs, put a toe into the steadily growing market for favours and gifts emblazoned with the official Club badge.

Ironically, the first boom in the market for Club merchandise, which owed much of its rapid growth to the development of conscious identity among the teenagers on the North Bank, was undermined by the perceived danger during the 70s and early 80s of wearing colours to football at all. The possibility of identifying yourself as a target for potential trouble-makers – themselves 'unmarked', dressed in the latest 'casual' fashions – was enough to convince many fans that the best place for their colours was a bottom drawer at home, at least until the next year's Cup final.

The change in mood inside the English football stadium after the mid-80s and the growing sophistication of the merchandising arms – now recognised as an essential complement to gate-receipt revenue – of leading clubs like Arsenal coincided with a general social trend towards sportswear as leisure clothing. The times sparked a remarkable (and, for the clubs, profitable) upswing in 'dressing up' for football.

Fashion, while never allowed to become a tail wagging the Arsenal dog, had taken a firm grip on Highbury and its customers by the time the 80s closed. Almost overnight, it seemed, every sports shirt on the North Bank became an Arsenal team shirt. As the age of the shellsuit dawned, the Club shop was poised to take advantage: quilted jackets, training tops, t-shirts, polo shirts, sweatshirts. Football was this market's perfect medium.

A half-page of scarves, rosettes and pennants in the programme during the mid-60s has become a 30-odd page full-colour brochure for the mid-90s. Merchandising is now a vital component of every football club's financial plan, with even Arsenal's gate receipts now accounting for only around 50 per cent of the Club's income. While some dads on the North Bank complained about having to fork out for the boy's new kit each Christmas, the immense popularity of the Arsenal team shirt – a ubiquitous corner-stone on which the contemporary football fashion empire has been built – seemed to suggest that the Club had managed, by and large, to judge the market to perfection. The success over the past two years, of the Arsenal World of Sport complex at Finsbury Park stands testimony to that. Stuff that wasn't even invented when boys were making their own rattles in woodwork class, is now available, in home and away colours (Fleece-lined? Reversible? On interactive video?), and selling well!

All those people would be coming out the station and straight up on to the North Bank. They come in their working clothes – hats and boots and mufflers you know, overcoats – I remember seeing them come with their overalls still on, they'd all have been working Saturday. Everybody worked Saturday morning, everybody worked till 12 o'clock Saturday.

Charlie Robinson

HATS OR CAPS?
Recently I have heard of the revival of the old argument as to which is the most suitable style of headgear for the football spectator. I should fancy that the verdict on this question would be almost unanimous. In the seating parts of the ground the question is not so urgent, but it is important enough with regard to the standing and crowded sections of the ground. Now, to my mind there is no doubt that, however

serviceable and smart the bowler and the soft hat may be, what one really likes to see on the head of the man in front in a tightly packed crowd is the plain, common-or-garden cap. So convinced am I on this point, that I would like respectfully, but seriously, to suggest to patrons who attend matches in other forms of headgear that they would be doing a great service to other spectators, especially those of few inches, if they adopted this humble, but eminently suitable, covering on match afternoons.

AFC Programme, 20.12.30

A mac and a cap. They all had caps on. When we went away we had all the colours on.

Tom Jales

'The Jolly Boys' all decked out in colours. Red and white rosettes were undoubtedly the fashion of the hour.

Islington Gazette, 29.4.30

You weren't frightened to have your colours in them days, you didn't have all them coloured shirts and that but you always had a rosette, or funny hat on or something.

Charlie Robinson

On the way to the scene of the conflict I met a filming procession consisting of an Arsenal fan and friends covered in red from head to foot and carrying a copy of the Cup in the same colour and half a hundred followers all similarly attired.

Glasgow Evening News, 26.4.30

I had a great big heavy wooden rattle. Solid hard wood with a metal cog in it. And to hold it up and go round, you had to take a wide circle, otherwise you wouldn't get it round, it was so heavy. I was taught how to do that! And those trousers! My dad worked for a tailor, he made them for me, the red and white striped trousers. My daughter's got this bell. My dad's bell. This big silver bell. I used to ring that. My dad had it chromed, with a leather strap riveted to it. Didn't get many with them!

Rose Jales

Stand easy and really enjoy the game from whistle to whistle without the dragging, tired feeling which typifies *STRAIN*. Feel 100 per cent fit from morning to night by simply wearing a *LITESOME* Supporter – every man from 16 to 60 needs its comfort, its protection, its support. That's why tens of thousands would not be without their *LITESOME* Supporter. Every man's essential need. From chemists, outfitters, sports shops, etc.

Sheffield Wednesday Programme, 30.1.46

After the war, it all went dead. People stopped dressing up.

Tom Jales

When I was in the RAF and kick-offs were half past one, quarter past two, I couldn't get home in time if I was on a 36-hour pass. So I used to come home, in uniform, dump my kit and say: *Hello, mum. I'm off to football. No time to change.* Forty-nine, 50 this would have been.

Frank Hummell

After the war, I remember going to games in my uniform. When we were demobbed we were all given a civvy suit. You have to remember, clothing was very scarce then. Clothes rationing went on for a long time.

George Williams

Early 50s, everyone had a flat cap, you know, the old cheese-cutters. Scarf – they just had the red-and-white bar scarf. The old macs, shirt and ties, lace-up shoes and trousers. Everyone looked the same. It was a bit like, well, I went on holiday to Romania a few years ago and on the buses they've all got these drab grey or brown macs, they'd all got a cap. That's what it was like. Eastern Europe, to me, was like a time lapse.

Chris Thompson

Nobody wearing their colours, that's another thing. We didn't have scarves. We went straight from work and all the men always had a raincoat over their arms and nearly all the men wore hats as well, or caps. In fact you still see that generation now don't you? I mean, we walked back the other day with somebody and he was in shirt and tie and tweed jacket you know. I suppose it's the casual gear. The only time they dressed up was for top games and then everybody went over the top and the Club used to let the really dressed-up ones run round the track.

Maureen Hewlitt

TIES

An official Club tie has been approved by the Executive Committee, and it is hoped that supplies will be available by the time you get this magazine. The ties are a jacquard weave with woven motifs of the Club emblem incorporated. The design is being registered and can only be purchased by members through the Club, the ties will not be on sale in any shops.

The price of the ties is 8s 3d each, post free, and they can be obtained at the Club Room on Tuesday nights, or by application in writing to the Honorary Secretary.

BADGES

Club badges (prices 2s 6d post free) can be obtained from the Club Room on Tuesday evenings, or by application in writing to the Honorary Secretary. Members are asked to state on their applications whether they require the stud type (for men) or the brooch type (for ladies). Will any members writing for more than one badge please state the name and membership number for which each badge is required. Junior members (under 16 years of age) are entitled to a badge at the reduced rate of 1s 6d each, but it is necessary for them to state the date of their birth on application.

SCARVES

A limited number of red and white woollen scarves is available for our members, and these can be obtained at the Club Room on Tuesday evenings at the cost of 6s 3d each.

BERETS

Red berets (suitable for either sex) are now available, and these can be obtained from the Club Room on Tuesday nights at a cost of 3s each, or by application in writing to the Honorary Secretary at a cost of 3s 3d (including postage and packing).

GunFlash **5**, 1950

I have never really been a fervent football supporter; for if, by a loyal fan, you mean one who dresses up, whirls his rattle, sends balloons flying, and, in short, behaves much as a child at a fancy-dress birthday party, then you don't mean me. That description includes me out. Some of the imbecilities to which soccer fans will go in the support of their team makes me shudder with embarrassment. I have often felt the blush creeping up on me when travelling around on my reporting duties, I have had to mix on the station and in the train with a bunch of grown-up babies who took huge delight in showing themselves off.

Ralph Finn, *Sport Magazine*, November 1952

We had red and white balloons. We'd all congregate on the halfway line at away games and let them go to announce that we were there, you know.

Frank Hummell

It used to be good on the Cup games. The people used to come in their fancy dress and they'd parade round the ground. It was lovely, very enjoyable. People all dressed up in their clothes, people cheered and counter-cheered, friendly booing – nothing nasty – it was a real carnival atmosphere.

Geoff Gilbert

That bloke Dave Stacey used to dress up. Top hat, white trousers and a red coat. He'd walk round the pitch before the game. He used to have a big shield and on it, it said: *We the Arsenal supporters say: May the best team win.* White shoes, white socks, white trousers, red coat with a long tail and a red and white top hat. He used to walk round, with this bloody great shield and a rattle, giving it all that. You saw him at England games, too. (See plates 12 and 13.)

Steve Shaw

When I was a kid you had rattles, bells. You'd buy your scarf. Rosettes were frequent which you don't see now. Arsenal golliwogs which you used to pin on and badges – little stars with all the Arsenal players inside. I mean to own an Arsenal shirt would have been unheard of, you couldn't get hold of one.

Steve Shaw

Rosettes and woolly hats with a little pompom. And I had my bell. I couldn't take that now. It'd be an offensive weapon!

Tina Evans

People always wore rosettes. I had a red rosette, because when I went to the Peterborough–Arsenal Cup game and they lost 2–1, I got about eight rosettes off the terrace after that, people slinging them away. They lasted me about ten years those rosettes.

Maurice Gran

I was at school at the time of rosettes. And I had a very wide woollen scarf my aunt knitted for me. It was stolen eventually by some Chelsea fans who beat me up for it. Scarves, rosettes, I even had a rattle for a while. We did it in woodwork, it was one of their standard things, but they were on the wane then.

Al Fresco

I mean there'd been like a tremendous surge of affluence in the country between, like, the beginning of the 60s and the beginning of the 70s hadn't there? People were much better dressed. In our day, fashion wasn't anything that kids had ever heard of, but by then, it was all about putting the right gear on.

Roger Hewlitt

There was no sort of set uniform like there was in the 70s. In the 60s it was just a matter of people dressing in the fashion of the day, rather than the fashion of football. You always wore your scarf, but not the college type with the name on it, just basic red and white, you know.

Laird Budge

I've been sort of smacked and punched and things when I've been walking from the train station to the ground, and occasionally back on the North Bank, occasions when one lot of supporters have felt a bit brave and charged through. Nine out of ten of the people who have turned tail and run and I'd certainly put myself among them an' all, but we all liked the look of it. I mean we all wore Doc Martens and the braces and the Ben Sherman shirts.

Mick Essen

I tell you what I have got – I've still got it now. You remember the Double year, the silk yellow and blue, with the FA Cup and the Football League Championship on – still got that in a case upstairs in the attic in my house. I remember wearing that. It used to be tie these scarves on your wrist, through your bell loops and things. I don't know about when you used to come but, the white vegetable coats, I call them greengrocer coats. We used to put *George Graham* or *Frank McLintock* and all the team names and things like that on there. I was talking to my pal the other day and he's still got his, up in the loft. He's got all the yellow and blue patches on and red and white down there, it's unbelievable.

Paul Johnson

When I was up the back, I used to have really long hair. It was that time, late 60s, early 70s, when you had to be one thing or the other. Mods had gone and then the Skinheads were coming in. And there was a residue of hippies. It wasn't vogue for hippies to go to football but there were lots of long-haired guys up the North Bank. I remember one day when some blokes set fire to the back of me hair!

John James

In the 70s, there was a couple of stewards there who used to get stick for the way they dressed and that, the way they looked. Flares, things like that. That was always a wag.

Steve Winfield

When I used to go in the 70s there were Badger and Mary, I don't know if you remember them. The bloke used to wear a hat and a black suit, badges all over it so that he looked like a pearly king and he would say his name was Badger because he had all these badges. Mary was his wife, and they used to drape a Union Jack at the front. You used to see them everywhere and there was a feature on them in one of the programmes. They were on *Thames News* in 1979 before the Cup final.

Al Fresco

It was probably into the 70s when there started being a problem with wearing colours.

Eddie Mason

It was bobble hats without bobbles for a while. Then it was silk scarves. Then it was tea-cosy hats and the really trendy thing was to have a two-colour one. You had a red Arsenal one and then had an away one, maybe in green and blue, or you had a red Arsenal one and you had a Scottish one the other side, say Dundee United. They seemed to be the most popular ones, or Arsenal and Celtic, Arsenal and Rangers, Arsenal and Dundee United – those tea-cosy hats. About silk scarves, I don't know why, and probably I let it go later than other people because I'm not the most fashion-conscious of people, but when I started going to away games they were the thing. When I started going to a lot of away games outside London, everyone was wearing silk scarves tied round their wrists. That was 1977. I used to have a red and white silk scarf on that wrist and a yellow and blue one on that wrist, that was another superstition that was. They had to be worn in a certain way. Yeah, yellow and blue scarves were: *If you wear away colours you're a truer fan.*

Al Fresco

I remember bringing a friend who was an Everton supporter. I said: *You wait till you get in there, you'll see every single bloke of my age will have the Charlie Nicholas haircut!* Everybody had the haircut, including myself I have to admit. I remember going into the hairdressers once and when he said: *How do you want your hair?* And I just said: *Like*

Charlie Nicholas. He goes: *Oh, yeah. We know.* You went in and asked for a Charlie Nicholas and they knew what you wanted.

David Court Jnr

And then, I suppose, replica shirts. I think they were starting in the late 80s. I think it was becoming a thing then to wear replica shirts. I mean people were wearing sports shirts – not just football shirts – as everyday wear. That's something that changed in the 80s. What was previously leisure-wear – tracksuits, shellsuits, all that sort of stuff, sports shirts – became acceptable to wear into work. Clubs picked up on that, and it's still going on here today. Most people wear replica shirts now – they're the thing. I've got one now, which I wear when I play. It's just the changing fashion isn't it? I mean, most people at most clubs, if you want to identify yourself with your club you wear a shirt, and if you're a real fan you wear the away shirt, because real fans go to away games. You don't have to go to every away game but you go to away games so, therefore, to show that you're a true supporter you wear the away shirt.

Al Fresco

The team shirts? You want to be your hero if you kick about on a Sunday morning. With the shirt, you feel more a part of it. I'll wear it to every game. I do wash it though! And then after the season it becomes a bit of memorabilia, doesn't it? You've got to wear your shirt. Not many people wear scarves now but everybody's got one. I wear mine because I always have, the same scarf. But I don't think they sell as many now. If they can sell a shirt they can make more money, can't they? I'd like to have one of them from the 70s, red with short sleeves, white with a little red band and a little white band round the neck with the little cannon. I'd like to get hold of one of them. You can get some of the old ones can't you? Like the 30s ones. You can tell the people who stand up the back because they're the ones who don't wear any jackets over their Arsenal shirts. Because it's hot and because they want to show off who they support.

Guy Thomson

I hated the new away shirt but then I thought how ironic it was that the Arsenal are the most traditional, old-fashioned fuddy-duddies in the world and yet they've actually produced *the* modern shirt. I love the fact it's become the biggest-selling shirt ever.

Richard Stubbs

This is where merchandising has come in. I mean, now, 50 per cent of people going to Highbury are wearing all the Arsenal clobber – shirts, jumpers, all this.

Steve Shaw

Premier League football kicks off today and every young fan will be imitating their heroes in the nation's parks first thing Monday morning. And, as any football-mad kid knows, there is nothing as embarrassing as mucking about in last season's kit.

British parents fork out a small fortune to keep their children looking like a mini-version of Vinny Jones or Peter Beardsley.

And clubs can't help cashing in – by constantly changing the colour and style of their football strips. Take Arsenal, for instance. As you can see from our two pictures, last season's kit appears very similar to the new one. The only real differences are the new position of the logos of both the club and the manufacturer, plus the stripes on the sleeve. As our table shows, for these subtle alterations parents are having to find £44 for a kit.

Daily Mirror, 1992

First game of this season I was walking down from Finsbury Park and all the young fellows were wearing Arsenal shirts. Not last season's, mind, the new ones! I don't know how much they are, £20? £30? They're spending fortunes!

Dennis Evans

I've got glasses, underpants, socks, French letters. I've got cannons all over the place!

Steve Shaw

It all has to match. I wear blue jeans, my white polo neck, team shirt, jacket and if it's cold I've got an Arsenal hat and gloves. If I'm going away, I've got green jeans that go with my away top. You have to wear the shirt, the jacket, the scarf and the hat. If I see something in a shop that's of Arsenal, I have to get it. I work during the summer now. I wanted to get the new tracksuit top and every time I got fed up of work and wanted to go home, I'd just think about that tracksuit. I bought an Arsenal shirt and wore it to school. I had to keep my cardigan over it because if my teacher saw it she'd make me take it off. And when we won the title I was wearing red and white ribbons in my hair and my teacher goes: *We can tone down on the Arsenal ribbons, can't we?* She knew I wouldn't take them out!

Julie Wheeler

It's just fashion, isn't it? I mean, that's all any of it is. I don't know who decides it or, I don't know, if people get bored with things. I liked inflatables. When did you last see a whole crowd with inflatables? I mean, they only lasted half a season and the best one was Grimsby with Harry the Haddock, that was fantastic. I don't know, maybe we were a bit too cool at Arsenal, we never quite went into them the way Man City or Grimsby did.

Al Fresco

My brother and I were watching telly and there was a guy in an Arsenal shirt, I think it was the European Championships – and he had this pair of shades on and we just said: *Oh, look – typical Arsenal!* I think they're a bit flash! Designer gear flash, the younger ones anyway. I've got a funny feeling you see more people wearing sunglasses when it's cloudy up the North Bank then you would, say, at QPR.

Amanda Caspari

After we won the League I had a tattoo on my shoulder. The tattooist wouldn't do the lettering: *AFC*. He said: *You'll go off them. It's just because they've won the League.* He was French and obviously wasn't into football. I tried to explain to him: *You just can't change team. Even if you want to. There are times you want to be a fan of someone else. You can't.*

Natasha Horbacki

CHAPTER ELEVEN

'You're an Arsenal Fan, You're Arsenal'

THE NORTH BANK MELTING POT

The story of the North Bank tells a story, too, of much that has happened to the Borough of Islington since Arsenal built their new home in its north-eastern corner in 1913. Stretching north from the City and the industrial fringes of the East End, Islington was then – as it is now – a densely concentrated residential area which Henry Norris was astute enough to recognise as the perfect environment in which to develop a reliable audience for League football. Despite the nearby counter-attractions of Tottenham Hotspur, to the north, and Clapton Orient, to the east, football at Highbury was an immediate success with its new audience. This was achieved in the face of misgivings forcibly expressed by some local residents prior to the move, who feared for the sobriety of their Saturday afternoons in the wake of the roughnecks a football team next door would inevitably attract. They probably had in mind the denizens of some of Islington's notoriously anarchic backstreets, such as Campbell Road in Finsbury Park and Queensland Road behind Drayton Park. It seems, however, that the problems encountered by Highbury's neighbours had more to do with the size of the crowds that arrived on their doorsteps every other weekend than with the character of those crowds.

The largely working-class population of Islington was hungry for entertainment: by the time Arsenal were attracting 50,000 in the late 1920s, the Borough was also supporting *two dozen* cinemas and several theatres and music halls. The local audience, a tram ride or walk away, could be filled out with those from further afield who took advantage of the proximity of Gillespie Road Underground station. Excavations from the new Piccadilly Railway had provided foundations for Highbury's terraces. Now supporters spilled from its trains on to the Laundry End.

During the 1930s, apart from special occasions like Cup-ties, Arsenal enjoyed an almost exclusively metropolitan audience. Long-distance travel was expensive and time-consuming and the motor car had yet to make its mark. Of the two 'ends', it appears the Laundry End was the more cosmopolitan of the terraces because of its convenience beside the now-renamed Arsenal Tube station. The Clock End backed on to, and attracted a crowd from, Islington's heartlands – Holloway, Dalston, Hoxton, and the Caledonian Road. The terraces of the period would, generally, have made room for a higher proportion of 'neutral' football supporters, followers of other London clubs who would take the Underground to Highbury on Saturdays when their own teams played away. Likewise, many Arsenal supporters remember taking the bus up Seven Sisters Road to watch Tottenham every other week.

Although the glamour associated with Arsenal attracted a famously cosmopolitan and well-heeled crowd, this finds its more accurate reflection in the construction of the lavish East and West stands and their occupation by a percentage of season-ticket holders wistfully admired by secretary–managers elsewhere. Although the mix of 'blue' and 'white' collars in Islington was reflected on the terrace, silk topper and flat cap occupied very different worlds at Highbury as elsewhere. The Laundry End was the crowded home of the working and lower-middle classes while Arsenal attracted royalty and the glitterati to the luxury of the stands. During the 30s, the Club was responsible for broadening the appeal of the game beyond its traditional audience, without doubt. But it was still the railway porters, pattern-cutters and errand-boys who continued to crowd, nearly 20,000 at a time, on to the Laundry End.

The Second World War had a profound effect on the demographics of the Borough and those of its local football ground. The bombs which the Luftwaffe dropped on north London created the first ripples in a pattern of migration which spread outwards from Highbury – and from Islington – and continued to do so, for different reasons, throughout the post-war period. Driven out, at first, by the Blitz to safer suburban environments shared with friends and family, many never returned – the first emigrants in a general shift by better-off working families out from the dense and deprived urban centres to the outlying suburban districts and, then, the new towns to the north and east: places like Watford, Hatfield, Harlow and Chelmsford. This process continued to accelerate into the 60s but, importantly from the North Bank's point of view, many of these families maintained links with their old way of life, returning to Islington by the improved road and rail networks to be at Highbury on Saturday afternoons. For a new generation, born and raised 50 or more miles from N5, going to Arsenal remained an essential part of their lives and identities.

And as the traditional football crowd moved away from Islington, immigrant groups moved in to take their places. During the 50s, Irish, Greek and Cypriot supporters who had settled in the Borough – the former around Archway and Holloway in partciular, the latter in Finsbury Park – found themselves places on the North Bank. Many of the newcomers arrived as Arsenal fans already, the Club having been synonymous with English football all over the world for two decades. On the home end, they joined ethnic groups who had been standing on the North Terrace since the 1920s, Jews particularly – drawn from the garment industries of the East End and the residential areas north of Finsbury Park. These were later joined, come the 1980s, by Afro-Caribbeans – a growing presence in the Borough and attracted, too, by the young black players breaking into the Arsenal team.

Recently, the continuing gentrification of large areas of Islington left its mark on the North Bank as well. Middle-class spectators, interested not only in football but in the unfamiliar culture of the North Bank, now began to choose to stand rather than sit. The sense of involvement, the noise and colour of the event – as well as the sport – could be enjoyed as safely on the terrace as on a seat. To the end, the North Bank's story reflected the Borough's own.

Television and improved transport facilities have had their own effect on Highbury's crowd, of course. With the spread of televised football since the 60s and the simultaneously increasing ease of travel, the big clubs have become able to attract audiences from enormous distances beyond their traditional catchment areas. Arsenal and other London teams, especially, have benefited from the general trend. The 'walk round the corner' to the North Bank was, for some, an adventure in time and distance of epic proportions.

The North Bank of recent years comprised an extraordinary mix of ethnic, social and cultural backgrounds thanks, on the one hand, to the nature of the Borough in which Woolwich Arsenal chose to settle and, on the other, to the remarkable and well-publicised success of the club Henry Norris brought to Highbury. That mix is something that the North Bank deserves to be remembered for: a model of informal, good-natured and good-humoured co-existence. It was cosmopolitan to an extent not seen on any other terrace in the country. Not always as passionate or as loud as some might wish but, by the end of its story at least, the North Bank enjoyed degrees of tolerance, intelligence and open-mindedness of which all who stood there could and should be proud.

'SOMETHING IN COMMON'

Just in line with the penalty area, inside of the first post so you had a clear view across the goal. My spot. My land. It felt like my land, I'd paid for it enough times.

Richard Stubbs

In a way it's like a sort of family, although you don't necessarily stand next to the same people when you go. It does happen in a lot of cases, people meet there and stand in the same place. It's still like sort of a large family. You feel like you're part of that. You know it's more or less the same people who go, and if you take friends along who haven't been there before, it's like you try very hard to make sure they have a good time, because you want them to be impressed.

Mick Essen

That's the amazing thing about football and football fans: all of a sudden you have something in common with another person. If you both have a really strong feeling about it, there's a really strong bond between you even though in other circumstances you wouldn't maybe speak to that other person. There's this common denominator. It happens to be Arsenal and it happens to be love!

Emma Young

Football is a social life. You follow the team. You meet different people. They introduce you to different areas of London. It was a big part of growing up.

Vidos Neophytou

Everybody I know goes to every game. One story: those semi-finals against Liverpool in 1980. I think it was at Coventry. I've got a group of mates I've stood with for donkey's years. I went up on my own and I got in and saw this bloke I recognised from the North Bank. I'd never spoken to him or anything but I asked him if he'd seen my mates. He said: *Yeah. They're just down there!* The group of people I stood on the North Bank with I would very rarely see anywhere else. That's the thing about football, isn't it? You come together, become really good friends, experience some amazing moments together and then you go away again. It's football friends.

Richard Stubbs

I just think that they were true, true Arsenal supporters, real Arsenal supporters, supporters that will go to every game, and you'll find most of the people that travel away are North Bank supporters, the diehards that are going to go to every match that they can go to. I go to most of the home games, one away now and again, I'll go if I can, if I can make it. I think the extra vociferous element, they'll go up and watch them playing Newcastle or wherever it may be, they'll be there.

Frank Warren

Going to football, going to Arsenal particularly for the big teams, is a love/hate thing. It's not something you do casually, you can't treat it like going to the cinema.

Andrew Allerton

The thing with Arsenal is you either love the Club or you hate it. And I love it.

Alex Froso

I think the 'lucky Arsenal' tag came from their style. They could be defending a lot and it would seem like the other team was all over them, then Alex James could pass to one of the wingers and it would be in the net. You can be most dangerous when you're defending with someone like Hulme who was renowned for his speed. Hulme and Bastin scored umpteen goals between them. We hardly needed a centre-forward.

George Williams

Most football supporters are paranoid and I think Arsenal supporters are as bad as any I have come across. I certainly am. I mean, I certainly have a *Everybody hates us* view of football which wasn't there in the 50s. I said earlier Arsenal had a style then, the Club had a style, and I don't think people disliked Arsenal. From the 30s, when they first introduced the stopper centre-half, people had a criticism about the style of play, which carries on to this day, but people did appreciate the Arsenal. *The everybody hates us* thing, I think, has been a gradual thing over the years, like the violence and the terrace hooliganism, I think it's crept up. I think it's developed with communications. I mean, the newspapers were a lot less flamboyant in the 50s, they tended to report things as a factual happening. Over the years they developed into picking on the more sensational issues. As far as I'm concerned the big papers, *The Times* and *The Telegraph* have a high moral tone to their football reporting: *There is only one way to play football and if you don't play it then that is it.* It wouldn't matter if Arsenal played it better than anyone else in the world, they would still criticise. That's my paranoia. But I do believe that the press has developed that along the years. Football in the 50s was reported as a factual straightforward event you know. But over the years it changed.

John Platt

I've always suffered for being an Arsenal supporter. Around here, Hatfield, unless they're Arsenal they all fall in line and knock you. You'd go into the pub and if they'd lost you'd get slaughtered and if they'd won, you'd be ghosty. But when I was up the North Bank, it was like you were with your own, everybody was together. You're not looking to defend yourself.

Laird Budge

I love the fact that they're the establishment. I love the fact they're traditional. I love the fact everyone hates us. Everybody wants to have a go at us. I love it.

Richard Stubbs

The Stretford End was a big disappointment – I don't know how they got their reputation. The Holte End's a big terrace – the biggest – but they could do better. The Kop I respect. Some of the smaller northern clubs, I've found, are more vocal than London. The north in general are more vocal. I think Arsenal when they want to be are as loud as you can get. But it's only certain occasions when they're on top form, where some northern clubs, like Blackburn for example, they can raise the roof just for a corner, you know. I suppose we expect more.

Paul Jerrams

I don't think supporters down here are as passionate as the ones up north, like Leeds. Externally, I mean. I mean, we all feel the same, we want to win, but outwardly Arsenal's not the greatest amtosphere, is it?

Mark Burdis

I've had a lot of contact with people like Plymouth supporters and Exeter supporters, it's where I used to come from and, obviously, their expectations were a lot lower. We expect a good team performance every time we watch our club play, and they don't. They can come up here, I travelled up with Plymouth fans when we beat them 6–1. We got lots of stick, there were two or three of us, we had a lot of stick from them. They went down one end, we went down the North Bank, and after the game they had had a great day out: *Oh great game, that was* – a 6–1 stuffing! Can you ever imagine us enjoying a 6–1 stuffing? – *We came down and we were taught how to bloody play the game today.* We didn't get any stick on the way back at all! I think all genuine football supporters love their club the same, you know. I'm sure if they know their team then they know when they're playing badly, they know when they're playing well. Each ground has probably got their slaggers as well, we just seem to have a lot of them at Highbury. If things aren't going well then you hear it from the crowd, you know, which is bad.

Rob Ashman

I think Arsenal fans' capacity for irony and disaffection has served them well in the long term. I've got this theory that Manchester United and Leeds, in particular, would never have got themselves into the messes they got in if their fans were as London fans were, who just wouldn't put up with it. When you go to those places, they've just got incredible support – we never make noise like that. The down side to that is you tend to put up with any old shit and *we* don't put up with any old shit. They take the piss out of us because we're whingers. But I think that's good, I think it's a healthy thing. It's the closest football fans get to being discriminating consumers! They're bright enough to know when things aren't good enough.

Nick Hornby

I think my feeling about the Arsenal is that they're very, well, what's called in medicine *emotionally labile*. They go from euphoria to depression and when they're depressed – I mean Alan Smith is the best example of that when he's down and he goes for ten weeks in a row without scoring, you can see his head hanging. I think it goes back a long way. But when they've had a bad sequence it reinforces itself, the crowd is depressed and disillusioned by it, and to get them going it has to be on a sort of knife-edge where the crowd feel that they're going to make a difference. It often happens when we have a run of six or eight or even ten bad games, then they come out of it and have an absolutely unbeatable run for 20 games. It's when they're on that sort of cusp between the down and the up that the crowd can make that big difference. Every so often when it's into the beginning of their good run, it takes a bit of a while to get their spirit going and it can happen that the crowd by singing and chanting can carry them through. They're a very moody side and a very moody crowd as well, I think. I think that when the team is down the crowd is down, they reinforce each other. I mean its like a kid, you know, like the six-month-old with colic who has tears streaming down his face and two minutes later it's all over.

John Yudkin

Looking back on it now, it used to go in ages. Younger ones at the back, going down to middle-aged regulars at the front and older people on the side. And right at the front there'd be the nippers. It was different for the younger blokes. You'd go down and have a sing, see your mates, chanting, it was your team and everything, where the older people would appreciate the football more. When you're younger, you just want them to win in a certain way. The old ones would still be going on about Logie and that. They were still there in the crowd.

Steve Winfield

That's what football is, actually, it's the mix of all ages. You go to pubs and there's the 15-year-olds' pub, the 20-year-olds' pub, there's the old geezers' pub, or whatever. But football mixes it all and I hope seats won't stop that.

Richard Stubbs

When I was old enough to go on my own, my mum let me go in the Schoolboys' and I was happy there for a couple of years. Then I became very, very anxious to get on to the North Bank but I was really scared, and I stood there for about six months sort of looking at it and thinking: *Well, if I went in that bit, that probably wouldn't be so bad!* I remember very clearly, my heart in my mouth, paying 25p instead of 15p to go on the North Bank and I stood middle towards the bottom. Then as I got older and I grew a bit I went middle top and then the next few years, when I was post-wannabe hooligan, halfway down left and then the last few years top right, just on the edge of the roof with a group of friends. Sometimes there'd be two of us – but everybody else knew where we'd be so some weeks there'd be 15. Now that's all gone. I've got a season ticket and we've got a spare one – but it's not the same is it?

Nick Hornby

There was a migration as you grew up. At first, I'd stand behind the goal. I was only little – I didn't mind watching through the net, watching Jim Furnell and other goalies and their little rituals. And then you wanted to get into the North Bank, when you got bigger. If you could stand on the back you could, well, you were the accepted crowd. Then you tended to move back into the middle again and then out along the side. It was great over on the side. You know, you were still 17 but going on 40. You were close enough to the atmosphere to touch it but you were a bit remote from it, too. You had the atmosphere but you could watch the game. And, of course, on the big games you were all shouting and cheering them on.

John James

Well where I stood the last three or four years, on the top side, ages range from something younger than me to 30-odd. People that slightly knew each other used to stand there every week, who you'd see at away games sometimes and out of the ground sometimes. If you were to get a map of the North Bank and how it was and ask people where they stood, they'd know people there and those people would know people there and around there. I mean it was a really nice atmosphere. It must be 50 people I used to sort of at least say hello to just around where I was standing, 20 of them I might know their names, five or ten, you might meet again outside.

Josh Yudkin

One match last season we took someone along who hadn't been to football since the 70s. He'd stopped going because of all the trouble. After the game he said that the atmosphere on the North Bank – all the children, the women, it wasn't all white or all blokes – he said he'd never felt that. He'd never felt so comfortable. And we were in the right rowdy bit!

Natasha Horbacki

'WHERE HAVE YOU COME FROM?'

I don't think you could define a North Bank 'supporter'. Not in a nutshell. They come from all walks of life, don't they? All a mix of nationalities and race.

Lenny Brandon

I grew up in Holloway. The people I went with, there was eight of us, I met them through football. We played for a team over Regent's Park. It was a Tottenham steward managed us, as it happens. But most of us were Arsenal and going on the North Bank was like our social thing. Whenever we were together it was all football.

Steve Winfield

I was born in Caledonian Road, so I've always been in walking distance of the Arsenal. We used to walk along the Cally and then down St James Road – it's Mackenzie Road now. We always used to walk there and back. I still walk there now. In fact, if the wind's in the right direction you can hear the shout from here. I'll get home and Joan will say: *What happened about ten past four? Oh, that's when we scored!*

George Williams

He always stood on the North Bank, me dad. From 1920 onwards he stood up that end. If you lived down that end, if you lived in Finsbury Park or you lived at Manor House you came in that end and that's why you were there. We always did. It's a funny thing, we still go to the Arsenal that same route. Although we sit now, we go that same route, the Finsbury Park way. I always come in that end. I don't know, I think the funniest thing about football is, whether you sit or stand, you always go to the same place. I don't know why that is. We used to go through the same turnstile, up those stairs to our position, and there we would stand.

Maurice Gran

My cousin took me to my first match when I was nine. I'd never been up that way, near Highbury, before. I come from Hoxton which is north London even though a lot of people class it as east. It's a part of Hackney. I would say it's 60 or 70 per cent Arsenal, 30 per cent Tottenham with a few West Ham chucked in.

Paul Jerrams

The first game I went to was a reserve game around 1952. Our next-door neighbour took me. We lived in Stoke Newington and we walked down and I can remember being in awe of it, you know, all the people. My dad was a Leyton Orient supporter, he came from over that way. But I went to school locally and I was a football fanatic from the word go. And it was always Arsenal. In those days it was local. By 1957, when I started going regular, we'd moved to Enfield but I knew a boy whose dad went every week so I used to go with them. And I still stand in the same spot, on the right-hand side just outside the roof – near enough to run in if there's a downpour. It was a tradition wasn't it? My friend's dad, his dad had stood in that same area in the 20s.

John Platt

The only unfortunate thing about the job was that during that time, Arsenal didn't do a lot in the football line, didn't win anything. I was born in Highbury and lived in Highbury New Park until 1975. I used to come to Arsenal before I joined the police. It was an added benefit of the job.

PC Roy Beasley, retd

Supporters were more local. In the 50s we were the exception, coming from outside. I suppose it started happening in the 50s and 60s, people like my mum and dad who got bombed during the war and had gone out of London. The war started sending people out of London but they'd still come in to watch their team. But it was still localised to an extent, there wasn't the media coverage, the television. I mean, if you go down Watford High Street on a Saturday now, you'll see kids wearing Watford and Arsenal shirts, and other London clubs, but also you'll see Man United, Liverpool and Leeds, the glamour clubs, because the media has opened it up. It wasn't like that then. I can remember going into school the day after the Munich Air Disaster. I was in tears, I was crying but nobody else was. It affected me because I'd been to that Arsenal vs Man United game the week before. Even the teachers couldn't understand but I'd seen those players on the Saturday. If half the Manchester United team got wiped out today, every kid would know about it because of the media coverage. It was in the papers and on the telly but it only meant something, really, if you'd seen those players play.

Tina Evans

We used to go to Charlton one week and Arsenal the next. You see, because of the Woolwich connection, so many people used to come over from south of the river that, by and large, Charlton were at home the same day as Tottenham so there wouldn't be a clash with the Arsenal.

Chris Thompson

The boys that I used to come with lived in Northampton, Luton, Milton Keynes, in that area. I talk to people: *Where have you come from?* They say to me: *We've come all the way from Luton this morning to come back out on a charter to Manchester.* There is definitely a percentage of people that come from far away, whether it be St Albans, whether it be Luton, whether it be Southend, Canvey Island, wherever. We have got a lot of outside-London fans. I think it's been steady. If I look at my memberships, the majority I would have to say, obviously, is N5, N1, but a hell of a lot are from Hertfordshire, Suffolk, Sussex, Essex.

Paul Johnson

One of the themes of my book is that I was this suburban boy and I was always desperate to be a north London boy and I used to pester my dad to move to Highbury. He used to say: *I don't think you'll like it. What will you do when you grow up and don't like Arsenal any more?* At that time, I very strongly had the feeling that everybody came from around the ground. But then I noticed, particularly when I went to Cambridge, that I'd get on the train at Cambridge, there'd be 20 or 30 Arsenal supporters. By the time the train got to Hitchin, it was absolutely packed and from there on in you could hardly get on the train. And then four or five years ago, achieving my ambition and moving to Finsbury Park, I noticed that Saturday afternoons I walk out of my front door, I'm the only one! It's all cars, coming from the Home Counties. All those terrace houses round here, they've completely changed their meaning. When you look at a house like that now you don't see the same thing you saw 30 years ago – I mean, I grew up in a small, detached house in a small, detached town and when I looked at the houses when I was a kid I thought: *Poor people.* Now I look at them and I think: *Rich people.* There are people paying £100/150,000 to live in this street and they're not interested in going. People have pushed further and further out. I think TV has made it easier to support a team that's not your local team. And I think, if you live in Maidenhead or Watford, or Hitchin or Slough, you feel a bit pissed off with what life has allotted you in terms of your football teams. You think: *Why the hell can't I support Arsenal?* I mean, for me, it was dead cheap to get there – it was 30 pence on the train, it was easy to come and watch them – and I thought: *Well, I don't want to watch Maidenhead United. I want to watch Arsenal – or Chelsea or Tottenham or QPR, who other kids at school were watching.* And all the other things I wanted from football – the excitement, looking at the clothes and the haircuts, the rumour-mongering, the whole culture of football was missing (from my local teams).

Nick Hornby

On the North Bank, I'd imagine people have roots in north London, even though they may be coming in from Hertfordshire or wherever. They've moved out or moved to south London. When my grandfather went in the 50s it was very much a north London crowd – Islington, Hackney and Harringey. But it's inevitable people gradually move out – it's something that's happened to London since the war. I think that's one way that football's very important. It's a way for people to retain their roots. It gives people a sense of community they'd otherwise lack.

Andrew Allerton

I've been following Arsenal for as long as I can remember but I didn't get to a game until 1983 because it was such a long way to come, Horsham, near Brighton. I couldn't afford it, you know, and I had a Saturday job, too. But I finally said: *That's it I'm going to a game.* My dad went a bit mad because hooliganism was really knocking about then. I went up there on the train, it took about an hour-and-a-half and when I got there – I'd seen it on the telly – but when I went up those steps and on to the North Bank. I thought: *Oh, yes. This is the place to be.* The Arsenal fans, like the Kop or the Stretford End, they *are* the North Bank. That's where all the noise comes from and I wanted to be in all the noise. I thought it would be loud and a bit squashed and it turned out to be loud and bloody squashed. You know there was that trench that runs across about halfway up? Well, I stood against the bar just above that. I never stood there again! You get everyone comes forward. I got crushed to death. But it didn't matter because we won.

Then after I finished college, I thought: *I've got to get up to London*. My brother lived up here. I didn't know where but I thought I'd find him and I did. I had to move to London so I could go and see the Arsenal. Now, I'll only live in north London. It's nice here too, you know, but that's a very very big part of it.

Guy Thomson

I grew up in Norwich but as soon as I'd done my A Levels, I moved down here for work. And I had some friends. I lived all over the place. Bethnal Green, Marylebone, in rented places. But as soon as I decided I was going to buy a flat, we're going to these estate agents and they're going: *Well, what sort of place do you want?* And I said: *I didn't care as long as I can walk to Arsenal*. It had to be Stoke Newington, Highbury or Islington, basically. That was my main criterion. Not how many bedrooms but how easily can I get to the ground!

Stewart O'Brien

You get where it's handed down. My daughter Jenny comes down with me. Because I go and watch Arsenal, she does. She starts off watching a London side, born and bred up here in Northampton.

Chris Thompson

We've received a very interesting letter from Margaret Shillam from Nottingham. She told us about a trip her father and 31 other supporters from Suffolk made to see our famous title-winning side of 1931. There wasn't an Arsenal Travel Club in those days! Margaret says the fans put away sixpence (2.5p today!) a week to save up for their spring trip to Highbury. They could only afford to come once a season.

AFC Programme, 10.9.83

Well, Andy will come over to my place. First thing when I see Andy is when he walks through my gate. I see this red and white shirt and he's there and he's like this: *Come on!* We'll have a cup of tea nine o'clock, quarter to nine, get in the car, get sorted out. Off we go and straight away we'll be talking about who's playing, any problem that may have come up that week connected with Arsenal. We normally have a couple of sing-songs up the A373, before we hit the M5 just to get started. There we are, just driving along, getting our emotions up. We actually get on very well anyway, which is very good. It's always like an away trip. It's a great day out. You can get away from it all, you know. Everything else you've got in life, you can forget that day. The day is Arsenal. It's therapeutic at Highbury, it makes me feel so good. I shout off every aggression that I've got in me, come away well happy. What we used to do was stop off at Heston, have a sandwich and a drink, drive up round the North Circular and get to the ground about one o'clock. That was when you paid in and there was always the chance that we'd be locked out. I always used to allow for a bit of time, possibly for a breakdown and to get to the ground. I didn't mind because I could get into the North Bank and that would be it. Very few people there, you'd sit down read the programme, you'd begin another packet of peanuts or something. People we know would start arriving, local lads would get there about twenty to three. The usual shaking of the hands, *Hello mate*, if somebody had a baby or somebody's pregnant, that would be got out the way and then: *Right, what do you think about today?* A chat about the prospect of the game, the team would come out and then football. The game would finish, we'd scoot off. Always wait for the final whistle but then straight away. I'd get back about nine o'clock you know, that's not a bad time.

Rob Ashman

I think there are so many people now, with better transport, that come from outside. Some of the accents that you see, you turn round and think: *He's come a way*. What time do they set out to come from there, you know, what time are they going to get home? Brilliant! That's a good supporter, that's nearly week in week out, you know with the better transport and that.

Steve Winfield

My father's parents moved to England from Russia, my mother's parents from Warsaw, both about 1905/1907 and they settled in Stepney. They later moved to Hackney and Dalston, which meant when my mum and her family – my dad was never interested in football – when my mum was little she and her sister and her older brother were all Arsenal supporters. My mother used to go a fair amount in the early and mid-30s. Alex James was her favourite player, she was about 15 or 16. Her sister married another Hackney Jewish schmutter business guy who was also heavily into Arsenal, my uncle Morry, who used to take me to football. And apparently there was a very large number of immigrant Jewish people who were following the Arsenal in the period between the wars.

John Yudkin

The thing about Arsenal is it's on top of Holloway Road, which is on top of Archway which is on top of Kilburn. So there's always been a heavy Irish contingent. Like me. I mean, my dad don't watch football but his sons do and their sons do. Thousands of people in the stand – *his dad's Irish, he's Irish, his grandparents were Irish* – thousands! And that ten years when we had so many Irish players in the team, you go to Ireland now and you've still got loads of people who are Arsenal because of that. I don't know if that will fade away. Arsenal, Man United, Liverpool and Everton are the big clubs in Dublin. Tottenham don't get a look-in! And we're still right on top of the biggest Irish community in London.

Mark Burdis

Watching a team every week, it's natural you're going to start supporting them. And the more successful they are, the more games you're going to have to do. The more money you earn! No, seriously, I'm a staunch Arsenal fan now – even though I'm from Scotland – and have been for years.

PC Alan Smith

It wasn't something that I was particularly conscious of but, looking back on it, there weren't many black people at the games. Although there was one black guy I can remember. Apparently he was one of the troublemakers. I'd heard of him before and later on I saw who he was. But, generally, there was no hostility towards me as a supporter. I was really quite comfortable, going down there and watching the game. When I first came into the Arsenal team there were about half a dozen black players in the First Division. Racism wasn't a problem at Highbury but away from home, especially up north, it was tough. In a way, though, it was complimentary because you knew they were trying to put you off your game. So it didn't really worry me that much. When I started playing for the first team, I remember someone shouting out from the crowd, the usual racist things, as I was warming up on the touch-line. This voice kept shouting out this stuff and I thought: *I've got to turn round and check this person out.* And it was a black girl. I couldn't believe it! Shouting out all this racist stuff. I just couldn't figure it out at all. There may have been one or two instances of racism towards opposing players. I don't remember them distinctly. They would have been small pockets of people. Nothing that ever worried me, really.

Paul Davis

When I first started going there weren't a lot of black kids that went. A couple went with us. Definitely more now with Ian Wright, Kevin Campbell. There was a time when you used to get booing and monkey chants over there but you never get that now. That's all gone. It's just ignorance. And other people won't tolerate that now. And I think you'll find there's more Asian people going now where four years ago they wouldn't.

Mark Burdis

It's all to do with the community. I mean, 20, 30 years ago there weren't many black kids round here. Islington Boys Club there was one black kid out of 60 or 70 kids who used to go down there. But as the population changes round here, so does the support of Arsenal. And you get people move. Say a kid grows up in north London and he moves to east London, he's not going to change his team, is he? It all builds up. Lots of people come in, there's some link with Arsenal, they come to watch the football. You know, it's like I can't imagine a kid who was born, bred and raised in Manchester would support Arsenal. There's always a connection along the line. Their great uncle takes them over there or gets them a programme or a scarf or something. And they grow up with it. It's very rare a kid would change his team.

Vidos Neophytou

There's a big Greek contingent, Cypriots. They are fanatics. They're mad. I think they go just to let off their steam. You know. *You crazy bastard, ref!* And it's half time, you know.

Mark Burdis

With the Greek and Cypriot supporters, well, it's entirely to do with where they are. They're in the heart of north London – Green Lanes, Finsbury Park, around Highbury, it's a very big Greek community. It's all to do with the community, really, they live in the area. Funny enough, you go back to Cyprus and geezers who used to live over here, they still support Arsenal. And you go there for a holiday and you'll get people who've never been over here, they start asking you questions about the Arsenal. (Their uncle lived here for years or something.)

Vidos Neophytou

Before I left Cyprus I used to watch the Greek Cypriot team, Apoel, who've played Arsenal a couple of times. I'd been going to football since I was seven. Now I'm 57 and I've been going to Highbury for 38 years.

When I was in Cyprus, I used to read and hear about the Arsenal because in the early 50s they were one of the best-known clubs in Cyprus. When I came to this country, I used to live in Peckham and I started to learn my way around, you know, on the buses. I used to have to get three buses to get to Highbury – the number 1 to the Elephant, then get on to Warren St or Goodge St and get the 29 to Finsbury Park. About one-and-a-half hours travelling. But I loved it. I had Arsenal in my blood. When I first came to Highbury, it was incredible. In Cyprus you watch games, there are 2/3,000 people. When I came and saw the thousands going into Arsenal I was shocked. I couldn't believe it. I remember a Spurs game with 62,000 packed in like sardines. I loved it.

Alex Froso

My brothers never go to Arsenal or my dad. But my uncle, he was a building worker, he had football as part of his social life. He'd finish work on a Saturday morning, go down the pub for a couple of pints and then over Arsenal with the blokes he was working with. He was introduced to it through that.

Vidos Neophytou

Because of my involvement with Greek social clubs and in the Greek community, we've estimated there are ten to 15 thousand Greek Cypriots who follow Arsenal. When I go to friends' houses, the majority of the kids are wearing Arsenal shirts and so on. It gives me pleasure to see the Club still growing within the Greek community. We have some go to Chelsea, some to Tottenham and a few to West Ham but the majority of the Greek community go to Arsenal. People of my age, when they came to England they already knew about the Arsenal – 30 or 40 years ago – we didn't know about Spurs and Manchester United. And Arsenal, today, is still the main team back in Cyprus. My ambition, when I go back, is to open an Arsenal supporters' club in Cyprus. I'll have to fly back for all the home games!

Alex Froso

Well this is just from somebody we stand with: his name's Pete Quatere which is a really odd name, but he's Belgian. He's stood in the same spot for well over 40 years with his father – and his father's now dead. They've got Belgian cousins. And one

Saturday some friends of the Belgian cousins came over to England and they wanted to see a game and these cousins just said to the friends: *Well, Pete and his father stand* – and they told them where they stood, which was actually the pillar on the left-hand side, the front pillar. All they had was a photograph of his father when he was eight years old and they came to Arsenal and they found them and he was 60 years old then.

Maureen Hewlitt

I had been an Arsenal supporter in exile since the late 60s when I first came to London from Germany on a four-week holiday in August 1972, as a schoolboy aged 16. One of my main reasons for my trip was football, although I sold it to my parents as a language holiday in England. Although the football season had not started, one of my first excursions was to Highbury, deserted on the day but for a hostile groundsman, who refused me a look inside. But I crept in through an open side door and had my first look at the stadium, which struck me as a beauty compared to the wide open continental stadiums of the time, with their wide running tracks. I immediately picked out my spot on the North Bank where I wanted to stand for the first home match one week later – and where I should stay for 20 years. As the match day drew closer, I became more and more excited and bought my first Arsenal scarf in preparation: red and white bars, real wool! It was this very scarf that I left tied to one of the pillars close to my spot, when I left the North Bank for the very last time at 6.05 p.m. on 2 May this year.

Arsenal had won their first match of the season away to Leicester and were entertaining Wolves the following Tuesday. I approached Highbury from Finsbury Park at about six p.m. and – as I got closer – could already hear the chanting and the atmosphere building up on the North Bank. But nothing had prepared me for the experiences of that night: the emotions, the passions and the originality of the North Bank. Ritual chanting – and indeed vocal support in general – was still largely unknown in Germany and the incessant noise from the North Bank was exhilarating and overwhelming. I took some time to learn the songs, don't forget I was on a language holiday, especially *You'll Never Walk Alone* proved tricky, but I was totally gripped by this experience and the feeling of loyalty, togetherness and mutual aim of the North Bank. Arsenal won 5–2 and I had become an addict on day one. I stayed for another three weeks and saw three more home games (two wins, one draw) and when I left already considered myself a regular.

I was a confused young man at the time from a well-to-do upper-middle-class family, bad at school, with little obvious ambition, a drifter. But the Arsenal, and the North Bank in particular, changed all this. My ambition was now to return to London as soon as possible to satisfy my new addiction. I became extremely interested in English at school. It had previously been one of my worst subjects. I took up a subscription to the programme, started buying Sunday newspapers for their sports coverage and listened to the BBC World Service sports report every Saturday. I also became very interested in every other aspect of English life, such as politics, history and literature.

It took me one-and-a-half years to get back on the North Bank at Easter 1974 and when I next returned in 1975 I had started a university course in English

literature at Stuttgart University. My next move was carefully planned and involved
a year abroad at University College, London, and more importantly the North Bank,
Highbury. I went to every home game of the 1977–78 season and many away games,
and became indistinguishable from the rest of the North Bank, but for an ever-so-
slight German accent. I started making friends at my spot halfway up the terraces
behind the left goalpost, some of whom are still around and run into me at strange
places like Lisbon and Liverpool.

Songs were no problem now I had mastered the language – I actually graduated
with a first-class degree – and I look back at that season as the happiest year of my
life. The team was doing well (Cup final, League Cup semi-final and challenging in
the League) and the North Bank was always in good voice and full. The best-ever
atmosphere for me was against Man City in the League Cup quarter-final (attendance
59,000). It was so tight on the North Bank, which was seething and constantly
moving like one big organism, to finally erupt when we scored the winning goal. I
remember everything from that night, counting out the seconds on my stopwatch to
my friends before the final whistle.

Well, I never looked back. I went on for a second degree in English and came
back to the North Bank many times every year. This lasted till 1986 when I became
a young investment banker at a big German bank, specialising in (what do you think?)
the UK stock market. I was now in the position to satisfy my addiction regularly and
started to attend most big matches and during our Championship seasons, even many
midweek matches, taking the first flight back early next morning. Singing on the
North Bank provided a big contrast to my daily life, but was even more enjoyable for
that.

I always knew it had to end one day, but feel very sad about the insensitive way
in which things were handled by the Club, who did not really seem to care too much
about the destruction they brought upon a part of the lives of their most devoted
supporters. It all looked a long time away, when the plans were first announced, but
it was with an increasingly heavier heart that I trekked to Highbury. I thought for an
entire year what it would be like on the last day and even dreamt about it.

I even convinced my fiancée to attend a home game (Liverpool 4–0 in April
1992) with me, so she would also know what I missed. I had successfully introduced
many friends to the North Bank over the preceding 15 years.

I was the first one in the ground through 'my turnstile' on 2 May and one of the
last people out, unashamed of my tears.

I bought a bond, ruefully, to secure a seat near my old spot behind the left
goalpost, because I could not bear the idea of giving up this part of my life. But I
would have rather bought ten bonds to preserve the most treasured square foot in my
life for the future. Things will now never be the same, but hopefully just a little bit.

Michael Schoek

I could not sing all the chants because frankly I had a hard time understanding every
word of them, but I remember feeling at home among the Gunners fans. I especially
remember all the little things that we did not have here in Italy: the girls going around
trying to sell the lottery tickets, the programme vendors, the smell of food and

exhilarating joy when it appeared to look certain that Arsenal would win that game. I remember thinking about that importance of the game to myself, and I was living 350 days a year in Bologna, so I could just only imagine how important the Spurs game was to all who lived among Spurs fans all year! I can also recall stopping to eat something at a kind of bar-eatery in what I think is Gillespie Road, but I'm not sure. My heroes at that time were Willie Young, Liam Brady and Alan Sunderland, who will always have a place in my memory because of that late goal he scored at Wembley in the FA Cup final against Man United. In fact, I still get shivers down my spine whenever I play the tape of those final three minutes on my VCR, which I do regularly.

Roberto Gotta

I've only been standing at the North Bank four times but it has made a great impact on me, and will always have a special place in my heart. Living in Sweden made it difficult for me to get to London and Highbury. Even though I've been an Arsenal fan since I was seven, I'd waited 20 years to see the 'Home of Football' for the first time.

Magnus Falkehag

A thing that's unique about the North Bank is the different accents, different regions of the country you get there. I put this down to Arsenal's being unique in London because we're not *Tottenham* Hotspur, we're not *West Ham* United, we're just Arsenal. It's not Islington, it's not North London, it's an entity. It's an institution. You go up the North Bank. As long as you're Arsenal, it doesn't matter if you're from Islington or Bristol, you're an Arsenal fan, you're Arsenal.

Mark Burdis

'A GAME OF THE PEOPLE'

In the 50s, it was very much the working man's game. That's where the basis of the support was. There wasn't the same interest, I don't think, from people with money or businessmen. The big crowds were because it was the working man's sport.

David Court

Most women like me would not go to football – it's a social class thing. I think women who come from mostly middle-class backgrounds would not go to football. Traditionally, football is a working-class sport to go and see. Your father – if he's, say, a vet like mine – is more likely to go and watch rugby I suppose. I mean, I'm making completely broad generalisations, but that's my impression, knowing my friends and their backgrounds.

Amanda Caspari

I get the feeling that it's changed a bit over the years. I think that it's become the done thing for somebody who has not been interested in football to go along to be seen to be doing something that's proletarian. I think that the sort of middle-class supporters in the North Bank has increased enormously over the past five years.

John Yudkin

We are getting people that can well afford to do other than they do, go and stand on the North Bank. In other words, you're getting some people with middle-class families and very well-paid jobs that could afford to sit in the stand that want to be on the North Bank. That happens relatively regularly. A chap came the other day, a business person, and we sat in the directors' box and his son came in and had lunch with us and then disappeared, I said: *Where's he gone?* And he said: *He's always on the North Bank.* Now he actually had a seat in the directors' box but wanted to be on the North Bank. It's a meeting place. People come from everywhere and meet on that spot and meet their own people.

Ken Friar

There was this great effort Thatcher and the Tories had attacking working-class community gatherings whether they were trade unions or football. There seemed to be this attempt to make everybody privatised, having a video instead of real life.

Richard Stubbs

I personally think you're getting a different type of punter now. I think they have made very little secret of the fact that they have been trying to attract a different type of punter. If you can attract your person who's going to give you ten grand a year for an executive box, you've got that dough. You don't know how many of us are going to turn up. I think they honestly thought they'd be playing in front of 29,000 each and every week this year. It ain't happened. They are business people, aren't they? They're looking to take the thing upmarket. Football's always been, if you like, a working-class game for working-class people. I don't know what's going to happen next year. Maybe they will lose some of these guys forever. The image is going to change totally. All these sort of commercial packages and all that, you're going to lose the grass-roots.

Chris Thompson

It's a rather Arthur Daly idea of what constitutes the right crowd isn't it? Very sort of second-hand mid-80s idea of the people they're trying to get to.

Maurice Gran

I worry that the hidden agenda on all this is, well, I'm getting the distinct feeling I'm not wanted any more. I mean, it's delivered as an attack on standing and we've all got to do that because Taylor says so, you're going to die if you stand there. I'm not sure that the feeling at the back of this isn't: *Well, I don't think we want the terrace supporter any more.* Under the guise of complying with safety regulations, I don't know that market forces aren't being trained on someone other than us. You can go too far with conspiracy theories but I think they're looking for other markets, lucrative TV contracts that don't require us 'yobs' on the terraces. We're untidy, we're messy, we make a lot of noise. There's this backdrop of wanting to get us all out of the ground. But the danger is that you'll kill the goose that lays the golden egg. The value of our support is something that's been totally undervalued.

John James

If the aim of the clubs is to bring in a different audience, then the audience they want to bring in is the connoisseurs. The trouble is that it's only about twice a season that you feel like applauding anything that happens on the football pitch from either side. That's why it won't work – the partisanship is absolutely the point of football. It can't work any other way. If you had a European Super League and you had a division of 16 teams and you came to Highbury 15 times a season to watch AC Milan, Real Madrid and pay £25 to get in, then you can see it happening then. But all this other stuff – the Coca Cola Cup against Millwall – it's just ludicrous to expect the connoisseur to be attracted to anything like that. In a way it's very heartening to see people knowing more about the game and appreciating what the other side are doing but, paradoxically, in the long term it's very depressing for the future of the game in this country. It's a paradox football has got itself into and you can't really see how it's going to get itself out of it.

Nick Hornby

CHAPTER TWELVE

'Not as Many as Today but Quite a Few'

WOMEN ON THE NORTH BANK

There may be questions asked about the principle of setting one corner of this book aside to look at women's experience of the North Bank. Of course, women have taken their places on the terraces since the beginning of the story, as is clearly shown by the significance of their contribution elsewhere in these pages. Indeed, it should be remembered here that women playing football was enormously popular in the early part of the century. Teams based in the northern mill towns, especially, drew crowds which, had the Manor Ground's matched them, would have made Arsenal's move to north London a matter of little or no urgency. A football culture which had no problem with women playing the game themselves, I'd suggest, would find nothing untoward in women crowding on to the terraces to watch men play. By the time, though, that Arsenal had established a presence at Highbury in the mid-20s, the women's game had proved itself unable to sustain its profile as a spectator sport.

How many women watched football in the early days on the Laundry End can only be a matter for conjecture. Certainly, minimal specific provision was made available for members of 'the gentler sex' by way of facilities. It could be argued that this would have troubled women no more than it did their male contemporaries, for whom such considerations were of little or no relevance. Men, though, could take advantage of the anonymity of the crowd and, in time of need, relieve themselves when and where they stood.

Despite the fact that the domestic and economic arrangements of the inter-war family unit may have militated against their presence, many women were certainly on the Laundry End with their menfolk to marvel at the Arsenal of the 30s. Although men and women were aware of each others' different attitudes — *Sorry about the language, Mrs* — most of what made Saturday afternoons special could be enjoyed no less by women and in a relatively safe, good-natured environment. After all, if there were limited options open to the working man of the 1930s when it came to cheap, accessible entertainment, the choice was even more restricted for his mother, wife or daughter.

Women, then, were standing on the North Terrace before and after the war, even if for many men football, like the pub, was somewhere to go to avoid female company. That Highbury was, like other grounds, an overwhelmingly male environment, however, is clear from the 'special words' addressed to female spectators in Club and supporters' publications. This marginalisation was further exacerbated by the changes in crowd behaviour experienced during the late 60s and 70s. Some teenage girls became an important part of the North Bank's raucous new youth culture but older women and children were felt to be particularly at risk as the terrace increasingly came to be seen as a dangerous place. It does seem that many women did stop going – or weren't taken – over a 20-year period up to the early 1980s.

Since then, the change has been dramatic. By the time Arsenal won the League in 1989, large numbers of women had returned to the North Bank, or started standing there for the first time. The Club itself had been responsible for this in part, developing the Junior Gunners and Family Enclosure schemes to help draw back to the game the audience it recognised had been lost over the previous 20 years. This helped establish a cycle of renewal, whereby people were attracted to a change in the Highbury ambience and then, by their presence, contributed to that change themselves. Shifts in the pattern of women's employment and their control over their own incomes were also significant here, as was the effect of widespread change in the way new generations of young women were deciding on their places in society at large.

The renaissance of women's football, to which the Club has successfully devoted important time, expertise and resources, came too late to have an obvious effect on life on the North Bank. It has been an important part, however, of the general pattern of change outlined briefly above and will, without doubt, have a role to play in defining the relationship between female spectators and football at Highbury in the future. In the early 90s, at Arsenal and elsewhere, football remains 'a man's game'. To what extent that may change in the coming years is a matter for speculation. For now, what is certain is that the game is accessible to – and being enjoyed by – more women of all ages, and all backgrounds, than it has ever been before.

'CALLING ALL LADY SUPPORTERS'

Walking along Gillespie Road last Saturday night with Manager Chapman, long after the Sunderland match was over, two tiny little girls, aged about eight or nine, politely asked: 'Who won the football match?' 'Arsenal, by two goals to none,' said the genial Herbert, while I rather detected a tone of satisfaction. 'Hurrah! Arsenal at the top of the League,' the two kids yelled in unison as they suddenly ran off down the street. A pretty little incident because it was so unexpected to us, and spontaneous on their part, but one of importance because it shows that the nippers of Highbury, potential supporters of the future, have the welfare of the Club at heart, and that they are taking a keen interest in the Club's fortunes even at the tender age of eight.

AFC Programme, 5.12.25

Manager reported that the plans for the extra ladies' lavatory accommodation on the ground, had been prepared and passed by the local authority, and that the work had been commenced.

AFC Board Minutes, 11.11.27

There was quite a few used to go to football. Not as many as today, but quite a few. They'd feel safe, yes, because there was no trouble or anything then.

Tom Jales

Oh yeah. Sometimes, in the 30s and that, I've seen women down here with half a dozen kids.

Ron Pottage

I don't remember many women in the crowd. Not as many as there are today. Maybe there were more up in the stand.

George Williams

Before the last war, they used to come with their girlfriends and young wives and stand on the terracing, simply because they couldn't afford a seat.

Bob Wall, *Arsenal From the Heart*

It is many years now since I was at school on the Lake of Geneva in Lausanne, Switzerland. Even so I still remember the time when I was deputed to ask the Headmaster if he would allow a party of us to go to Geneva one Sunday to see Switzerland play Italy. The goalkeeper of our school team was an Italian from Milan and our excuse for the request was his sister intended to make the journey from Italy in order to see the match. I also tried to stress the fact that the viewing of such a match was bound to have a good instructional effect on our school team. Permission was granted. Accustomed as I was to the English crowds of those days, it was with no small degree of amazement that I noticed the large feminine element sitting, and standing too, among the big crowd. In later years of course the popularity of the FA Cup finals at the Empire Stadium, Wembley, and the bi-annual meeting of England–Scotland there, brought a great increase in British feminine interest but it was really not until the Arsenal Football Club converted the Gillespie Road Ground into the present palatial Arsenal Stadium, with such clubs as Tottenham Hotspur and Everton following suit, that the fair sex started to follow football in this country with any real degree of seriousness. Hysterical hockey on ice, stench of speedway petrol and other inducements certainly are set up as counter attractions but once the football fever gains hold – well, we have at Arsenal a lady from Crewe who holds a season ticket, a gentlewoman from Portland who does likewise and my own wife will give up anything but her Saturday afternoons at Highbury. It should be noted that the lady from Crewe most often attends both home and away matches with one of our own sex and another young female fan never misses a home match on a real 'lone wolf' basis, so it would seem that the gentler sex can truly be numbered now among the most loyal and enthusiastic fans of our great game.

AFC Programme, 8.11.47

There weren't many girls then, in the 50s. Or women. I don't really remember seeing any. I suppose it was unusual, going as a girl, but I didn't think it was because I just remember at home, from Saturday right through to Sunday evening, it was just the games being talked over the whole time. And in fact I don't really remember seeing a lot of women until very recently, you know, the last ten years, I wouldn't say much before then. I still think it's strange when I see them. I also think the reserve games, you see loads of women going there on their own.

Maureen Hewlitt

We had an old girl down here that they used to have to take home every week. She'd get pie-eyed drunk every first-team match. What was her name? Florrie, was it? An Arsenal supporter, she was always drunk. Her whole family wouldn't have nothing to do with her. In the end the Arsenal give her a seat!

Ron Pottage

You very rarely got women coming along. But one I remember was 'old Flo'. She used to stand on the North Bank. She used to stand just to the left of the goal and could just about see over the railings. Used to go to all the away games. Absolute Arsenal nutter.

Steve Shaw

You used to see her outside the players' entrance. We all knew her. And sometimes she'd be there during the week.

Dennis Evans

There was a friendly atmosphere. I can remember an old lady who used to bring sweets for all the kids around. She was a Dennis Evans fan, but that was a memory from the latter part of the 50s. I once stood with a young lady who claimed to be Len Will's sister. Her bad luck. He was not first-team material.

Peter Leslie

And there was that one old dear on the North Bank always used to have a flask with her. And some of the language. I don't know what she had in that flask!

Ron Pilcher

There was one old couple, an Irish couple, who used to be there. She was an Arsenal supporter and he was QPR. He'd turn up and she'd shout: *What the f-ing hell are you doing here?* And she'd call us over and try and get him thrown out!

Ron Pottage

There used to be that little old dear, didn't there? Right down the front in the left-hand corner. She was great. She used to have a helmet with her so she'd obviously come on her moped or something. She used to stand there in her corner and she was the loudest one. She'd be going: *You're playing like a bunch of girls, you bunch of fairies! Wake up!* She was brilliant.

Emma Young

There's this one woman, you hear her everywhere. I've even heard her on the radio: *Come! On! You! Gunners!* She's always there. I've never seen her, I don't know what she looks like, but you always hear the voice.

Julie Wheeler

I took women on the North Bank – some of them I never saw again! It was mostly people took their daughters, probably hadn't got a son so they dragged their daughter along. There's far more of it now than you used to see.

Laurence Marks

There was hardly any women then. In the group we went with I can't remember any other woman being there, when I first started going. More women started coming late 60s/70s. It was younger women wanting to go with their boyfriends. Before then it was the young men went off to watch their football on Saturday afternoons and didn't dream of taking their girlfriends with them. But then the 60s and 70s were more rebellious years and all of a sudden, I suppose, girls started saying: *Why can't I come?* And there's far more now than I've ever seen.

Tina Evans

Late 60s, there used to be a lot of girls over there. I remember one group of girls who used to come all the way over from south London. Every game.

Vidos Neophytou

Now, you would say there were, last season, there were one in ten or 20 people on the North Bank were women. When I started going in 1960 it was more like one in 200. On a Saturday, basically, it was a man's domain. He would go to football. People like Christine, my wife, she's avid West Ham. She's like a new breed, women coming in who really follow football. But in those days, no, you have to think hard to remember seeing a woman at a game. Twenty or 30 years ago, a woman would be with her husband at the game and it would probably be a one-off thing.

Eddie Mason

It used to be there were more older women and less younger. Now there's more younger ones. It's brilliant. I love it. It was nice for a while to think that you were slightly special but that's not what you really want.

Natasha Horbacki

I mean I go now with Roger to home games and I go to the away games with the young lads at work, very kind of them taking me. They promised they'll come to the old people's home when I'm there and take me out. I love away games.

Maureen Hewlitt

I can't explain it. I really enjoyed it. Looking round at the people, this lot ranting and raving. I come out the game and I'd really enjoyed it. I hate football on telly but I love it at the ground. There's the atmosphere, the people around it, you hear their comments. I love it.

Sam Hobb

You have to queue to go the toilet now. You never used to have to do that. That's a sign that there are more women. Before you could always go straight into the toilet and come straight out. There's a big queue now, and that's really good. I go to the toilet and I think: *There's all these women here!* And the funny thing is there's women in high heels, women in this and that, all dressed up to go to the Arsenal. Older women as well.

Emma Young

'TRADITIONALLY A MALE PRESERVE'

Naturally, as the scorer, Bastin was the hero of the game. At Snow Hill Station a woman kissed him impulsively and called him one of those soft names that women use. And I do not think it was his mother, either. Bastin seemed to take it as a matter of course. Fine life, a footballer's!

Daily Express, 14.3.32

In the 30s, if we got there and there was a really big crowd, especially at away games, I'd say: *Let me go first*. And I'd go through. *Excuse me, please! Excuse me, please!* And then the 15 of them would come through behind! But because I was a woman, everybody would part. Mind you, after you'd gone they'd say: *Damn cheek! Shut the gate up*, they'd say, *or they'll all come through!*

Rose Jales

CALLING ALL LADY SUPPORTERS!!!
Owing to the increasing number of lady supporters in the Club, it has now been decided to give them space of their own each month in *GunFlash*, so now it is up to us to make our part the best feature in the magazine, and perhaps, who knows, even the men may read it!

Many people may wonder at the growing popularity of this great game with the women followers, when it has long been regarded as a man's sport, but, after all, it is as much for the women to support their favourite team as for the men. Although some of us do not know all the finer points of the game, we can always learn. We know that for the married women it is difficult to see all the matches, because of looking after 'hubby' and the children, but it is a great thing for a wife to take an interest in her husband's sport and oh, it makes it so much easier for the husband!

For the younger girls, it is a good, clean, healthy sport to follow. I wonder what some of your views are as to why you follow football? I should be interested to know and it should make good reading, so why not write and tell me?

We want to make this part of *GunFlash* entirely for women only, and through this medium to help each other. In these days when we have to make a little go a long way, some of you may have suggestions to offer in the way of cooking. Useful hints for the home would also be welcome, thereby providing useful to us all, so don't forget to send me your pet recipes and household hints.

Ladies' netball, table tennis, and darts are being organised, particulars of which appear on the social page. Now you young girls, come and 'Have a Go' at netball, and show what the girls in red and white can do!

Send your ideas and suggestions to me so that we can make this feature a 'Rip Roaring' success.

'Gunnerette', *GunFlash* 6, February 1950

My mum used to tell me, I used to get a little lecture, when I first started going: *Now, Tina, you're going to hear a lot of swearing. Men do this when they get a bit incensed when they're watching football. I don't want you to take any notice of it, you're not ever to repeat it.* And I'd say: *Alright mum.* But that was the bit I loved most. Mind you, I must admit the language wasn't as bad then, in the late 50s, as you hear now. My mum used to think *bloody* and things like that were bad which now go in one ear and out the other.

Tina Evans

All these blokes, my dad and his mates, me a little girl. They plied me with everything I could possibly want. And I was a little girl, you know, and little girls don't go to football matches but I did. In my primary school, football was the big thing and I had one up on my class because I used to go to matches. I used to really love it. There were so many people, it was so loud and you could really shout. And I remember I used to ask questions all the time, the most ridiculous questions. I'd get really into it. It was really part of my childhood.

Natasha Horbacki

Me and Dawn (my daughter), we go up on our own and I know John (my husband) gets a bit concerned. But he knows we won't do anything stupid. And for me it's so familiar, it's like a second home – I know all the streets around there, we know all the stewards – I don't feel any danger in it at all.

Tina Evans

Being a woman, a small woman, I go to matches on my own but I wouldn't stand on the North Bank on my own because – I don't mind the crowds – but the worry of getting pushed over. I remember a Tottenham game before they lowered the capacity, and my feet just didn't touch the ground. It doesn't panic me, though I can imagine it would panic women, but I'm *always* smaller than everybody else so that didn't bother me. The only thing that did worry me was just before the start of a game when the crowd and everybody would be coming in from Avenell Road and pushing in and you'd get shoved across – trying to maintain my space at that time, no matter how much I crossed my arms or stand so as to make myself big, you know, I can't maintain that space – I get pushed around. I get cross more than anything – I don't get frightened. Before they lowered the capacity the view wasn't too good but then a couple of games last season (91–92) I had an unobstructed view. I couldn't believe it. But you know what happens, you can start off in a good position, but then when they score and everybody leaps around you can find yourself halfway down the terrace, somewhere completely different and then you haven't got a good view at all. But I tend to have to stand on my toes all the way through the game anyway! I always stand immediately in front of a barrier, with my back to the barrier I think it's safer. I do worry about getting pushed over but I don't think about it all the time during the game.

Amanda Caspari

My mum used to start to me: *Make sure you get to the toilet before you go in there. For a start, you'll be hard pushed to find a ladies' toilet, and they're appalling.* They're not much better now! I always took her at her word. Never dared to go to the toilets at the Arsenal!

Tina Evans

Last season (91–92) I did notice there were a lot of women on the North Bank – more women are going now than when the capacity was higher. I never talked to anyone about being on there. I used to talk to two couples, parents, I suppose, with the daughter and the son-in-law. They'd always be laughing because the people I was with would disappear down the terrace when we scored and they'd often hold on to me! Mostly it was complaining about the toilets. That's when you get women talking. You could always tell people who hadn't been before because they'd be saying: *Oh, sorry, they don't flush.* If you've been going for a while, you don't bother to apologise any more. You know bloody well they're not going to flush anyway! I don't know about the ones on the west side, I think they were better, but our side, it was like a small public loo – three toilets but they never lock and they flush every ten times or something like that. There was always a huge long queue. And there was always a man outside selling hot-dogs right by the door! Not the cleanest place to be selling them!

Amanda Caspari

I always remember a bloke called Christmas. It was bloody cold. There was a couple of girls in front. He said: *Ain't it cold, missus? Do you mind if I put my hands under your arms?* So she said: *Yeah, alright.* That's what he done. Winter warmers! It was entirely different then. If you did that now, you'd expect a punch on the nose.

George Stinton

When women and children did go, they were always treated well: *Can you see? Are you alright?*

Tina Evans

Any bad language, someone would turn round and say: *There's a lady down there*. And they'd say: *Sorry, madam*. And that would be it. They'd always apologise!

Rose Jales

A lot of men used to take their wives with them. I took my wife to stand over there before we got married, while we were courting. There was no problem with that. Do you know, if a woman fainted in the crowd, they would pass her down to the front over their heads and you'd never even see her knees.

Sid Butler

So the inevitable has happened! Two young ladies from Barnsbury have written to ask for the formation of a ladies' football team. This is a debatable question. It is an accepted fact that there are sports in which women may play without losing their feminine charm, but, having regard to our sex, is football the right game for women to play? I do not know how many of you heard Peter Wilson broadcasting on this subject recently, but he was obviously not very much in favour of women trying to play football. Of course, I do not agree always with all that men say, but for once I feel I must bow to their better judgment. Can you imagine the Gorgeous Gussies, turning out in their red-and-white lace panties!!! Nevertheless, girls, I am pleased that you are sufficiently interested to put your ideas forward. In response to my request last month for your opinions as to why you were followers of football, most of you have written to say that your husbands, brothers or sweethearts make this their Saturday afternoon recreation and you like to join in with them. Of course, once you have visited Highbury, the fever grips you! Many of you have made friends there, and with the formation of the Supporters' Club (and now our own page) you are able to enjoy a regular 'get-together'. Most of you have a soft spot for the Compton brothers and 'Wee Jimmy', but, for the information of our men readers, we do not go to see the men's knees!!

I note that several of you have purchased red berets and have embroidered them with *Up the Gunners*; and added white tassels. What about you other girls following suit and getting them ready in time for Wembley.

GunFlash 7, March 1950

You see, then, there were two sections – the nursing division and the ambulance division and never the twain met. It was terrible.

Ron Pilcher

Of course, then, we weren't allowed to come down, they used to say *we don't want women down there*. This was run by Camden, the old railway division of the St John's.

They didn't have any women and they didn't want any women, not at football. They were a right funny old crowd. They would have a female division, a nursing division, at one end of the hall and the male division at the other end of the hall and they weren't allowed to fraternise. We don't discriminate now. The St John have got more female members than male. That's been true since the war. The war you got quite a few men who'd be interested, coming out of the army. But very few young men join the brigade now. And if they do once they get a regular girlfriend, if the girlfriend's not in the brigade, you've had it!

Shirley Haxell

I was with my girlfriend. Whenever I was going out with a girl I'd always take her to Arsenal. I remember once I was going out with a Swedish girl, very tall, very glamorous, blonde Swede, my father and mother objected to her! Took her to the Arsenal around 68 or 69, I suppose. Because she was a very attractive blonde, as we worked our way to where we wanted to stand, there was a great shift and moving from the centre and there were blokes actually there that weren't watching the match. It was really funny. So after her every girlfriend I ever went out with I took at least once. They never wanted to go twice.

Laurence Marks

Early 50s there were very, very few women. There must be more going now than there's ever been. Can't remember any then. The only woman I can honestly remember seeing at a football match was when we played Everton, the old lady came round dishing the sweets out. Done up, top to toe, you know, in blue, velvet dress right down to the floor. Big basket of toffees and she dished them out to the kids. Remember Dairy Maid caramels? Well, the woman on the wrapper of one of those would wear a bonnet that came down and had a white peak, really old-fashioned. Like that.

Chris Thompson

Another person who was warmly greeted by the North Bank was a particular *Make Money with Arsenal* ticket seller. She was a tall, fair-haired lady who used to wear a low-cut t-shirt. This prompted whistles of delight and appropriate sexist comments from the North Bank. People down the front would rush forward to buy a ticket but stop about a yard short, thus forcing this lady to lean forward to sell the ticket – *aaahh!*

John Deasy

In my time up there, you didn't get many women. Down the front you would but not up the back where we were.

Steve Winfield

Football has traditionally been a male preserve. I've been on the North Bank plenty of times with women but while the majority of people on the North Bank, certainly the hard core, the topside and the middle are male, then it's still going to be more of a masculine world. It's not my position to give a female point of view. But, as I say, I've taken girlfriends to the North Bank. Does that change your experience in any way? No it doesn't. It gives you someone you know to hug when you score, I suppose, doesn't it? It never calms me down. The one thing that calmed me down was my mother. We were talking about it the other day, that I had to cut out some of the swear words. She came to that one game, that was the thing. My uncle brought her along and I had to watch what I said – you know how it is with mums – but with other women I still go as mad as anything. No I don't think women on the North Bank necessarily makes any difference, I mean they scream and shout!

Al Fresco

We started going, this was about ten years ago, I was about 13. It was, like girls didn't go to football, girls didn't understand about football. It just wasn't the done thing. But we always used to sing. We were always going to go on the pitch. We'd take the piss out of the police. We used to have a really good laugh. We didn't go with boyfriends. We weren't standing there with boyfriends with their arms round the back of us or anything like that. We were just two girls by ourselves and when we started singing, we'd be singing louder than any of the blokes around us to the point where they looked embarrassed!

Emma Young

For a while there were five or six of us, my sisters used to come. Well, there's not much you can say to that, that many feisty girls who are obviously into it!

Natasha Horbacki

They'll say things like: *Oh, it's nice seeing girls at football*. When what they really mean is: *You should be at home cooking dinner!* But I think we were so into the football we didn't notice that much. And the people around you, they'd always look after you, offer you sweets and fags or a cup of tea.

Emma Young

I'm very careful what games I take my girl to. You can look after yourself to a certain extent, but I wouldn't want her to get in any hassle. And it's still in the back of your mind, the hooliganism.

Guy Thomson

I once went up there and there was a crowd of blokes who I'd seen up there every week – older, in their 40s – and we were standing where they usually stand, but they were pretty late in, and they were really pushing and shoving me to get to where I was standing. I was getting really upset. I mean they were being quite threatening but they do it in a clever way, they sort of laugh and shove and push. There's a lot of them and they're gradually muscling you over. And also if I were to say to someone very tall in front of me, you know, *can I come and stand in front of you?* – it's funny, you get it more with older blokes you know, they wouldn't move: it's almost like, *well, you shouldn't be here* whereas the younger ones don't seem to mind so much – they'll say: *Oh, go on then, you go in front.*

Amanda Caspari

I mean, when Sam came, we all looked out for her. If she came, we'd get there a little bit earlier to get on a barrier so she could get a good view. People were respectful. Big guys would move out of the way so she could see. You knew the people around you and they'd co-operate.

Paul Hobb

I was never worried taking my daughter to the ground. Where we stood we were all friends, all Arsenal supporters and I have never had any trouble.

Alex Froso

It's different if you're not with a bloke. If you're with a boyfriend they treat it like: *You can't go near her.*

Natasha Horbacki

In the late 50s, if my mum didn't go, I would sometimes go and sit in the East Stand with my dad. And it was different. They just ignored you, like you weren't there. They'd talk to my dad but I was ignored. I didn't like it. I much preferred to be standing. They used to talk to me on the terraces.

Tina Evans

I'll tell you something interesting and I don't know if it's because I went on my own. When I used to stand on the North Bank, I was usually with people, not necessarily talking to them but with them. I actually found it more threatening sitting in the East Stand. I was in the Upper Tier amongst season-ticket holders, and I found that more difficult. I found they were all turning round to have a look at me, because I was a woman and on my own. That never really happened on the North Bank and I've walked around the North Bank on my own – like, looking for my brother who I was meeting up there – and I never felt that pressure that I did up in the East Stand. It's almost like women are more *allowed* to stand on the North Bank.

Amanda Caspari

CHAPTER THIRTEEN

'And This is How It's Followed on, You See?'

FAMILIES ON THE NORTH BANK

There are people out there who aren't interested in football: who neither understand the back-pass law nor want to; who presume Arsenal's massively popular 1991 replica away shirt to have been a mistake in the dyeing process; who can't see the point of travelling hundreds of miles to be at a game which is being shown live on TV; who can actually conceive of something else worth doing at three o'clock on a Saturday afternoon. The depth of the football supporter's attachment to the game and to a club may, perhaps, defy the innocent bystander's powers of belief. The back-pass law certainly isn't a good place to begin to explain why football means so much to so many. Family is a better place to start.

A survey of Arsenal fans conducted by the Sir Norman Chester Centre (the leading body for football-related study and research in this country) recently expressed in percentage terms a home truth that football supporters have always known. Just over 60 per cent of respondents first came to Highbury in the company of a relative, 38 per cent in the company of their fathers. Those numbers are a window on to the importance of football, of *going down the Arsenal*, to thousands of people's lives. It's a passion handed down through generations, carrying with it the senses of continuity and identity which make the family mean so much.

The North Bank has, for 80 years, offered an informal environment where football can be the vocabulary with which to celebrate a family's intimacy or with which to build bridges where common ground doesn't otherwise exist. Going to football together reinforces and defines the ties of family. Going with family can give the afternoon at football, in turn, a resonance beyond the game itself. Every father or mother taking a son or daughter to Highbury for the first time will still remember the first time they were taken as a child. Four generations of a family could often point to a corner of the North Bank that was 'theirs' for 80 years. The patchwork of parents and children is extended further, too, by the complications of courtships, marriages and friends. Love of the Arsenal, the afternoon's traditions on the North Bank, are often the only distinguishable common social thread to knit this patchwork of relationships together. In a very real sense, many families on the North Bank were *Arsenal* families.

For the youngster introduced to the North Bank, perhaps from the Schoolboys' Enclosure or – more recently – the Junior Gunners, the terrace served as a backdrop to the trials of adolescence. The importance for teenagers, from the 50s onwards, of establishing an identity within the crowd on their own, independent of the company of older relatives, says much about how the process of growing up was moving away from traditional, more tightly structured patterns. That the patterns were changing, however, did not diminish their importance. The change as observed on the North Bank simply offered a specific model, as in so many other instances, for social change that was taking place, simultaneously, in a wider context.

The teenage years are not the only time of life during which football is not only something which the family does together but provides a setting in which developments within the family can take place. Of particular importance – and no little charm – are the marriages that have been made, if not in heaven, then in the next best place. One of the little-recognised virtues of the anonymity found in the heart of any big crowd is the surprising degree of privacy that is to be had there.

Of course, the family dramas played out on the North Bank are not restricted to a particular area of the ground. The interaction of family and football has the same significance for father and son in the East Upper as it does for those on the terraces. However, the spiralling cost of football and the advent of the all-seater stadium do pose a threat to the continuity of families' involvement with football, a threat which the North Bank's informality and accessibility, in economic terms, did much to keep at bay. Arsenal seemed to have recognised this when setting up the Family Enclosure of recent years for members of the already hugely successful Junior Gunners scheme. At the time of writing, the Enclosure offers under-16s a season ticket at less than half the price of its adult counterpart. The policy is one that deserves the highest commendation, recognising as it does the importance of the loyalty to the Club which is passed on when football is part of a family tradition. Subsidising those kids is, without doubt, an investment in Arsenal's future. It is of vital importance to the Club's sense of continuity with its own past that the continuity of family traditions – which may be interrupted by the loss of the North Bank on which those traditions flourished – is encouraged to take root elsewhere. This is not simply an emotional appeal to a sense of natural justice but makes long-term economic sense as well: subsidise a nipper for the first eight years and you've got a regular customer at Highbury for the next 80! The West Stand's Family Enclosure deserves a counterpart in the new North Bank Stand. The families who stood on the old North Bank for generations deserve that, too.

'I STOOD THERE WITH MY OLD MAN'

It's what their dads have done and what their dads have done and their grandads, and so on. It just says: *You've got to come to Highbury and you've got to stand on the North Bank.*

And from the North Bank you progress like an apprenticeship, so that's where it all starts.

Paul Johnson

My father used to follow them when they were down in Woolwich. He lived down there, big family, he had seven brothers and two sisters. And, of course, when they came to Highbury, he came too. He always told me he took me to the first game at Highbury. I don't remember it! My mum used to go with him in those days but my dad told me that in 1913 my twin brothers had the mumps so she couldn't go that day. So my father took me! That first game, against Leicester Fosse.

Arthur Peakell

My dad took me. Well there was two of us, you see. And my mum said: *I'll have one, you take the other*. I was the noisy one. So my dad took me to Arsenal. I was about five and I was born in 1916, so it was 1921 or 22.

Rose Jales

My dad first went to the Arsenal in about 1920. My brother, who was the generation of the late 40s, 50s team, he went to the Arsenal. My dad at that point had a sweet shop in Hackney, and I remember one Saturday afternoon he took me too. He said: *We're going out today*. He didn't tell me where we were going. I remember clearly, we arrived at the South End of the ground, and I had no idea where I was. I was only about three or four. And we went to the North End where we always stood and I watched my first game. That was in about 1952, Arsenal v Cardiff. I suppose he took me because of the Cardiff connection – my mother hails from Cardiff and we used to spend a lot of time there. So I always used to go up there, unless there was a game with a very very big crowd in which case he wouldn't take me. He had this little blue stool, and I remember he'd get me in the turnstiles and he'd do something with the bloke: I think it was about a shilling to get in and he'd give the bloke sixpence for himself if he'd let me in the turnstiles. We always went in the same position just to the right of the goal and he put the stool down and said: *Would you mind letting this little boy watch the game?* He put the stool down and I would stand on it and watch the game.

Maurice Gran

My dad took me in 58, 8 November. I'm not very good at dates, but I remember he took me just after my eighth birthday. In those days it was a thing just to get on a train. It's not like nowadays, you know, kids of ten and that go anywhere with football now. I know it was a bit of a poor game. Me dad was Arsenal. It's always passed down ain't it? My dad was an Arsenal supporter and he took me up there and me brother was an Arsenal supporter. He come from Hornsey, but we'd moved to Hatfield. I was football mad anyway and then he took me up there and that was it. I was sold, just because of the atmosphere. Looking back on it, it was a boring game but for a fellow my age then, you were in a crowd of 30 to 40,000-odd people, it was just totally different circumstances. I just remember a couple of players. I remember Jack Kelsey because he was a biggun and the only other player I can really recollect was Vic Groves.

Laird Budge

The thing about my old man, he used to sort of, how can I put it, he'd pretend he wasn't too bothered. I'll do it to a certain extent now. I don't want to get too much into it. I want my boy to feel like a good Arsenal supporter – and he is – but I don't want him to go spoiling the rest of his life because of it, it's got to be kept in proportion, and that's what my old man was like. He'd say: *Well, I always wanted to support Tottenham anyway*. It was his way of sort of hiding it you know. But I remember when we won the Double, a few years later, he was like crying his eyes out.

I mean, when I started secondary school and found friends that obviously supported the Arsenal as well, we started going. I mean, Dad started going: *Well you can go to the home games on your own*. I got to the stage I was a bit embarrassed. Like my kiddie now, he's only 11 but he's got to that, yeah. He don't like walking down the road with me, his neighbour's going to see him.

Mick Essen

I grew up in Norwich. It was a London family and there's a lot of Arsenal fans on my mum's side, it's all Arsenal, but a lot of them live in Australia now. When I was born, for a christening present, I got a red and white teddy bear. There was never any question. I mean, my two brothers were Chelsea. One of them's defected to West Ham now. But I had this teddy bear from the Arsenal side of the family and when I got old enough to think about football, when I was about six, I looked at my brothers and thought: *Chelsea? No, that's not for me. No. Mum's Arsenal so I'll support Arsenal*. And I always have. My dad took me to my first game. He was quite excited, he hadn't been to a football match for ages. He had me sat on his shoulders. It was against Norwich, we won, Ray Kennedy scored with a header I think. And I'm going: *Did you see that?* And I've got my hands over his eyes, hanging on to his head: *Did you see that?* And he goes: *No, I didn't*. He was really pissed off! Brilliant!

Stewart O'Brien

He'd go out and he'd sometimes buy me a programme or something. I'd ask him all about it. It was Brighton and Hove Albion in 1979. He was taking this guy Daniel, a friend of the family who was about 17 at the time – and they were on their way out and my dad just said to me: *Are you coming with us then? Are you coming to Arsenal?* I just couldn't believe it. I was now old enough to go. I was four-and-a-half! I sat on his shoulder, sort of thing, half standing to see properly, and I knew we won, can't remember the score now, just from the noise when we scored. The whole time I was there I couldn't believe I was actually there, because of the shock of him asking me to go. I went to a few games later on that season with him on the North Bank, and the season after I started bringing a little stool to stand on.

Josh Yudkin

I started going, my mum says, when I was about three or four. I've got really young memories of being at Arsenal and sitting on the bar, all that kind of stuff, with my dad and his mates. Right crew of them used to go, they used to play football together on a Sunday and they'd go down to Arsenal in their van. All the lads and the little girl. I was the first child, my brother was still a baby. I really got into it. My mum used to dress me up all in red and white, ribbons in my hair, the whole business, every match. They'd perch me on the bar. They used to do mad things, like they'd have a packet of fruit gums each and they'd wedge the whole lot in their mouths and see who could get rid of them first. My dad had been going since there was all the violence when Tottenham used to come and try to take the North Bank. He stopped going. His mates still go but now they've all got suits and season tickets.

Natasha Horbacki

First time my dad took me was down the Clock End. We got there late so we just went in anywhere. It was all quiet and I could hear all this noise coming from the North Bank. I'd seen it on the telly and people said it was the rough end but I just went: *Dad, dad! I want to go down the North Bank.* I went on and on, so next time he took me.

Julie Wheeler

My dad took me to my first game. It was against Tottenham. My dad's a Spurs supporter, actually, but I made him take me on the North Bank. It was great.

Dawn Hicks

I was about ten when I first started going. I was born in 1919. My brother Ted was nine years older than me and, looking back, I must have been a bit of a pest. He had his own friends and that, and I was a different world – kid brother, a bit of a nuisance, I suppose – but I don't recall he ever said that at the time. He always seemed quite happy to take me to the Arsenal with him!

George Williams

I was born in 1947 in Monmouthshire (now Gwent). My mother had been re-deployed from her home in Canonsbury during the war and met my father, an engine driver. In those days few people had television and all I really knew of sport was rugby and athletics. I saw my first football match at Newport County in 1959 when relatives came from North Wales – my father being a rugby supporter had never taken me to football.

My mother and I frequently came to London, via British Rail free passes etc, but I knew nothing of the Arsenal just up the road. Then on one visit – Christmas 1960 – my father and I accompanied my grandfather and uncle to see Arsenal play Sheffield Wednesday.

I was transported to another world. I think the greatest impact was floodlights, I had never been under floodlights before. Huge stands, a mass of noise and colour. I was changed! – from now on, I was a football man.

Steve Thomas

I was nine years old and my cousin Perry took me on the North Bank which for me was such a thrill, all the colour and noise; my cousin put me up on to his shoulders so I could see the game above all the crowd. After some time, he could hold me no longer so the rest of the match for me was just a sea of bodies and a wall of noise.

Paul Jerrams

I remember me and Pops, I call my grandad Pops, when we used to drive up to the ground I used to enjoy it. Right from the beginning, getting in that car, putting all the scarves out and you go up the motorway, see all the opposing supporters. Pop used to sing to me all the way, you know, Arsenal songs. Sing away, whistle away. And all the way up he used to tell me stories, stories about what it used to be like. I was so interested and there were one or two stories I liked the most and I used to make him tell me them every week! There was one I liked because it was rude. I can't remember what ground it was, but all the blokes at the back used to stand and pee on people down underneath. I used to love the way he told them. And whatever team we were playing he would say: *Oh, so-and-so, years ago.*

Dawn Evans

My old man tells me we were at games like the Man United game before they got killed in the crash. He reckons he was taking me and sitting me down in front of the fence and that. But the first time I remember was about 63, we were playing home to Wolves and we lost. It was the start of the season, it was a nice hot day. I think maybe I just about reached the age when I could take a bit of notice about what was going on. I can do it now with my son. He's 11 now and, although he's been going for a fair old while, if you ask him about some of the first games he went to he probably wouldn't remember them, whereas now, the last couple of years, he can actually watch what's going on. Before I'd take him and I'd take his mate, whoever his best mate was and they'd chat about the game, or they'd be chatting to each other about school or whatever. Now he's actually into the game. He gets upset if things go wrong and he's cheering when they do well. He's that little bit older now.

Mick Essen

My dad took Tina, our daughter. He was a dead ringer for making the family go. He said to me they were going to buy her a signet ring for her birthday. It was midweek they were playing Burnley and I was working, and he said to get her to have an afternoon off school and bring her over. He bought her the ring and then he said: *Right. Nanny's going home and we're going to go somewhere. We're getting on the bus.* And as soon as she got on the bus she said: *Oh, grandad, you're going to take me to the Arsenal!* She'd heard so much about it. She was five-and-a-half but she'd already got the bug. Up till then, we'd moved out here to Watford and we used to go into London, leave Tina with my sister and we'd go. But, oh! When grandad took her there, it was the be-all and end-all of her life: *I've been to see the Arsenal*. It was better than going to see the Queen! (See plate 39.)

Rose Jales

My grandad used to take me. He made me a wooden stool, with a little handle on it so I'd be able to see. And the very first game he took me to, 1955? He bought me this ring, it was like a Christmas present the end of November and then took me to the Arsenal. I can't remember when Arsenal wasn't in my life. My mum and dad got bombed out during the war and they moved out to Harrow Weald near my dad's sister, always intending to go back. But they got used to it, so, for as long as I can remember, it was train up to Euston, bus to the Angel, into Chapel Market — Manzie's — for your pie and mash and liquor for dinner. Then I used to go with my nan to my aunt's who lived in flats in Holloway Road, from when I was a tiny tot, while they went off to football — mum, dad, grandad, my uncle. They'd come back from football all full of it — it was a big family gathering, my cousin would go, too. Then one day, my grandad took me to a jeweller's at Highbury Corner and bought me this little signet ring, I was six and I still always wear it. We'd gone through the usual routine and I knew I was going to get this ring. We came out of the jeweller's and I assumed I'd be going with my nan. But grandad said: *No, you're coming with me.* I said: *Where we going grandad?* And he said: *We're going a on little trip.* So, of course, we got another bus and started walking and I saw all the crowd, I'm going: *Are we going to Arsenal, grandad?* And then we came down into Avenell Road. I was overawed. I'd never been in such a crowd. I could never imagine such a crowd. We lived out in the sticks and I thought a crowd was what I saw in Chapel Market! And the noise! It was like a roar. So many people and the buzz of noise. Grandad kept saying: *Are you alright?* I think he thought I was going to be sick or something? And then when we came out, my mum and Ada met us — *You didn't know where you were going, did you?* From then on, I was clamouring to go again and my grandad was thrilled to bits that I'd liked it. So when I was eight or nine I started going regularly.

Tina Evans

I love Arsenal so much that when I had my daughter, my first child, I named her after the Club. I named her AFC, Alexia Froso Costas. I used to take her to Saturday games. I had her there on my shoulders when she was two years old and then I used to take a little stool for her to stand. She grew up always to love the team and it was her ambition to be a doctor or physiotherapist at the Club. Well, she works there now and loves everything to do with Arsenal. I can't tell you how happy I am about it.

Alex Froso

I got one boy's nine, one's four. I took them on the North Bank for the last game. The younger one, obviously, it passed him by a bit. But when I was their age, all we ever used to do was play football. Kids now have got so many alternatives. You don't see kids playing football in the street now, do you?

Lenny Brandon

I wanted my kid to go up there, find his way up there, on his own without me. He's only been there once. I took him there last year for the Sheffield Wednesday game. Up till then I'd taken him where he'd be guaranteed a view, like along the side. I said: *I'll take you once because you won't have another chance.* It was only just outside the roof, but he still got the feel of it. There was still plenty of space, we weren't doing particularly well, and he loved it, loved it. If anything, it was probably a mistake because he's probably going to think, as he grows up: *I wouldn't have minded doing that a lot more!* That's how our family think: *Part of growing up, isn't it? A definite part of growing up.* I would have liked him to have done it with his mates as well, as he would have done. That's what would have happened next, standing up with his mates there. If he'd grown up a bit more, he'd have wanted me away. For safety, I wouldn't let him go on his own, but once he was inside the ground that'd be fine. I'd have met him outside afterwards. It's part of growing up, you know.

Mick Essen

I've got a little sister who every now and again I'd take her to football. I'm sad that I can't do that anymore. There was one match we went to, we had eight children with us. We had them lined up on a bar on the North Bank. And we'd ask people if we could have this bit of bar, if they'd guard the kids from behind. We had complete strangers being really protective.

Natasha Horbacki

I took me mother once. She come from Birmingham. It appears when they were kids they walked all the way from Birmingham to London! Her and her mother and her brother. So Arsenal were playing Birmingham, when Birmingham were in the First Division, I took her there and Arsenal scored and she said: *Good old Brum!* She got the teams wrong didn't she? Fanny Maria – that was my mum's name – great old girl, wasn't she?

Charlie Robinson

Going with my son David was nice because it brings back memories of when you're younger. I know there are plenty of older people on the North Bank, always have been, but you normally go through a progression: you stand at first and then sit and stay like that. You don't normally go back the other way where you stand again. The catalyst of that was simply that I had children who wanted to stand.

David Court

'THEY ALL CAME TO OUR WEDDING'

We met at football. I was about 18. I'd been going since I was five. We met on the train going to Luton – we didn't have cars then, went everywhere by train. On the train with Les Jessop, the fellow who played in the band. On the specials, you only talked football! From the time you got on to the time you got off!

Rose Jales

I met my wife through the Supporters' Club. There was a crowd of us who used to stand together and go to away matches. I met her down at the social club the Supporters' Club had down in Canonbury Park. Her and her girlfriends, a lot of them were potty about footballers. So the boys and girls started going to matches together and that's how marriages took place: courting on the terraces, or up the back of the coach! When Arsenal played up in the north-west, the secretary often organised a weekend in Blackpool. In fact one Christmas Day we were away to Blackpool and Jessie and I went off for the weekend. I was in my early 20s and it was much to the disgust of my own family. It was the first Christmas I'd spent away from home.

Frank Hummell

I tried to get me missus in there and all. I took her to a game, I took her to the North Bank and they played Man United at the end of the season. Arsenal won 4−0 and Radford scored a hat-trick that day. And my missus fell asleep up the North Bank! She was my fiancée then, and we were down the centre where she was leaning against the pillar and she fell asleep in the second half. That's the only time I've taken her. I ended up marrying her, luckily, but I've never taken her since. I thought: *If she's going to become my fiancée, I might as well take her up there, and try to get her interested.* She honestly fell asleep and that was it, then. Obviously, I went with half a dozen of me mates and I hadn't noticed it. I mean, I was into the game, like, and she's leaning against the pillar, and my mate says: *Have a look at Wendy*. And she's just leaning back. You know, what the noise must have been, you can imagine what it must have been like that day, so I never took her again. She never asked to go again, to be fair.

Laird Budge

Me and my wife met through the Arsenal. A big Cup game against West Ham − we lost 2−0. I was in the pub beforehand, drinking with friends, you know, and I took her out down Hackney Road that night. Shame. If we'd have won it would have been a good night. (You can imagine − down there it's all West Ham.) But it went on from there. Every other Saturday after that. We progressed from there. To be honest, that was when we stopped going to the North Bank and went up the Clock End. I think you was worried about the pushing and shoving. We were only 19/20 and it still had that feeling up there, things you wouldn't want to see again. So we moved.

Steve Winfield

No, it wasn't the sort of place you took your girlfriend. I married her, but when I went out with her she hated football. That part is quite enjoyable, actually, watching her change. Well, I took her once because it wasn't fair that she should be knocking it without experiencing it: *If you don't like it, then I can't moan!* But she went the first time and loved it, fell in love with it. She couldn't believe the atmosphere and all that. She'd been used to, like, Donovan concerts and you know sort of the Round House

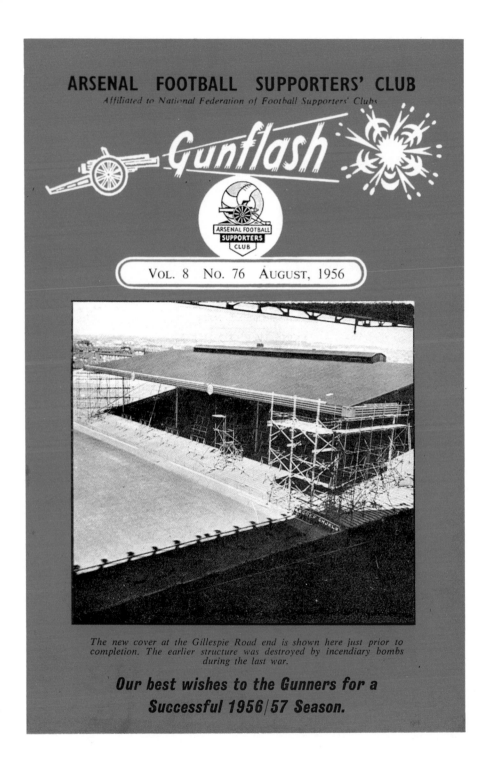

ARSENAL FOOTBALL SUPPORTERS' CLUB

Affiliated to National Federation of Football Supporters' Clubs

Gunflash

ARSENAL FOOTBALL
SUPPORTERS
CLUB

VOL. 8   NO. 76   AUGUST, 1956

The new cover at the Gillespie Road end is shown here just prior to completion. The earlier structure was destroyed by incendiary bombs during the last war.

Our best wishes to the Gunners for a Successful 1956/57 Season.

(Plate 33) 'It was like a palace.' Gunflash, *the Arsenal Supporters' Club magazine, celebrates the completion of a new roof over the North terrace at the beginning of the 1956–57 season*

(Plate 34) 'Now supporters are proud of young players who've come through.' Two early examples of the success of Arsenal's youth system which began to come good towards the end of the 60s, David Court and, with the ball at his feet, Jon Sammels (Colorsport)

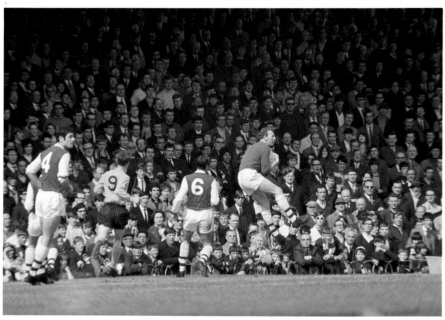

(Plate 35) 'A real respect.' Bob Wilson, Player of the Year in Arsenal's Double-winning season, 1970–71 (Colorsport)

(Plate 36) 'They'll sing: "We're the North Bank" wherever they are.' Arsenal fans at the Heysel Stadium for the European Cup-Winners Cup final, May 1980 (Colorsport)

(Plate 37) 'All of a sudden you have something in common.'

(Plate 38) 'Oh, let them get on with it.' A grandstand view from the roof of the North Bank
(Doug Poole)

(Plate 39) 'It's like you belong to something.' Tom and Rose Jales, supporters since the 1920s, with daughter Tina and granddaughter Dawn, celebrate victory in two Cup finals in 1993

(Plate 40) 'Our piece of barrier. Superb!' Rob Ashman and his mate, Chris, in a corner of Devon that will be forever Arsenal

(Plates 41 and 42) '2 May 1992.' Out of control (above) as Ian Wright completes his hat-trick against Southampton and, in control (below), measures taken as North Bank fans finally leave the ground

(Plate 43) 'All the memories and they just come and bulldoze the place.' The North Bank a few days after the final home game of the 1991–92 season (Evening Standard)

(Plate 44) 'I'm glad I've got one now.' Advertisements for the Bond scheme on the North Bank mural, behind which a new stand took shape during the 1992–93 season

(Plate 45) 'I think the new stand will be very nice.' The North Bank Stand, August 1993
(Match magazine)

at Chalk Farm and places like that, so she was a bit taken. It wasn't even a particularly good game, it was an end-of-season game, but she loved the atmosphere then and has done ever since.

Mick Essen

When my oldest was courting he said: *Can I bring Carol down Sunday dinner?* She comes from Bournemouth. We said: *Yeah!* She came down, we're having dinner. All of a sudden, I said: *You come from Bournemouth?* She said: *Yes.* Michael goes: *You'll have to watch it, Carol. It's Arsenal or nothing down here!* I said: *Oh, leave the poor little cow out of it, let her alone!* He goes: *No way, dad. Anyone comes in here* . . . Well, now, she's Arsenal mad. Then Peter, when he got married, she come from Barking. Brought her here for dinner. She's gone: *I'm West Ham, Jack.* I said: *I don't want to upset your dinner but you better change that.* She said: *I know. I've been told!* Now she's Arsenal. They've got to be Arsenal.

Jack Hobb

First time I went was a Tottenham game. I'd been going out with Paul for about a year, 18 months. I'd never been to a football match before. On paper, I'd always followed Tottenham. I came from a Tottenham family. My dad wouldn't take me, my brother wouldn't take me, so I went with Paul. I really enjoyed it. Paul was a different person at football. Every other word was a swear word and I thought: *God!* I knew his brothers there, too. It was a different Paul. Ranting and raving. We went home and I was just shell-shocked!

Sam Hobb

When we first met, I told Sam: *If we're going to carry on, you've got to know that Arsenal is my life, that's it. If you come with me, you're going to hear so much foul language out of my mouth you're not going to believe it, but for those couple of hours on a Saturday your whole world changes. That's your team, your life. No matter how I behave, that's part of my life. If we lose I'll have the hump for the rest of the night.*

Paul Hobb

Something else happened which I've never forgotten. I won't go into the relationship I had with this girl right, but we were very close. She was going away to college in Sheffield and we had to decide whether we were going to make a big commitment or not. Now I won't go into all this. But one week I decided that I wanted her, I wanted to make a formal commitment: *You're mine, I'm yours.* I decided that I was going to phone up and tell her all this. Now that night we had an evening game at home, it would have been 81–82. I was living in London at the time. My brother had been home and he said: *By the way I've got a postcard for you.* And this was at half time, he turned round and said: *I've got a postcard for you.* I put on my specs and I was reading this from Julia and on it she told me that she'd decided she was going to get engaged to this bloke, she had been going out with him and that. I remember sitting there through the whole of the half time absolutely torn apart. Every time I think about that happening, it's the North Bank and the postcard, you know, it happened in the

North Bank. I'm almost pleased it happened in the North Bank.

Rob Ashman

I remember one couple who used to spend the hour-and-a-half before a game snogging in the middle of the North Bank. They were almost soldered together during the game. I think they got married in the end.

PC Alan Smith

But the moment at the North Bank that I really will cherish happened at my last visit to the North Bank. At half time in the game against Man United in 1992 me and my girlfriend got engaged.

Magnus Falkehag

They all came to our wedding. One of them was still at my mum's house four days later. He wouldn't leave till the beer ran out. Les Jessop brought his band down. We had red and white walking-sticks when we came out of the church, which we knew nothing about, tied together. One would have a football. The next one would have football boots. They'd all sorted it out.

Rose Jales

We held the wedding reception in Rosa's Café in City Road. We were married in St Mary's Church in Upper Street. The vicar said: *Hurry up.* I said: *What for?* He said: *I want to get over Highbury.* So I said: *Why didn't you tell me before, I'd have come with you!*

Tom Jales

I remember him and mother going on a holiday once and they went down to the West Country and they took me to Bournemouth, Plymouth – I mean every day there was a game, my mother loved it! – she couldn't bear football! And they got back in time to see a home game at Arsenal, you know. He just loved football. Where was he the day I was being born? Oh God, he went to Arsenal and left my mother. And it was a reserve game! My poor mother's never forgiven him. And they also got married on a Sunday because of Arsenal on Saturday. My brother was the same.

Maureen Hewlitt

'IT'S ALWAYS BEEN FOOTBALL'

All the men had raincoats, most of them wore caps. Everybody was smoking. There was no swearing 'cos the dads wouldn't swear in front of the children and the children certainly wouldn't swear in front of their dads.

Roger Hewlitt

My wife knows Arsenal is the other woman in my life. That's my other front room. I'm as relaxed there as I am in the front room. It's a lovely feeling. Saturday morning's a ritual to me. I can't get out of bed quick enough. I got a lovely wife, but Saturday mornings I can't get up quick enough. I sing in the shower, because it's Saturday, it's football and I'm away, here we go! On Saturday afternoons, my wife's going to go shopping, I'm going to football, and the whole thing's a ritual. I get up Saturday morning, I'm in the shower first, have a nice big greasy breakfast and I get myself all nice. I'm daft, I'm not going out with a girl but I'm always going to wash me hair, always have a blooming shave!

Steve Whitman

A two-foot strip of concrete between the fence and the steps where the roof ended on the Avenell Road side – this tiny strip was home to the Trevett family every other Saturday. My father Jim and his brother Richard fighting over the best sweets, my sister Mandy trying to ignore them and watch the game, and sometimes even my girlfriend Julia would stand there shivering in the cold. Also there each week was Danny and his mate who only stood there so they could laugh at the unfortunate people who slid on the notoriously slippery steps, spilling the tea they had spent half an hour queuing for. Every week it would be the same. Uncle Richard would tell the same jokes, distracting your attention just as the game exploded into life. Just as Limpar or Merson attacked the full-back, bearing down on the North Bank goal, Richard would be persistently tapping me on the shoulder until finally I could take no more and I would have to turn and face him. *I only wear this cap*, he would grin as the rest of the crowd craned their necks to see the ball fly into the box, *because the cap makes me taller. That means I can see the game better.* Well I suppose height was never in the Trevett genes. Sadly the humour is pretty slight as well.

Ian Trevett

He'd always come straight from work and go back again after. I always went over on my own and came home on my own!

Rose Jales

There used to be a little bar at the top of the North Bank, in the corner just above the steps to Avenell Road. I was left to savour the memories of my visit, while the adults had a few beers.

Steve Thomas

My first Cup match was a fourth-round tie at home to Norwich in 1954. Arsenal lost, 5–2, and so was I. Somehow I got separated from my brother. I drifted with the crowd towards Gillespie Road while my brother went to Avenell Road. I found a cop and told him that I was lost. I was taken in a police car around to Avenell Road where my frantic brother and father were waiting outside the entrance. I was told that I was beaming.

Peter Leslie

After the war, my father had a season ticket. So he used to sit but I'd stand. He would take me there on the bus or very occasionally we might get a lift in a car from a friend – if you had a car then you were lord of the manor. So he used to take me there but we never actually stood together, strangely enough.

Geoff Gilbert

My dad, when he worked in the furriers, had to work half day Sunday to get two hours off on Saturday afternoon to come down to Highbury. Then when the match was finished at five o'clock, we'd go to have a cup of tea and he had to get back to work. He'd had his two hours off on Saturday afternoon, then he'd have to make it up at the other end, in East End sweat shops. But those two hours off on Saturday afternoon meant exactly the same as what they meant to me and you and the kids that will go until Arsenal cease to be.

Maurice Gran

Winning always was my problem with the Arsenal. When they win, I'm so happy. I don't care if I haven't got a penny in my pocket. My missus would ask how they got on: *Won 2–1*. She'll say: *Thank God, I'll have a nice night tonight, then*. I was just the same as my three boys are now. In this house, if they lost, you could cut the atmosphere with a knife! Not a word would be spoken.

Jack Hobb

All of my family supports Arsenal. Because the boys in the family used to ask what big uncle was doing and, when they're told the big uncle is going to Arsenal, they grow up to support Arsenal. We have a family in New Zealand, my sister, she has three boys. The three boys are Arsenal and the grandchildren now, they're Arsenal. We have to send them the uniform. For the kids, three or four years old, Arsenal kids. I used to take my godson, who lived in Gillespie Road. I picked him up every Saturday. He still goes now.

Alex Froso

I couldn't wait to get home, after the first game I couldn't wait to tell people. I went on about it all evening. My dad had to tell me to shut up in the end. I just had to let people know how good it is. My girlfriend gets peed off about it now.

Guy Thomson

My brother went to medical school at Middlesex Hospital and there was a long period of about two or three years where I very rarely saw him. But I always saw him on the North Bank. That was our meeting place. On match days I would see my brother. That's something I remembered about that particular era. I would always be looking at the crowd waiting for him to come up. I'd see his head, like.

Rob Ashman

My dad died in 75. He was going right up until the week he died, and then with dad dying, funnily enough, they stopped going. The group disintegrated. My brother stopped going, his friends who he used to go with stopped going. They used to play cards every Friday night, that had to stop, and then they stopped going to the Arsenal.

Maurice Gran

There was a guy called George Nichols in our street, who used to go over Arsenal, and he was like the Pied Piper. All the kids' dads were up the pub on a Saturday you know, and George Nichols would take us, hundreds of kids from the street, all round Westbourne. Me mum'd think I was going with George, that was fine. There used to be a little green gate at the Arsenal between the North Bank and where you used to have the school kids. So what you do is you pay in the Schoolboys' and the commissionaire would be there, and there would be George and there would be like 25 screaming kids going: *That's my dad!* You know, black kids, Asian kids, white kids! And the commissionaire's going: *Hold it*, you know. You'd charge the commissionaire, and you'd always get in. We always went with him, always. He used to get us in basically, then we used to stand where the gate was, on this side, but he used to stand on the opposite side, on the first pole, so we knew exactly where he was before we went home. But we'd just leave him to it and dash off. There was times when, you know, parents couldn't afford it, simple as that. I was talking to one of George's sons about two months ago, and I said: *I remember your dad when kids couldn't afford it, two or three kids. He'd go: That's sweet, and he'd take us up there, and pay for it.* Honestly, and he done that many times, he took different kids. He said: *It's alright*, and paid you in.

Mark Burdis

In many ways, standing on the North Bank with my stepfather was my way of getting to know my stepfather. I never really went with my father, then my mum had a few years off from going and then a stepfather comes along. When you're 11 or 12, it's a confusing time – it was an ideal way to get to know each other. You know, I think a thing about the terraces, anyway, is people lose their inhibitions, all sorts of people are brought together.

Andrew Allerton

As I've got older, you know, I've grown more aware of the game. I've done coaching and that and I like to look at that side of it, the football. It still amazes me what watching breaks you down into! You think: *I'm just going to watch this game.* You're playing someone who's not very good and after about ten minutes you're shouting your head off. I remember I went up the North Bank when they got beat by Villa in the Cup and I remember there was a bloke in front of me and as they come out he's going: *This is Graham Rix and this is that.* His boy's the only son, and as the game was going on he's going: *Yeah, yeah, he's going to pass that ball over there.* He's all sort of indoctrinating. He'd go from being a real sort of pleasant, even type of parent. He'd gone like everybody else had – they got slaughtered that night – and it just turned him into just a dumb little idiot by the end! But I mean that's what football does to you.

Laird Budge

Before going back with my kids, I'd never stood on the North Bank as a partisan supporter. It was a strange feeling being in there, I guess. It was something I hadn't done for quite a few years. It took a bit of getting used to I suppose – two or three games standing thinking: *Is this really what I should be doing at my age?* But having said that, all David's friends were known to me and it got to the point where if I wanted to go, say, on my own, I'd know where to find this crowd of guys to stand with even if David wasn't there. They were friends of the family, I guess, and I didn't feel too old because I had kids their age myself. My eldest daughter would come with us, and at one stage we were bringing our youngest daughter with us, in which case my wife would invariably come along as well!

David Court

I have to say when I used to take the children when they were little, I never felt worried about being on the North Bank. I mean, people go on about being worried about being crushed. But you didn't feel insecure.

Roger Hewlitt

The only time I've got worried was when I went, just me and my grandad, and grandad was getting on a bit. If there's a big crowd you can see as you come out over the corner of the North Bank and you come down the steps. You see down below, all the crowd and I think: *Oh, I don't want to go into that!* and I'll go: *You alright, pops? You alright?* I'm worried for him in the crowd. But I know people around, even now, once they see, they'll make a little space. But he hates it, you know, he says: *Yes, yes! I'm alright!*

Dawn Evans

I work with a bloke who's a Tottenham supporter. But all his family are Arsenal: mum, dad, brother, rank paid-up Arsenal. Now how does that work? He must have rebelled as a kid.

Peter Hobb

Yes, Arsenal goes back a long way in my family. Grandparents on both sides were Arsenal, my father, my stepfather, my mother. I was never ever going to support anyone else!

Andrew Allerton

Everybody's involved. We even drag dad along to one match a season! Even though he hasn't really got it – he's dispassionate about it where we are passionate.

Dawn Evans

It's always been football in my family. My dad used to go and my brothers. The end of Hoxton where we lived, it was all Arsenal. It's always been a close community with the Arsenal. The Arsenal has always been in my family. When I met the missus, at the time I was courting her, I'd see her Saturday night. On Saturday it'd be me, her brother-in-law and one of her sisters. The husband'd go: *Highbury, Jack? I'll meet you down there. Right-o George.* And off we'd go. End of 48–49 this is. If the Arsenal won, we used to come from Highbury, up Riversdale Road, into the first pub and we'd go to every pub until we got to Hoxton. We'd won, we were happy. Beer was 6d a pint. Nothing to worry about. We'd get home about half past seven at night. Now the game's finished maybe at four o'clock. The missus'd say: *Alright?* I'd say: *No, I'm going home to get ready, I'll see you down there in about an hour's time.* I'd go home and get changed. Get back there and her brother-in-law would come in: *Wasn't it a game, Jack?* Her two brothers who weren't so much football fans would say: *But how come it took you so long to get home?* My mother used to say: *How can that girl stand you?* I'd say: *The Arsenal won, mother!* That was all that mattered. And then, of course, when I got down the pub with the missus, have a few more drinks and someone would start an argument about football! I never took Irene to football, she never liked the crowds. She'll go now though, to watch my little grandson play football. He's on Wimbledon's books. Anyway, we were married and had our boys. The first was Michael – he's 43 now – and I used to take him over the reserves at first and then the first team. We'd sit him down the front there. By the time he was at school, he was eight or nine, he'd go: *Can I go over the reserves?* I'd say: *Who are you going with?* He'd say: *I'm going with Dennis and so-and-so.* So I used to give him half a crown and he'd go. You wasn't afraid to let your children go there. He'd come home full of it. First-team games, I'd take him because of the crowds. Then along comes Peter and as he grew up I used to take him over. Then they wanted to go on their own, so off they went. They were always getting in arguments at school about: *Arsenal are the best.* We had a brother-in-law who was a Tottenham man. If the Arsenal lost, he used to come over: *See the Arsenal got beat.* Michael and Peter used to go mad. When the Arsenal won, they used to tell him off. I used to say: *Look, football's football. No arguments. Not in the home.* The boys would go: *Alright, dad. But he's not getting away with it!* Finally, Paul was born. When he was five or six, I took him at first. Then he went with Michael and Peter. I'd see them by the turnstile after the game. *Alright. On the bus and home to your mother!* And this is how it's followed on, you see.

Jack Hobb

I've never really subscribed to that *football is the family game and you've got to take your wife and little girl* point of view. As far as I'm concerned football is for the blokes, a few beers beforehand. But in the 50s it was a more 'family' thing, more dads and sons, you know, and that was all round the ground. And of course there was no hooliganism then, people were quite happy to take their children. They weren't frightened. Away supporters came, but not in any numbers, and they mingled. It was quite good. You'd have the wags in the crowd and you'd get a bit of banter going, but there was never any animosity.

John Platt

The 60s were the rebellious years, weren't they? They were the first generation of rebels. They wanted to do their own thing. They didn't want to stand with their dads and grandads. They wanted their own place. I think the North Bank was where they all went.

Tina Evans

Around about 85–86, things started to change. We're gradually getting back to the way things were when I was a boy. I think so, personally. The police are doing their part, the Club are doing their part, we – as first-aiders – are doing our part. What we've got to do is start to bring the families back with the children. If you don't fetch the children back, you have lost the Club because they are the supporters of the future. When there was all that trouble it was because the kids were away from mum and dad. We used to come with them – we were all together – but later they used to think: *Oh, no, I'm not going with my dad!* And out of sight, out of mind. But now they're gradually coming back. I should imagine when the Club is settled and people have got their seats, there'll be a different atmosphere.

Frank Martin

I think standing up is a growing-up phase of going to football. You're going to miss the dads with the nippers on their shoulders. The generations that's going to come through now is going to miss all that. Like the Junior Gunners – I think that's great what they do there – but they're the next lot who'd be wanting to go and stand on the North Bank. I think that's part of being a fan, an Arsenal supporter. Everyone's stood there, even if it was only once. Or it was a secret! I used to tell my dad I was going to the Clock End, not such a big crowd, but you'd go up to the North Bank because that was where you all went.

Steve Winfield

People should have the choice if they want to stand. It's going to price a lot of people away from the game. Kids aren't going to be able to go to football. We used to go to Arsenal for the afternoon, five bob all in. Now, the cheapest seat'll be £12, £3 on the train, £2 for the programme. *Can I have £18 to go to football, dad?* A ten-year-old? The grass-roots will disappear.

Lenny Brandon

When you're having to sit, or pay £8 or £10 to stand, not many people can afford to take their kids now. Twenty pounds plus your programme and a drink is a lot for one man. If he has two or three kids, it's impossible. The last three years the price has gone sky high. In some grounds they charge half-price for children, which I think is a good idea. It helps to bring children back to the ground. At the end of the day, it's the children who will be following Arsenal when we're gone. If we had half-price for children, dads could bring them. It'd be a day out, he could teach them and the kids would follow in their father's footsteps, like my daughter followed me.

Alex Froso

Here am I, a house, a mortgage, wife expecting a baby – my standard of living is probably above the average – and I'll be struggling to afford football, you know, bonds and season tickets for me and my kids, I'm being squeezed out. And I think of all those people, all those fathers and sons and uncles who for generations used to sit on the terrace for an hour-and-a-half before a game. I know those times have gone but I think we need to keep the essence of that.

Phillip Bloomfield

CHAPTER FOURTEEN

'There Will Be Nothing Like It'

THE NORTH BANK, 1987–92

While each of us continue to have our own little moans from week to week, we are all aware that it's impossible to overstate the change George Graham has wrought at Highbury since becoming manager in 1986. His sense of purpose, his commitment to Arsenal, his belief in the teams he sends out every Saturday and the ambitious terms in which he defines the goals he sets for them, have driven the Club back to the very top of the domestic game. After one false start, European competition presents the next hurdle and you'd be a fool to bet against the gaffer taking it in his stride. The last days of the North Bank cheered six seasons of high achievement – two League titles and a Littlewoods Cup – which set standards of consistency not enjoyed at Highbury since the 1930s. The team that won the Championship in 1991, while perhaps not as sporadically exciting as its counterpart two years before, will be consigned to posterity as one of Arsenal's greatest ever, along with Chapman's side of 1931 and Bertie Mee's Double-winners of 1971. George Graham took Arsenal by the scruff of the neck from day one and put us, as the song goes, back where we belong.

As crowds had rushed to marvel at Chapman's team, so Graham's Arsenal sides drew newcomers in the wake of their success. Casual supporters, women, Afro-Caribbeans and members of Islington's gentry all found their way on to the North Bank of recent years to watch the new Golden Age unfold. Inevitably, the consistent level of achievement raised the levels of expectations in the crowd dramatically, in a way that reminded many of a similar change in attitude among supporters during the later years of the 1930s. In 1989, every Saturday on the way to the League Championship – at least until the penultimate week – seemed like Christmas Day. Two years later, many supporters had already come to expect victory as the natural order of things and voices were quick to be raised at the sight of any sign of weakness. The North Bank became a calmer, less passionate, more critical place to watch football during its final years. It also became safer, more tolerant and more sophisticated.

Apart from the effect that the new cycle of achievement had on the terrace fans, there were factors beyond the football on display which would also leave their mark on life on the North Bank near the end. One was the obvious decrease in the threat of violence at Highbury and elsewhere, the reasons for which will be returned to. Another was the richer mix of age, race and sex that began to find a home on the terrace, attracted to the team's success and by the North Bank's reputation.

The appearance of fanzines on the terraces for the first time was the latest chapter in a story that had started with the formation of the Supporters' Club in 1947. The fanzines celebrated and promoted an increasing sophistication on the North Bank and around the ground. They offered fans a platform on which to rehearse the sense of humour, the arguments about team selection and the prognostications on the future which had been the stuff of terrace conversation for decades. That they appeared at all was evidence of the increasing accessibility of information technology. The amount of time and effort involved in putting *The Gooner*, *One Nil Down*, *The Echo Echo* or *An Imperfect Match* together and on the street were evidence of the North Bank's continuing love affair with Arsenal Football Club, however critical a stance the magazines may have taken on specific issues. That those four publications, and the others that have come and gone, should have such different editorial and production values and still co-exist is evidence of how mixed a crowd the North Bank had become. The fanzines were a symptom, too, of the less passionate, more ironic – even cynical – attitudes that the terrace which they sprang from had started to enjoy.

At the same time, it was possible to detect a new-found sense of solidarity and articulacy among football supporters following the events at the Heysel Stadium in 1985, the formation of the Football Supporters' Association, and the co-operation between clubs and fans in resisting the Government's preposterous ID-card scheme. From the mid-80s onwards, the right to a voice and opinions of their own became an idea, for fans, whose time had come. Their attitudes and ideas were suddenly of interest to politicians, administrators, academics and journalists who had ignored them for decades.

The impracticality of the ID-card scheme, which was the Government's answer to the crisis provoked by the Heysel outrage, and the scant regard for the civil liberties of ordinary fans enshrined in its proposals, were a clear reminder of what Whitehall knew or cared about football supporters. In the event, however, despite the hard work of the clubs, the fans and some politicians to counter the scheme, it took the Hillsborough Disaster to actually remove ID cards from the agenda.

The events of 15 April 1989, indeed, proved to have an impact that would change the identity of every football ground – and every spectator's experience – forever. As soon as Lord Justice Taylor, in his report on the Hillsborough Disaster, had set out his recommendation that all leading clubs should have all-seater grounds within four years, the argument was over bar us shouting. Given Taylor's recommendation that the terraces should close, it was a political imperative that legislation should be pushed through whatever fans, the clubs or other interested parties might have to say. Any Home Secretary, given such advice and declining to implement it, would have been offering his political career as hostage to the safe conduct of every spectator, at every football ground, for the foreseeable future.

From outside too, of course, the all-seater proposal made perfect sense and looked long overdue. The football grounds of Britain had suffered decades of neglect and now was the time to force the game to put its houses in order. Many of those actually involved, however, at the local level – the clubs, the police and the fans themselves – saw matters from a very different perspective. Their arguments, though relevant, rational and deeply felt, were all to no avail. The matter was done and dusted the moment Lord Taylor put his signature to the report.

Seating was the recommendation that made the headlines. That was why it was the one proposal that would be implemented however strong the arguments against. Lord Taylor's report was a long and very thorough piece of work of which the end of terraces was only part. The bulk of the report was a well-meant and well-thought-out analysis of the contemporary politics and practice of football-crowd safety. Taylor uncovered, and attempted to correct, decades of neglect and irresponsibility. The irony, for those who were to lose their places on the North Bank as a result, was that they supported a club whose pro-active and energetic policies on crowd safety and control had ensured that much of what Taylor would recommend was already in place at Highbury well before the Hillsborough Disaster happened. Arsenal already devoted to these matters the priority, the time and the personnel without which, it must be said, neither Taylor's nor anyone else's recommendations will really ensure that football grounds are safe. The policy that had been in place at Highbury for some years was based on close, regular and constructive liaison with the police, safety engineers, the local authorities and the first-aid organisations. Basically, what those bodies – with their own specific and specialist experience, and particular responsibilities – wanted, they got.

Trouble on the terraces at Highbury had not been a major problem for five or six years. The North Bank, indeed, thanks to effective segregation and a change of mood, had been no problem at all. There was one incident during the period, involving Millwall supporters visiting Highbury for a Cup-tie, which pushed security arrangements to their limits and the situation – inside the ground, at least – was successfully kept under close control. During the 80s the police and the Club showed themselves ready to co-operate with each other; stewards were taken on and trained; engineering work – the lateral fences and the surveillance posts on the North Bank, for example – was undertaken when, or before, the need arose.

The North Bank of the late 80s and early 90s was a safe, friendly place to watch football. A great deal of credit must go to the Club and the police for this. But the change in atmosphere, the dissipation of the threat of violence, was due as well to a change of heart and change of mind in many North Bank supporters in the months after the deaths at the Heysel Stadium. Violence, while still actively sought by a committed minority (as it is today), was going out of fashion. Come the summer of 1988, many of the 'faces' on the terraces, in conflict only weeks before, could be seen in London night-clubs gobbling Ecstasy and loving each other, as the first wave of rave culture broke into view. As the threat of violence ebbed, more families, women and children started – or returned to – standing on the North Bank. Their presence, in turn, helped relax the atmosphere behind the goal still further. A happily non-vicious circle was in place. Later on, Hillsborough itself had a profound impact on the mood of terraces across the country. The need for a sense of proportion and a sense of responsibility was made starkly obvious, cutting across the passion and commitment, even, of the most close-run Championship for years.

In terms of crowd safety, too, Arsenal's policy meant that much of the Taylor Report was already current practice at Highbury. The Club had, since the early 70s, commissioned a company of independent consultant engineers to issue a safety certificate. Examination, recommendation and improvement were carried out each year with a care and stringency well beyond any legal obligation in place before Taylor made his recommendations. The St John's Ambulance Brigade, like the police, had benefited from Arsenal's *what you want you get* policy and, by 1989, the numbers of staff and facilities available at Highbury already matched standards Taylor would establish, for football as a whole, the following year. The North Bank played its part here too. Many St John's volunteers remember the good-natured co-operation of the terrace fans of recent years as a return to what had seemed to them a bygone age.

This is not to say that the Taylor Report was irrelevant to Arsenal. However, it deserves to be remembered that sound policy and good practice at Highbury – and the growing sophistication of the North Bank – meant that the importance of the Report's substance had been recognised and, to a great extent, implemented well before 15 April 1989. While the appropriateness of the new legislation to the overall situation in British football is more difficult to contradict, in the specific circumstances relevant at Highbury the abolition of terraces was both unnecessary and, for the most part, undesirable. This is a book about the North Bank and it is a part of telling its story to recognise that the End's disappearance was imposed, uncalled for and unwanted. In a wider context, of course, our home end would be seen as a single example on which to enact across-the-board legislation which, by its nature, ignored the relevance of local conditions and culture. It was therefore inevitable that the North Bank's history would be rushed to this hasty all-seater conclusion. Arsenal and Arsenal fans were among those who had to pay for others' inability – or unwillingness – to move forward until Hillsborough meant they had to.

Arsenal were quick to recognise the inevitability of change. A new all-seater stand to replace the North Bank was on the drawing-board within a year. Proposals for a debenture scheme to help finance the new stand were put to the supporters as the team paraded the League trophy to a delirious Highbury in May 1991. The Club showed admirable decisiveness in their readiness to respond, constructively and ambitiously, to changing circumstances, having quickly recognised the implications of the Taylor Report. However, both the designs and the funding proposals for the envisaged all-seater stand can be seen, with hindsight, to have betrayed the insensitivity of too-great haste. Over the coming year, often bitter conflict was to arise over both issues.

In the early days, especially, Arsenal's bond scheme seemed to be presented as a stick rather than a carrot with which to raise some of the nearly £20 million which the new stand was going to cost. It appeared to many that the Club's most loyal supporters were being presented with Hobson's choice: find £1,100 or £1,500 (to buy the right to buy a season ticket for the next 150 years) from somewhere – to help replace a terrace that you never wanted to leave – or you may not be able to watch

Arsenal in the future at all. Some felt the goodwill of North Bank fans was simply being exploited. Enough people were upset and angry for the Independent Arsenal Supporters' Association to be established in the summer of 1991. Debenture schemes are a perfectly acceptable way for organisations like football clubs to defray the cost of significant capital investment. Indeed, an important proportion – around a third – of the cost of the new North Bank Stand will have been met by this means when it opens in the autumn of 1993. However, Arsenal's bond issue was something of a disaster, especially in public-relations terms. To fund the new stand in this way was, quite properly, the Club's decision to make. But time and effort spent consulting supporters – especially those to be displaced when the North Bank disappeared – would have been of enormous value, financially and politically. Much of the debate was to do with the presentation and restricted accessibility of the scheme. Ways and means could have been found – indeed were to be found later on – to make the bond more supporter-friendly and, at the same time, to reassure those who weren't in a position to consider participation in the scheme that they had a place in Highbury's future. Instead, many North Bank fans felt that they were being shown the door as the Club went after a vaguely defined 'new' high-spend, business-class consumer. Often angry confrontation ensued. The articulate and well-publicised anti-bond campaign – centred on the North Bank and fired up by the apparent injustice of Highbury losing its terraces at all – became bitter, personalised and confused. Certainly, the campaign had an effect on how the debenture scheme developed later on. But this was at no little cost to the fund of goodwill felt towards the Club by many North Bank loyalists. A political issue became, at the same time, a moral and emotional issue for all involved in the debate. The depth of feeling, unbridged by constructive dialogue, led to personal recriminations which drove the two sides further apart. Now, hopefully, with the new stand open, the bond scheme a limited success, and fans having found a voice of their own, angry conflict can become a rational exchange of views which can only be to the Club's – and the supporters – benefit in the future.

The original designs for the new stand also met with the accusation that they took no account of how other people involved might be affected by them. The new proposals appalled some local residents who set up the Group for an Alternative Arsenal Stand. GAAS included architects, local councillors and journalists who campaigned long and hard to get the Club to reconsider. While unable to succeed in getting their alternative design considered, GAAS's opposition to the original plan – like IASA's to the bond scheme – gave Arsenal the necessary impetus to look again at the problems. A second look at original ideas which, in the rush of circumstances, had not been analysed as objectively as they might, certainly paid off for the Club. The stand design which eventually received planning permission, while still not achieving the impossible and pleasing everyone, is a creditable compromise in environmental terms. Furthermore, its unrivalled facilities, superb views and genuine sense of integration with the rest of Highbury's buildings mean that the North Bank Stand will be the finest in the country: a landmark in stadium architecture with an impact to compare with that made by Waterlow Ferrier's West Stand in 1932. After all the arguments, the outcome is very impressive indeed.

May 2nd 1992 was the day on which, to all intents and purposes, this history came to an end. The North Bank was packed for the last game of the 1991–92 season, its numbers swelled by many who left their seats or places elsewhere in the ground to be there with the regulars on the terrace's last day. The sense of loss, the hopes and fears, that people brought to Highbury that Saturday afternoon, hung over the North Bank and the first 45 minutes of the game itself. The second half, however, thanks to a remarkable display from the End's newest hero, Ian Wright, transformed the afternoon – in 30 memorable minutes – into a celebration of the joy, the sense of belonging, that comes from standing on your terrace to watch the football team you love. As each goal of Wright's hat-trick flew in, isolation, frustration and disappointment were submerged in the boiling pot of 15,000 people's excitement. A charge crackled around the North Bank as it had on countless afternoons and evenings since September 1913. Fifteen thousand people inspired by one man in a red shirt and those 15,000 roaring inspiration back. A bloke with a football out on the pitch and a tumbling mass of the ages, races, sexes and cultures crashing around on the terrace: man and crowd living for each other, celebrating the point of it all, here – at this moment, in this enclosure – in this noisy and anarchic corner of north London. The North Bank was a beautiful place to be: the best of people, best of friends and best of times.

Millions of people had stood on the North Bank, relishing moments like those, since before the First World War. It was left to a couple of thousand – many knowing little, many knowing much, of what had gone before – to stand guard over the terrace's last hour of friendly occupation: arguing, singing and just being there, until a thin blue line swept across the steps to make way for change and an uncertain future.

At the start of the 1993–94 Premier League season Arsenal will open a two-tier, all-seater grandstand at the north end of the ground, named after the terrace it has replaced. Whatever the future holds for football, for Arsenal and for the fans who'll take their seats in the new North Bank Stand, the past belongs to the voices and the footsteps of the old terrace, some few of which have been recorded here. There'd be no stand, there'd be no Arsenal, had families over generations, over 80 years, not made the North Bank home. That continuity, traced by people's feet and stitched with people's dreams, is lifeblood to the sense of tradition that has made Arsenal quite unique. Lose that – the sense of who we were and where we've been – and we lose the thread we need to secure our football's future.

'A DIFFERENT KIND OF SUPPORTER'

Electrifying, there was nothing like it. There will be nothing like it. As much as this stand's going to be the best stand in England, Europe whatever: Arsenal–Tottenham derby game, shouting till you're hoarse, big stand, you're covered, brilliant! You'll never replace it, never ever replace it. It made me tingle, made the hairs on the back of my neck stand up, when we used to score, that's all I can tell you.

Paul Johnson

Forty years ago, programmes cost three old pence, now £1, 80 times as costly. To stand cost one shilling and three pence, now £5, 80 times as costly. To sit in the stand in block Z was seven shillings, now £8 – only 20 times as costly. It looks like the terrace supporters have had a rough time!

R.J. Sheen, *AFC Programme*, 18.11.89

It was great, much better than I thought it was going to be, because everybody comes up and says hello and talks to you.

Dawn Hicks

I moved to up there from the 18-yard line because I wanted to be on the telly. All the time I went, I wore my white bobble hat and I could see it on telly. I thought if I moved up a bit more, they'll see me more. On the Club video, I'm on every single home match. One game, Oldham I think, you see Lee Dixon come down and even before he's crossed the ball you see this red coat – that's me – just jumping for nothing, just bouncing about. I didn't even know I was doing it at the time.

Julie Wheeler

The last few seasons I've noticed there's been a lot more youngsters on the North Bank. Schoolkids, really, 14–18. When I first went it was a much older crowd. Arsenal had a hard-core hooligan element who you stayed clear of but you knew who they were. But during the 80s they seemed to fizzle out and you had the younger ones taking their place, who are a different kind of supporter. I can't see them being there in ten years time. I could be wrong.

Jim Smith

Since I was about 12 people have been going to me: *Oh, you'll grow out of it by the time you're 15 or 16.* But here I am now and I think I'm worse! I know more about it now. Everything I do is just Arsenal, Arsenal. Where I work, they call me Mrs Merson. Or this bloke, when he sees me he just goes: *Alright Arsenal?*

Julie Wheeler

Julie used to come up to me at school and whack me and say: *See you at 12 tomorrow.* But then it got earlier and earlier, 11, half past ten. Now we're the first ones there. We sit outside where we've got to go in, read our programmes. Watch people go past and talk to them. Sometimes foreign people come and take photos. When the turnstile opens, she rushes in, because she's got her season ticket, while I pay, and she saves our place. We'd go over and talk to 'Julie's Fan Club', these people we know – they stand behind the goal. Except once they start talking they never stop. Or they come over and talk to us. About Arsenal or about Paul Merson because they know he's Julie's favourite.

Dawn Hicks

There was a lot of smoking dope started going on up the North Bank mid-80s. A lot of people were puffing round by us.

Lenny Brandon

What's happening on the North Bank? No, this isn't another moan about hooliganism, or chanting (actually I like the chants). My theory is that there's a growing number of people who come here on Saturday afternoons with the sole intention of sampling the gastronomic delights of the refreshment hut!

This must be true, or why else would so many people wait patiently for the match to start, then spend the next 90 minutes pushing their way to and fro determinedly through the crowd, without even noticing what's happening on the pitch! I can only conclude that the thought of a tea or burger must become increasingly desirable the moment play kicks off.

Sophie Bane, *AFC Programme*, 17.12.88

Our latest thing has been sweets. It sounds ridiculous. I mean, I'm not a Woolworth's Pick 'n' Mix man but you can see them as a sort of modern art: *What do you buy? What d'you take? When do you eat what? What are you left with? When d'you share them round?* Sweets have been the main thing the last two or three years. I've still got this old packet of Nuttall's Mintoes we haven't finished. But the big thing are Woolworth's Pick 'n' Mix because it takes quite a creative effort to put that mix together.

Richard Stubbs

One game that sticks out is that game against Man United in the Cup when Brian McClair missed that penalty in the last minute. That sticks in my mind for atmosphere. I don't think, really, we were expecting to win that. We couldn't really believe we'd got into a winning position. And him missing that penalty was the icing on the cake.

David Court Jnr

I shall never forget McClair's penalty miss in the FA Cup when Lukic's hands became about 15 feet wide. It was like that Kenny Everett thing. But it was the North Bank. The North Bank kept it out. One of the few times the North Bank kept a goal out. There was no way he was ever going to score. Absolutely sublime moment.

Richard Stubbs

My favourite game was when we played France in the Championship year. I enjoyed that because there was nothing riding on it. Because I get dreadful before Cup games, nervous, I go to the loo about 100 times, and we have to drink out of special mugs in the morning. Now you see last season we decided we'd cut this out. We've got two old mugs we drank out of on a Saturday and we thought: *This is stupid!* And we didn't do anything last season you see, so this season we've gone back to drinking out of them. I love evening games, I think you get the atmosphere the grass looks so green, I love it. And I like seeing all the men coming straight from work in suits and their raincoats. I thought that was a fabulous game because if they'd beaten us it wouldn't have mattered. It was the French national team. I thought it was a lovely game, I really enjoyed that.

Maureen Hewlitt

You talk about atmospheres. When we won the Championship in 1989, I've never seen so many people panic in my whole life. They were so nervous. With three or four home games to go. People were shaking. If we hadn't scored after ten minutes the Championship was over! And when we played Derby. We got beat 2–1. That was it. We'd thrown it away. We were just nervous wrecks. And the Wimbledon game we drew 2–2. When they equalised there was just silence.

Peter Hobb

The Championship year, 1989, the game at home to Derby that we lost, before the draw with Wimbledon. I turned round and there was this bloke – it was a boiling hot afternoon and he'd got jeans on and his t-shirt tied round his waist, he was a mass of tattoos – he'd got his head on the railings and he was sobbing. The old earring, Skinhead – just sobbing. I wanted to go and cuddle him. I felt awful. I mean, we all thought we'd blown it didn't we? If you'd have seen this bloke on a dark night you'd have been terrified but there he was, head on his hands, sobbing. He didn't care who heard or who saw.

Maureen Hewlitt

The one game I was catatonic was the Derby game in 1989 when we lost 2–1. The result was all that mattered. I went home and went to bed. What people don't realise is, that it's not 'them' it's 'you'. Alright, the Arsenal lost, but that symbolised every time when I could have been a contender. Every time when you haven't done what you could have done.

Richard Stubbs

I really started to go and stand regularly again, the season we won the League in 89. And that was funny because the crowd were willing the team to win it, they had it in their grasp but they didn't seem to want to do it for some reason. It was very frustrating standing there. I could identify with the players to a degree, willing them to do things you thought in those circumstances you might do yourself. Certainly the games when they played well there was a terrific atmosphere. The crowd knew they were going to win a Championship, which was something I'd never been involved in as a player – I just missed out on the Double side – but you did actually feel you were part of the effort if you were in the crowd. The empathy, the camaraderie of everybody being together made you a unit – the team, the crowd, the Club. You could sense that on the terraces. They were part of the effort. I felt it myself towards the end of the season, you got more and more involved and became caught up in it. It was like being part of something I'd never been part of as a player. Not chanting and singing like the choir, but when goals went in you'd have that same feeling of exhilaration. (See plate 29.)

David Court

When we won the League in 89 it was the most cosmic thing that had ever happened. Better than any orgasm ever.

Emma Young

Do you remember that afternoon of the Hillsborough Disaster? We were at home. I can't for the life of me think who we were playing. The whole atmosphere on the North Bank changed within five or ten minutes. Everybody had a transistor and from five or six people, it went ten–12 injured very quickly. And then two or three dead. *Oh, no.* You think: *I've just come into a big crowd myself.* And it really hit home how bad it was. The feeling on the North Bank was, I don't know, mundane, subdued. We had to win that game but when we did it was sort of: *So what?* That afternoon on the North Bank was very, very sad.

Paul Hobb

You know when Hillsborough happened, that Newcastle match at home. I was there with a kid, he was seven. Just me and him. He sat on the bar in front of me. And at half time, everyone was going: *Fucking cunts!* Because we didn't know what had happened. Everyone thought it was like Heysel. People were going: *Oh, they should be chucked out of the League.* And I just remember looking down, at the end when we realised what had happened – they said all those people had died – and I looked at this kid and I thought: *This is awful* and I've been in that situation, that crushed, when you couldn't breathe. But I don't ever want to not do that, not take this child and feel safe. If anything happened at Highbury you could put them on that pitch. I remember walking round that day. There was no singing, even though we'd gone top of the League.

Natasha Horbacki

That was one of the saddest days of my life: 15 April 1989. It's engraved on my mind. I mean, I would give up every trophy we've ever won to have that not have happened. It's a wider thing, it's about football. When something like that happens it's not just about your club. We beat Newcastle, Marwood scored and we went top but I remember thinking: *This whole thing doesn't really matter.* I'm very proud of the dignity the Club showed. And the fans, especially the North Bank. We cancelled our games and when we came back, we played Norwich and there was a minute's silence which was impeccably respected. You could've heard a pin drop. And after it finished the whole of the North Bank broke into: *You'll Never Walk Alone.* Hillsborough will never be forgotten and I think that's more to do with the fans than it is the clubs. Fans will keep the memory of those people alive much longer than any organisation like the FA ever will. We all said: *Every FA Cup game should kick off at five past three instead of three o'clock, as a reminder of when it happened.* Things like that. Our mate had an idea that the new North Stand should be named after the youngest person who died. It's the fans who keep that kind of thing alive. Whenever we go to Liverpool now we take bouquets of flowers to leave at the memorial.

Stewart O'Brien

As you know today is our first game since the Hillsborough tragedy, we could not play our game against Wimbledon so soon after such a tragic day for so many. Our hearts are still heavy, but life must go on, however, what we must not do is forget. We must ensure that no such disaster occurs again.

Today we will observe a short silence before the kick-off and perhaps you will say a silent prayer for those who died and those left bereaved. There will be a collection for a fund to help the bereaved and I am sure many of you will want to make a contribution. The Club has already made a private donation.

We have always taken pride in our stadium here at Highbury, and we believe it to be one of the safest grounds in Britain. We have spent over £1 million in recent years on safety improvements. It is not perfect and we are pledged to continue to improve the ground for both comfort and safety.

One of the reasons Highbury has a good safety record is the excellent understanding that has always been maintained here between the police, the management, the stewards, the staff and the supporters. I know that this understanding and relationship will continue and Arsenal will always be our pride and joy.

Peter Hill-Wood, *AFC Programme*, 1.5.89

Without a doubt you supported the Club when I first started, and the team were part of the Club. It was Arsenal, then you had the team. Now, you support, first and foremost you support the team and you don't support the Club. *It's my team.* You never seem to hear people talk about my Club, because now they talk about my team.

John Platt

When we weren't as succesful as we have been of late it was a different kind of crowd. The same people, obviously, but different noises, a different atmosphere. They expect more now that we're successful, expect it to carry on, so there's added pressure to do well.

Paul Davis

I mean Arsenal seemed to become like a Tory club up the North Bank. Nobody really gets going in there like they did in the old days. I found in the last couple of years up the North Bank, people were expecting more and not giving so much, you know.

Laird Budge

The crowd's changed. Football has, everywhere. You get your nights. You get your games. But I think people have calmed down, to be honest. There's so much football on telly. We've had so much success. I don't think the fervour's there. In any ground, now.

Peter Hobb

I changed over the years. I used to think that you can never knock the Club. I thought people who did should have been taken away and shot. I've grown, hopefully, a bit more sensible as I've got older, and now I think supporters, even the idiots, are entitled to their say. They're paying their money through the turnstiles and even if you don't agree with them I wouldn't knock them, they're Arsenal supporters. I don't agree with who they think is a good player or who the manager's picking or selling or buying, but I wouldn't stop them from saying it. I've argued with them for hours, but I wouldn't stop them from saying it because they're entitled to.

Mick Essen

I mean, if the opponents score a good-quality goal that you'd applaud if your team did it, well, I applaud them, you know. I don't know about other people.

Guy Thomson

I think we have a good club. We are well behaved. But I think we are stronger away. At Arsenal sometimes it goes quiet.

Alex Froso

I think people's devotions to teams are less polarised than they used to be because they see more football on television. They've got more comparisons to make, they know much better how their teams fit into the overall scheme of things and I think also, dare I say it, people don't care quite as much because there are so many other things to take up that part of their lives, which I don't think is a bad thing. I think it's a fashion and maybe things will change in 20 years and there'll be more partisanship again. I think it's also to do with the relationship between the players and the club and the supporters and the club. In many ways supporters are much more involved now I think than they ever were. They've demanded to be more involved but also I think the relationship has changed because they now see the clubs for what they are. There is not that sort of same master-servant relationship, that unquestioning faith in their club.

Simon Inglis

I mean, if we lose, I'm not interested in football, I don't want to watch it! I can't bear it, can you?

Peter Hobb

Every game I go I get excited like it's my first time, looking forward to it. I go on at people, saying: *I'm going up the Arsenal.* And they go: *We know, we know.* I just get so excited.

Julie Wheeler

In 90–91, when we won the League, I decided I wanted to try a season of the back. I got to know loads of people up there. It was great because that's where all the singing comes from isn't it? Down the front it's so quiet. Everybody sort of says things under their breath. If I take my girl, I'd go down there because it's quiet and you know there's going to be more room, you know you'll get a space. But up the back, you get knocked around a lot more. You have a great time. Everybody says exactly what they think. I used to sit on the barrier right at the back. The police'd come along and say: *Get down.* They look away and you get back up again. You'd be crushed up with your knees in front of you. Then as soon as something happened, you'd suddenly have all this room in front of you because everybody's just hurtling forward. You know, looking around, a lot of the people up there weren't even watching the game. You're watching everyone else and talking. It's funny. It's a real bad view, you can't see what's going on. It's just being there, you know. And the singing up there, having the noise all around you. It's fantastic.

Guy Thomson

Now I'm a student and I'm going to be a student for another four years. I've already done two. It's no joke, you've got no money. But every season, we used to work at Highbury to get our season ticket. You used to be able to paint at Highbury over the summer and they thought, because we were girls, we couldn't paint. So me and Nat we'd paint for half an hour and then sit down for two hours and they'd go: *God! You've done a great job, girls!* They'd make us tea, we made friends with everybody. We painted the red bars on the North Bank. After we won the League, we painted those red bars red. We weren't touching any paint that wasn't red! And for that we could get a standing season ticket for the North Bank. There was a spot that would have been there now where one of us kicked over a pot of red paint and it just stayed there. We pretended to clear it up but we wanted it there, our big spill of red paint. And it was there for three or four seasons because it was red gloss lead paint. When they were relaying the pitch, they were putting the goalposts back up and they were too long. He cut them off at the bottom and gave them to us. We've got the bottoms of the North Bank goalposts. Our prized possession. Our bit of the North Bank.

Emma Young

The Bank Holiday afternoon we won the last League Championship and Liverpool were playing at Forest. Four of us was down early. We went for a drink at the White House in Green Lanes, outside – you couldn't get in – and Forest scored. Everybody went mad. I was shaking like a leaf. I thought: *I've got to go to the ground.* I didn't know what to do. I got on the North Bank, pacing up and down. I had more wees in that half an hour than I've ever had in my life. A guy came in and he had a portable telly. Everybody was going to have a look. Before that, Liverpool had equalised. And I just watched his face. If Forest were attacking, you could see it on his face: *Go on! Go on!*

And they scored. He's got the telly in one hand, he's sort of juggling with it. The whole North Bank went mad. There was thousands of people there even though there was two hours till kick-off. That last five minutes were the longest of my life, watching that guy's face. He was a chubby-faced guy with a beard, little woolly hat with a bobble on. If he walked in now, I'd know him. I was staring at his face. If Liverpool are attacking, he grimaces. If he smiles, Forest have got it away. I was pacing, holding my head!

Paul Hobb

It was noisy. When we scored I got picked up and thrown in the air. I loved it. I love shouting and everything. I love it when Paul Merson or Anders is coming down the wing and there's hardly any noise and then it all builds up as he goes to cross it. I love that. And if a goal comes at the end of it, you just go mad.

Julie Wheeler

I don't know if you've ever read John Berger's book *G*. There's a line in it something like: *Life is islands of ecstasy amidst a sea of ennui*. Now anyone who goes to football a lot knows that's what football's all about. Anyone who doesn't go imagines it's frightening or it's this or it's that, whereas in actual fact it's usually incredibly tedious. But you do get these odd moments, like when Ian Wright scored those two goals against Forest, where you think: *This is why I'm here*. And nothing compares to it, really, to that moment of ecstasy. That's what keeps you going year after year.

Richard Stubbs

'THEY'VE GOT IT PRETTY SUSSED'

We've always spent a great deal of time and money and everything else that's been necessary in making sure that we can control what goes on inside the building. We've got 220 stewards here, we've got hundreds of police, we've got commissionaires, we've got all sorts of additional staff, the best part of 1,000 people now involved in running the business on a match day, so we've done all the things that we know we should be doing. I mean they have already been done, we spend thousands upon thousands on it every year.

Ken Friar

The stewards here at Arsenal are trained. I wouldn't do it. They take a lot of stick. I wouldn't put up with the amount of abuse they get, no chance. Perhaps it's 'cos I've got no patience. I think that the numbers have increased and we must have something like 250 stewards in all, to help with the segregation, to help with people finding turnstiles, their seats, stop them from drinking where they shouldn't be.

Paul Johnson

I mean, everywhere's got stewards now, haven't they? I think they're a bit heavy handed. People can accept being told off by the Old Bill, but not when you've got a steward telling you. The police have got it pretty well sewn up now. You don't get opposition fans in the North Bank now. But I do think people resent the stewards pushing their weight.

Lenny Brandon

It's an educational thing, really. Somebody starts singing and other people just don't think. Like when they were having a go at the stewards last year. They didn't decide to knock down the North Bank. They don't get paid, they love the club as much as we do. But people were going: *You're a bunch of wankers.* It's just ignorance, really. Couple of people start it up and everyone joins in.

Stewart O'Brien

That Cup game against Liverpool in 1988 that we drew nil–nil. We'd gone up there and drew 1–1 and they beat us in a third game. I remember queuing up outside the North Bank that day. It was absolutely packed. It was before the Hillsborough thing but when Hillsborough happened I remember looking back on that night in particular. The queue was so large to get in the ground – I don't think it was all-ticket for some reason – it went from the Avenell Road turnstile, down to the corner of Avenell Road and then snaked back on itself. What you had was people jumping across the queue. The police weren't really doing anything to stop it and, of course, once someone starts, they all start. People are thinking: *I'm not going to get in. I'm going to stand my ground and push my way in.* It got quite frightening. I was with two girls at the time and it wasn't a very nice experience for them. There was a crush. In fact, once you got inside, it was so packed we couldn't get to where we usually stand, because it had taken so long. That was probably the last really massive crowd they had down there. The general feeling was that people were being fairly responsible. You know, with the Hillsborough thing, I'm sure it was just a few people spoiling it for the rest. On the whole, people were just trying to ease things off but it was so difficult – with 15 minutes to kick-off and you don't know whether they'll put the kick-off back – and you want to get in. There was the feeling, too, that the quicker you got in, the quicker you'd be out of the crush. A lot of things compounded it but the main catalyst was the few who can't control themselves and have to be in before everyone else.

David Court Jnr

The St John's have always been round there. They're probably the thing that hasn't changed at all. I remember when someone got injured last season, I forget who it was, I think it was an away player. They were trying to get the ambulance boys to bring the trolley on and the two guys didn't look as though they could run. For as long as I can remember they've been around, to the best of their ability.

Chris Thompson

It's changed because of Hillsborough. We're now supposed to have one first-aider per 1,000 people.

Shirley Haxell

This is one of the grounds that's had that sort of coverage (one first-aider per 1,000) all the way through. We've been very fortunate. We've had three main divisions and always had a good working relationship with the stewards and the police. We all work together. The supporters? They're alright. A bit of friendly joshing, you know: *Oi! Get out the way, I can't see!* You always get that. But you can't pick where your casualties are going to be, can you? There's no animosity there, it's all friendly. And if you had to go into the crowd, they tend to clear a way for you to get through.

Stan Carroll

I think things started getting quieter here when the police stopped the drinking. The police are very good. One sign of trouble and they're out. One of the most common problems is people fainting because they haven't had enough to eat. You just bring them in, lie them down and give them a glass of water. You get the other medical conditions come up. They may have had it for three days and they come to football and then decide they need treatment. Fatalities, we will usually get about one a season.

Shirley Haxell

Since the Taylor Report we've always got the London Ambulance Service here, 'on scene', just in case.

Ron Pilcher

People still rely on you. *There's a first-aider! Quick up here!* And you get in: *Are you alright, son?* It's a nice feeling to say: *They rely on you.* And you're part of the Arsenal. I mean, I've seen people with blood pouring from them. But as soon as we get there, they'll say: *It's alright now. It's the St John's. We're safe.* It's a funny feeling, it's a great feeling. I just wish I'd been doing it years ago.

Frank Martin

One would have to look at one's safety record because you have to judge these things by fact and not opinions. Our safety record stands examination, in my view, by anybody. We've always been certified as a safe stadium, examined regularly by the football licensing authority throughout the year and the local authority, We're certified and have been for years since before it became a requirement. We were certified with an architect's certificate many, many years ago. That goes back probably 30 years. A fellow called Thomas Brown used to do it and that was done before it was a requirement to do so. We've always felt that there is a responsibility not only to the supporters but to ourselves to ensure that we are happy with what's going on. Our record's been very good. I think we're going through the pain barrier just now and the old saying that there's no gain without pain I suppose is probably true and one day, who knows, we might all say that all-seaters are a good thing. For the moment, sitting where I sit, it doesn't look particularly good.

Ken Friar

⚽

There's continuity here. The fans will see some of the same faces on a regular basis, certainly from season to season and, in some cases, from one decade to another. It's an unusual policy, the fixed-post policy. Other clubs may have one or two people doing the same job every week. We've got 38 fixed-post officers. In later years there would have been one sergeant and six PCs just on North Bank safety. When I first came here it was two and 12 for North Bank rowdyism, back in 86.

PS John Birt

Back in the late 70s there were three home games where you knew there was going to be trouble: Tottenham, Chelsea and West Ham. You knew there was going to be trouble in the North Bank those games. The other games you felt sure that the away fans wouldn't be able to take the North Bank, but those three games you knew there was going to be a concerted action by the hard core of away fans trying to take the North Bank. That started to die away, I think, from the mid-80s, certainly after Heysel. That was why the Arsenal–Millwall FA Cup game was shocking, because it was like going back in time, it was like going four or five, six, seven years, back to the bad old days. You know, they were smashing up places on the way and all the rest of it. I anticipated that there might be problems. I didn't travel on the Tube that day, I went on the bus instead. They were smashing up Tube trains, beating people up left right and centre, it was awful, and you wondered why you'd ever gone to games where there had been the potential for that. It was the worst atmosphere I've ever been in at a football match. Because it was post-Heysel, and we felt we'd gone beyond that.

Al Fresco

I think the trouble's died away now en masse. You've just got the geezers who want to do it now, there's not the hangers-on there were.

Lenny Brandon

You still see the same little crowds of troublemakers over there, back to when we were kids. They don't live in London. They sort of want to keep a name as being violent. I've known them for years. Still the same ones. They still go over there, sit in the seats. But it's as if it was still 20 years ago to hear them talk, Forty-year-old men running with the 20-year-olds. It just makes you laugh. They haven't changed. Still go in the same pub, talk about the same thing: *Oh, look. We done him.* It's sad to see it but you do get it, at every club. The older ones who lead on the younger ones.

Vidos Neophytou

Ten or 12 years ago, if you were working on the North Bank, you used to get to know the troublemakers. That was great, you'd know that little group. The same on the South Bank, they would know their little group. Now, the idea is that the football officer would make it known to all officers attending who to look out for. After cameras came in, there weren't the attempts by large groups of away fans to get into the North Bank to cause trouble. You might get people forming up into a group of 50 or 60 just to sing, but they were there just to make a point rather than to start a fight. The whole idea of violence inside the football ground, that there was going to be a fight – *Where's the fight going to break out first? Is it going to be the North Bank? Is it going to be the South Bank?* – that died off. If a fight broke out, it was a surprise to people, they wouldn't have expected it. If they've only been coming to football a few years, a lot of people won't ever have seen a fight on the North Bank.

PC Alan Smith

During the summer we have installed a new closed-circuit television system in the stadium. It will be operated by the police, have high-density resolution with 'close-up' facility for identifying individual problems and will not only assist with crowd control, but continue to make your stadium one of the safest in the country.

AFC Programme, 23.8.86

A football supporter has been fined £500 and banned from going to matches at Highbury for a year after video cameras caught him throwing a coin during Arsenal's 2–1 home defeat by Manchester United on Sunday.

The Times, 27.1.89

I don't know about controlling it, but CCTV has pushed it away from the grounds. Most of the trouble we get now is outside the stadium. And that's true in most places. Obviously, you still get sporadic incidents inside the ground but CCTV has been very important. If people are going to misbehave now and they do it in the stadium, they know they're going to be filmed doing it. There's a good likelihood they'll get caught, so they don't bother. Nowadays it's places like railway stations, up and down the Euston Road or in Highbury Fields, well away from Highbury. The camera really has been a boon to our service. It was introduced here about 86, 87. It all followed on from Heysel, the Liverpool and Juventus incident. They were already talking about it and that hurried it up, with financial help from the Football Trust. Obviously, there's been an increased emphasis on policing generally over the past few years. CCTV has been the main tool in displacing trouble from the grounds.

PS John Birt

Occasionally you get someone just going mad on the one occasion, but I've been involved on the football hooligan side for five years now and 95 per cent of them have got a criminal record not regarding football. Generally they're going to be male and under 40, but the football criminals at Arsenal come from all walks of life, all backgrounds – the worst estate in south London to the flashiest house in north London. They would say that, at heart, they love the Club. They're doing this for Arsenal. Which is crap. They support Arsenal but they're doing it because they like a fight. If they weren't doing it here, they'd be doing it in the High Street on Saturday night and, in a way, it's better if they do it here where we've got plenty of policemen, and the public tend not to be involved.

PC Alan Smith

Nowadays we have officers specifically dealing with football criminals, which really didn't exist, on an official basis, as little as eight or ten years ago. Officers whose sole job is to work on football and football hooliganism seven days a week. That's a network right across the country. We've got two officers here at Holloway just for Arsenal. Most Premier League clubs have at least two officers who work full-time. Again, this followed on very much from Heysel. If Arsenal went up to Manchester United, they might have taken in those days, 6–8,000 supporters of whom 200 or 300 would be 'undesirables', shall we say. The officers up there wouldn't know one from another. Everybody spoke with the same accent. Nowadays we're armed with photographs of convicted hooligans, exclusion orders. We will present that intelligence to officers up there and they will, in turn, brief their own officers as to what to look out for from Arsenal. Likewise, we get the same service from them down here. Except for officers from Liverpool. They don't take part in the system. As far as they're concerned they don't have a problem up there and their senior officers won't waste money on it.

PS John Birt

There has been a very close relationship with the police. They've got a dreadful job to do when you think about what they've got to handle and they do extremely well. Since I've been here we've always had a good relationship with them. You have to work at getting on with people. Clearly there are differences but what you do, you work at it, and hopefully everything ticks smoothly. We work at it. We have differences of opinion with the police but we don't fall out over it. We debate, we argue our corner, they argue theirs and, in the end, we come to a joint decision. They're very good indeed and as I say we always try to be helpful to them.

Ken Friar

Since the mid-80s, there's been a steady decrease in the number of policemen on large-area terracing. As the problems decreased, we could decrease the number of people there.

PC Alan Smith

I was at an Arsenal–West Ham game and there were fights going on all over the place. There were West Ham supporters walking through the North Bank, looking for anyone wearing an Arsenal scarf and starting to beat them up. You thought: *Well, what are the police doing about this? They're policing the ground, why aren't they coming and stopping this?* Now, they do. It's better policed, maybe because of close-circuit television or whatever. I suppose in those days people seemed to get away with it and get away with it regularly, whereas now you wouldn't expect to get away with it. I mean, if I walked into some terrace now and started looking for opposition fans and started smacking shit out of them, I would expect to have to do a runner pretty quickly or the Old Bill would be on to me. It wasn't like that in those days. They never caught them.

Al Fresco

The relationship with the police is better down the front. They do look for trouble sometimes. You'd be standing at the back sometimes and you could feel eyes on you. You shout something out at the ref – he can't hear you, you're so far away for God's sake – but you'd feel eyes on you. Then as soon as you look round and they see you looking, the police think: *What's he up to?* But I tell you, I don't understand these people who get chucked out about five minutes before kick-off. I don't know what they'll have done. But what a waste of time! What a waste of money! That was more down the Clock End. The North Bank was completely trouble-free.

Guy Thomson

I don't know why they didn't trust the North Bank. The night we won the League against Man United, the police ringed the North Bank because they thought there'd be a pitch invasion when they were awarded the trophy. All the people who ruined it come on from the Clock End. But they wouldn't trust us.

Paul Hobb

Sometimes the police can be obnoxious but generally they do their job don't they? I mean, Arsenal's a good ground to visit. They've got it pretty sussed. There's never any trouble inside the ground. It's a friendly Club, really.

Mark Burdis

'A STEP FORWARD'

Well, there was unrest among the fans before George Graham became manager, But that was over disappointments on the pitch. There have been misconceptions about the North Bank stand and why we have to build it. I'd prefer to see the North Bank stay a terrace, because I know how much it means to our supporters. However, we must go all-seat by 1994 because of the Taylor Report. That's something outside our control.

Peter Hill-Wood, *AFC Programme*, 11.4.92

The Government have forced something on the football clubs that they didn't need and they've got to carry the burden. The Club can't pay for everything. Even if they did, *we* would have to pay for it in the end. They're going to charge us for it because there's no Government subsidy – this isn't Italy.

Geoff Gilbert

If I had a son, I'd say come along to the game, this is where you stand, where you *feel* the game. If you're sitting up there, it's all very well, you've got a better overview of things, but you're not here to get an overview of the game, you're in here to feel what it's like to be with all these people, on a Saturday afternoon between three and five o'clock, and learn the game.

Maurice Gran

You can't beat atmosphere. Atmosphere makes events, adds to everything, I'm sure players rise to the occasion. If there's tension, there's atmosphere. Standing up when I was a kid there, it was just being involved, you felt involved, and I think that's what it is. If you're supporting the team, you've got to feel involved. I don't feel involved when I go now. I go and watch the football but I don't feel, I suppose, as passionate and involved as I did. I think on the North Bank you're part of it. Up here, everyone's got a few quid, they're sitting up in the seats. Down there, we are the boys, the ones who matter. You feel part of it don't you, in there? Especially when you're a youngster, you want to belong, you want to belong to that, or feel that you belong to something, and I think that's all part of it. That's going to be sad when that doesn't happen. I don't think you're ever going to recreate that. I don't think it's the Arsenal's fault, it's the Government legislation's fault.

Frank Warren

I think it's quite a simple thing really. Sitting is passive and standing is active. When you're standing, everybody there's thinking: *I could do that* or *I could run round there* or *I could . . .* I mean you know you can't but I think you see yourself doing these things. If you're sitting you're distancing yourself from it, that's why I don't like sitting. If you get next to somebody who's really obnoxious – and I've noticed people moving away from me! – at least you can move, but if you're in a seat, especially if you're a season ticket, you're stuck in front of some moron, you know you've probably got it forever. I think that's bad news. It's more participatory when you're standing, I think, really. All that surging used to be because you became part of what the action was on the field.

Roger Hewlitt

Well, I got these season tickets through Tom Whittaker after the war. We had them for years until they got too expensive. But it wasn't the same in seats. The atmosphere's gone in the seats. I suppose it's on the terraces, you're closer together and football supporters are natural comics – you hear all sorts of jokes. Someone shouts out something and you're all in hysterics. Up in the stand you can't let yourself go. It's going to be a sorry day for football when we go to all-seaters.

Tom Jales

Well, I've always worried that all-seaters were Thatcherism by the back door. But then I look at Italy. They're all-seater but they seem to have a lot fun. People can adapt, like they always have, I suppose. But I worry if it's going to be the football I've always known, and know, and want.

Richard Stubbs

It may be that the best days have come and gone – you're not going to get 60,000 at Highbury any more, so consequently you're never going to get that monumental scale of support and atmosphere. All-seater stadia are a fact of life now, but I think it's sad in some ways. You're going to find not so many pensioners are going to come, not so many kids are going to be able to afford to come. From what you hear, Glasgow Rangers have a great atmosphere, so I'm sure once the new stand is there you'll have an atmosphere, they'll do the business. But they'll be people earning in their 20s, 30s and 40s. You're going to cut out the pensioners who's been going for 50 years and cut out a lot of the kids whose parents can't afford to take them. There'll be something missing. I mean, I've been sitting for several years myself. I suppose you have to say that's progress, It's going to have to happen. You won't have that communal thing, the moving, swaying mass, will you? The edge, the danger of it, really, I suppose. Probably in 50 years' time, people will say: *Why the hell did they put up with that?* Well, because they loved it, it was in their blood. It was important – their team, their community, the atmosphere of the crowd, the drama. It takes some beating.

Steve Kazmarek

Basically, if standing is more important than football, it doesn't really make sense. If you're a die-hard and say: *I really enjoy standing with my mates;* then you might as well say: *My mates and I think we'll all go and stand in a phone box for two hours on a Saturday afternoon!* You've got to be a little bit logical about it.

Laurence and I went to watch Valencia play when we were working in Spain for a few weeks. What they had in Valencia, which I thought was brilliant, you sit on the terrace with a cushion. It's only terracing, but the sight lines are better. You got into the game and either you've got your own cushion or you rent a cushion which you fling on the pitch when you don't get a penalty. On top of the stand, on the roof of the stand, was the terracing and if you wanted to stand, you stood on the roof. You try invading the pitch like that. And there were about 2,000 standing on the roof of the stand.

When you go to American football, for example in 82 we went to watch USC in the Olympic Stadium. That was the day I became jaundiced about football. We were sitting down with a group of people that we spoke to, people that say *Hi*, you know. You went downstairs and there was more space. In fact, although USC is in a dodgy part of Los Angeles, none the less it was still a great atmosphere. It wasn't to do with standing or sitting. The English working class is not much good at having fun sober, and so the standing up and all that intermingling, and pretending you're coal miners coming up from the shift and all being pissed together, these are all artificial makings of a 'good time'. In America you meet people who can enjoy themselves sober. It's quite a revelation.

Maurice Gran

I never thought I would agree with Lord Justice Taylor's recent report. Until the home game with Tottenham, my own opinion was that making grounds all-seaters would kill a great deal of the atmosphere, especially at Highbury.

That was until 1 December. I was standing in the centre of the North Bank as usual but had to leave at half time, like many others around me, because of being

320   THE END

constantly crushed by people pushing from behind. Normally it's not bad but because of the volume of people packed into the North Bank that day it was unbearable.

Now I can see how the Hillsborough Disaster happened and why grounds are being made all-seater. The ones doing all the shoving thought it very funny and even after several requests from those being crushed, they still continued. So just remember one thing if you're one of those who thought it very funny: *It's thanks to people like you that soon none of us will be able to stand on the terraces.*

Nick Robinson, *AFC Programme*, 21.12.91

Me and my mates are going to go for seats in the new stand. As far as we're concerned, we've got no option. You've got to sit down, haven't you? I mean, you get all these people saying: *Oh, it's great to stand, knee deep in piss, getting cold.* No, it isn't! Them days have gone. You're not going to bring them back. I don't want that. I want a bit of comfort. Why shouldn't you? That doesn't mean you have to change the atmosphere. I'll give you an instance: Ibrox. Glasgow Rangers. They've got the most modern stadium in Britain. Has it cut down on the atmosphere? Not one iota. Forty thousand every week. All-seater. Like Highbury will be. Still a fantastic atmosphere. I think it's got to be a step forward. Look, we're coming up to the year 2000, you know.

Peter Hobb

From a player's point of view, all-seater stadia aren't going to change the atmosphere. I've played in enough grounds where it's all seats and the atmosphere's still there. You're going to have less people in the ground in England and Scotland, capacities are being reduced when seats are put in. That may make a bit of a difference. But, by and large, I don't think it's going to detract from the atmosphere.

Liam Brady

I really liked Tony Adams until last season when he couldn't be bothered to say anything about the North Bank, and yet he's had a column in the programme every week. It was: *Keep up your support, we need it.* OK they were gagged at the Club, I realise that, but couldn't the lot of them together have just said something?

Maureen Hewlitt

I don't think it's something players really think about. I haven't had a real conversation with anyone about it. They just play the game, you know.

Paul Davis

I like seeing the players as people. They say you see the pattern of the game better up in the seats, but I suppose I don't know enough about that. I like to see them rushing towards you, falling over. I like to see the expressions on their faces, that sort of thing. I like to feel involved.

Maureen Hewlitt

There's a different atmosphere when you're standing. It's more fun. When you stand you're part of the game and I do like to have a good shout. You're all standing there together and once that goes, the game is not the game anymore. On the terraces you get a *feel* of the game.

Geoff Gilbert

You got your education on the North Bank. It went into your blood. And even if people move to a seat later, they've still got that. It's like a legacy. And that's how you get a throughput of fans into a club. I mean, the Junior Gunners is a great idea, stuff in the programme and fostering the youth and all that. My boy loves all that. But you can't take away the actual process of being up there. And whether it was because it was cheap and accessible or because you wanted to stand there at the North Bank or the Clock End – it was a necessary part of your apprenticeship. They say that's an old-fashioned view – that all-seater stadia are the way forward – but I don't think those people understand the culture of supporting football.

John James

We've got seats in the West Stand, me and Sam. It's just not the same. I think I've had arguments with about five people, and we're only a month into the season. I can't take these people who, five minutes into the game: *We're the worst team on earth. Slag, slag, slag.* As they come out of the tunnel they pick their player – it's been Merson, it's been Anders, it's been Winterburn. There's a geezer behind me picks a different one every week. I can't handle it. I've had to tell them. First game, one bloke sitting next to us, I've said: *I'm not going to be able to handle you for the rest of the season.* He's gone: *Oh, I suppose you're from the North Bank. Well, you get a better class of supporter in the seats!* He's called us North Bank yobbos. Sam's sort of gone: *Oh, no. He's going to hit him!* Just as well she was sat next to him, really!

Paul Hobb

I didn't believe that, in general there was this enormous kinship. I know there's a certain amount of flexibility lost when there's no standing, but we used to stand in broadly the same space as I used to when I was at school. You see people, that you've seen for weeks, but you didn't talk to them very much except to comment on the day, you know, or if you came in late you ask what the score is.

Maurice Gran

When I was a kid we used to queue up for ages to get in and stand on the same spot with the same group of people. Standing on the terraces, the patter was just unbelievable. Of course, kids of the next generation won't know about that. They'll be sitting in a seat – which is great. People will lose that atmosphere – but with the new regulations things will have to change, are changing rapidly. But there is something about the terraces that creates an atmosphere whether at times it was the fighting, or the stick you get from opposing supporters. It will take something away from the game. But nowadays, too, the game's about big money and there's more money in bums on seats than there is in people on the terraces.

Charlie George

You know my involvement with IASA, we looked at a lot of things about safe standing. We won all the arguments. Standing is safe. We've had accidents, but think of the accidents that might happen. Seating is not automatically more safe.

John James

It's something that should be there, even now. I don't think there's any reason why it shouldn't be there. At any of the grounds, I don't see why there shouldn't be a section where you can stand, if that's what you want to do.

Mick Essen

I think the hooligan element, the demise of that, is probably because kids now if they want to go and use a lot of energy, they go to a rave, they take their Ecstasy tablets and they want to love everybody, and it gets it out of their system. You don't hear of it now. Although they're making grounds all-seater and so forth, I think that is now unnecessary. I know that what happened at Hillsborough and so forth were tragedies, but football has changed dramatically in the last four or five years. You have only got to look at the game.

Frank Warren

I think you should have the option to be able to stand and I resent that it's that lot that's created this problem. I think Liverpool people take football too seriously. I wouldn't condemn them completely for Heysel because that could have been just a mindless minority. It was a dreadful disaster and ruined our reputation. But Hillsborough, that done them in. The North Bank was important to me, it was your inauguration, as a kid it was where you wanted to be. I resent that because of Liverpool or their supporters, it's impossible now for future generations to go there. It's sad, really. I think that was a one-off situation with a one-off mentality. The whole country over-reacted.

Eddie Mason

I think it's more dangerous in seats. I mean, if you had a fire or something everybody would be pushing, you'd fall over seats where on a terrace you could all just run or move away without any obstacles stopping you getting out.

Julie Wheeler

We will lose 10–15,000 supporters and the feeling of standing, that experience for the younger ones. In seats, when something exciting happens people stand up anyway which causes more problems, arguments happen in the seats now.

Alex Froso

People will get fed up if they have to sit in the rain and if the wind's right, no roof will keep people at the front dry. It's like the East Stand. When they built that in 1937, the seats came right to the front. So many people complained they were getting wet sitting there, they changed it to that little bit of standing, didn't they?

Frank Hummell

All-seater stadia make our job difficult in different ways. That's a personal opinion, as opposed to an opinion of the police force. We find if people start fighting in seats – we had a couple of minor outbreaks this season – it's very, very difficult getting to the people who are doing it. When you get there, you're on your own. You might have four officers in a line behind you but, effectively, you're on your own with someone who may well be intoxicated or whatever. It's difficult to get them out. You're limited with space. It's difficult to get a proper balance or purchase. I don't think it's a very well-thought-out piece of legislation. It's certainly not the answer to the problems which were occuring in the past. Since the Hillsborough Disaster, the capacities of standing terraces have gradually been reduced in line with the Taylor recommendations to a point where it's now virtually impossible to get overcrowding on a section of terracing. Obviously, in a concerted effort, they could all push in one direction, and eventually a number of people *would* be forced up against crash barriers, frontal fencing or radial fencing, so it would be *possible.* But that's just a non-existent thing as far as I can see. I'm not saying it's wrong to reduce capacities. I came here in 73 for a sixth round Cup-tie against Chelsea and there were 63,000 here and I never saw a ball kicked the whole game. I was only 12 and I'm still not very tall but I just stood there and looked at three people's backs! I wouldn't advocate going back to that for one minute. But I think an effective job could have been done just by reducing the capacities on terracing. Again, I have to say that's a personal opinion not the opinion of the police force. All-seaters are not the answer. You will still get problems in seated areas, like you did at Wembley for the England v Holland game. A modern, all-seater stadium and you had hooligans running amok along the dividing line with the Holland supporters.

PS John Birt

I feel the move to all-seater is something that's got to happen. The conditions of most of the stadiums over here are terrible, really bad and outdated. I feel it's come time when people should sit down to watch football, more comfort, more facilities, toilets, eating area. It's overdue and I think it's a question of time before people adapt and look back and wonder what all the fuss was about.

Paul Davis

We had to grow up from the terraces, didn't we? I mean, we were second-class citizens, really. Obviously facilities had improved, but not that much. I suppose when you're younger you don't know any different or you can't afford a seat. Mind you, you wouldn't have gone anywhere else even if you could.

Lenny Brandon

Supporters have responded extremely well elsewhere to the better facilities. We've put in new facilities in various parts of the stadium, they've been very well treated. We're hoping that when the North Bank is opened next year, it will be superb, that it will be one of the best in the world. We're hoping that people will react to it, enjoy it. We're going through a very difficult phase. Once that's over we're hopeful that people will accept that it's been inevitable, we've had no choice, and they will use it and enjoy it.

We're getting supporters coming in now and we have this computerised system where you can select your seat, they want to know exactly where they stood. They want to take us out there and show us where it is, because that's where they want their seat. There's a great affinity with these things, there really is, I understand that. You have to remember, I've been a kid here, so I know what it's about.

Ken Friar

What do clubs like Arsenal do? Do they dig their heads in the sand and say *no, we'll keep the North Bank ad infinitum?* Or do they plan for the future? This is why I still believe in the basic precept of the Taylor Report. Conditions at so many football grounds are so poor, and we've got used to them and we've accepted them because that's football. The only way to kick clubs up the arse and to get them to really revolutionise their grounds is to force them to go to all-seater because it forced them through a whole system of thought processes which they've never gone through. I think the side-effects of it are depressing and sad, but I still maintain in ten years' time that this will blow over, that a lot of people will be looking back and will say: *God, do you remember, we used to stand! How did we do that?* in the same way I now think: *God, we used to drive cars without seat-belts.* It's a a a change, just in the same way that the guys on the North Bank now go to different pubs, wear different clothes, go to different kinds of cinemas, they're used to different kinds of fast foods and all that sort of thing, totally different from the experience of their counterparts even ten years ago. What they're going through with football now is exactly the same and of course we kick and we fight because we don't want to let go, but I think it is a progression, and I think it is for the better and I genuinely feel that our football grounds will be better places for it. You guarantee that football grounds will be serviceable in 20 years. If we'd have done nothing, if we'd have just said *we'll reduce the capacities of the terracing*, which was effectively saying *don't make any improvements just try and make them a little bit safer by reducing numbers*, the North Bank would have been falling down and would have needed vast amounts of work. The other thing to say about it is that it's actually much more difficult to maintain areas of standing and costly in terms of barrier testing, in terms of concrete maintenance, all that sort of thing. You can handle the crowd better, you can handle refreshment facilities better, because you know how many people you are going to have. You can book them in advance on a credit card and know that you can turn up five minutes to go and you've got your place. Now I value that personally, I know a lot of people don't and they would regard this as yuppification, but everything is being gentrified. The multi-screen cinema that we go to now has air conditioning, the toilets are much cleaner. You look at the toilets on the North Bank and a lot of these other places and, unless you are a hardened football fan, they are pretty disgusting. I think football clubs have put up with it because they don't know anything else, they don't imagine that football grounds can be any different. I think it's going to be a huge culture shock when football fans go to America and see what conditions are like at the stadium and the way they are treated. And the other thing about the Taylor Report which a lot of people forget is that the seating recommendations were only two paragraphs. There were 70 other recommendations and all of those are being implemented and they are changing the environment of football grounds beyond recognition. There will come a time when Arsenal will have first-team matches and there will be 20 policemen inside the ground and the people you will be dealing with on the new North Bank will be stewards who will be employed by Arsenal. They will be friendly and they will be nice to you and they will treat you like a customer. It's already happening and the change is incredible. That's happened in the last two years and it wouldn't have happened without Taylor. Other changes on the way that tickets are issued – the Taylor Report is full of all these sorts of things, the way that medical facilities are provided, that kind of thing. It's almost like football, even without the seating, would have changed completely. Fans wouldn't necessarily have noticed it, it would have been a gradual process. My memory of it is, you see pictures of the 50s and even the 60s, a couple of policemen patrolling round the outside of the ground or walking round the touch-line and that was it. No fences. Then we went through this horror period from about the mid-60s to Hillsborough when grounds became like fortresses and we grew up with it, we sort of didn't even notice it, and then suddenly we saw people crushed against those barriers at Hillsborough and we thought: *What have we done?* Not only have we let the barriers go up but we've let the police take over the running of football grounds, which is part of the reason that Hillsborough occurred. The other reason was that the local authority didn't do their duty and Hillsborough has changed that completely. All over the country, people are having to revamp entirely the way they view football grounds, so my argument is that Hillsborough has changed everything. Hillsborough was really the last disaster of a string of events and a series of appalling oversights which were allowed to occur because basically they could get away with it.

Simon Inglis

I do honestly think the fans have got to appreciate – how can it be done? What are the alternatives? Do you still want a winning team on the pitch? Can you still have a winning team if all your income goes into fulfilling what was said by the Taylor Report? What ways can it be done? Much as we would love to say in our romantic way: *We should still be standing.* I mean, Christ, will we never really learn the lessons? I had to present *Grandstand* on the afternoon of the Hillsborough Disaster. I mean, to my dying day, I'm scarred by watching the people die in front of my eyes – the cameras were on them as I presented all afternoon. They were on the terraces. That could happen on the North Bank – don't you tell me it couldn't. It could happen on any terrace in the country where a mistake is made or something goes wrong. You can't take that risk. Surely we're approaching the day and age in which you can enjoy football in a seat? Some of my best memories are of standing at football matches, but

I just think we've got to move. You can't have Hillsborough and Heysel and other tragedies without saying: *Come on, enough is enough. If it's one life, it's one life too many.*

Bob Wilson

I think more people would've been killed if we hadn't gone all-seater. We had a disaster about every 15 years and that's not a price that was worth paying. I'd rather sit than die!

Nick Hornby

I thought David Mellor said a very sensible thing the other week. Speaking as a politician, he said: *After Hillsborough, any Home Secretary just could not not accept the findings of a Taylor Report. It would have been on their shoulders for the rest of time.* And a bit of me understood that.

Richard Stubbs

I don't think it's right that people should be told what's going to happen to them. I'm for letting the public make their minds up. A lot of clubs' supporters might want all-seater, a family attitude that wants all-seaters in. But I think the public are the game, let's face it. If we don't have a public, a strong public, the game will dwindle. So I think the public have got to be asked: *What do you want?* At each club. I think they would respond. I think they would tell you what they'd prefer. If they want a bit of terracing, it's possible to make that terracing safe. Without it I think you're taking a lot of the character, the history, away from certain clubs: the North Bank, the Celtic End. I think the Celtic End could be seated here but we've got the Jungle here, which is similar to the North Bank or the Kop. I mean we play at Ibrox now which is a tremendous stadium, all-seated, but as soon as things start going wrong the seats get battered, you know. People take it out on the chair! I think the whole thing causes a lot of conflict. It should be possible to say: *You can stand there. And it will be safe.* I certainly think the public should have their own say in this.

Charlie Nicholas

It's a difficult subject. I think in England we're held back a lot by tradition. I went to America last year and watched a couple of baseball games in their stadiums. And you think: *This is fantastic. The stadium, the facilities, everything is superb. There's nothing like this in England. And why can't it be like that?* But then you come back and you think: *Well, that's not really what football's about.* Football's a game steeped in tradition, and maybe tradition is what holds it back in some respects, but standing behind the goal to watch your team is part of football and that's the way it's always been. And that's the way I'd like to think it's going to continue but obviously it's not going to. I can't help thinking that all this all-seater stuff, there's more to it than putting safety first. Hillsborough was a terrible thing to happen but I think it could have been avoided by methods other than having seats in there. The Government said they were going to bring it in but I think that if teams like Arsenal, Man United, Liverpool and Everton, all the big clubs had turned around and said: *Well, no, we're not going to stand for this*, I don't see how they would have taken their licences away. I don't think they would have done it. If there'd been a united stand by the clubs against the Government I don't think it would have happened. But they went along with it and now I think they're aiming for another kind of customer. It's taking football away from the people who made football what it is, really. This isn't just Arsenal, this is everywhere. Putting seats in, they're trying to make football into something it's never been. But football fans have put up with a lot over the years and they keep coming back. I can't imagine if Arsenal are playing on a Saturday people are going to say: *I'm not going to go because I've got to sit in a seat*. They'll put up with it in the end.

David Court Jnr

'SIGN FOR THE ARSENAL'

I feel that if a club is trying to do something because it's in the club's best interests, hoping that their supporters will go along with them, action and reaction being equal and opposite, it would be more likely to turn the fans in the opposite direction. That's a way of life, I think. There are very few instances where clubs have gone in a particular direction and actually created a quantum leap in supporters' attitudes to match.

John Yudkin

The bond really has come about because of the legislation. It didn't introduce the legislation. I think everybody knows the Club's viewpoint: *We'd much prefer to keep what we've got, rather than do what we're having to do.*

Ken Friar

In a way I agree completely with the bond scheme. If we're a family – I know we're not because we don't have equal rights – but if we are a family it's right that you turn to the family to raise the money. What I don't understand is why the people who sit in the East or West Stands which were built donkey's years ago should get their season tickets without paying a subsidy for the North Bank. Why should we, potentially the least well-off and the most committed, have to pay for it? If they'd just made it that everyone chipped in, I think people might have understood it a bit more. The fact that they picked on the people who stood on the North Bank and wanted to *use* their commitment was wrong, although a part of me felt: *I'd rather they did that than go under*. How do you pay for these damn things?

Richard Stubbs

I mean, obviously, we're always going to see it from the little person's point of view on the North Bank. Maybe we can't see the wider issues. But I cannot understand why they didn't have proper discussion with people. At the end of the day, they own the Club. People either pay their money or they don't. I don't see why discussion would be such a threat.

Roger Hewlitt

I mean, how much market research did the Club do? How many people coming through the turnstile did they shove a piece of paper into their hand and say: *What do you think about changing this stadium into all seats? What are your views? How do you think we should handle this? What should we do?* You know, nothing was done, was it? We're offered a *fait accompli*. I will not buy a bond. I do not want to be put in a position where I'm stuck next to Harry Smurf from Enfield for the next 150 years giving me bloody bunny all the way through the game, arriving 15 minutes late, walking past, then getting up to go for a piss, then coming back with his hot-dog dripping with mustard, then getting up early to get out because he wants to get his cup of coffee and then leaving 15 minutes before the end of the game. I don't want that. I don't want to be put in that position. Just because I've got my name on the back of my seat? *Please!*

Phillip Bloomfield

I know there's been a lot of controversy about our new stand with the fans but I'm not sure if it's all-seater they're unhappy about or the way it's being done.

Paul Davis

Last year, those who stayed behind for demonstrations, they were the real North Bank supporters. They were the people who came week in and week out. I think that's how we started to feel about ourselves. Which is not to say that people in other parts of the ground, like the Clock End, don't feel that. But, yes, I think there's a strong sense of *we're full-timers*.

Al Fresco

I'm the football liaison officer at Highbury, dealing with policing arrangements generally at the stadium. The biggest thing with the North Bank for me were the demonstrations organised by IASA during the 91–92 season. That caused a great deal of work for us, which we didn't object to. The local policy from the senior management at Holloway was that they were happy for people to make their point, as long as they did it in an orderly manner. (And weren't abusive to anybody – which they didn't strictly adhere to.) We had a number of meetings with the organisers and, generally, they were happy events – although the circumstances were sad for them, particularly because they didn't really get their point across to the people they were trying to get their point across to. But I think we had a reasonable relationship with the people involved. One or two things we weren't happy with, like setting fireworks off from rooftops behind the North Bank. But we spoke with the organisers as a result of that and we got a response, it was discontinued. They were genuine people with a grievance and they had a right to make their point. We were happy to let them do that. It got a bit out of hand on the last day of the season. I think they felt they were going to stay there for the rest of the night and obviously the Club weren't prepared to allow that. We didn't have the manpower to commit to policing it and, consequently, we had to clear the stands. That was just one of those things. So that was the main thing. Every match we had to prepare for a possible pitch invasion off the North Terrace. It takes a lot of manpower (two double serials, two sergeants and ten officers, that's 60 men) to line one particular end of the stadium – and a lot of work getting the officers briefed for each particular deployment. That, really, was my main concern specifically relating to the North Terrace while I've been football liaison officer.

PS John Birt

I've bought a bond, so next year I will be sitting down for the first time in 50 years of supporting. You were put on the spot very quickly weren't you? The end of the season before last, they'd just won the Championship. They weren't daft. They tried to sell these bonds straight away on the back of it. We had two days to make up our minds. We all said: *What are we going to do? Are we going to get a bond? What are we going to do next year?* So five of us decided straight away. We thought there was going to be a massive demand, which never happened. We panicked, really, you could say. Now, there's still thousands of bonds to be sold. I'm glad I've got one now. I'm looking forward to next season, even though I didn't want to stop standing and I didn't see why the fans should have to pay. I mean, weren't we paying enough? We were all paying for terrace seasons. How much have I put in over all those years? Why should I have to suddenly put in £1,500? I was able to pay mine out of my redundancy money. I suppose I would have found a way to pay anyway. But my son and lots of our other mates just couldn't afford it. (See plates 24 and 44.)

Frank Hummell

It's not just football clubs making a profit out of the fans paying more money. A lot of the money is going into the players' pockets and, if you want Anders Limpar and Alan Smith and all these players to turn out, the Club's got to afford to pay their wages. I think the players get off very lightly from all this to be honest.

Simon Inglis

If you want quality players, you have to pay the price. What fans don't realise is that unlike in Italy, where the stadia are communal, here we have to pay!

Geoff Gilbert

What you've heard about bond schemes and who's been getting the information through the post – I know a couple of people who went down to try and get plum seats in the new North Stand and were told they'd already gone to local businesses. I think if you're asking people to find £1,000 before they pay for admission – I said it in my book, there's this grand theory that you've had all this trouble with young working-class males, for the last 25 years and, as far as the clubs are concerned, they're being asked to turn their ground into a fortress and they come and smash it up and they can't afford to pay very much money. There's this great idea that if we have a different crowd, they won't cause trouble and they'll pay twice as much to go. Well, there's a logic in that and, I think, if I was running a football club from a pure business point of view, I'd be tempted by that, too. The catch is that there aren't people who are going to come very often. This is the crucial thing for football. I agree that stadiums had to go all-seater. Looking back on it now, I've been in too many near misses, Hillsborough near-misses. If we'd built new grounds, the Taylor Report wouldn't have been necessary – they could have accommodated terracing quite comfortably. But having made that decision, to go all-seater, there are various ways of going about paying for it. For example, if they'd been imaginative about it and said let's have a moratorium on all transfers for the next three years, or million-pound-plus transfers, you use your youth team and you use the squad that you've got and everyone's in the same boat – well, I think that would have been interesting, would have done a lot for football. I mean, soon after the bond was launched, we spent two-and-a-half million on a forward we didn't need and you think: *What's going on here?* When you're asking the fans to pay for the North Stand, how does that work? It's not simply that it's morally wrong, it's that they're making financial mistakes. I think that's where the protests should have come – that it was bad business. It was a bad idea and they didn't understand how football worked – and that to break the link with supporters who've been going for 25, 30, 50 years is a disaster because it's bad business. If you alienate all those people, where are you going to find another 40,000? There'll be a few of us left when all this is sorted out and then they're going to have to find a new generation – seats will be really expensive – who'll be worked up enough to want to go for the next 20 years.

Nick Hornby

With hindsight, we've been guilty of not getting the PR right. I can understand why fans were upset. But there will be significant advantages to bond holders – reductions on season tickets for several years, for instance, as well as the most modern facilities when the new stand is completed.

I understand the fans' feelings. As I said in the press, if you can afford to buy a bond, then it's a good scheme because you will get benefits, and I think we should have emphasised the advantages more forcefully. If you can't afford that sort of money, then obviously it is less attractive. But there will be approximately 7,000 tickets available on a match-by-match basis next season, and many thousands more when the capacity rises to 37,000 for 1993–94.

You could say the opposition to the scheme has concentrated our minds. We've tried to make the idea more palatable to the fans. I think it will be fully subscribed when supporters see the advantage, though that may take a while. But raising £16.5 million for the North Bank is a monumental process.

Peter Hill-Wood, *AFC Programme*, 11.4.92

'2 MAY 1992'

It's a great pity that the North Bank's been lost. It's a tragedy for the kids who want to stand there with their mates. I used to feel really a part of it all, stood there with my pals. It's a great pity. (See plate 30.)

George Williams

It was a very difficult situation because part of me wanted to really let go, wanted to invade the pitch during the match and stuff like that and really get the issue going. The other part of me wanted to keep my job and not get a police record and all the rest of it, be banned from Arsenal for the rest of my life and stuff like that. Personally, I don't think there was any more I could've done. I was at all the demonstrations and I didn't leave the North Bank until the police pushed me off. I mean, we didn't go until they actually steamed in and pushed us off. I don't know, I felt all along we were fighting a lost battle that we weren't going to win, that we weren't going to get the Taylor Report overturned. Even though West Ham and other crowds were demonstrating, I still didn't feel we were going to get the Taylor Report overturned. But you did it for the same reasons that you went to the North Bank in the first place. You did it because you're affirming your identity by doing it, you were saying: *I know I'm not likely to win but I'm going to stay behind, I'm going to make my feelings known and I'm not going until I get kicked out.* You were saying: *At least I was there, at least I did something.* I don't know, it was our last affirmation wasn't it? There's a part of me that's quite happy to sit down. When I go to a match like Arsenal–Man United and you've got 10,000 fair-weather supporters, I'm not going to be pushed out of my space by the bastards or when somebody farts, you can't fucking move, you're not going to be placed in that situation. There's part of me that maybe wants a bit of comfort, but there's another part of me that knows it's not going to be quite the same. The absolute madness, the euphoria that you got into on one or two occasions a season, you're not going to get that sitting down.

Al Fresco

I think to be truthful I am football daft for Arsenal. I'll do anything really. I must admit that I'm a bit ashamed that really I didn't do anything. We should have done something. I mean, I signed a couple of petitions or something, but nothing where you think to yourself: *It's your Club, you should have put a viewpoint over.*

Steve Winfield

It was the first time I'd been back on the North Bank to watch a game since I was about 16. It was a bit weird. But I felt I wanted to do it. I just crept in at the side. It was strange. It was quiet, we were playing Southampton, because I was at the side there weren't many people around. If I'd been in the middle there'd have been more noise. The quiet I felt was because it was the last game. The North Bank is a lot noisier than that when I'm down there playing. Something like the North Bank being knocked down, that's been there for so long, I wanted to be up there for the last game to see how I'd feel about it. And to say I was there on the last day. It was strange being up there watching the team when perhaps I should have been down there playing. I find it hard to watch the team playing anyway; standing there on the North Bank on the last day made it even more difficult!

Paul Davis

The last game, we were all sitting there. I mean, I would never fight with the police or anything. They were going: *Get up!* Everybody was just sitting down. They were pulling people up. They pulled me up by my arm and I'd had an injection the day before. It was really sore. I said: *Please could you let go my arm?* I was really calm. No way would they let go. I thought: *I'm really going to lose my temper.* I mean you're really upset. Everyone was just upset. It was unnecessary. When they came over it was if there was a riot going on or something, so many came down. As we were going out, this bloke had hurt his arm. He was lying on the terrace crying. He was about 15 and in real pain. I bent down and said: *What's happened? I'm medically trained, just tell me and I can help you.* He laid with his head on my lap. Police came up and said: *Move along!* I said: *I can't. He's hurt.* They just went: *Move out the way, we've got him now.* He was carried off over the pitch. We were the last out and when we turned round for our last look, it was just blue, police everywhere. It was horrible.

Natasha Horbacki

It was sad the season had to end like that with people demonstrating but it was the end of the North Bank. It's like someone in your family dying. They've just taken it away.

Dawn Hicks

Everyone was there together, all people that you sort of knew. And now you might see them, you know, around the ground. But they'll be all separate. Because the North Bank to me was like one big voice just shouting. Now it won't be one big one, it'll be all little separate ones going in. The North Bank was like the leader of the ground, if you know what I mean.

Julie Wheeler

I hate the fact the North Bank's been knocked down. As far as I'm concerned, demolishers came, against my will, and knocked my house down, knocked *our* house down. All the memories and they just come and bulldoze the place. Terrible. (See plate 43.)

Richard Stubbs

I said to my mate Andy one day: *I think we ought to have a piece of barrier, right?* The thought of the North Bank just going, and that's it, I just had to have a piece that I could hold, you know. I just wanted a piece of it. So we wrote a letter to George Graham, sent it off. I was working nights at that time. When I came home one Thursday morning or Friday morning, Mr Beattie (the clerk of works) phoned me up at ten to nine. *Hello*, he said, *I've got your letter to George Graham here. I phoned you up because you've got to act fast. They're starting over the weekend and it will be done in a week. I'll give you the name and address of the company doing the demolition. You phone them up, speak to Mel and he'll organise something for you.* So I phoned up and 'Mel' was off making sandwiches. Phoned him back and eventually got on to this Mel, who didn't seem to be very interested to be honest with you. Eventually he said: *Yeah, yeah, you come up, yeah, no problem. You come up and see me.* And I said: *Look we'll just go on the North Bank and get a barrier.* He said: *Oh no, no. You've got to come and see me, you've got to come and see me, right?* I could only make it on Monday, so I then had a panic on to get a van. Fortunately my wife's sister's boyfriend owns a workshop in Honiton and he's got this big van, you see, so I got Tina phoning up her sister to arrange it – *yes he'd do it,* I had to pay the geezer – I think I gave him £35 but he'd do it. Took him away from his workshop for a day which we shared, we spread the cost.

So, on the Monday morning at nine o'clock Chris comes round and we're away. It's funny, although I never really knew what I was going to come away with, I somehow knew that I was going to get our piece, I had it in me that it belonged to me. We got to the ground and it was the west side they had all opened up. I go in and there's a bloke with a yellow hat on and somebody's talking to him and he goes: *Well, Mel.* So I wait till he's finished: *Mel, I'm the guy from Devon come for a piece of barrier. Come with me* he said. So we walked up the west side, get to the top, and there's this thing digging away. And he said: *There you go, help yourself.* And all there was, was mangled pieces. There'd be a piece with two legs and a four-foot piece of barrier sticking up from it, it was bent here and bent there, it was just rubbish, it was all crap, basically. I asked: *Is there any chance you could cut me out a piece? No no* he said: *pick something up and get off the site. You haven't got a hat.* I just couldn't believe it. We had a word with this driver: *Is there any chance that you can dig out this barrier for me?* So he started to nibble away here, nibbled this bit and nibbled this, to get this one, and as he tried to pick it out, it all bent up, and he just went: *Nah, sorry.* I looked across to the other side and right over the other side of the North Bank there was a piece laid down, ten foot long and with six legs on it, and I said: *Come on Chris we're going on the other side.* Chris said: *Mel told you to get off the site,* I said: *Chris, we're going.* So we walked down, got back in the van, drove right round and all the gates were shut. Pushed one of the gates, it opened and there was a canopy. I went underneath the canopy and started to walk up the steps, and I was met by another digger there doing the same thing as the other driver and I had a word with him: *Look, is there any chance that you can lift that piece up for me?* And he said: *Well, you shouldn't really be on the site you know, I'll get shot if my governor sees you.* I said: *Look, I've had a letter from George and I've had a word with Mel right –* I was dropping names – *And they said to come over and see you.* And he said: *I dunno.* Then two other guys came out of this bit of the North Bank and I said: *It's alright. I'll go and have a word with them.* So I walked up to these two blokes, young bloke and another bloke. I think they were both Irish and I said to them: *Look, is there any chance you can cut me out a piece of barrier?* They said: *So what they doing here then?* I said: *Well they're going to build a two-tier stand and all that sort of thing.* And they said: *Are they really?* And I said: *Is there any chance that you could cut me out a piece of barrier? You know: What did it used to be like here then?* He was going on like this. At the time I was thinking: *My time is running out. Sooner or later somebody's going to see me and that'll be it.* And eventually they said: *Alright then, which piece do you want?* So I said: *Come with me* and we walked up the steps, which would have been D, which is where I always went in, walked up the steps, went to this piece of barrier. I said: *I want this.* They had oxyacetylene cylinders down the bottom, so there we were humping these cylinders down the steps, they were bloody heavy. We carted the lead over and it wasn't quite long enough. We had to go back down the steps so we were humping these cylinders back up there and when it was long enough he said: *What do you want exactly?* I said: *If you can cut the legs off as far down the bottom as you can, cut the barrier off there, right, that would be superb.* He said: *Yeah, alright then* and started doing it, I couldn't believe it. So I'm standing there watching them, very proud, getting my piece of barrier. I was standing behind this fence watching them and all of a sudden I see Mel again at the other end, and he was just having a look around. So I immediately stood behind one of the pillars. If he saw me, I'd be off the site, wouldn't get my piece of barrier. So I'm looking round the corner, like this, and every now and then he's looking over like this, you know. He's gone away. I thought: *Great! Come on lads hurry up, I must get this.* And then a younger sort of bloke came up and said: *What the fuckin' hell are those two doing?* and I thought: *Oh, here we go again.* Obviously they weren't supposed to be doing that, so I said: *Well they've cut me out a piece of barrier.* You know, I didn't want to want to get them in trouble. He said: *Get off the site.* I said: *Shit!* He said: *Get down those steps.* But I could not leave without it. So we went down the bottom of those steps again and I didn't know whether they were still cutting it out or not and I was waiting there and waiting there. Then I saw the two guys come back to the stairs with that supervisor and then they went back again. I thought: *Well, what I'll do, I'll wander back, I'll smoke this fag.* And as I'm going back up the stairs – by this time they were putting tape down the bottom to stop people going past that point – the next thing I know these two guys appear at the top of the steps with our piece of barrier. So we're immediately running up the steps, get hold of this piece of barrier and it's bloody heavy you know. We carried it all the way down hill, they carried it outside for us and we got it on the van. I said to one of the Irish blokes: *Look, I really appreciate what you've done, you know. Buy yourselves a drink.* So we were tying up the barrier in the van and I said: *I've just got to pop up to the Gunners Shop and get myself a pair of shorts.* On the way up there I see George Graham driving round the corner in his car. I go: *George, George!* He stopped and I've opened up his passenger side and I'm in there, and there's George Graham, and I said: *George I'm the bloke from Devon, piece of barrier down there, thank you very much!* He's shaking me hand and he's saying: *That's good, really good!* I said: *George I've been coming here for 29 years, they've taken away my North Bank.* The look on his face told me he knew what the North Bank meant to Arsenal, the look was: *What can I do? It hurts me as well.* I walked away, thinking: *At least we've got a piece.* Not only had we got a piece, we've got our piece. Our piece of barrier! Superb. We managed to get it home. You imagine: *That's the valley, you've got another hill up there. We're building a large pond area here, and the barrier's going to go in front of that, and it's going to be overlooking the valley.* (See plate 40.)

Rob Ashman

'PROBABLY THE BEST STAND IN THE COUNTRY'

Even today, if I take someone to Arsenal as a guest I will try and get there early and go to one of the cafés to get them to savour the atmosphere which you don't really have at Villa Park. I loved all that, that there were shops all round in the Arsenal colours, the Gunners Café and the pub, because it was like you were entering a community. I don't know of other grounds where it is quite so pronounced – it's all around you. It is the only ground that has that sense that you don't know it's there until you hit the corner of Avenell Road and Gillespie Road, That adds to it enormously. I mean, it's like coming across a hidden gem. I think the other thing about Arsenal which I've always felt, was what a grand place it is and I really mean that. You sense that you are entering an institution, a sporting institution and there are very few stadiums like that in the world. I think like the Bernebau, Real Madrid, you feel that this is a powerbase and that it has an aura. You couldn't be anywhere else except Highbury, when you're in that ground. Tottenham fans won't thank me for saying it, but I've always felt that you could put Tottenham anywhere in Britain and it would just be a football ground. Arsenal, I think, is special because of the 30s associations, the design of the exterior, everything down to the picture of the ball with the motif, the advertising hoardings, the brickwork that links the whole ground together at street level which is a clever piece of design. I think that because all football supporters have in their mind what Arsenal was, even though it may not necessarily remain that way (that's not for me to judge), I think you feel that you are entering a place of great history that would stir any football supporter from anywhere in the world. There are very few places, the Bernebau is one, I think, the San Siro is another and I think Ibrox may be another. I think when you enter Highbury or even when you're just approaching it, you have this sense of history. I always feel when I'm walking around the ground that it's a club that knows that it has this heritage, which is why building the North Bank in the way that the original scheme envisaged would have destroyed it. To me, it would have said: *Well, what a shame. Arsenal has turned out just like any other club in the country.* The fact that they've gone for this architect, they've gone for a very expensive lavish design is deeply reassuring to me because, at least architecturally, I feel that that heritage is safe.

Since Herbert Chapman instilled at Arsenal, in the 30s, this corporate image, it hasn't changed. And it shouldn't change because that is how you recognise Arsenal. When you look at the North Bank or the stands and you see the emblems, the Gunners and the A-football-C emblem, and you see the Gunners symbol on the front of the ground and at the side of the stand, it's instant: *That is Arsenal.* There are very few corporate motifs within football that carry that kind of weight and I was genuinely worried that this development at Highbury would destroy that, it would cheapen it. I think it has at the Clock End and I think they realise that now. They realised that was a mistake and, hopefully, in the next 15, 20 years when they have recovered from the enormous financial blow of the North Bank – it's going to set them back years, there's no question, there's no way a club like Arsenal can carry £15 million worth of development and not suffer – they'll revamp the South Bank. I believe that they've just started to look at it, although I don't think they can afford to do it, the idea of building a mirror image of the North Bank Stand. (See plates 25 and 45.)

Simon Inglis

You felt you were all there for the same reason, you were all together. It's brilliant that feeling. And you had that nice little path across the back, and another one about a third of the way down and then all the little paths going down to the front.

Maureen Hewlitt

It's a good view at the North Bank, you always get a view. And you're right near the pitch, you're in the game, you can smell the grass.

Mark Burdis

What happened was that when we were looking at the design of the stand, it was put to us that we should have pillars. It was also pointed out that to remove those pillars would cost something approaching £1.5 million, but I think the board unanimously agreed that we wanted to provide the very best facility for years to come. I think people deserve that. Therefore everybody swallowed hard and bit the bullet and off we went. I'm sure it will be probably the best stand in the country, when it's finished, because we've been all over the world to look at other stadiums, we've been everywhere, the whole architectural team's been around. We've got a project team of architects, civil engineers and they've been everywhere. To be totally frank, we've stolen the best ideas that we can, because they're available. The original stand was of a very similar design to the one at the other end of the stadium, the South End, it had wings on it, but by a process of going to the planning authority, taking the views of all of those involved, particularly those of the local residents who had an input, it was eventually agreed that a new design should be put forward. This is a different design from the other one. I think everybody agrees it should be superb when it's finished.

Ken Friar

I was very involved with the people from GAAS — the Group for the Alternate Arsenal Stand. Really good people, a couple of architects, really bright people. They gave Arsenal their blueprint of a plan. They worked so hard to get them to improve that stand. It *was* changed but nowhere near to what GAAS wanted. GAAS's plan incorporated seating for thousands more people, there was an area for a possible return to terracing in the future. We had to fight the Club every inch of the way. GAAS actually gave them their design and said: *Look! We can make you more money!* And they wouldn't give. That was to do with pride and ego. They couldn't have some little ad hoc group of architects telling the Arsenal what to do!

Phillip Bloomfield

I think, if the new stand is anything like as good as I hear, people are going to turn round and say: *Cor, blimey! I'm a part of this. This is my Club.*

Bob Wilson

'THEY'RE GOING TO WONDER WHAT IT WAS LIKE'

I always said when I'm too old to go in the Junior Gunners, when I'm older and with my friends, I'll go up the North Bank. No chance of that now!

Dawn Evans

I think we've always tried to anticipate what's going to happen and I think that the Club, long before I came here, has always been one of the leaders in what it does, going back to the days of Herbert Chapman when he got us to be the first club to have a Tube station named after it; the first club to have a 45-minute clock (that albeit disappeared); we were one of the very first to install floodlighting; the first to install undersoil heating, things of that nature. I think we certainly want to be innovators. I think there are times when you've got to be leaders and I think the Club has recognised that since before the 30s.

Ken Friar

What will football lose if it loses the terraces? Passion. You sit in your seat — I've done it — and you see the game but you also enjoy the spectacle, the atmo-sphere. Who's going to provide that passion, the atmosphere, when the North Bank's gone?

John James

Everything that they've done recently, strikes me as being so shortsighted. I wouldn't say it to anyone who wasn't an Arsenal supporter. I'm finding it so hurtful, everything they're doing. All that about the stand that they're building now, it was just, like, push it straight through without any consultation. I think what hurts me the most is that it was *always* like that until Graham came, became manager. Then, all of a sudden, I thought: *This is really good, they're actually taking great efforts to make this into a family club.* My kids were so made up when they first joined the Junior Gunners. There was personal attention. I know there wasn't, but it didn't take much to make them think that. I thought: *This is great*, coinciding with kids coming through like Rocastle and Quinn and Hayes and so forth. I thought: *This club is really good now, it's really making an effort.* It's gone, just gone, the effort they made — I could talk for a long time — but it's all gone, just disappeared, and it hurts a hell of a lot.

Mick Essen

I'm very disillusioned and I just wonder if the Club can ever get us back to feeling the way we did. I'll always support them. I'll always go. I can't imagine what other people do on Saturday afternoons. But, I don't know. All those years that people stood there on crumbling terraces, lousy loos and bad weather. That counts for nothing. All they're bothered with is deals over television rights.

Roger Hewlitt

I could stand on there when a game wasn't going on, and have a well good time. It was home. And now it feels like you're not wanted anymore – you're being made to stand somewhere else or sit. I'm sure people in the Kop or the Stretford End or the Shed will feel the same.

Guy Thomson

I've come to the conclusion that the only way to get a good atmosphere is to go away. The following's good and the atmosphere's always really good. I think the only way people are going to get that camaraderie of the North Bank is by travelling away, really.

David Court Jnr

There's definitely a hard core of away fans who've got passports, really, saying they're away fans, and I reckon a majority of them are North Bank supporters. They'll sing: *We're the North Bank*, wherever they are. (See plate 36.)

Paul Jerrams

In 20 years' time, the whole idea of terrace culture will seem very important and will be something that future generations will wish they'd been around for, rather like I might wish I'd been say 20 in 1967 in the middle of psychedelia or something. Or, I don't know, I might wish I'd been 20 when Elvis first started and rock 'n' roll first started, and I think people are going to feel that about football terraces.

I think in future times people are going to look back and maybe look at old films where people go absolutely mad on terraces, when a goal goes in or something, they're going to wonder just what it was like. People who never experienced that, they're going to wonder.

Al Fresco

What we'll lose when the terraces go? There's two or three things. Noise. Highbury's never been a particularly noisy ground, but those nights – Anderlecht, Chelsea in the Cup, Championship nights, the atmosphere where players have said they felt the ball being sucked into the net – when you've got a stand full of north London car salesmen, you won't get that. Concern. At half time when you're a goal down and the buzz goes around the terrace about how we're going to sort this out. It may be that people there in the future will be as interested in seeing whether Ryan Giggs will get a second goal as they will in whether Arsenal can turn it round and win. The community thing. I don't think Arsenal any longer represents the aspirations of the local community, those days are gone, but football grounds are their own community anyway, people coming from other parts of London, other parts of the country – it doesn't matter if you're from Maidenhead ɔr Gillespie Road – to get there and be part of an Arsenal community. And I think we're seeing the destruction of an Arsenal community. It's not so much that people will miss their knees being straight rather than bent, it's that culture. And the way things are going, that's going to go and it's going to make an enormous difference to all of us.

Nick Hornby

When we did the Double, the best-paid Arsenal player that season got £17,500. Today that might be worth £80–90,000. I don't think much more. So that's how different it is, how much it's escalated. That's why clubs are in so much trouble, because the demands of players and their agents are so great, a club like Arsenal can no longer survive just on money at the gate, which is frightening I think.

Bob Wilson

Don't forget the stadium held 73,000 at one stage and the same physical parameters last season held forty-four-and-a-half, and next season will hold 37,000 so you can see we have come a long way. We'll have lost 36,000, 50 per cent with the same physical limits to the stadium.

Ken Friar

I don't know what the future of actually going to matches is. I can only look at it pessimistically, that people will drift away because the price is being hiked up. I mean it was only a few seasons ago that it was £4 to get in and you can't tell me that the Government's reckoning of inflation is 100 per cent, that all prices have doubled since then. Arsenal used to be cheaper than other London First Division clubs, but not anymore. I always compared it to cinema and now cinema is much cheaper. I mean, local cinemas are half the price.

Al Fresco

I think it's something the clubs may well have wanted to do and they used the Taylor Report as an excuse to do it. I think it's money-motivated. Whether it will rebound on the clubs or not, I'm not sure. I suppose with the crowds of 60,000 of 20–30 years ago now going to be restricted to 38,000 at Highbury, they may think we can afford to let a few fall by the wayside and have half the old crowd who can afford season tickets and so on. Where that leaves people who can't afford to do that – I suppose they'll have to buy satellite dishes to watch a game of football, which is never going to be the same as watching it live.

David Court

My season ticket last year was only about £60. I'm a Junior Gunner and we had money off of the coupons from the year before. So on top of that, it'll take about £10 for my train fare, my programme and something to eat. I won't spend all of it. I work on a Sunday. Sometimes it gets on my nerves but I think: *I've got to so I can go to football next week.*

Julie Wheeler

The cost is getting more expensive and the seating available will be smaller so, ultimately, the people watching will be different. It's sad that a lot of people aren't going to be able to afford to watch football but the way I look at it, things have to move on. I think people stand because that's what they've been brought up to do. If they were brought up to sit down they'd sit down. It's a big change but I think, in the long run, it's a change for the better.

Paul Davis

Football used to be the working-man's game, which didn't used to cost a lot of money. They're pricing people out of it now. People are saying: *I can't afford it. My wife and family come first.* Football's going to lose the ordinary man in the street.

Steve Shaw

I think all-seaters had to come. It'll cut the crowd down quite a bit but I think the new stand will be very nice. My mate's bought three bonds. He used to live in Maida Vale but he's down in Bristol now. He's offered them to his pals to use, you know.

Arthur Peakell

I remember we queued up – must have been for a Cup game – a few years ago on a Sunday morning, to get tickets and when you got your ticket you had to go over the back of the terrace and out the other side. Nice Sunday morning, sun was shining, and I just stood there and looked out across the ground. I can get goose bumps just looking at that place, it sends shivers down my spine. There's something about it. I know it sounds stupid, but you can feel the ghosts of people long gone. You think: *How many million people have stood where I am now?* All those people who have come here over the years. And I think that's really awe-inspiring. What is it? What is it that has made my dad go for 72 years? If you asked him, he'd have trouble putting his finger on it. What is it makes you keep going, keep going? It's like you belong to something. It feels like your home.

Tina Evans

Sources

'WE HAVE HAD OUR TROUBLES', THE LAUNDRY END, 1913–30

AFC Board Minutes
AFC Programme
Charles Buchan
Daily Express
Islington Gazette

Rose Jales
Tom Jales
A.G. Kearney
Morning Post
Arthur Peakell

Ron Pottage
Percy Sands
A.E. Smith
George Stinton
George Williams

'THEY COME TO MARVEL AT THE ARSENAL', THE LAUNDRY END, 1931–39

AFC Board Minutes
AFC Programme
George Allison,
  Allison Calling
Cliff Bastin
Phillip Bloomfield
Sid Butler
Ken Friar
Geoff Gilbert

Brian Glanville, *Arsenal*
Jack Hobb
Frank Hummell
Islington Gazette
Rose Jales
Tom Jales
Reg Lewis
Frank Martin

Arthur Peakell
Ron Pottage
Charlie Robinson
S. Claude Stevens
George Stinton
Bob Wall,
  Arsenal From the Heart
George Williams

'OUR GROUND HAS BEEN REQUISITIONED BY THE PUBLIC AUTHORITIES', THE NORTH TERRACE, 1940–46

AFC Board Minutes
AFC Programme
Frank Hummell

Tom Jales
Reg Lewis
Frank Martin

Bill Shankly
The Warden's Post
Tom Whittaker,
  Arsenal Story

'A DIFFERENT ENTHUSIASM',
THE NORTH TERRACE, 1947–56

AFC Board Minutes
AFC Programme
C.H. Blatch
Charles Buchan
Dennis Evans
Ken Friar
Geoff Gilbert
GunFlash
Shirley Haxell
Maureen Hewlitt
Jack Hobb
Frank Hummell

Simon Inglis
Reg Lewis
Doug Lishman
John Macadam,
    Daily Express
Frank Martin
Bill Needs
Arthur Peakell
John Platt
Ron Pottage
Cardew Robinson
Charlie Robinson

Graham Selkirk, *Sporting Record*
Steve Shaw
A.E. Smith
    Sunday Graphic
Ken Taylor
Chris Thompson
E.J.G. Thompson
Bob Wall,
    Arsenal From the Heart
John Yudkin

THE BEGINNING OF 'THE END',
THE NORTH TERRACE, 1957–70

AFC Programme
PC Roy Beasley, retd
PS Jack Birt, retd
Lenny Brandon
Laird Budge
Mark Burdis
Stan Carroll
Dave Chesterton
David Court
Daily Sketch
Daily Telegraph
Mick Essen
Dennis Evans
Tina Evans
Al Fresco
Ken Friar
Alex Froso
Harry Gee,
    Press Association
Glasgow Mercury

A. Green
Geoff Gilbert
GunFlash
Shirley Haxell
Maureen Hewlitt
Roger Hewlitt
Peter Hobb
Frank Hummell
Simon Inglis
Islington Gazette
Tom Jales
John James
Howard Kaye
Steve Kazmarek
Leicester Mercury
Laurence Marks
Frank Martin
Eddie Mason
Bertie Mee
Bill Needs

Vidos Neophytou
North London Press
Tony Pigden
Ron Pilcher
John Platt
Ron Pottage
Charlie Robinson
Jon Sammels
Stratton Smith, *Daily Sketch*
Geoff Strong
Richard Stubbs
The Times
Steve Thomas
Chris Thompson
Bob Wall,
    Arsenal From the Heart
Frank Warren
Bob Wilson
Steve Winfield
Steve Whitman

'HELLO! HELLO! WE ARE THE NORTH BANK BOYS', THE NORTH BANK, 1971–86

AFC Programme
Andrew Allerton
Lenny Brandon
Phillip Bloomfield
Liam Brady
Laird Budge
Mark Burdis
Stan Carroll
David Court Jnr
J.W. Crotty
Daily Express
Paul Davis
Mick Essen
Al Fresco
Ken Friar
A.P. Fox
Maurice Gran
Shirley Haxell
Roger Hewlitt

Peter Hill-Wood
Jack Hobb
Peter Hobb
Paul Hobb
Nick Hornby
Frank Hummell
John James
Paul Jerrams
Paul Johnson
Steve Kazmarek
Malcolm Macdonald
Laurence Marks
Eddie Mason
Terry Neill,
    Revelations of a
    Football Manager
Vidos Neophytou
Stewart O'Brien
Ron Pilcher

Ralph Reader
Charlie Robinson
Adam Rose/Malcolm Dick
Jon Sammels
David Sartori
PC Alan Smith
Jim Smith
Richard Stubbs
The Times
Chris Thompson
Debbie Wakeford
Bob Wall, *Islington Gazette*
Frank Warren
Steve Whitman
Bob Wilson
Steve Winfield
John Yudkin

'BORN IS THE KING OF HIGHBURY', THE NORTH BANK AND ITS HEROES

AFC Programme
Andrew Allerton
Liam Brady
Phillip Bloomfield
Charles Buchan
Laird Budge
Mark Burdis
David Court
David Court Jnr
Paul Davis
Mick Essen
Dennis Evans
Tina Evans
Alex Froso
Charlie George
Geoff Gilbert
Maurice Gran
Maureen Hewlitt
Roger Hewlitt

Jack Hobb
Paul Hobb
Peter Hobb
Nick Hornby
Frank Hummell
Islington Gazette
Rose Jales
Tom Jales
John James
Paul Jerrams
Bernard Joy
Steve Kazmarek
Peter Leslie
Frank Martin
Harold Mayes
Joe Mercer
Charlie Nicholas
Stewart O'Brien
Arthur Peakell

John Platt
Ron Pottage
Jimmy Rimmer
Jon Sammels
Jim Smith
The Su
Steve Thomas
Chris Thompson
Guy Thomson
Julie Wheeler
George Williams
Bob Wilson
Doug Wilson
Steve Winfield
Colin Wood
Emma Young
John Yudkin

'WE HATE TOTTENHAM AND WE HATE TOTTENHAM',
THE RIVALRY WITH SPURS

AFC Programme
Andrew Allerton
Phillip Bloomfield
Liam Brady
Lenny Brandon
Daily News
Daily Telegraph
Evening News
Ralph Finn,
   Sport Magazine
Al Fresco
Alex Froso
Geoff Gilbert

GunFlash
Steve Kazmarek
Dawn Hicks
Paul Hobb
Peter Hobb
Natasha Horbacki
Nick Hornby
Islington Gazette
Paul Jerrams
Laurence Marks
Charlie Nicholas
Stewart O'Brien

Ron Pottage
W. H. Prescott, MP
Charlie Robinson
Steve Shaw
George Stinton
Richard Stubbs
Guy Thomson
Bob Wall,
   Arsenal From the Heart
Julie Wheeler
Steve Winfield
Emma Young

'TO URGE OUR BOYS ON TO VICTORY',
WORDS AND MUSIC ON THE NORTH BANK

AFC Programme
Andrew Allerton
PC Roy Beasley, retd
PS Jack Birt, retd
Phillip Bloomfield
Lenny Brandon
Beryl Brown
Laird Budge
Sid Butler
Herbert Chapman, *Athletic News*
Edward Costello
David Court
Daily Sketch
Paul Davis
Mick Essen
Dennis Evans
Tina Evans

Evening Standard
Al Fresco
Geoff Gilbert
Maurice Gran
GunFlash
John Harding: *Alex James*
Maureen Hewlitt
Roger Hewlitt
Jack Hobb
Eric Hoggers
Nick Hornby
Frank Hummell
Tom Jales
John James
Paul Jerrams
Graham Jones
Steve Kazmarek

Peter Leslie
Tony Madden
Laurence Marks
Eddie Mason
Bill Needs
Vidos Neophytou
John Platt
Jon Sammels
PC Alan Smith
Richard Stubbs
The *Sun*
Steve Thomas
Chris Thompson
Guy Thomson
Julie Wheeler
George Williams
John Yudkin

'TO OWN AN ARSENAL SHIRT WOULD HAVE BEEN UNHEARD OF', FASHION ON THE NORTH BANK

AFC Programme
Laird Budge
Daily Mirror
Amanda Caspari
David Court Jnr
Mick Essen
Dennis Evans
Tina Evans
Ralph Finn,
   Sport Magazine
Al Fresco
Geoff Gilbert

Glasgow Evening News
Maurice Gran
GunFlash
Maureen Hewlitt
Roger Hewlitt
Natasha Horbacki
Frank Hummell
Islington Gazette
Rose Jales
Tom Jales
John James
Paul Johnson

Eddie Mason
John Platt
Charlie Robinson
Steve Shaw
Sheffield Wednesday Programme
Richard Stubbs
Chris Thompson
Guy Thomson
Julie Wheeler
George Williams
Steve Winfield

'YOU'RE AN ARSENAL FAN, YOU'RE ARSENAL', THE NORTH BANK MELTING POT

AFC Programme
Andrew Allerton
Rob Ashman
PC Roy Beasley, retd
Lenny Brandon
Laird Budge
Mark Burdis
Amanda Caspari
David Court
Paul Davis
Mick Essen
Tina Evans
Magnus Falkehag

Ken Friar
Alex Froso
Maurice Gran
Roberto Gotta
Maureen Hewlitt
Natasha Horbacki
Nick Hornby
John James
Paul Jerrams
Paul Johnson
Vidos Neophytou
Stewart O'Brien

John Platt
Michael Schoek
PC Alan Smith
Richard Stubbs
Chris Thompson
Guy Thomson
Frank Warren
George Williams
Steve Winfield
Emma Young
John Yudkin
Josh Yudkin

'NOT AS MANY AS TODAY BUT QUITE A FEW', WOMEN ON THE NORTH BANK

AFC Board Minutes
AFC Programme
Sid Butler
Amanda Caspari
Daily Express
John Deasy
Dennis Evans
Tina Evans
Al Fresco
Alex Froso
GunFlash
Shirley Haxell

Maureen Hewlitt
Paul Hobb
Sam Hobb
Natasha Horbacki
Rose Jales
Tom Jales
Peter Leslie
Laurence Marks
Eddie Mason
Vidos Neophytou
Ron Pilcher

Ron Pottage
Steve Shaw
George Stinton
Chris Thompson
Guy Thomson
Bob Wall,
 Arsenal From the Heart
Julie Wheeler
George Williams
Steve Winfield
Emma Young

'AND THIS IS HOW IT'S FOLLOWED ON, YOU SEE?', FAMILIES ON THE NORTH BANK

Andrew Allerton
Rob Ashman
Phillip Bloomfield
Lenny Brandon
Laird Budge
Mark Burdis
David Court
Mick Essen
Dawn Evans
Tina Evans
Magnus Falkehag
Alex Froso
Geoff Gilbert
Maurice Gran

Maureen Hewlitt
Roger Hewlitt
Dawn Hicks
Jack Hobb
Peter Hobb
Paul Hobb
Sam Hobb
Natasha Horbacki
Frank Hummell
Rose Jales
Tom Jales
Paul Jerrams
Paul Johnson
Peter Leslie

Frank Martin
Stewart O'Brien
Arthur Peakell
John Platt
Charlie Robinson
PC Alan Smith
Steve Thomas
Guy Thomson
Ian Trevett
Julie Wheeler
Steve Whitman
George Williams
Steve Winfield
Josh Yudkin

'THERE WILL BE NOTHING LIKE IT', THE NORTH BANK, 1987–92

AFC Programme
Rob Ashman
Sophie Bane
PS John Birt
Phillip Bloomfield
Liam Brady
Lenny Brandon
Laird Budge
Mark Burdis
Stan Carroll
David Court
David Court Jnr
Paul Davis
Mick Essen
Dawn Evans
Tina Evans
Al Fresco
Ken Friar
Alex Froso
Charlie George
Geoff Gilbert

Maurice Gran
Shirley Haxell
Maureen Hewlitt
Roger Hewlitt
Dawn Hicks
Peter Hill-Wood
Paul Hobb
Peter Hobb
Natasha Horbacki
Nick Hornby
Frank Hummell
Simon Inglis
Tom Jales
John James
Paul Johnson
Steve Kazmarek
Frank Martin
Eddie Mason
Vidos Neophytou
Charlie Nicholas

Stewart O'Brien
Arthur Peakell
Ron Pilcher
John Platt
Nick Robinson
Steve Shaw
R. J. Sheen
PC Alan Smith
Jim Smith
Richard Stubbs
Chris Thompson
Guy Thomson
The Times
Frank Warren
Julie Wheeler
George Williams
Bob Wilson
Steve Winfield
Emma Young
John Yudkin